CONTENTS

Preface

This book was conceived in May 1981 on our first visit to the Imperial War Museum. We went there with a variety of preconceptions – one of them being that the Museum would have, amongst the paraphernalia of war, only a few pictures and that these would be dull or jingoistic. We found instead galleries hung with trench landscapes by Paul Nash and Wyndham Lewis, shelter drawings by Henry Moore, paintings of the Blitz by John Piper and Graham Sutherland, and of wartime production by Stanley Spencer, Mervyn Peake and L. S. Lowry, watercolours of the war in the Middle East and Western Desert by Edward Bawden, Anthony Gross and Edward Ardizzone.

This was only part of a unique and little publicised national war art collection of some twelve thousand works, the majority concentrated at the Imperial War Museum, with important subsidiary collections at the Tate and major provincial galleries – a collection of whose evolution there was no published account.

Our book sets out to explain who commissioned the pictures, when and why; which artists were employed and why they were chosen; where they went and what their instructions were; what were the conditions under which they worked. We have explored the reactions of the artists themselves to the official war art schemes, and to their experiences of war, and we have described the ways in which their pictures were used both for historical record and for wartime propaganda. Artists have been treated according to their importance in the official schemes rather than in proportion to their current fame; where we have included critical evaluations of official war art, these reflect the opinion of the times in which the pictures were painted rather than present-day tastes.

The amount of material available is immense, and we have had to be more selective than we should have liked. It has not been possible to chronicle all the wartime activities of every artist involved (though we have supplied as much detail as possible in footnotes), nor to catalogue every picture acquired under the auspices of the schemes. Most importantly, we have not aimed at the sweeping conclusion: where some five hundred artists of every stylistic persuasion are involved, generalisations as to the nature of war art, the impact of war on artists as individuals, or on British art as a whole, the differences between the art of the First World War and that of the Second, and so forth, are open to innumerable qualifications. Some artists, for example, found in their official appointments a refuge from the war, others were thereby exposed to considerable hardship and dangers they would never otherwise have had to face. For some, official employment spelled financial salvation; for others it was so badly paid as to constitute a form of national service. War was to some artists simply another subject; for others it was the turning-point.

Our aim has been simply to describe and illustrate the history of official British war art in the twentieth century – which is synonymous neither with an historical account of war as a subject for art, nor with a general description of the activities of artists in wartime. The book is concerned exclusively with fine art; posters, cartoons, medals and war memorials fall outside its scope, as does the work of the 'specials' – the newspaper illustrators whose war reportage was crucial before the development of photography. It deals only with the art initiated by official agencies and paid for out of public funds; more specifically, its subject is the distinct but related official war art schemes of the two World Wars and the years since Nuremberg, administered by the propaganda organisations of the First World War, the War Artists' Advisory Committee and the Imperial War Museum. It does not discuss the military art commissioned throughout the century by the Armed Forces outside these schemes.

Our principal source has been the mass of unpublished material in the files held by the Art Department of the Imperial War Museum – a remarkable archive to match the collection of pictures. All the pictures reproduced are from the IWM collection unless otherwise indicated; measurements are given in inches throughout, height preceding width. Full acknowledgement of the enormous amount of help we have been given is to be found at the end of the book, but we should particularly like here to thank the staff of the IWM's Art Department for their patience and encouragement over the last two years.

London, 18 June 1983

PART I

THE FIRST WORLD WAR

C. R. W. Nevinson, *A Group of Soldiers* (oil on canvas), 36 × 24

CHAPTER ONE

Prelude

ART is at the best of times an insecure profession; and though in the years before 1914 the art world in London was thriving, the Great War tipped a balance already precarious.

For the older established artists – men like Walter Sickert, Philip Wilson Steer and John Singer Sargent – professional life continued much as before. Conscription was no threat to these older men, nor even to younger but equally successful artists, the stars of Augustus John's generation, provided they had the necessary contacts to keep themselves out of the firing line. William Orpen, for example, a close friend of the Quartermaster-General Sir John Cowans, found a safe berth in the Army Service Corps at Kensington Barracks, from which he was able quite comfortably to continue his flourishing trade in society portraits – his sitters including, in 1916, the QMG himself.

The patriotism of these artists was largely satisfied by various forms of artistic war work, mostly for fund-raising purposes. At Christie's the Red Cross organised a series of auctions of blank canvases donated by artists who undertook to complete them in accordance with the purchasers' wishes: Augustus John, saved from the rigours of active service by an ailment he described as 'housemaid's knee', painted Lloyd George – 'a hot arse who can't sit still'; and the charity received £10,000 for the canvas on which Sargent painted a portrait of President Woodrow Wilson.

For artists less securely established, however, war meant the progressive contraction of an already limited market. Henry Tonks, Professor at the Slade School and a father-figure to many young artists of this period, recorded, as early as September 1914, a marked increase in applications to the Artists' Benevolent Fund. Some artists were protected by loyal patrons – Edward Marsh and Lady Ottoline Morrell being among the most active. A few took the little work that was forthcoming from illustrated periodicals like the *Graphic* and the *Sphere*. One at least was given a commission that provided both sufficient income to live and exemption from military service: Eric Gill's employment on the Stations of the Cross in Westminster Cathedral continued until mid-1918. But for many, poverty loomed: William Roberts was reduced to borrowing money from friends – he later recalled an embarrassing half hour spent skirting round the subject with Augustus John, who eventually produced the princely sum of half a crown.

For artists in this position the Services, ironically, provided a refuge. There were those who objected to military service on principle, most conspicuously the painters associated with the Bloomsbury Group, who obtained exemption on pacifist grounds and were, in Wyndham Lewis's acidulated words, 'all doing work of National importance down in some downy English county, under the wings of powerful pacifist friends; pruning trees, planting gooseberry bushes and haymaking, doubtless in large sunbonnets'. Less high-mindedly, Jacob Epstein saw the furtherance of his own artistic development as the greatest service he could render the nation: 'My life has always been war, and it is more difficult I believe for me here to stick to the job, than to go out and fight. . . . Really I am too important to waste my days in thinking of matters military.' The majority of younger artists, however, lost little time in joining up: the *Studio* published regular lists of soldier-artists as a record and an example.

Financial necessity was not, of course, the only spur. Most, like any other volunteers, felt it their patriotic duty: thirty artists joined the Royal Army Medical Corps *en bloc* in response to an impassioned plea made by the commandant of the 3rd London General Hospital, at Wandsworth, in the bar of the Chelsea Arts Club. Others, particularly the 'moderns', saw the war as vital to their artistic growth. 'You must not miss a war, if one is going! You cannot afford to miss that experience,' wrote Wyndham Lewis. For the English Futurist, C. R. W. Nevinson, war was the supreme stimulus: 'There is no beauty except in strife, no masterpiece without aggressiveness.'

The Artists' Rifles attracted many, among them John and Paul Nash, and Charles Sergeant Jagger – all of whom saw active service. A less vigorous recruit was royal portraitist John Lavery, who at fifty-eight joined the Artists' Rifles in a fit of ardour, only to find himself drilling in the quadrangle of Burlington House with 'a scrubby lot of painters, sculptors, actors, musicians, hairdressers, scene shifters, etc. of all ages'. At his age, enthusiasm was not enough: '. . . the second or third route march did for me. I had to call in the doctor, whose verdict was – "My dear sir, go back to your paint pots, you will do more for your country with your brush than with your rifle." . . . In the end they went to the trenches and I went to bed.' Artillery regiments absorbed Wyndham Lewis, William Roberts and Colin Gill; Bernard Meninsky was a clerk in the Royal Fusiliers. C. R. W. Nevinson joined the Red Cross, Henry Lamb retrained as a doctor and, with the Spencers, Stanley and Gilbert, enlisted in the RAMC (though Stanley later transferred to one of the fighting regiments of his home county – the Royal Berkshires).

Not surprisingly, many of these volunteers found themselves side-tracked into art-related jobs. Camouflage was a principal employer, but draughtsmanship and modelling had other obvious military applications – aerial maps and technical diagrams for demonstration purposes, topographical drawings to assist the big guns in range-finding, and target figures for small arms practice: the Imperial War Museum possesses a fine Orpen target head. In the 'tin noses' room at the 3rd London General Hospital, the sculptor Derwent Wood shaped wafer-thin masks of flesh-coloured electroplate, working from photographs, for men with appalling facial injuries. Stanley Spencer, no asset as a soldier, took the chance to endear himself to his sergeant when instructed to paint 'the letters indicating men's and sergeants' latrines. . . . I made a big letter 'S' for sergeants and painted some dog roses round it.' Paul Nash's CO, similarly solicitous of his men's welfare, requested from him 'a life-size figure of a man scratching himself to describe an anti-bug powder'.

Despite the hardships of life in the trenches and the military restrictions on sketching, many soldier–artists did try to work in their spare time, both to preserve their pre-war reputations and to supplement their army pay. The pictures they sent home found a ready market with a public avid for first-hand information about the war: even after the early fog of censorship had cleared, and war correspondents had been allowed to the Front, the images of war which filtered home were hazy. As the war progressed an increasing number of paintings and drawings found their way into exhibitions, at this stage 'unofficial' shows at private galleries. Among them were some of the finest works to appear during the war. Two in particular, *The Kensingtons at Laventie** and *La Mitrailleuse*, aroused intense interest at a most opportune moment for the proponents of official war art, in the spring of 1916.

The Kensingtons at Laventie, first seen at the Goupil Gallery, was the work of Eric Kennington. After six months' service in the Line with the 13th London Regiment (The Kensingtons), he was invalided out in June 1915 and worked on *The Kensingtons* during his convalescence. It depicts a moment in January 1915 when his platoon was forming up to return to billets – an old barn in the Laventie district – on the verge of exhaustion after four days and nights in front-line trenches in twenty degrees of frost and almost continuous snow. All the soldiers depicted are recognisable: the figure in the blue balaclava is Kennington himself. Emotionally powerful and executed in brilliant colours, the work is also a technical *tour de force*, large (54 × 63) and painted in reverse on a sheet of glass, and it was hailed as 'decidedly the finest picture inspired by this war as yet by an English artist'.

C. R. W. Nevinson, whose *La Mitrailleuse* was first shown at an Allied Artists Association exhibition in March 1916, had also been invalided out of the services in June 1916, with rheumatic fever. His picture, portraying man dehumanised as an integral part of the (then) most perfect example of lethal military efficiency, the machine-gun, was described by Walter Sickert as 'the most authoritative and concentrated utterance on the war in the history of painting'.

The popular success of pictures like these, and the genuine artistic merits of many of them, helped both to fuel and to justify the growing agitation in artistic and society circles for artists to be sent officially to the Front. This pressure, which reached its peak in the early summer of 1916, had a broad base: interest in war art as such was buttressed by the more general demand for records of the unprecedented national sacrifice and effort in all its aspects. The suggestion had been made by John Buchan that every regiment should have its own official historian; literary figures of the calibre of George Bernard Shaw and John Masefield were being sent to prepare eye-witness accounts of the Front; the Canadian War Record Office had been set up in 1916 by Sir Max Aitken to amass and preserve documentary material of historical value; and a Committee for the Medical History of the War was established by the RAMC. This anxiety to record and remember was to be manifest in the enthusiasm which greeted the foundation of a national war museum in March 1917.

Pressure came also from artists themselves. The tendency of many, if not most, artists to assess every situation in terms of its artistic potential would have engendered a natural desire among those not in the Forces to witness the war. 'The average artist will probably want to go to the Front,' wrote Sir Kenneth Clark at the start of the Second World War, 'not simply out of curiosity or bravado, but because he may there discover some of that emotional stimulus on a grand scale which is inevitably lacking from his everyday work' – a statement equally applicable in the First World War. By 1916 French and German artists had already been given access to their respective Fronts, and requests for similar facilities multiplied rapidly to reach the irritant level

*An asterisk in the text indicates that this picture is reproduced in the colour section.

– though curiously no collective representations seem to have been made by professional bodies such as the Royal Academy or New English Art Club.

Against this general background certain individuals stand out as leaders in the movement for official art – in particular William Rothenstein and Lady Cunard. Though in 1916 Rothenstein had not yet been appointed Principal of the Royal College of Art, he was nonetheless an influential figure in the art establishment as artist, educator and patron. As early as 1908 he had been propounding the novel doctrine that the only answer to the decline in private patronage of the arts was the employment of artists by the State: officially sponsored war art was for him a logical step. After a visit made to the Front in 1915 as a guest of Belgian Army Headquarters, Rothenstein returned 'full of enthusiasm for the scene of war. I implored my friend Colonel Repington [a war correspondent on *The Times*] to plead at the War Office that artists should be allowed out to France.' Repington, a 'curtained intriguer' in both political and military circles, invoked the aid of two of his most powerful contacts – Lord Northcliffe and Emerald, Lady Cunard, society hostess and patroness of young talent.

Lady Cunard was already ahead – Repington reported her to be 'full of fun and of the scheme of painters' and poets' visits to the Front. She has quite a long list of artists who want to go'; and in the summer of 1916 she generated a great deal of publicity for her scheme. Northcliffe, by his own account, did no more than speak of the scheme at GHQ 'several times' – but he seems to have given more positive support by publishing in *The Times* a letter from Rothenstein calling for 'Help for Artists' in the form of state patronage: 'If art be in truth the noble and inspiring thing our foremost statesmen annually assure us it is, it should be of service in time of war as well as in time of peace.' This was followed by an editorial recommending the dispatch of artists to the Front, which shows every sign of having been inspired by Rothenstein.

Interestingly, Northcliffe also cited Philip Sassoon (cousin of Siegfried) as an active proponent of official war art. Sassoon had an educated interest in art, and the money to finance it; his house at 25 Park Lane was a meeting place for both artistic and political luminaries, as well as his own 'graceful and rather decadent inner circle'. There is little other direct evidence of his involvement in war art, but as Haig's private secretary he was certainly in a position to argue the cause of official artists at GHQ.

It has been suggested that the official war art schemes were the direct result of this type of pressure. This is misleading. The stumbling block for both Lady Cunard and Rothenstein was the intransigence of the War Office, which controlled all visits to France. Their reluctance to provide facilities for a flood of artists to go to the Front could be neither circumvented nor surmounted through unofficial channels; and if grounds beyond an instinctive suspicion of 'artists' were needed for denying access, they were provided by the Battle of the Somme which opened on 1 July 1916, with a total casualty list of 57,470 soldiers for that day alone.

The first artist to go to France was not a painter particularly favoured in society circles, nor was he sent as part of a grand plan for artistic involvement in the war. His was intended as a 'one-off' appointment and, most importantly, it was not for the purposes of record or memorial, but in pursuit of an end of which the Cunards and Sassoons might well have been disdainful – propaganda.

CHAPTER TWO

Wellington House

U NTIL the spring of 1917, Britain's official Government-run
propaganda effort was directed exclusively abroad.[1] It began,
in some haste, in response to the intensive German
campaign waged from the beginning of the war for the support of neutral
countries, most particularly the USA – a great prize, and one
which Germany stood a fair chance of winning, in view of
America's large immigrant Germanic population and an
influential Jewish lobby opposed to Russia, and, by association, her
allies. During the first two years of the war a fierce propaganda
battle was fought for America; Alexander Woolcott characterised
it as 'the time of strain when the American people were trying to
hold onto their neutrality much as a voyager in the English
Channel tries to hold onto his breakfast'. Even after America had
ranged herself on the side of the Allies, the struggle continued – the
British striving to maintain American enthusiasm for the war at the
highest possible pitch, the Germans to decrease her war effort
by fomenting pacifism and distrust of Allied aims.

This was the first modern war to involve whole nations,
not merely their armies. Public opinion and civilian morale
had suddenly become vital factors in a nation's
fighting strength, and in each country propaganda was
directed both at the policy-makers and the general
public to whom the policy-makers were answerable
– and to whom they looked for the labour for war
industries and manpower for the Forces.

There were no precedents for manipulation of
public opinion on this scale; 'that the State
should advertise itself was an idea which had
occurred to few before the war . . . advertisement was thought
to be the work of the vulgarian'. Propaganda techniques evolved
and altered during the war as rapidly as its objectives. Initially
the main priority was to establish Germany's guilt and justify Britain's
entry into the war – for example, by presenting the Bryce Report, 'objective'
evidence of German atrocities during the invasion of Belgium. Later it became
more important to placate allies who suspected Britain to be serving only her
own ends: France in particular, after the decimation of

Max Beerbohm, *Mr C. F. Masterman preserving his ideals, 1911*
(watercolour), Ashmolean Museum. Oxford

[5]

her Army at Verdun during 1916, frequently accused Britain of failing, through both incapacity and unwillingness, to bear her share of the burden. Various propaganda motifs were deployed throughout the war: warnings of Teutonic 'frightfulness' and the hideous consequences of German victory; ridicule of repeated German claims that this victory was inevitable; attempts to mollify aggrieved neutrals suffering from such side effects of the British war effort as the naval blockade of the Baltic.

Under the overall control of the Secretary of State for Foreign Affairs, foreign propaganda was broadly divided between 'news' and 'comment'. Responsibility for news – which provided the immediate means of influencing opinion and countering German assertions – rested with the News Department of the Foreign Office and the Neutral Press Committee at the Home Office. 'Comment' was under the aegis of a special department set up secretly by Cabinet Minute at the end of August 1914 under Liberal politician Charles F. G. Masterman, at that time also Chairman of the National Health Insurance Commission. For purposes of cover the new department was located at the NHIC offices in Buckingham Gate and it was by its address there that the department came to be known – Wellington House.

Masterman assembled a brilliant and youthful team of writers, academics, journalists and civil servants. The department was organised on a geographical basis, with each section producing propaganda tailored to the needs of its respective area. Although some articles were produced for insertion in the foreign press, particularly in the USA, Wellington House was principally concerned with separate publications – reproductions of official documents and speeches; pamphlets and books on subjects ranging from the most general (*How Can War Ever Be Right?* by Gilbert Murray) to the most specific (*Cotton Contraband* by Lord Milner); and newssheets and periodicals printed in huge quantities and many languages. Annual output totalled between ten and twenty million items, sent all over the world without cost to the department through the transport and distribution network of the British shipping companies.

The two key features of Wellington House publications were quality and secrecy. Valuable lessons had been learnt from the failings of German propaganda, which was mostly crude and hysterical, and Masterman adopted a low-key approach, with the emphasis on literacy and sweet reason. Arnold Toynbee and Anthony Hope were both on the staff, and among those outside who contributed their services were Conan Doyle, Ford Madox Ford, Hilaire Belloc, Henry Newbolt and John Buchan. Secrecy was an essential corollary to this approach. While 'news' needs official backing to carry conviction, 'comment' is more likely to be accepted if it is believed to be independent.

Sheltering behind its uninformative name, the department kept its true purpose concealed both abroad and at home throughout the two and a half years of its existence. None of its publications carried a Government imprint, utilising instead the imprints of right-thinking independent publishers. They were for the most part offered for sale (on the Victorian principle that you value only what you have paid for); where distributed free they were sent via personal contacts to forestall the suspicion generally provoked by unsolicited literature. The distributors invariably posed as private citizens obeying a patriotic impulse: Sir Gilbert Parker, MP and novelist, corresponded weekly on the department's behalf with over ten thousand of the most powerful men and women in America – Senators, Congressmen, teachers, industrialists, society leaders and newspapermen (William Randolph Hearst among them), exerting a subtle influence and securing valuable exposure in syndicated newspapers for Wellington House material.

By 1916 pictorial propaganda was becoming an increasingly important part of Wellington House's work. After a slow start, war films had become popular: the first to be released was *Britain Prepared*, in the autumn of 1915. Photographs were being sold and exhibited all over the world: four thousand a week were dispatched to the foreign press and others were circulated as cigarette cards, calendars, bookmarks and lantern-slides. Pictures were used to illustrate newssheets and periodicals in several languages, including Hindustani and Chinese. Masterman commented, 'The enormous circulation of pictorial papers reveals, as much as the crowds at the cinematographs, that there are millions of voters . . . in all countries who will not read letterpress but from whom the demand for war pictures is unlimited'. In April 1916 a pictorial section was established within the department and one of its first acts was the creation of a new all-picture publication, the *War Pictorial*. By mid-1916 this was being produced in five separate editions – 'Latin', North European, Russian, Japanese and English (for American consumption) – with a circulation per issue of 300,000.

These illustrated publications depended on a steady flow of suitable photographs, which in 1916 was difficult to sustain. There were too few official photographers on the Western Front and too limited a range of subjects: the flat, empty landscapes of Flanders, trench scenes, numberless troops going 'over the top', and so on. The inevitable monotony was compounded by the Censor's insistence on removing significant detail or recognisable landmarks.

The simplest solution would have been to supplement photographs with line drawings, after the fashion of commercial illustrated papers. Two factors made Wellington House aim higher. One was the presence within the department of several figures then eminent in the art world – Eric Maclagan, later Director of the Victoria and Albert Museum; Campbell Dodgson, Keeper of Prints and Drawings at the British Museum; Thomas Derrick, an artist and teacher at the Royal College of Art; and Alfred Yockney, one-time editor of *Art Journal*. The other spur to ambition was the availability of machines utilising the photogravure process, enabling pictures of greater complexity to be adequately, even well reproduced.

The decision to use artists rather than illustrators or cartoonists to supply the badly needed pictures was actually taken by Masterman himself. Official war art was thus initiated by one of the most interesting and ill-fated figures of the time. Masterman's physical appearance was itself remarkable. His contemporaries recall him as 'incredibly untidy', with frayed cuffs and boots laced with string. 'He droops all over . . . I could not resist his similarity to a fish. He will extend to you a moist and tapering hand, his dark hair hangs down on either side of his face, there is physical melancholy in every parabolic line of his frame, and his small mouth and sharp nose seem the only determined solidified parts of his gelatinous anatomy. . . .' But this eccentric and indolent exterior belied a brilliant intellect: Arnold Bennett remembered, 'On any topic . . . you had the sensation, when he talked, of his brain reaching out and seizing on essentials like a pair of nut crackers.'

Several facets of his character – liberal ideals crossed with a streak of Puritanism, unshakeable loyalty to principles and people alike – reflected his evangelical upbringing in a family with a Quaker background. His career at Christ's College, Cambridge was conventionally distinguished; President of the Union in 1896 and editor of the university magazine *Granta* in 1897, he took First Class Honours in both Natural and Moral Sciences and was elected a Fellow of Christ's in 1900. His early philosophy is summed up in a letter to his wife: 'Don't let's ever tolerate the cruelties and injustices of the world. Pray for the fire within adequate to burn up the sins of the whole world.' He toyed with the idea of taking Holy Orders; instead his idealism found practical expression in campaigning for social reform, slum clearance in particular. He set up home in a tenement block in Camberwell, the better to understand what he was fighting for, and expressed his views forcefully in such books as *From the Abyss* and *The Condition of England*. Journalism provided a further outlet: in 1903 he was Literary Editor of the *Daily News*, moving later to the *Nation* in the heyday of H. W. Massingham's editorship.

By 1906 he had been elected Liberal MP for a working-class constituency in West Ham and, once in Parliament, he rapidly developed personal influence quite disproportionate to the actual posts he held[2] – a reflection perhaps of his belief that 'You can get anything you want done in this life if you don't mind someone else getting the credit.' He followed this principle as David Lloyd George's confidant and adviser – 'My line is to lie low and not try to speak and get Lloyd George to rely on me; then I can get things done.' Lloyd George rehearsed his speeches to Masterman; the two families went on holiday together; and Masterman played a vital part in the drafting and passage through Parliament of Lloyd George's controversial pre-war social legislation, including the famous Budget of 1909 and the National Health Insurance Bill of 1911. In 1912 Masterman was appointed Financial Secretary to the Treasury, and in 1914 he joined the Cabinet as Chancellor of the Duchy of Lancaster.

His ascent had been spectacular: he was by this time being widely tipped for Prime Minister. But on his way up, as a passionate advocate of social reform and, in particular, as Lloyd George's scapegoat for the unpopular National Health Insurance Bill of 1911, he had made some choice enemies – among them the demagogue Horatio Bottomley and, more seriously, Lord Northcliffe.

These were given their chance by his appointment to the Cabinet which, at that time, obliged him to resign his Parliamentary seat and seek re-election. He lost not only the first by-election but also a second, falling out fatally in the process with Lloyd George. In 1915 he was forced to resign from the Cabinet and for the rest of his life political failure was compounded by increasing poverty and ill health.

Masterman's tenure as head of Wellington House coincided with the steep decline in his fortunes: the direction of neutral and Allied propaganda was his last important appointment. His sponsorship of war art was typical of his work in the department – resourceful and imaginative. He knew little about art, but he had infinite experience of exploiting the talents of others; official war art in its early stages was entirely a product of his readiness to experiment.

CHAPTER THREE

Muirhead Bone

M ASTERMAN's first artist was Muirhead Bone, a Scottish etcher who in 1916 was one of Britain's leading draughtsmen. Having taken up drawing and etching at twenty-two, after four years of unenthusiastic apprenticeship as an architect, he quickly established a reputation as a London Piranesi for his drypoints of city scenes. 'His special province was the rendering of great masses of buildings under construction or demolition, with all the attendant paraphernalia, in such a manner that out of superficial chaos there emerged a beautiful and ordered design.'[3]

He was in no sense in the vanguard of contemporary art. The characteristic for which he was perhaps most noted was an almost photographic accuracy of representation – sometimes, in Shaw's words, 'too true to be good'; and he settled on the right wing of the New English Art Club at a time when the New English itself was drawing nearer to the middle of the road. But he had remarkably eclectic tastes and sympathy with work completely unlike his own (he was a particular champion of Stanley Spencer and Jacob Epstein), and his enlightened views were to be crucial in shaping the course of official war art.

In May 1916 Bone, though only just inside the age limit, was confidently expecting to be conscripted. Some time previously, a canvas he had donated to the Red Cross for auction had been bought by one of London's leading literary agents, A. P. Watt, who was on the staff of Wellington House. While discussing with Watt his plans for completing the blank canvas, Bone mentioned his impending call-up. It is not clear whether Bone knew of Watt's connection with official propaganda work, but with the idea of war art very much in the air in the summer of 1916, Watt at once recognised Bone's potential value. On 19 May 1916 he wrote to Masterman recommending that Bone be sent to France without delay: his drawings would greatly enhance the new *War Pictorial* and his international reputation might help it to penetrate even into Germany itself.

Muirhead Bone on the Somme, 1916

Fortuitously for Bone, Masterman's senior art adviser was Campbell Dodgson, a long-standing friend and admirer, who pointed out the wisdom of sending Bone, an artist whose forte was ruins, to record the devastation of France and Flanders. Masterman was convinced: in mid-June he persuaded the War Office to refrain from conscripting Bone, and GHQ to have him attached to their Intelligence Branch in France, with all the necessary facilities in the way of accommodation, transport, and security clearance.

Bone's services were to be entirely at the Government's disposal for six months:[4] the British Museum was to have unlimited choice of the originals and Wellington House was to have the right of free reproduction for propaganda purposes for the duration of the war. In return Bone would be paid £500 per annum, plus travelling expenses and the right to make etchings from his drawings (potentially a far more valuable form of remuneration than his salary). As a civilian he would have needed a conducting officer if he was to avoid continual harassment, so he was commissioned an Honorary 2nd Lieutenant – though he would have preferred a rank more befitting his age: 'Frankly I feel the matter of my bald head . . . and my one pip!'

These terms represented good value for Wellington House; Bone at this period could have expected an annual income of at least £3–4000. Nevertheless he cheerfully accepted the appointment which was offered formally on 15 July 1916 and, after a short delay whilst his uniform was being made, he travelled to France on 16 August 1916 at the height of the Somme offensive. In a chauffeur-driven car he toured the British Front from the Somme battlefields in the south – Maricourt, Fricourt, Montauban, Mametz Wood, Contalmaison, Trônes Wood, High Wood, Delville Wood and Pozières – through Arras and on to Messines and Ypres in the north. He worked quickly in pencil, pen, charcoal and chalk, laying in such watercolour as was necessary back at billets, and by 6 October had sent home approximately 150 finished drawings.

He was working with remarkable speed and concentration, but found it hard to produce the type of picture originally anticipated. 'I'm afraid that I have not done many ruins. . . . But you must remember that on the Somme nothing is left after such fighting as we have had here – in many cases not a vestige of the village remains let alone impressive ruins!' His work covered instead a wide range of subjects, almost all to be found *behind* the lines – the work of the medical services; the repair and maintenance of big guns; soldiers off duty, eating, smoking and playing football. Some of his best drawings illustrate the setting for war rather than war itself: troop movements in the Picardy landscape – columns of men and lorries on their way to the Front, hospital barges taking the wounded away from it – and the shattered towns behind the line. Bone made several drawings of the 'Virgin of Albert', the gilt statue on the tower of Notre Dame de Brebières, Albert, which had been knocked sideways by a shell and was leaning precariously over the street. The superstition had grown up that when the Virgin fell the war would end; the statue was finally toppled during the German advance in April 1918.

His attempts at the 'action picture' were in a small minority, though they did include two of his best-received drawings – a distant panorama entitled *The Battle of the Somme* and the enormously popular *Tanks*, the first drawing to be made of these war-machines after their first use in combat on 15 September 1916.

Muirhead Bone, *Tanks* (charcoal), $21\frac{1}{2} \times 29\frac{1}{2}$

As the weather became bleaker, military activity slowed down and outdoor sketching became more difficult. Bone was anxious to turn to munitions: 'To tell truth I feel that these scenes of great works are peculiarly my own and I would much like to have a "go" at them and to prove that I could do them better than Pennell!'[5] He returned to England in December 1916 and spent two months in the munition factories of Coventry, Chilwell and Middlesbrough, producing pictures like *Mounting a Great Gun* and *An Aeroplane on the Stocks.*

At the beginning of March 1917 he was sent to the Grand Fleet at Rosyth and worked for three weeks recording daily life at sea, from oiling and practice firing to stretcher drill and *A Cinema on Board a Battleship, HMS Repulse.*

In mid-April Bone returned to France to find that conditions on the Western Front had greatly changed. GHQ now briskly dismissed the Somme battlefields as 'a little stale' and suggested that he might profitably concentrate on the area to the east of the old British Front, 'recaptured' after the German withdrawal behind the Hindenburg line. Operation 'Alberich', the systematic total devastation of this evacuated area by the retreating Germans, provided Bone with all the ruins he had previously lacked. He produced dozens of remarkable drawings: the town hall at Péronne, its clock lying in the ruins of the tower; churches with their ancient stained glass blown out and statues methodically decapitated; châteaux with orangeries no more than rows of neatly sawn stumps. After six weeks he had had enough: Bone came back to England

[11]

Muirhead Bone, *The Great Crater, Athies, May 1917* (charcoal), 22 × 30

to concentrate on shipbuilding and was not to return to France again.

In the yards of the Clyde, on home ground, he produced what he considered his best war drawings – 'splendidly generalled armies of dutiful details', in scenes like *A Ship-Yard – Seen from a Big Crane* and *Building a Cross-Channel Train Ferry*. For this type of picture he had almost limitless energy and could work undistracted in the most difficult conditions, sketching in a notebook strapped to his hand with elastic, carrying on the design with perfect accuracy from page to page.

He was then bundled back to the Fleet to turn out a series of naval panoramas requested by the Admiralty, but by August 1917 it was becoming clear that he was dangerously overworked. On 18 August his wife wrote angrily, 'I watched him the other day looking at his pencil as though he didn't know waht to do with it. . . . Isn't it possible for the Authorities to consider that 500 drawings in a year ought to be counted for an artist's righteousness and to let him have space to draw breath?' As is disturbingly apparent from the progressive deterioration in his handwriting, by September Bone had worked himself into a virtual nervous breakdown and was to be effectively out of action until the spring of 1918.

This frenetic work rate was partly due to Bone's own temperament, partly also to the constant demand for pictures from Wellington House – initially for its illustrated papers, but subsequently for a separate publication launched in December 1916. Bone supported single-handed ten issues of a volume entitled *The Western Front*[6], each containing twenty pictures selected by Campbell Dodgson.

The introduction and short description of each picture were written by C. E. Montague, chief leader-writer on the *Manchester Guardian* and the model for a generation of young journalists. H. G. Wells described Montague as 'a curious mixture of sixthform Anglican sentimentality (about dear old horses, dearer old doggies, brave women, real gentlemen, the old school, the old country and sound stock: Galsworthyissimus, in fact), with a most adventurous intelligence. He was a radical bound, hide bound in a conservative hide.' In 1914 he was forty-seven, with seven children, and had been a consistent proponent of the *Guardian*'s anti-war line. But once war had actually been declared, he dyed his grey hair and enlisted in the Sportsman's Battalion, prompting from war correspondent H. W. Nevinson (father of C. R. W.) the much coined *mot*: 'We had often heard of men whose dark hair had gone white through fear but Montague was the only man whose white hair had turned dark through courage.' Thwarted of active service by an explosives accident in camp, Montague was attached as an Intelligence Officer to GHQ to write propaganda, censor war correspondents' despatches, and conduct 'distinguished visitors' about the Front, which he did with a notorious disregard for personal safety.

Montague was disparaging about his descriptive notes on Bone's drawings, dismissing them as 'drivelettes'. But he knew intimately the country which Bone was depicting, and the introductions to the trenches issues provide a vivid and moving complement to the pictures. There were allegations in the press, however, that the text and drawings in *The Western Front* made war more palatable by depicting only the destruction of property and glossing over the sufferings of men. Some critics considered Bone too detached, his battle scenes too distant – 'like a peep at the war through the wrong end of a telescope'. (He explained later: 'I did not like to imagine war scenes & so only drew what I saw & then only when I had a chance to draw it . . . I am afraid [this] resulted in rather prosaic work.') Others found his trench and dug-out drawings unacceptably cosy, with their name-boards ('Ye Rat Hole', 'The Ritz') and flower-pots. Montague wrote defensively, 'Perhaps it is hinted that we are all in a league to hide . . . some extreme, mysterious horror which is . . . war "as it is" . . . which, if leaked out, would make the world lay down its arms on the spot.' In his diaries he proved himself more than capable of describing the abominations he had seen. Very occasionally they creep into the text of *The Western Front* – in *Ruined Trenches in Mametz Wood*, 'perforated helmets, fragments of shell . . . broken stretchers, boots not quite empty' – but never into the pictures.

CHAPTER FOUR

Francis Dodd

T HE ten volumes of *The Western Front* cover a huge variety of war subjects, with
one major exception – portraits. From the outbreak of war German propagandists,
in a flood of pictures and articles, diligently nurtured a mystique of energy, courage
and efficiency round their military leaders. Masterman lamented, 'From districts like
California and South America I get letters at frequent intervals asking why on earth
we make no display of our Generals, whereas the Germans are always booming theirs
as geniuses which are unconquerable. We cannot help the ordinary people having
more interest in personality than in principle, and we must use this as the Germans
have used it, with skill.' He responded as best he could with photographs, but after
one critic had described the King, the Queen and Field-Marshal Haig, photographed
in *War Pictorial*, as 'stuck pigs', he resolved to try a higher art form and proposed
two series of portraits, one of generals and the other of admirals. Muirhead Bone, not
primarily a portraitist, could help only indirectly, as he was later to do so often, by
recommending another artist – Francis Dodd.

Dodd's appointment neatly illustrates the importance of personal contacts as a factor
in Wellington House's early selection of artists. He was Bone's brother-in-law and letters of support came from Campbell Dodgson and another old friend and flatmate of
Bone, Charles Aitken (subsequently the first Director of the Tate Gallery); no other
portraitists were seriously considered. But Dodd's qualifications were not in doubt.
At forty-two he was over military age; he worked rapidly, in a 'vigorous and manly
style', and he used charcoal and watercolours – much better suited than oils to the
embattled conditions in which he might find himself. He did not command the four-
figure fees of society painters like Orpen and Ambrose McEvoy but was nevertheless
an artist of some eminence, having been a member of the Royal Society of Portrait
Painters since 1911; and he was equal, in social terms at least, to the task of handling
Britain's military supremos. Ernest Gowers (then the Chief Executive of Wellington
House) found him even-tempered, unassuming, discreet and enthusiastic, with a well-
developed sense of humour, 'a valuable addition to any mess'. (He was, however,
inclined to the portly, and his uniform gave him cause for complaint: 'Oh for a smaller
waist, the late Sam Browne (Col) (God rest his soul) has a deal to answer for in the
Recording Angel's Book'.)

Dodd was appointed in December 1916 on terms similar to Bone – £500 p.a. plus
expenses, in return for the pick of his output and the right to reproduce it for the
duration of the war. However, Masterman had had to draw on all his political experience and connections to overcome the opposition of the Treasury, which doubtless
saw this second art appointment as the thin end of an extravagant wedge.

Dodd went to France in February 1917 with an exhausting schedule before him.
In eight weeks, motoring between the various headquarters of the British Army on

the Somme, he disposed of thirty-one 'victims' – fighting generals and a miscellany of chaplains, medical officers and support staff – catching a quick likeness in charcoal and adding watercolour later.

Several of the more glamorous personalities were, however, unavailable, and he was

Randolph Schwabe, *Francis Dodd* (etching), National Portrait Gallery

[15]

obliged to complete their pictures on his return to England. Viscount French sat for two portraits, a favour unlikely to have pleased Dodd, who found him vain and disagreeable and possibly expressed his feelings by portraying the Field-Marshal mounted in a field of cabbages. After one of the sittings he observed gloomily, 'I will . . . ask the old boy for another go at his mouth tho' all I could do would not give him much of a look of genial friendliness.'

The most conspicuous absentee was Haig, whose picture, as Commander-in-Chief, was obviously vital to Masterman's scheme. Dodd was required to fabricate one and did so with the aid of photographs for the head and his wife's brother for the body. Despite its spuriousness the portrait pleased Haig, who sent a telegram of congratulation. Not all the portraits were as well received. Dodd's object was accuracy and he soon experienced the phenomenon described by William Rothenstein: 'I usually found that each of my sitters thought twenty-three of the twenty-four drawings excellent likenesses; the twenty-fourth was his own.' General Cavan (whom Dodd in later years described as 'an ass . . . naught but a sergeant-major') passed his portrait round his staff, 'in order to arrive at an unbiased judgment . . . none of them recognised it.' The independence of mind of a general's staff may perhaps be questioned, but the picture was suppressed. Least appreciative of all was General Hunter-Weston, who wrote apoplectically, 'Does the Propaganda Department desire to destroy all confidence in the morality and intelligence of the Generals of the British Army and Navy? That these pictures are not the least like the originals is bad, but the fact that they make it appear that the originals are both unintelligent and in many cases evil-looking is much worse.' He went on to praise in glowing terms a portrait of himself by de Laszlo, which he felt should be substituted forthwith. Masterman was more than equal to the challenge and wrote with the utmost suavity, 'You will, I am sure, understand that it would have been very difficult for us to have included . . . a portrait by Laszlo, in view of his internment.'

Shortly before Dodd's return from France in April 1917, permission had been received from the Admiralty for the series of Admirals. Both Dodd and Masterman anticipated trouble in their attempts to advertise the Senior Service, with its tradition of stoic and gentlemanly reserve. Sir Douglas Brownrigg, Chief Naval Censor, reflected later, 'Considering their attitude towards having their portraits done, it is surprising that they didn't wear *yashmaks*.'

It must be a tribute to Dodd's charm that, with few exceptions, his naval engagements proceeded smoothly. He found Beatty fidgety and Halsey self-conscious, but his most serious problem was a severely practical one – the green parrot sported by Rear-Admiral Osmond Brock which 'was always dropping turds'. His reminiscences of the sittings make entertaining reading. Of the parrot-fancying Brock he records, 'Was at Hoy when Kitchener was lost. . . . He was in charge of sweepers & warned Admiralty that mines were in the fairway before Kitchener sailed, but the warning was disregarded. Said that some sailors did climb the cliff but were exhausted and took shelter in the hay cocks, died there & were not found till months afterwards. It all sounded remote and queer.' He was intrigued by Admiral Startin – 'A queer, god-fearing pugilistic-minded man . . . Fisher put him ashore because he would dive overboard to rescue drowning sailors instead of stopping on the bridge in command' – and delighted by

Francis Dodd, *Field-Marshal Sir Douglas Haig, GCB, GCVO, KCIE* (charcoal and watercolour), $14\frac{1}{2} \times 10\frac{1}{2}$

Admiral Bruce – 'A "character", always slept under the Ensign as bedspread'.

 Nevertheless, his finished pictures did not find universal favour with his sitters. Many may have been expecting the formal and heroic treatment in oils accorded their predecessors in high office and were disappointed by the literal, unromantic drawings Dodd offered. Vice-Admiral de Chair objected: 'The head seems put on too far forward . . . Anyone who sees this picture without having seen me would say I was round-shoul-dered with a back like a turtle & about 7ft 6in high!!' More plaintively still Admiral Bethel wrote, 'My womenfolk don't like it. They say the forehead is too high & suggest you might put a cap on it . . . I shan't have much peace if something isn't done.'

Dodd does not seem to have been much moved by these criticisms, but his life as a portraitist of warriors was beginning to pall. By the end of 1917 he had spent almost eight months travelling between the home ports and the Grand Fleet, working at high speed to complete 105 portraits – as he put it, 'every admiral on this side of Glory'. Most seriously he was getting stale, bored by 'Red Tabs and Brass Hats'. At the end of March 1918 he resigned, without opposition from Masterman, who by now had acquired more admirals and generals than he can have anticipated.

The portraits were put to good use, most immediately in newspapers, foreign and domestic. But Masterman's most sustained effort to exploit them took the form of two publications – *Generals of the British Army* and *Admirals of the British Navy*, each in two volumes and published, like *The Western Front*, by *Country Life*. Each volume contained twelve colour portraits, whose selection and ordering from among Dodd's copious output raised nice problems of protocol. The brief biographies which accompanied the pictures also promoted discord, as neither War Office nor Admiralty were prepared to tolerate any element of the controversial. Montague, though a close friend of Dodd's, was not approached; his aversion to the 'Red Tabs' of the old Regular Army was well known and it was considered more prudent to entrust the generals to John Buchan. Even he found the War Office attitude inhibiting and described his efforts as 'wretched stuff – simply dull military history'. (Montague was not unsympathetic: in a letter to Dodd he wrote, 'What a cornucopious distributor of laurels is Buchan – quite unavoidably no doubt, for I suppose you cannot say semi-officially "Quite a nice fellow, this, but came rather a cropper at –" . . . *Your* judgments can be much more frank, thanks to the purblindness of the great.') The naval biographies were even less enthralling and Masterman demanded testily, 'Can you provide something more unimpeccable . . . Jellicoe's life, e.g., seems grotesquely jejune!'; but he was aware of the resistance from the admirals themselves – 'It must be dealing with the facts: they won't stand the "proud strong man" business.'

Admirals and *Generals* were distributed and publicised widely. Home sales were satisfactory, at between 4000 and 4500 copies per volume. In addition, 1500 copies of each volume were distributed free to libraries, clubs and other public places where they might attract attention, and 5000 copies of each volume were printed for circulation in America. Interest in the pictures can perhaps best be gauged from attendances at a joint exhibition of the works of Dodd and Bone in the north of England in mid-1918 – 63,000 in six months.

Dodd had catered no more than Bone for the public's taste for drama and sentiment. He provided for the nation an interesting, thorough and honest record of its war leaders – too honest, perhaps, for propaganda purposes, but invaluable for posterity. His work disappointed many in its obvious lack of glamour – 'the most putrid thing I have ever seen. No wonder Jellicoe got the sack'. But one critic at least saw the real worth of his approach: 'The faces are mostly those of elderly, weary men, grimly intelligent, with well-opened steady eyes. It is not the joy of battle that their expression reveals, but the pensive determination of human men who have steeled themselves to terrible responsibilities.'

Francis Dodd, *Admiral Sir John Rushworth Jellicoe, GCB, OM, GCVO* (charcoal and watercolour), $13\frac{3}{4} \times 10$

CHAPTER FIVE

The Department of Information

HAD circumstances not conspired to effect a radical reorganisation of the various propaganda departments in the spring of 1917, it is probable that Francis Dodd would have been the last official artist to be appointed. In January Wellington House had received a request from General Sir Archibald Murray, Commander-in-Chief Middle East, for an artist to record the Palestine campaign, but despite the high level of the request Masterman had made no approach to the Treasury, anticipating that they 'would not sanction any further artists after Dodd'.

Since the beginning of 1916 the War Office had consistently been critical of both the policy and administration of the multifarious propaganda bodies under the loose control of the Foreign Office. On 22 December, ten days after Lloyd George's appointment as Prime Minister, they delivered a summary of their criticisms and proposals, confident of a ready audience. Propaganda was an integral part of Lloyd George's 'total war' policy. Moreover, he owed his own appointment in part at least to a well-orchestrated publicity campaign and he was perfectly well aware of the power of the press: his response to the dispute between the War Office and the Foreign Office was to appoint a leading journalist, Robert Donald, editor of the *Daily Chronicle*, to investigate.

John Buchan, National Portrait Gallery

In his report, delivered on 9 January 1917, Donald proposed the formation of a new Department of Information incorporating all the existing propaganda departments in a single efficient unified structure. He advocated placing greater emphasis on news and less on comment. He also suggested the names of various political figures for the influential post of Director, but none of his nominees was willing to accept the honour. When the Department of Information was set up by War Cabinet Minute on 19 February 1917 the post went instead to the forty-two-year-old John Buchan.

Although his appointment as Director of Information was very largely due to the intercession of Lord Milner, now a member of the War Cabinet – Lloyd George himself had not been enthusiastic – Buchan did have useful attributes for the job. At the outbreak of war duodenal ulcers had prevented him from joining up; instead, as director of Nelson's, he initiated *Nelson's History of the War*, most of which he wrote himself. His success as a military journalist encouraged Northcliffe to appoint him special correspondent for *The Times* to cover the Second Battle of Ypres in 1915, and this brought him into close contact with GHQ in France. In September 1916 a writer was needed to draft official communiqués, and General Charteris, head of Intelligence, wrote, 'I feel sure it is better to get a man who is accustomed to phrase turning more than is a mere soldier – and no one can quarrel with Buchan's literary tastes' (Buchan had by this time written *The Thirty-Nine Steps*, 1915, and *Greenmantle*, 1916). At the same time he was being employed by the Foreign Office; in June 1916 he had been given control of a somewhat mysterious 'Intelligence' section, with the rank of Lieutenant-Colonel.

He was thus acceptable both to the military (Haig was a personal friend from South African days) and to the Foreign Office – a rare accomplishment. He had a thorough knowledge of military affairs, and the contacts to ensure the requisite flow of information, from the Front at least; by 1917 he had also established a considerable reputation as a novelist and had made useful friends in society partly through his wife, Susan Grosvenor, and her family.

It was nevertheless unexpected that as a middle-ranking and relatively young officer in Military Intelligence, almost completely lacking in political experience, Buchan should have been put in charge of foreign propaganda – a post which later in the war was to attract men of the calibre and stature of Beaverbrook and Northcliffe. It is especially surprising at first sight that this should have happened over the head of Masterman, whom many considered by far the more powerful intellectually. His political expertise was unquestioned, and this was conspicuously a political post; he already had two and a half years of successful work in propaganda to his credit. His passing over was a symptom of the general decline in his fortunes, and especially of the soured relationship with Lloyd George. He went from Director of Propaganda at Wellington House to Assistant Director, Literature and Art, and his salary was reduced: this was in fact the point of no return. He seemed resigned – 'It doesn't matter much what happens now – we all have to be content to work under other people if necessary'; and he did at least like and respect Buchan to whom he was distantly related by marriage.

Under Buchan's control the DoI was organised into four sections (incorporating Wellington House) with a central executive, under Buchan himself, based at the Foreign Office. The Intelligence Section was responsible for collecting and evaluating information; a Technical Section handled transmissions by cable and wireless, press articles and cinematograph films; the Administrative Section was in day-to-day charge of the propaganda effort in different countries. The fourth section was Masterman's Literature and Art Section, still based at Wellington House but no longer bearing its name, and significantly altered from the old autonomous 'Wellington House'.

It had lost overall responsibility for propaganda in America to the new British Bureau of Information, set up quite openly in New York after America's entry into the war. Films, press articles and the distribution of propaganda had also been removed from its sphere of influence; it was now merely 'a very large publishing establishment, which issues every form of book, pamphlet, magazine and picture'. Pictorial propaganda was accordingly promoted in its scale of priorities – the monthly circulation of *War Pictorial* was increased to 700,000 – and despite the reduction in its other activities Masterman's section was to remain the most costly branch of the Department. As pictorial propaganda expanded, war art expanded with it, and it became necessary to delegate responsibility for the day-to-day administration to a specific official: the choice fell on Alfred Yockney, originally employed as an assistant in the Eastern and Moslem Propaganda Department of Wellington House, but an art journalist of many years' experience. From the middle of 1917 until the end of 1920 he was to be more intimately involved than anyone else with the nuts and bolts of official war art.

A. N. Lewis, *Alfred Yockney* (pencil), 13 × 9, reproduced by kind permission of Mrs Sue Yockney

Though Buchan made no claims to be particularly knowledgeable about art, he was to support all the war art proposals made by Masterman's Literature and Art Section and even initiated one or two appointments himself, moved partly by a belief in art's value as propaganda, and partly perhaps by a sense of its topicality.

Besides this general aura of good will, his principal contribution was the protection his post provided against Treasury obstructiveness. The old Wellington House had previously had no separate Vote (its funds coming largely from the National Health Insurance Vote), and consequently needed Treasury sanction for every appointment made. The new DoI had both its own official funds, which Buchan could administer without reference to the Treasury, and access to the Foreign Office's Secret Service Fund for 'work which in the public interest should never be revealed to the public'. At least one war artist – Paul Nash – is known to have been financed from the latter source.

The long-term effect of this financial emancipation was an impressive list of artists in DoI employment; the immediate result was the granting of General Murray's request for an artist in the Middle East.

CHAPTER SIX

James McBey

W HEN the Commander-in-Chief's request was first considered in January 1917, Campbell Dodgson had a nominee in mind: 'I can think of no artist more suitable for drawing in Egypt than James McBey . . . A man who is so good both at black and white and colour, drawing and etching, should find military subjects in Egypt a congenial sphere of work.'

McBey, born in 1883 and raised in a tiny village outside Aberdeen, spent the first decade of his working life as a bank clerk, the sole support of his mother and grandmother. The work was both gruelling and dull, and he was possessed by the fear that his own acute short-sightedness was the precursor of the disease that was progressively blinding his mother; on his own admission he became adept at manipulating balance sheets, preferring to make up small deficits from his meagre salary rather than pore for hours over the columns of microscopic figures.

In a moving fragment of autobiography he has described these dour early years, lightened only by an obsessive determination to become an artist. Untutored, he read his way through the art section of the Aberdeen Free Library and taught himself to draw. A treatise on etching inspired him to make his first plate out of zinc-copper bought cheap from a plumber; he ran off the proofs on his mother's mangle and realised that he had found his perfect medium.

After eleven years at the bank he had with great difficulty saved £200; in 1910 he turned his back on hard-earned financial security, left his job, and spent his savings travelling to Holland to study the landscapes of Rembrandt's etchings. The following year he moved to London where he acquired a reputation not unlike Bone's, as a very hardworking and conscientious draughtsman in the nineteenth-century tradition 'of which a high degree of skill and a professional craftsmanlike approach were the cornerstones'. A visit to Morocco in 1912 produced work which revealed him as an accomplished watercolourist, and by 1914 he was well established, a remarkable example of self-made success.

James McBey, *Portrait of the Artist* (chalk and watercolour), $13\frac{1}{4} \times 9\frac{3}{4}$

McBey's early attempts to join up at the outbreak of war were foiled by his poor eyesight. He was eventually commissioned in January 1916 as a 2nd Lieutenant in the Army Printing and Stationery Service and posted to Rouen, where his duties depressingly resembled the drudgery he thought he had escaped. Sketching was forbidden, but he nevertheless made surreptitious studies (some of them tiny drawings in the palm of his hand)[7] which he worked up afterwards on a larger scale; later he was able, legitimately, to make two series of etchings while on leave, one of munitions works at Harfleur, *France at her Furnaces*, and another of the Somme battlefields. These were exhibited in London and it was their popularity, coupled with the success of McBey's first exhibition in New York, which ensured his acceptability as a war artist.

His appointment began on 21 April 1917, initially for a period of six months, but extended successively until February 1919. He retained his rank as 2nd Lieutenant and received a salary of £500 p.a. plus expenses; use of his work went to the Government for the duration, and the British Museum was to have any of the originals it wanted. McBey's brief was 'to make drawings of appropriate war scenes in Egypt and Palestine for the purposes both of propaganda at the present time and of historical record in the future', and he was given a complete set of *The Western Front* for guidance. Of all the official war artists he was the only one to approach Bone's prodigious output, executing 299 drawings, watercolours and oils over a twenty-one-month period.

By the time McBey left for Egypt General Murray had been replaced as Commander-in-Chief by 'Bull' Allenby, an old-style cavalry general from the Western Front, whose personal support and understanding of T. E. Lawrence did much to bring the Arab irregulars into active and valuable co-operation with the British Army in their campaign against the Turks. Lawrence's inspired guerrilla raids in the Hejaz and in the deserts to the east of the Jordan made the Middle East a place of romance and adventure to the British public. McBey followed the main body of British forces in their advance north from Suez through Palestine, the Lebanon and Syria, and so was never able to capture any of the individual incidents of Lawrence's war, but he met and painted the man himself and some of the Arab chiefs, and his work was undoubtedly enhanced, both during and after the war, by the association.

True to form McBey started to sketch the moment he boarded ship in May 1917, and the detailed notes he made on the back of each drawing impart a strong flavour of his wartime journey to the East. '*On the Troop Train: the Second Day*. "Fed up" after 48 hours' continuous journeying . . . the spontaneous and demonstrative "God speeds" of the Rhône Valley no longer awake response . . . *The Gun Sentry*. On the windy platform rigged in the stern a sentry stands beside the gun. After sunset, on a quiet sea the wake, zigzagging to the horizon, shows the course for miles astern . . . *The Arrival in Port*. Egypt at last! The destroyers, having nosed ahead like dark ferrets all the way from France, stop and, as the transport passes them, are seen alongside for the first time. From the crowded decks rousing cheers are given for the gallant . . . bluejackets as they drop anchor.'

McBey arrived in Egypt in the midst of Allenby's preparations for the push north up the Gaza Strip and on to Jerusalem. Thus his first few weeks were occupied with subjects in Port Said, Cairo and the Canal Zone – wood, fodder and frozen Australian meat being unloaded, and bread being baked in huge quantities at regimental bakeries;

James McBey, *Dawn: Camel Patrol Setting Out* (etching), 9 × 15

Armenian refugees in a camp near Port Said, weaving and dyeing cotton for the Red Cross; horses being shod and rehabilitated at a veterinary hospital on the edge of the desert; the Suez Canal itself, 'scooped across the desert by the finger of God'. Five invaluable days were spent on a long reconnaissance patrol into the Sinai Desert with a contingent of the Australian Camel Corps. The men, almost all rough-riders from the outback, at first regarded the artist with some incredulity, but McBey's doggedness and application to his (albeit unmanly) work in the appalling summer heat of Sinai earned their respect and he was invited to share all the pleasures of their company, including 'a plate of onions at 6 p.m.'.

This early waiting period was very fruitful and McBey maintained a steady flow of drawings, but when the advance started he encountered his first real difficulties. 'I beg to apply for the use of a car. . . . For three months I have carried on with none but chance transport . . . and the results I have to show are disappointing considering the trouble taken and the considerable fatigue undergone. After walking more than say a mile in soft sand it is a physical impossibility to produce a good drawing, a performance which under even favourable conditions demands considerable nervous strain.' In this campaign of constant movement, lack of transport meant unique opportunities missed; McBey arrived too late for the fall of Gaza and wrote despairingly to Masterman, 'The finest material of the whole time I have been here is around me and near me but completely out of my reach.'

He did, however, witness Allenby's historic entry into Jerusalem in December 1917. Though relatively unimportant militarily, the occupation of the city had always been a symbol of Turkish (and Islamic) primacy in the Middle East: its capture, following the fall of Baghdad and Mecca, was a clear sign that Ottoman power was crumbling.

Moreover, for the Christian world Jerusalem was 'the prize that countless Crusaders through the centuries had striven for in vain. . . . As a timely Christmas present came the redemption of the place to which the thoughts of Christendom turned at Christmas-tide.' The Allied response to Allenby's achievement is encapsulated in McBey's drawing *The Black Watch Guard on the Church of the Holy Sepulchre, Jerusalem* – 'For the first time since the thirteenth century, Christians guard some of the Holy Places of Christendom.'

The DoI was understandably eager to turn to immediate propaganda use McBey's pictures of Jerusalem. An exhibition had already been organised for January and February 1918 at Colnaghi's and Masterman was anxious to incorporate the Jerusalem series, but it was March before they emerged from GHQ, Cairo. By this time any impact they might have made was lost in the shadow of the massive German spring offensive on the Western Front.

From the propaganda point of view McBey must be accounted one of the DoI's failures: throughout his appointment, much impeded by delays at GHQ Cairo in censoring and photographing the drawings, the Department seems to have been incapable of taking advantage of his prodigious output, despite its obvious potential. Two booklets along the lines of *The Western Front* – one on Egypt and one on Palestine – were suggested but never implemented, and the only publication during the war was *The Desert Campaigns*, published (probably independently) by Constable & Co., a short essay which included only eleven of McBey's drawings. Of his other pictures, some were reproduced by the DoI in the *War Pictorial* and in newspapers and periodicals, but there were no exhibitions outside London despite repeated requests from provincial galleries.

In February 1918 McBey was at last given a car and driver, and during the year he made exploratory trips in the wake of Allenby's armies. One activity he particularly wanted to record was the work of patrol boats on the Dead Sea; after a baking and circuitous drive from Jerusalem, his first thought was to swim: 'It was delightfully buoyant but my eyes almost bled with the sting of intensely salt water. The sun was the only substitute for a towel. I had just begun a drawing when two large cars drove up. In the first was the Duke of Connaught and General Allenby, and in the other staff officers. The Commander-in-Chief stopped and said, "Making a survey?" (I was working on a survey plane table). "No, sir. Sketching." "Who are you?" "The official artist." "What, McBey? I did not recognise you." No wonder, for the Dead Sea water drying on my face had left a thick deposit of salt, giving me the appearance of Lot's wife. . . .' He also visited Bethlehem, Jericho and Jaffa and, before being defeated by recurrent bouts of heatstroke and sand-fly fever, attempted three sketching trips into the Jordan Valley, which he found 'a sinister place. . . . It is like being in a vast white oven with a lid for the sky resting on the Moab Mountains on one side and the Jordanian Hills on the other. I'm going to have a rake through the Bible tomorrow, as I'm inclined to think the Hebrew idea of Hell, on which we were all brought up, took shape from their living on the edge of this furnace.'

McBey was bedevilled not only by fever but by flies, sand, heat in summer with no shade to relieve the sun's glare, and torrential rains in winter – problems exacerbated by the need to be continually on the move, following up the advance. But the rigours of his apprenticeship as an artist had made him exceptionally determined and very adaptable, and his early experience of desert conditions in Morocco stood him in good stead. He adopted a technique of great economy, drawing rapidly on the spot in brown ink or pencil, with a faint wash of colour – ideal both for coping with the practical difficulties of the environment and for evoking the scorched wastes and brilliant light of desert scenery, succeeding, as one critic put it, primarily through 'the magic of suggestion'.

However, as the advance moved north the landscape altered and McBey pressed to be allowed to change his medium. 'We are now in very broken country, difficult to suggest in watercolour, and not made easier by the heat here drying the colours immediately they are put on paper, and buckling it.' Although swirling sand had not interfered with the use of watercolours, as it could be shaken off once the colours had dried, it had effectively prohibited the use of oils; now the deserts were receding and McBey requested oils and canvas for portraits of the successful military leaders. Allenby, Bulfin and Chauvel all sat for him, and on arriving at Damascus after its capture by the Arabs on 1 October 1918 he at last met T. E. Lawrence. After Damascus Lawrence left his followers and returned to England; McBey painted him on the day before his departure, seated in a room through which his guerrillas filed one by one to kiss his hand in farewell.

McBey also jumped at the opportunity to paint some of the Arab leaders, including the one Lawrence most respected, Emir Sherif Feisal. 'I lured him into a room away from the crowd of curious interrupters. Feisal sat wonderfully steady for about five minutes, then he suggested lunch. . . . A huge Abyssinian negro with swords, knives and automatic revolvers hung round his neck, stood immobile behind the Emir's chair. After lunch we had tea and coffee alternately. The sitting began again but little progress was made as Feisal was evidently uncomfortable. I suggested a rest, when he immediately rose and took from the bare wooden seat of his chair a brass door knob, which had been put there, by accident of course, and on which he had been sitting for half an hour. Thereafter the sketch was soon finished.' McBey also sketched Feisal's huge bodyguard and followed him with one of the fiercer sheiks of the Hejaz, the sixty-five-year-old Mohammed Ali-el-Manyed el Aden, who 'insisted that the word "fighter" should be written on the drawing before he would allow it out of his sight'. (Not all the portrait sitters took such a keen interest. McBey recalled an especially jaded Indian prisoner, for whom artists were the last straw: '"I was taken by the Turks at Kut," he said, "and the Germans sketched me; now I have escaped and you sketch me."')

After Damascus the retreat of the Turks became a rout and the campaign was brought to a rapid conclusion at the end of October with the capture of Aleppo, where McBey joined Allenby for the Armistice. Thorough to the last he wrote to Yockney in December, 'I badly want to see England, naturally, but I should like to know that my record was complete', and he stayed for another two months to finish to his own satisfaction his extraordinary pictorial history of the Palestine Campaign.

Whilst in the Middle East McBey had been unable to do any etchings. On his return he wasted no time in producing three series from his notes and sketches, the most famous of which, *The Long Patrol* (based on his Australian Camel Corps experiences), brought him international fame: in 1926, at the height of the print boom, the *Long*

Patrol etchings reached record prices at auctions on both sides of the Atlantic. In 1919, however, McBey could not have anticipated this success and, in pursuit of the funds to buy No. 1 Holland Park Road, his home for the rest of his life, he submitted to Yockney his claim for reimbursement of expenses. It is a document worthy in its precision of an ex-bank clerk, and quite typical of McBey in its modesty: for twenty-one months of continuous work he claimed £37 5*s* 10*d* for materials and, for the transport of self, paintbox and luggage throughout the Holy Land, £2 1*s* 6*d*.

CHAPTER SEVEN

GHQ & William Orpen

Colonel A. N. Lee,
(reproduced by
kind permission
of P. Murray Lee)

BESIDES seizing the chance to appoint McBey, Masterman wanted further to exploit the DoI's financial independence by extending artistic activity in France. For this he needed the sanction of the military authorities as artists were in effect specialised 'visitors' and all visits to the Front came under the heading of Military Press Control, the province of MI7.

In France, Military Intelligence (a contradiction in terms, according to Lord Curzon) had a sphere of operations far wider than merely the gathering of strategic information, including responsibility for 'the Press, censorship, Secret Service, mapping, ciphers, visitors and various odd little side-shows, like sound-ranging, telephone- intercepting sections and carrier- pigeons'. For visitors it provided accommodation – either at special visitors' châteaux (generally reserved for spectators more eminent than the war artists – politicians, literary lions and the like), at the press châteaux (where Bone was housed), or in billets with the troops – more convenient for artistic purposes than the châteaux miles behind the line, but far less comfortable. Intelligence arranged for transport, for access to appropriate spots on the Front, and for censorship at source for the material the visitors gathered.

Until February 1917 Intelligence had taken only one artist at a time; now the DoI asked for the creation of a permanent 'artists' establishment' and the 'utmost possible facilities' both for long stays like Bone's and for short visits such as GHQ had been granting to writers like Masefield, Bennett, Shaw and Wells. The Intelligence Chief, General Sir John Charteris, dealt with the proposal personally. His reply was cautious: he agreed to take a maximum of only two artists at any one time, subject to the availability of conducting officers and cars. He had noticed, he said, the tendency of artists to 'want to sit down and look at a place for a long time', which made it difficult for them to share cars with the more peripatetic correspondents – and he insisted that GHQ had the right to vet the names suggested. Most importantly, to forestall a flood of applications from 'the whole tribe of artists' eager to exploit the war's artistic potential, it had to be made absolutely clear that work at the Front was to be done for the Government and not for private ends.

Under the new 'Agreement with Artists' (drafted by Dodgson), the Government protected its interests merely by retaining for the duration copyright in any pictures produced and, as a further deterrent to self-seekers, offering no salary. The DoI had little interest in acquiring pictures, either for itself or for the British Museum; thus the new artists, though unpaid, kept possession of their works and were to have the right to sell them after the war.[8] Other points were left to be settled in each individual case: the payment of expenses; the length of visit (these were intended to be short appointments, and a visit of three weeks was suggested, but artists almost invariably stayed longer); and honorary military rank – wisely left unspecified, as it increasingly became a bone of contention between the military and propaganda authorities.

In fact, the new terms made the post of official artist *more* and not less attractive than it had been under Wellington House; if the artist was of any repute at all, the right to retain and sell his pictures was worth far more than a salary of approximately £42 per month. Nevertheless the War Office and GHQ raised no objections, and the new arrangement started amicably with the first two posts on the new establishment going to artists originally suggested by the military authorities themselves – William Orpen and John Lavery, both successful society portraitists, and both Irish.

Some observers saw the choice of two Irish artists as a propaganda move in itself, designed to demonstrate Anglo-Irish solidarity in the face of the German menace and counter the very different impression left by the Easter Rising. However, Orpen and Lavery both maintained a public indifference to the Irish Question – Orpen claiming not to know what the question was. Both were expatriates, and neither was particularly identified with Ireland or the 'Celtic Renascence' – Lavery was more closely associated with the Glasgow School, and Orpen was reported as saying, 'I am unknown in Ireland. It was the English who gave me appreciation and money.' (His accent, however, remained Irish: Wyndham Lewis wrote sourly of the 'quavering Dublin patter which he had taken good care never to get rid of'.)

Though it seems surprising now, when his reputation is only gradually being rehabilitated after forty years of neglect, Orpen was almost the biggest 'name' among the official artists. Pressure for his appointment came from the highest level – and he must have seemed eminently suitable as the first artist to be appointed on the new terms. In fact his term of office was to be the least staid or orthodox of all. Employed under an agreement which suggested a stay of three weeks, he was to work in France, more or less beyond official control, well into 1920. Other artists came and went but Orpen was a permanent, if unreliable, fixture in the background of official war art until long after the signing of peace.

He combined extreme proficiency as a draughtsman with a distinctive imagination and wit. While he was still at the Slade this won him the 1899 Summer Composition Prize for his *Play Scene in 'Hamlet'*, in which he included tiny portraits of artist contemporaries and older friends – William Rothenstein, Ida Nettleship, who soon afterwards married Augustus John, and John himself. Orpen, John and Rothenstein's younger brother Albert were known as 'the Three Musketeers', a nickname with a misleading suggestion of inseparability as John grew increasingly malevolent about Orpen's blossoming reputation, with good reason: William Rothenstein remembered connoisseur and gallery-owner Robert Ross claiming that 'people came into the Carfax [Gallery] and prostrated themselves before a John but always went off with an Orpen.' In 1910 Orpen was made an ARA and pundits forecast a steady progress to the Presidency; by 1914 he was firmly established as one of London's leading portrait painters.

As such, he was in great demand in fashionable circles. One of the most effective weapons in his social armoury was his size – little more than five foot and slightly built: Max Beerbohm unkindly depicted him as sitting down to paint and saying, 'Now I'll do a tremendously big fellow – I should think about five foot six.' Acutely conscious of his lack of stature, he did his best to present it as an endearing, rather than simply comic, even freakish characteristic, referring to himself as a 'migit', or, more often, in the third person as 'Little Orps' or, worse, 'Ikkle Orps', even 'Orpsie Porpsie'.

It certainly did nothing to cramp his style with women. He was married to the statuesque Grace Knewstub, and embroiled with several other sizeable ladies, most notably the American millionairess Evelyn St George – well over six foot tall and slender enough for the pair of them to be known round London as 'Jack and the Beanstalk'. Mrs St George was an ambitious and determined professional hostess, and it was through her that Orpen met Sir John Cowans, the Quartermaster-General, and Sir Douglas Haig. He had already made influential friends of his own – Lord Derby sat to him in 1912, and in the following year he painted Philip Sassoon – and these contacts were directly instrumental in obtaining him his appointment as a war artist.

Orpen was not unpatriotic; when war broke out he gave his black-and-white Rolls-Royce (plus chauffeur) for use as military transport and donated three blank canvases for auction by the Red Cross. But, on his own admission, he had no intention of fighting. In December 1915, shortly after the introduction of the Derby Scheme, the forerunner of conscription, he voluntarily joined the Army Services Corps; with Cowans' help he was commissioned as a 2nd Lieutenant in March 1916 and from May served uneventfully at the ASC's London headquarters at Kensington Barracks. Then came an invitation from the Canadians to work in France on portraits of both English and French leaders. This alarmed Lord Derby, now Secretary of State for War, who felt that if the French 'were to be beholden to anyone it was the British and not the Canadians', and he pressed for a pre-emptive strike.

On 30 January 1917 the *Daily Mirror* reported Haig as having 'appointed' Orpen as 'official artist with the Army in France' – a private arrangement between Orpen and the War Office, which would have had nothing to do with the DoI had not Orpen's departure been inexplicably delayed. By the time Derby applied pressure again, the new arrangement with the DoI prevailed.

Thus when Orpen arrived in France in the first week of April 1917 it was on the Department's terms. The Government was to have the copyright of all his work; he was to receive no salary, only his regular Army pay (no mention was made of his expenses) and he was to submit to all regulations made by GHQ. From the start it was clear that Orpen was not the conventional employee: he had been promoted from 2nd Lieutenant to Major and offered unlimited time in France (both efforts to equal the terms offered by the Canadians), and he brought with him not only his own batman but also a manager, Captain T. T. Aikman, to make all the time-consuming 'military arrangements'. He was given both a car and a chauffeur by Cowans.[9]

In *An Onlooker in France*, published in 1923, an account of his years as an official war artist, Orpen parades his abhorrence of bureaucracy. His first brush was with Intelligence, in the shape of Major Arthur Lee and his immediate superior, Colonel Hutton-Wilson; the latter was Orpen's especial *bête noire* and the most vicious abuse in *Onlooker* is reserved for him – but the day-to-day wrangles were with Lee.

From mid-1917 to the spring of 1919, Major (later Colonel) Lee was the man responsible for all the logistics of artists' visits to the Front and also for censoring single-handed all their work and that of the official photographers. The censor, by virtue of his job, can never be a popular figure, and it would be unfair to take all the war artists' railing against censorship as being personally directed at Lee. He was a hard-working, much harassed man, a solicitor in civilian life, conscientious to the point of pedantry. When war broke out he was thirty-seven and had been in the Territorial Army for fifteen years. He saw active service both in Ireland (where he won the DSO for his services in dealing with the Easter Rising) and in the Ypres Salient on the Western Front before being posted to GHQ, Intelligence. He had a certain consciousness of his own worth, but this was offset by a sensitivity to ill-feeling – at one point in his war diary[10] he remarks sadly, 'I heard that two of the war correspondents didn't like me (I thought they all disliked me!).' He was conventional in his tastes, proud of being Captain of the Section Cricket Club, and enjoying nothing more than 'a smack' round the mini golf-course that 'Maps' had improvised; he cultivated a small allotment outside his billet at Beaumerie-sur-Mer, and would work off ill-humour by hoeing peas.

He was a staunch defender of prevalent middle-class values – during the strikes of October 1919 he expressed to Yockney the hope that the Government would 'show the strikers that the poor old middle class can run the country without their help' – and displayed in particular the anti-semitism that was neither uncommon nor considered reprehensible in middle-class circles at that time. He regarded Sir Alfred Mond as 'an awful pig of a man, a hateful person with no manners. . . . It's a pity we can't run the Empire without the assistance of foreign Jews even tho' they be stuffed full of brains!' Nor did he care for other 'thrusters', particularly foreigners: he described Beaverbrook as 'quite rude and Canadian . . . not a gentleman in any meaning of the word. But clever . . .' 'Brains' were highly suspect, and he had a horror of the 'highbrow' – George Bernard Shaw he found 'a wild and woolly specimen'.

Lee, who by his own admission was 'not an arty man', was both convinced that artists were incapable of looking after themselves (he was to describe the formidable team of Sargent and Tonks as 'such children'), and determined that they should not be better off than the fighting man – 'although I was never one of those who said that all men of military age . . . should spend their serving time in the Line being killed and sticking trench knives into Huns, I did not believe that those selected for other less arduous work should have any more comforts than the Line people . . . just because they were lionised by Society at home.'

His attitude infuriated Orpen whose first act on arrival in France was to complain bitterly about his lodgings; he depicted Lee most unkindly in *Onlooker* as an officious toady – a piece of meanness which reflects worse on Orpen than on Lee as by 1923 the two had been close friends for at least five years. Even before the end of the war they were regular drinking companions (though Lee supplied most of the drink),[11] and possibly companions in more piquant pleasures as well: the surviving post-war letters from Orpen to Lee range from the suggestive to the mildly indecent. It is also worth noting that Lee was well-liked by several of the other artists and ended the war with a fine collection of pictures they had given him.

The immediate cause of Orpen's row with Intelligence was his failure to produce very much in the way of finished pictures in return for the facilities extended to him. Orpen exploded, 'This wonderful Colonel [Hutton-Wilson][12] expected me to work all day and apparently in the evening take what I had done and show it to him – the distance by motor to him and back was something like 110 miles!' At this stage (May 1917), Orpen was for the DoI 'a very big little man', whose pictures in the Royal Academy had been the success of the season, and Masterman wrote effusively, 'Please take your own time, do what you like, stay as long as you please and give us when you can . . . the opportunity of reproduction of that which you feel you can do best.'

However, four months later Orpen was still unforthcoming and Masterman, describing him as 'Irish and artistic', began to make unfavourable comparisons with the industrious Bone and Dodd. By September he had started pressing in earnest for pictures, partly to justify keeping Orpen in France – 'There is a certain jealousy by other artists of those who have been given facilities . . . and this jealousy can only be allayed by the demonstration of some of the work being used for national purposes' – but largely because he was faced with the immediate prospect of a shortage of pictures from the Western Front. Bone was back in England, and under pressure his copious output was drying up. More seriously, Masterman had learnt that he could expect nothing on the war in France from the second artist appointed under the new terms – John Lavery.

CHAPTER EIGHT

John Lavery

L AVERY's was another appointment looked on with favour at the War Office and GHQ. In 1917 he was sixty-one and an ARA, and a painter of wide range, with a fondness for the genre picture. His greatest commercial and social success, however, was as a portraitist; in 1911 he became the first President of the Royal Society of Portrait Painters. His reputation was not as dashing as Orpen's, but his connections were even more exalted. He had originally established himself after being appointed to paint Queen Victoria's State Visit to the International Exhibition at Glasgow in 1888, and in 1913 he painted a group portrait of the Royal Family at Buckingham Palace.

Like Orpen, Lavery owed many of his contacts to a forceful American female with social aspirations – in Lavery's case, his second wife Hazel. 'I do not know', he wrote, 'how many sitters, and wealthy ones, came to me on her account.' An exceptionally beautiful woman and a successful hostess, she dabbled in many fields and had powerful friends in all of them. In his autobiography, *The Life of a Painter*, Lavery remembers with pride Shaw sending her in proof *The Intelligent Woman's Guide to Socialism* for her comments, and claims that for her part in the negotiations leading up to the Treaty of 1921, by which the Irish Free State was created – a role which consisted mainly of bringing the opposing sides together over dinner – she had hopes of being made Vicereine of Ireland: certainly her portrait, by Lavery, appeared on Irish banknotes in 1923.

In consequence, his official appointment as a war artist (three years after his abortive attempt to join the Artists' Rifles) stemmed, like Orpen's, from an unofficial interest taken in high places. Early in 1917, while visiting the Duke of Westminster on holiday in France, he wrote to Lord Derby for leave to enter the British lines to paint, under the care of General Rawlinson (a keen amateur artist, whose portrait Lavery was completing). This was translated, first by the War Office and then by the DoI, as a request for an official post, and an agreement was made which seemed to suit all concerned admirably.

Lavery proposed to stay in France for six weeks during which time he would paint fifty or sixty oils of open-air scenes (he specifically excluded portraits). These would be the more useful to Masterman for being in colour, providing welcome variety from the black and white drawings of Bone and Dodd and, as they would be finished on the spot (Lavery estimated that his oil sketches would take him on average two hours), they would be available for immediate propaganda use. The Government was to have copyright but Lavery would retain the originals; the trip was to be entirely at his own expense, and he would receive no salary.

Lavery set about preparing a motor van in which he would live, and was due to leave at the end of June. Then, in a car crash during the black-out, both he and his wife were concussed and badly shaken. Lavery suffered for several weeks from attacks of amnesia and insomnia; but he would then have been ready and willing to go had it not been for Hazel. Throughout *Life of a Painter* his attitude to his wife is ambivalent. She was considerably younger than he was and from a smarter background; he could not understand (he claims) why she had married him, and he felt indebted to her for much of his success – even, perhaps, for his knighthood, which he suggests she achieved over dinner with Lloyd George at Philip Sassoon's. He constantly reiterates her beauty, charm and talents – at the same time hinting that she was vain, pretentious and neurotic. Following the accident she seems to have suffered from a nervous breakdown of some sort during which she was obsessed by the fear that Lavery would be run over; and though anxious to start for France, he was warned by her doctor, 'If you want to hasten your wife's death, go.'

His own account, so far highly coloured, becomes vague at this point, but the official correspondence reveals that the DoI hastily substituted a tour of the Home Front. On 3 August 1917 Lavery was issued with a Special Joint Naval and Military Permit, in theory enabling him to observe and depict every aspect of the war in Britain. In fact the permit carefully excluded docks, harbours, munition factories, captured ships or planes, and 'any other place or thing guarded by His Majesty's Forces', for access to which special permission was required. Lavery, expecting a genuine roving commission, was disappointed, and doubtless little cheered by the explanation: 'The reasons against issuing a more complete pass are that should you be killed by design or otherwise the pass could be used for enemy purposes.'

On the other hand the Special Joint Permit was sweeping enough to arouse suspicion at Rosyth when he went to visit the Fleet. The police thought it 'too good to be true' and regularly stopped him in the streets, after which 'children who had been told to look for spies became troublesome, calling me "the German spy painting oor brig" [the Forth Bridge] and throwing stones.'

Elsewhere authorities were sufficiently impressed to give him a fairly free hand. He found most of his subjects in the munitions works of Newcastle, Edinburgh and Elizabethville, the 'shell-making village' run by Belgian refugees, or with the Fleet in the Firth of Forth; he also produced some of the first pictures of Britain's air defences – aeroplanes taking off for test flights at Hendon, airships at Roehampton, and the kite balloons used by observers over the Western Front. The sitters for the few portraits he consented to do were very different from his usual fashionable clientele – a deckhand of the Northern Patrol, the skipper of the mine-sweeper *Granton*, and a young female shipbuilder from Wallsend-on-Tyne.

Lavery had painted 'war' pictures before his appointment – *The Green Park, 1914* (painted in the first fortnight of war, when the Park was already an armed camp), *The First Wounded in London Hospital, August 1914, A Mayfair Drawing Room, 1915* (converted into a convalescent ward for wounded officers), and others. His official paintings were of more obviously war-like and technical subjects, but the treatment was not markedly different. He was in fact a far from natural choice as a propagandist, regarding himself rather as a pacifist with distinct sympathy for the Germans as an inevitable consequence of his considerable pre-war following in Germany. Looking at war he saw only men 'blinded by rage and hatred . . . murdering each other, backed up by the churches in the name of patriotism and the sanctity of the home'. His readi-

John Lavery, *Elswick, 1917* (oil on canvas), 25 × 30

ness to serve was beyond question till the end of the war, but the lack of genuine enthusiasm and passion in his pictures could not be disguised and he himself dismissed them disgustedly as 'totally uninspired and dull as ditch-water . . . Instead of the grim harshness and horror of the scenes I had given charming colour versions as if painting a bank holiday on Hampstead Heath.'[13]

Lavery was good at feeling guilty – his autobiography is full of self-reproach – and he was convinced of his own callousness: 'I doubt if there are a more heartless crew than poets, painters and composers. We are encouraged in it by our lay brethren.'

Much of his later dissatisfaction with his pictures undoubtedly stemmed from the feeling that as an observer of other men's efforts he had not *suffered* enough during the war. Given his age, his attempt at active service, and the hardships he endured without complaint later in the war, he might seem to be blaming himself unnecessarily. But his harsh judgement was endorsed by C. E. Montague who found the pictures 'hopelessly dull and off-the-point . . . though I suppose [Lavery is] a worshipful person.'

Montague's acerbity was whetted by his own struggles to avoid the cheery commonplace in writing notes on the pictures. He had been commissioned to do this for a new publication inaugurated by Masterman when it became clear that Bone could no longer sustain *The Western Front* unaided. *British Artists at the Front* was a more ambitious production, geared more obviously than its predecessor to the art lover. Four artists were involved, one contributing to each issue, and the pictures were reproduced in colour. The format was similar – each picture was faced by an accompanying note – but in addition to the general introduction, which was intended to supply the context for the pictures and point their moral, a biographical essay on the artist of little apparent propaganda value was provided.

The Lavery issue of *British Artists at the Front* (eventually published in April or May 1918, as the second in the series) constituted the only use of his work for propaganda, because his broad handling of paint and his preference for even tonal values (even his reds were generally subdued) lent themselves particularly badly to reproduction in black and white. An apparent miscellany of Home Front vignettes, it suffered in commercial terms from concentrating on subjects with which the British public was already familiar – the Forth Bridge, framing an assortment of naval vessels: the Crystal Palace, scene of a review of the Royal Naval Division, and so on. But in his accompanying letterpress Montague highlighted a theme that was both novel and immediately relevant – the role of women at war. To accompany Lavery's pictures of women manufacturing tanks and turning shells he wrote, in the best *Guardian* manner, 'Women have travelled some way from the mild watercolours and crochet of mid-Victorian maidenhood. . . . What they have done in this war will surely be remembered for ever, not only helping to win it, but also helping all men in future to a nobler idea of comradeship with women.'

CHAPTER NINE

C. R. W. Nevinson

AFTER the conservatism of Masterman's first choices, his nominee to fill the gap left by Lavery's default was a surprising departure from form. Christopher Richard Wynne Nevinson was a modernist, something of an outsider, and a magnet for controversy.

He was born in 1889 into an aggressively Bohemian family, his mother a suffragette, his father, Henry Woodd Nevinson, though a pacifist, a noted war correspondent. In his flamboyant and passionately opinionated autobiography, *Paint and Prejudice*, Nevinson recalls a childhood clouded by conflict and a growing sense of exclusion. At the Slade, which he attended from 1908–12, he was both happy and seemingly successful until Tonks advised him with brutal candour to give up art. The life-long enmity this spawned makes entertaining reading – in *Paint and Prejudice* Nevinson places 'that old woman Tonks', 'poor virgin Tonks', or 'Henrietta Tonks' at the centre of successive (imaginary) conspiracies against him – but the episode did much to intensify the persecution complex from which he was to suffer all his life.

After leaving the Slade Nevinson studied in Paris, revelling in Montmartre café life and making close contacts with the French *avant-garde*; he shared a studio with Modigliani, met Picasso and became acquainted with cubist techniques, which were to remain a vital part of his artistic armoury until 1917. On his return to London in 1913 he threw himself into some of the more radical pre-war art groupings: he maintained a close association with Wyndham Lewis and the Vorticists, until in typical fashion he alienated them all through his over-exuberant espousal of Futurism.

This remarkable philosophy, part political, part artistic, had originated in Italy in 1909, and its disciples fervently devoted themselves to praising and portraying the dynamism of the modern mechanistic world – speed, noise, violence, colour, crowds, efficiency. Nevinson had been caught up during his Paris days with its prophets, Severini and Marinetti, and in June 1914 he and Marinetti together published an English Futurist manifesto – denouncing the 'passéist filth' which polluted the London art world, trumpeting the virtues of Futurism, and making some imprudent assumptions about their own position in the vanguard of 'vital English Art' – the effect of which was to ensure that at the outbreak of war Nevinson was left (if one discounts the youthful Herbert Read) in splendid isolation as the sole English Futurist.

The Futurists welcomed war as an irresistible force for good – the 'hygienics' of the world. '[Marinetti] must be in seventh heaven,' observed Wyndham Lewis in 1915, 'torn in mind as to which point of the compass to rush to – to drink up the booming and banging, to lap up the blood.' Nevinson saw in war a unique opportunity for the practical application of the art theories he had embraced: 'our Futurist technique is the only possible medium to express the crudeness, violence and brutality of the emotions seen and felt on the present battlefields of Europe.' Rejected by the Army

Eric Kennington, *The Kensingtons at Laventie* (oil on glass), 54 × 63

James McBey, *Cacolets* (pen and watercolour), $12\frac{1}{4} \times 20$

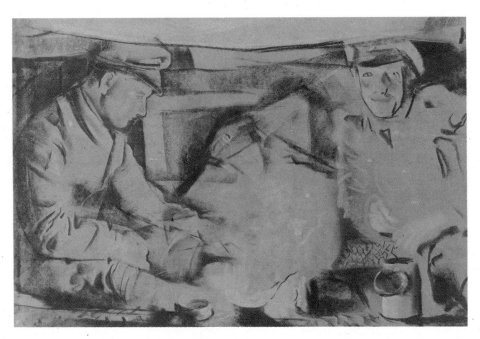

C. R. W. Nevinson, *The Road from Arras to Bapaume* (oil on canvas), 24 × 18

OPPOSITE BELOW, Eric Kennington, '*The Die-Hards*' (pastel), 19 × 25¼

John Singer Sargent, *Gassed* (oil on canvas), 90 × 240

BELOW LEFT, C. R. W. Nevinson, *Reliefs at Dawn* (oil on canvas), 28 × 36. RIGHT, Paul Nash, *Wire* (ink, pastel and watercolour), $18\frac{3}{4} \times 24\frac{1}{2}$

William Orpen, *Dead Germans in a Trench* (oil on canvas), 36 × 30

OPPOSITE ABOVE, Paul Nash, *The Menin Road* (oil on canvas), 72 × 125. BELOW, Colin Gill, *Heavy Artillery* (oil on canvas), 72 × 125

as unfit, he immediately joined the Belgian Red Cross and set off in pursuit of the Futurist ideal. During 1915–16 he turned out a series of pictures based on his experiences as an ambulance driver in France, using his own mongrel blend of Futurist and Cubist techniques. From Cubism he had learnt to condense and simplify, and he combined this with the slanting lines of Futurism and its multiplicity of successive images evoking movement to produce a remarkably effective method of depicting mechanised warfare.

The success of *La Mitrailleuse* and other war paintings (including his most insistently Futurist work *Returning to the Trenches*) prompted the Leicester Galleries to offer Nevinson a one-man show in the autumn of 1916. This proved enormously attractive to critics and public alike, particularly to soldiers on leave – a surprising popularity for a radical modern artist; but because Nevinson had taken neither Cubism nor Futurism to extremes, his pictures remained intelligible and unintimidating to the layman. A number of them were bought by the wealthy and famous – Arnold Bennett acquired *La Patrie* and Sir Alfred Mond *A Taube* – and his standing was further enhanced by the publication of a complimentary monograph by P. G. Konody, the influential art critic of *The Observer*. Konody argued that for the adequate interpretation of war on such a cataclysmic scale, a synthetic and not a literally representational approach was required, a modern and not a traditional artist – and he claimed that Nevinson had succeeded triumphantly in the role: 'He stands alone, in England, as the painter of modern war.' This opinion was endorsed by Arthur Clutton-Brock of *The Times*, who regarded Nevinson's work as the best possible illustration of his own thesis that man had become merely part of the war process, a cog in the machine.

Between them these critics set the seal on the twenty-seven-year-old artist's reputation in both England and the USA. When in April 1917 he wrote asking for employment as an official war artist, the DoI was happy to oblige – 'There is no doubt he has genius'. Nevinson's own account in *Paint and Prejudice* of an appointment received through the intervention of a string of generals is not substantiated by the official correspondence, which shows his chief advocate to have been Muirhead Bone, at that time a friend and admirer (though, like many of Nevinson's colleagues, later to become an object of hatred and suspicion, labelled 'Bonehead Muir').

Nevinson was appointed on the standard DoI terms. As his visit to France was only to be for three weeks (he actually stayed from 5 July to 4 August 1917), he needed no military rank, though to alleviate the suspicion his appearance as a civilian would arouse he wore the uniform of a war correspondent – 'a bastard affair' without badges or other marks of rank.

Nevinson was an artist with war experience, the first to go back under official auspices, and he found the Front much changed. The small British Expeditionary Force of 1914–15 had grown to a vast conscript army of millions making its final preparations for the Passchendaele onslaught which began on 31 July. In complete contrast also were his living conditions: instead of sleeping rough as a common soldier, he was classed with visiting 'Red Tabs' and VIPs, and billeted in the luxury of Château

OPPOSITE ABOVE, John Nash, '*Over the Top*' (oil on canvas), $31\frac{1}{4} \times 42\frac{1}{4}$. BELOW, P. Wyndham Lewis, *A Battery Shelled* (oil on canvas), 72×125

d'Harcourt, where he earned a fine reputation as a mixer of cocktails and welcome antidote to the last 'artistic' visitor, the vegetarian and ascetic George Bernard Shaw.

Slightly ashamed of his 'cushy billet', Nevinson worked hard on his visit and ranged widely along, behind and above the length of the British Line. Masterman had described him to Buchan as 'a desperate fellow and without fear . . . only anxious to crawl into the front line and draw things full of violence and terror.' On the eve of the Passchendaele advance he made an unauthorised visit to Ypres, irritating Intelligence profoundly. On another occasion, while going up to an artillery observation post in the front line, he was spotted 'and got shelled, had to stick glued against a bank for an hour wondering when Fritz would leave off. I wondered why on earth I had not devoted my time to painting "nice nudes" in a warm studio, instead of risking so much for a picture which will probably not sell, be accused of being faked and certainly be abused by the inevitable arm-chair journalist.'

He was among the first painters to treat aerial subjects; in an aeroplane over the trenches he displayed his usual capacity for taking things personally: 'I saw Archies bursting below me, though the pilot assured me that they were not firing at us, I still have doubts. . . . I have been shelled every time but one when I have gone up the line.' One night he floated over the Somme in an observation balloon: 'After the aeroplanes I had been accustomed to, the silence was painful. . . . Gradually the various sounds came to me from below: the hooves of the horses and mules, the engines of cars and lorries, the regimental band in Arras, and innumerable gramophones making an orchestra of the wildest modernism.'

His synthetic technique was well suited to this adventurous peripatetic approach. He claimed to be unable to compose out of doors and relied almost entirely on memory, making the scrappiest of notes and no careful sketches – 'Nature is far too confusing and anarchic to be merely copied on the spot,' he wrote. 'An artist's business is to create, not to copy . . . to my mind creation can only be achieved when, after a close and continuous observation and study of nature, this visual knowledge of realities is used emotionally and mentally.'

After his return in August 1917 Nevinson worked steadily towards a second one-man exhibition at the Leicester Galleries, this time under official auspices. The pictures from this period, completed, like his earlier works, with great speed and facility, include *Over the Lines*,[14] *Reliefs at Dawn*,* *Bomb Thrower*, *Roads of France*, *Survivors at Arras*, *The Mule Team*, *The Road from Arras to Bapaume** and *After a Push*, and they mark a transition in his work.

The DoI had hoped for dramatic pictures from Nevinson – stark inhuman images of war which would equal the impact of his unofficial work – and their immediate reaction was disappointment. 'On the whole Nevinson seems to have restrained himself – sometimes to the point of dullness,' wrote a disconsolate Thomas Derrick. Masterman attributed this unwonted and unwanted decorum to an anxiety to please: '[Nevinson] . . . has abandoned his own *métier* in order to produce *official* (perhaps dull) pictures' – and he urged him to 'develop his own genius – however bitter and uncompromising'.

Had Masterman known him better, he would have realised how uncharacteristic

OPPOSITE, C. R. W. Nevinson, *Swooping Down on a Taube* (lithograph), $15\frac{3}{4} \times 12$

it would have been of Nevinson to avoid giving offence; and that had he genuinely been striving to be propagandist, he would have been both more positive and more successful. Moreover Nevinson himself acknowledged that he had been given a free hand: 'My only instructions from you were to paint exactly as I wanted.' In later years Nevinson was to foster the image of himself as a rebel, victimised by establishment coteries and repressed by bureaucracy, and he wrote sardonically of his official employers, 'In time I fully expected the order to produce my works in triplicate.' This has given credence to the idea that they were in some way responsible for the change of pitch and direction in his war pictures, but in fact his official appointment of 1917–18 *caused* nothing: it happened to coincide with a change in his interests and merely provided him with the opportunity to express these changed reactions in his art.

Nevinson had experienced the horrors of war more fully than any other official war artist: his Red Cross work in France in 1914–15 had been a primitive, disgusting and bloody business. One memory, transcribed in *La Patrie*, haunted him all his life. In a railway shed near Dunkirk his unit found a group of French soldiers, some already dead, others terribly wounded, who had lain there unattended for over three weeks following the virtual collapse of the French medical service: 'They lay on dirty straw, foul with old bandages and filth, those gaunt bearded men ... some white and still with only a faint movement of their chests to distinguish them from the dead by their side. Those who had the strength to moan wailed incessantly – "Ma mère, ma mère!" ... "Que je souffre, ma mère!" The sound of those broken men crying for their mothers is something I shall always have in my ears. It was dark when we arrived. There was a strong smell of gangrene, urine and French cigarettes. . . . When a month had passed I felt I had been born in the nightmare. I had seen ... sights so revolting that man seldom conceives them in his mind.'

His later service in the RAMC was scarcely less horrifying: posted to No. 3 General Hospital, Wandsworth, a centre both for severe facial injuries and for shell shock, he worked for months on a ward full of mentally deranged soldiers and was later to express the opinion that mental illness was infectious. The effects of his experiences undeniably showed themselves in the collapse of his own health. The nervous and delicate child had become an unstable and sickly adult, his condition worsened by self-imposed over-work. The continuing appalling casualty lists from Passchendaele affected him deeply and by March 1918 he was on the verge of a nervous breakdown.

By the time of his official appointment Nevinson was beyond question losing all belief or interest in 'the beauty of strife': he made no attempt to witness the first few days of the Passchendaele campaign, preferring to depart for Paris to arrange for the transfer there of his 1916 exhibition. More particularly, his attention had been forcibly diverted from the glories of mechanised war. The static siege warfare of the Western Front had none of the Futurist virtues of speed, efficiency, colour or excitement; rather it was a display of *human* qualities. He became indifferent to the machine-like character of military organisation, interested rather in men as individuals – the victims of war.

OPPOSITE, C. R. W. Nevinson, *The Doctor* (oil on canvas), $22\frac{1}{2} \times 16\frac{1}{4}$

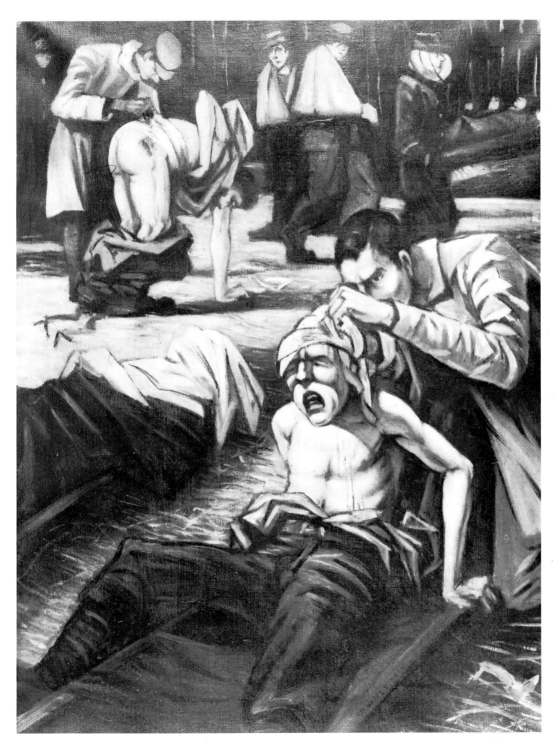

Even before leaving for France he had signalled his new priorities: he wanted his pictures to give 'the civilian public some insight as to the marvellous endurance of our soldiers and the real meaning of hardships they are called upon to face'. He was to harp increasingly on the theme of human sacrifice: of one picture, *The Doctor*, he wrote, 'I regard this picture quite apart from how it is painted expresses an absolutely NEW outlook on the so-called "sacrifice" of war', and described it as 'the last word on the "horror of war" for the generations to come.' (Though melodramatically expressed, Nevinson's concern was sincere and lasting: he painted in about 1934 a large allegorical canvas called *The Unending Cult of Human Sacrifice*).

A change of attitude necessitated a change of artistic technique. Osbert Sitwell described him as an explorer in the realm of style: he was convinced that 'the personality of a painter . . . enables him to withstand the test of any technical method.' His Cubist/Futurist technique of 1914–16 had been well suited to the mechanistic or dynamic subject – the machine-gun or the column of marching men – but to express human suffering and endurance Nevinson turned to a realism as sombre and intense as he could make it: his DoI series is evidence of a shift towards literal representation which was to find full expression in his 1918 commission for the Ministry of Information, *The Harvest of Battle*, and his subsequent rejection of all the 'isms' of experimental art.

Intellectually honest this change might have been, but it disappointed his admirers. He had lost the advantage of novelty: a novel attitude to war, a novel style, and the novelty of modern technology – the tank, the machine-gun and, in particular, the aeroplane – as subject matter for the artist. The new realism was quite simply not visually as attractive – less exuberant in design and largely restricted to the dingier colours of the Western Front – mud and khaki. Never again was he to achieve the marriage of subject and technique that had made his early war work so powerful.

Increased realism brought another, even less welcome response from the Censor. Like propaganda, military censorship had evolved in scope and complexity as the war progressed. For obvious reasons artists were prevented from portraying recent technological developments, operational techniques or points of strategic importance. But there was a plethora of other considerations: they could not risk offending Britain's allies, for example, by showing their forces in an unfavourable light (Martin Hardie's picture of the *Bathing Corner at Boulogne* was censored for displaying the French as unbecomingly frivolous, while his *Kaffirs Landing at Boulogne* was held back after 'native authorities' objected to it as 'accentuating the Kaffir features unduly'.) And they had to show due regard for civilian morale at home: the wounded could be depicted, even British wounded, but only in small numbers, apparently in good health, and well taken care of. After Passchendaele there was a complete embargo on corpses, British or German.

On points of factual detail the censor was unassailable, and Nevinson accepted without demur the instruction to correct the traffic flow from the left side to the right on *The Road from Arras to Bapaume*. But when Lee tried to suppress two paintings on principle, he found himself with a battle on his hands. One picture of which Nevinson was particularly proud was *A Group of Soldiers* (see facing page 1). He had taken all the faces from ordinary soldiers he had seen in the Tube, returning on leave, and when

Lee refused to pass it on the grounds that 'the type of man represented is not worthy of the British Army', Nevinson was roused to apoplexy: 'I will not paint "castrated Lancelots" though I know this is how Tommies are usually represented in illustrated papers etc. – high souled eunuchs looking mild-eyed, unable to melt butter on their tongues and mentally and physically incapable of killing a German. I refuse to insult the British Army with such sentimental bilge.' Nevinson's mortification was genuine: 'It seems awful to me that I should be dictated to by one man . . . especially as I know he would have censored all Rodin, Forain, Michael Angelo, Rubens and Goya as "too ugly".' But he was wrong to suspect Lee of merely applying his own 'particular aesthetic code of manly beauty' as a basis for censorship. Lee genuinely feared that 'if [the picture] ever gets into German hands I will lay a shade of odds that the Germans use it against us', as evidence of the degeneration of the British soldier. The War Office agreed with him, as did Masterman, the professional propagandist; but Buchan personally intervened and the 'monstrosities' were passed.

The second picture, *Paths of Glory*, immediately suspect for the heavy cynicism of its title, incorporated several foreground corpses: this time there was no going against the official line – that 'representations of the dead have an ill effect at home' – and despite Nevinson's expostulations ('Civilians at any rate know that war causes casualties, even if soldiers do not'), he was forbidden either to exhibit or reproduce it.

Despite the general sense of anti-climax, Nevinson's work was used as widely as that of any other official artist. Seventeen of his pictures were published in February 1918 in the first issue of *British Artists at the Front*, with a biographical essay by Campbell Dodgson and an introduction by C. E. Montague – who privately described his efforts as 'a ration of bleat' dished out for '20 systems of triangles and other lesser objects'.

Fifteen thousand copies of the volume were printed for distribution in England and the USA – and were ready in time for the official exhibition at the Leicester Galleries in March 1918 at which Nevinson showed sixty pictures, the product of seven month's intensive work.

It was probably the best-publicised of any of the exhibitions put on under official auspices.[15] Nevinson was a natural showman – in his own words, 'the soul of indiscretion'. Loftily he explained his attitude to Masterman: 'Personally I consider all advertisement vulgar and therefore I never trouble to differentiate between its various forms. . . . I prefer . . . to advertise well, rather than to paint the muck so beloved by the public.' Stung by Lee's claim that his paintings did not reach the man in the street, Nevinson promptly asked for an aeroplane in which to fly over London 'chucking out handbills. . . . If you will give me facilities there will be no "men in the street" but all will be in the Leicester Galleries.' Masterman demurred and Nevinson planned a second dashing coup – which both pulled in the public and, perhaps more to the point, irritated Lee – by pasting a strip of brown paper over *Paths of Glory* – marked CENSORED.[16]

CHAPTER TEN

Eric Kennington

NEVINSON was followed to France by the other young soldier-artist whose 'unofficial' pictures had been the success of 1916 – Eric Kennington. In some respects the two were not dissimilar. Kennington, like Nevinson, felt threatened by a scheme introduced in 1917 for the reconsideration of men previously graded unfit for military service and, alarmed at the prospect of tedious and 'inappropriate' home garrison duties, considered an official artist's job greatly preferable. Once he had been appointed he displayed, like his predecessor, a remarkable fluency in complaint.

Kennington owed his official appointment entirely to a genius, and a passion, developed during his time in the army, for portraying the ordinary soldier. 'If I am of use,' he wrote, 'it is in depicting British soldiers in their truest and noblest aspect; of that work I shall never tire.' He consolidated the success of *The Kensingtons at Laventie* with a series of drawings made during an unofficial visit to France in December 1916,[17] and exhibited at the Goupil Gallery in April 1917. By May, when his request for employment was first considered, his talents met an obvious propaganda need. Bone had drawn few individual soldiers, Dodd had drawn only their leaders, and Orpen, to the best of anyone's knowledge, had drawn nothing at all: on the other hand, the French had begun to make pictures not only of their own fighting men but also of ours, and Dodgson commented sedately, 'I think it is time one of our own men did this.'

Not all were convinced of Kennington's suitability. *The Kensingtons*, with its exhausted soldiers amidst the cold, dirt and debris of a shattered village, was hardly a good advertisement for the British Army in France, and both Buchan and Masterman heartily disliked Kennington's work. But others had faith that pictures carrying less weight of personal comment might have a real value: Thomas Derrick (who had already invited Kennington to contribute six lithographs – *Making Soldiers* – to a series entitled 'Britain's Efforts and Ideals in the Great War', of which he was the general editor),[18] remarked, 'I think they are much more likely to be popular than Bone's drawings because most people are more interested in soldiers than shell-holes.'

Kennington had other valuable allies – Bone, Charteris and Lavery – and in August 1917 he was appointed albeit on terms slightly less generous than usual. Having given the Government copyright in his work for the duration he was free to sell the originals, but he was obliged to give the newly-established National War Museum 'the first choice of any of his work as a presentation from him' – a proviso which was to cause much ill-will.[19] He was to have no car, no salary and no expenses, and was later to assert that he had been the Government's cheapest artist.

At the end of August Kennington went out to France. It is difficult to follow his movements precisely, as he rarely dated his letters and was usually prevented by the censors from giving an exact address, but he appears to have started work at Third Army Headquarters, where he was astonished by the warmth of his reception – 'Everyone is charming and I am having far too good a time.' His materials failed to arrive and for his first weeks he worked with map chalk and scrap paper[20] on portraits of 'odd men, such as Boche prisoners, black men' (tactfully re-labelled 'Indian warriors' when a selection of the pictures was published).

When he moved towards the front line, to Villars-Faucon, Kennington began to work mostly in pastels, an awkward medium from the DoI's point of view, easily smudged even after fixing, and quick to fade. But nearer the fighting he found the subjects he wanted – the common soldier and the conditions of his daily life in France. He drew signallers, Lewis gunners, raiders – *Raider with a Cosh* – fusiliers, a regimental carpenter, a Bantam sergeant,[21] and 'a man always chosen for dangerous work' – the *8th 'Queen's' Hero*. He sketched men at work – laying field telephone wires, preparing for a raid; in hospital (*Blinded Soldier, A Gas Patient*); and at leisure – talking, delousing, waiting for the rum ration or the tea to come round (*The Cup-Bearer*), and grousing (*The 'Die-Hards'*: If this is all the Tea we gets . . . roll on Breakfast-Time*). The minutiae of the soldiers' accommodation particularly fascinated him and he recorded every type of shelter, in descending degree of comfort – Nissen huts, reserved for officers out of the Line; 'Adrian' huts, used as casualty clearing-stations, with windows of oiled linen and beds made from wire netting and sacking stretched on plank frames; 'elephant' huts of corrugated iron, used for reinforcing dug-outs; bell-tents pitched in lines in the snow; lean-to's constructed more or less elaborately out of wooden ammunition boxes and biscuit tins, and infested with rats and lice.

Eric Kennington, *A Camouflaged Tent* (chalk), $7\frac{1}{2} \times 11\frac{1}{4}$

Earlier in the war Isaac Rosenberg had declared, 'I will not leave a corner of my consciousness covered up but saturate myself with the strange and extraordinary new conditions of this life, and it will all refine itself into poetry later on' – an attitude with which, *mutatis mutandis*, Kennington was much in sympathy: during his time at Villars-Faucon his only demands were for more time in which to respond to the inexhaustible stimuli of the Western Front. 'Give me six months,' he pleaded. 'Orpen has already had six months and Bone years.'

Kennington was obviously a man of considerable charm, but he had that single-minded absorption in his work which, though often condoned in artists, is regarded in non-creative people as selfishness. It is clear from his letters that he could be aggress-ive and irritable – as Bone put it, 'rather *difficile*' – and in October he was infuriated by being moved back from the Line. Later in the war he summarised well the dilemma of the artist in the battle zone – 'If [he] remains back he is safe and comfortable – and does not really see the war, & if he goes really "forward" he sees the war, and life is so disturbed and full of apprehensions, dangers and sudden changes that he cannot really apply himself to his work.' At this stage there is no doubt which of the two alternatives he preferred, and his complaints came thick and fast.

Because of his civilian status and lack of transport he was confined to camp where, without rank or even military uniform, he was continually harassed by vigilant NCOs. Away from the Front subjects were scarcer – 'I suppose you thoroughly realise that I was sent to this part because there was absolutely nothing doing here. . . . The only records of the Western War will be French.' Furthermore, in the use of such material as he found, he was restricted by the censor.

Kennington had a reverence for the hero which may perhaps be related to his own earlier inglorious departure from the Army. There is no evidence that the injury – sustained clearing a friend's jammed rifle – for which he was invalided out permanently unfit was anything other than accidental. Nevertheless, a bullet in the foot was the classic self-inflicted wound on the Western Front, and he is likely to have met with suspicions and insinuations calculated to make him place a high value on personal bravery. Whatever his motives, he was anxious to commemorate the 'nameless heroes of the rank and file' – and incensed to find that this was considered undesirable 'adver-tisement' of individuals. He had accumulated a set of portrait drawings, signed by their subjects, to which he attached great value; in the interests of modest anonymity Lee rubbed out the signatures. He was also in the habit of blue-pencilling drawings on the front: Kennington took this personally and complained bitterly that the censor regarded artists as 'things not to be encouraged (unless they are intimate with the great).'

Describing his stay in France, Kennington later wrote of 'the unique troubles of a soldier who has no rank, no badge or buttons, no unit, no pay, no batman, no billet, and an unmilitary dress – and no rations'. The key word is 'unique'; he undoubtedly felt, not without reason, that other official artists had been given bettter conditions – 'Bone had a commission and Orpen has a damned good time'. He was cheered in December 1917 by the arrival of friend and admirer William Rothenstein, who had

OPPOSITE, Eric Kennington, *Raider with a Cosh* (pastel), $24\frac{3}{4} \times 18\frac{1}{2}$

bought one of the studies for *The Kensingtons*, praising its 'mental vigour and probity'. The two worked happily together, first at Montigny Farm (where Rothenstein noted bemusedly that Kennington 'seemed content to draw tents and shacks and camp rubbish'), and later with the Jodhpur Lancers at Devise. Kennington later revealed that he had 'felt danger acutely' and 'been in much shell-fire' during this time; he also had a severe bout of trench-fever in January 1918 and accepted his recall in March 1918 without complaint.

This docility was in part due to his need to arrange an exhibition through which to recoup his considerable expenses. In June 1918 his one-man show, 'The British Soldier', opened at the Leicester Galleries. The catalogue is impressive, prefaced by 'Fulfilment', Robert Nichols's emotional hymn to the fighting man, and with an introduction by Robert Graves which anticipates *Goodbye To All That* in focusing on the glories of individual courage and self-sacrifice to be found amidst the grotesque ugliness of the Great War.

It might seem that Kennington had got precisely what he wanted – eight months of facilities in France at a time when many other artists were pressing to go out, and invaluable personal publicity in the form of the exhibition and his own issue of *British Artists at the Front*.[22] However, the captions for the exhibition catalogue had to be censored, like the pictures themselves, and the combined efforts of Lee and Yockney called forth a tirade of Nevinsonian vigour. Censorship, Kennington protested, 'is

Eric Kennington, *The Dismantled Elephant Hut* (pastel), $18\frac{1}{2} \times 24\frac{1}{2}$

always reducing us to the level of grammophones [*sic*] to say just what we are told to', and he appended a list of specific complaints. '*Via Crucis*. Must the soldiers endure hideous agony & the civilian not be permitted to think of it second-hand? You encourage civilian slackness. . . . *65*. I see you have cut the lice. . . . It is *staggering*. Tommy endures the persistent torture & his mother & sister must not think of the "disgusting little things". No wonder he returns from leave disappointed in us. . . . *90*. In this cut you destroy fun and truth which I have noticed are invariably frowned on by the censor.'

Kennington was further outraged to be informed that he could not sell his pictures to the Government at market price, having obviously failed to digest the implications of the clause giving first option to the National War Museum. Under heavy moral pressure he gave way, but not with the best of grace – 'Have read [the agreement] and shall hope to retain my watch and chain'[23] – and he did no more work as an official artist for Britain until the Second World War.[24]

Notwithstanding the diatribes, the DoI received from Kennington the use of some of the most evocative and persuasive pictures to come out of the official art scheme. In his introduction to the 1918 catalogue, Robert Graves wrote eloquently of their particular virtues, drawing some pointed comparisons with what had gone before: 'Here is no genteel amusement at the gaudy slap-dash camouflage on a big howitzer; no discreet civilian wonder at distant shells bursting along a chalk ridge or the long procession of ammunition lorries moving along the pavé road; no old-maidish sympathy for convalescents at the base hospital. Mr Kennington is not the embarrassed visitor in a strange drawing-room nor the bewildered old lady at her first football match . . . he has the trench point of view, and cannot forget how in the dark days of 1914 he gulped his rum and tea, fried his bacon, filled his sand-bag, ducked under his first bullet, stared into black night across the parapet and endured terror and misery as a private in the infantry.'

However, since then Kennington's official Great War work has been passed over – partly, perhaps, because of its limited scope. Kennington himself wrote of his visit: 'Did not attempt to depict any of the horror & tragedy, realising that it was too vast, & that I was not capable'; he concentrated only on 'the magnificence of the men', which resulted, as Dodgson complained, in a certain lack of variety. Again his pastel medium was not the most dramatic, and the DoI received no large oil to compare with *The Kensingtons*.[25] More importantly, Kennington's work was almost immediately overshadowed by war-related work done outside the auspices of the scheme.[26] He was to devote himself increasingly to sculpture, and his first major piece attracted much attention – the memorial in Battersea Park to the 24th Division[27] (in which Robert Graves was the model for the left-hand figure). And during the 1920s he was invited by T. E. Lawrence to be art editor for the first edition of *Seven Pillars of Wisdom*: the drawings of the Arab fighters he made for the book were to be his most widely known works.

CHAPTER ELEVEN

Paul Nash

W ITH the new system of short visits to the Front, artists who had already experienced trench warfare were at a premium; and it was a third young soldier-
artist, Paul Nash, who was chosen in succession to Nevinson and Kennington in the
autumn of 1917. (Nash knew both his predecessors well: Kennington from school
– St Paul's, and Nevinson from the Slade where Nash had studied from 1910–11.)[28]

In the period between his departure from the Slade and the outbreak of war, Nash's
style settled after an unconvincingly romantic start and he gave every appearance
of being simply 'a painter of park-like landscapes to the essentially conventional character of which he gave a poetic and stylish turn'. By 1914, as a member of both the
London Group and Bloomsbury's Friday Club, he had begun to acquire valuable contacts and patrons; thus his decision to join the Artists' Rifles seemed nothing but a
regrettable brake on a promising, if not particularly exciting career. Ultimately it was
to prove one of the most important steps in his artistic development.

From the Artists' Rifles Nash took a commission in the Hampshire Regiment in 1916,
and in February 1917 he was posted overseas for the first time, to the Ypres Salient
– 'the bulge, of course, round the romantic ruin of the town of Ypres . . . a stupid
bulge, but one of which the high command were inordinately proud; not because
it was of any strategic importance, but because a great many men had been killed
in its creation. It is obvious why a "salient" is an unsatisfactory place for the men
who are in it. They can be shelled from three sides, more or less, instead of one. But
this Salient was sacrosanct. . . . So it was kept intact as a monument of "doggedness".'

Even at the Front Nash had as quiet a time as the Salient could offer: 'There is not
much danger,' he assured his wife. 'Raids are not very feasible and the line is seldom
badly shelled.' Then in May 1917, while admiring a distant artillery barrage at night,
he fell into a trench and dislocated a rib – a painful but, as it turned out, profoundly
fortunate mishap: three days before the battle for Hill 60, in which most of the officers
in his unit died, Nash was invalided home.

The accident gave him, as it had given both Nevinson and Kennington, the chance
to work up immediately the notes and sketches he had made in his spare time at the
Front. In July 1917 the Goupil Gallery mounted an exhibition of twenty war drawings,
which revealed that Nash's art was taking a dramatic and original turn, as his feeling
for the *genius loci* responded to extraordinary new surroundings. It attracted much
favourable attention, winning him new patrons and confirming the support of the
old. One of the most loyal was Edward Marsh, whose modest private income was sufficient for him to indulge in the patronage of young artists and writers on a small but
invaluable scale; he had bought several of Nash's pre-war watercolours and with him
had planned an edition of *Georgian Drawings* as a companion to the *Georgian Poetry*
he had issued in collaboration with Rupert Brooke.

Marsh was also a rising civil servant, Churchill's Private Secretary at the Ministry of Munitions; and Nash, anxious to return to the Western Front as an artist rather than a soldier, wrote to him in July 1917 asking if he knew 'in any direct or indirect way that terrible man Masterman . . . Nevinson told me I ought to try and see him. Let me say at once I don't want one of those HQ jobs – driving about in a car and all that – merely a permit or special licence to draw in the line and facility for seeing all the different [sectors] . . . of course as ever I turn to you.' Marsh considered Buchan more likely to be sympathetic, and dragged him to the Goupil Gallery to inspect the pictures. He then wrote urging Nash on the DoI as 'a man of brains, humour and character which will support his specific gift – I mean, not one of the promising wasters whose little talents so often run to seed . . . I think it is safe to say that Paul Nash is one of "les jeunes" who are generally considered "to be reckoned with".'

Nash busily orchestrated further support himself, a campaign which elicited an endorsement from William Rothenstein and another letter, calculated to appeal even more to the DoI, from Francis Stopford, the editor of *Land and Water*. He reported that Nash's pictures had given him 'a much better understanding of German brutality and of the needless havoc and destruction which German armies are committing under orders in occupied territories' (a sentiment interestingly echoed by Roger Fry who, however, in describing Nash's war pictures as 'propagandist' intended no compliment).

The response from the propagandists was curiously unenthusiastic: Masterman declared himself 'not very struck with Paul Nash's productions', and Campbell Dodgson went further: 'Nash is decidedly post-impressionist, not cubist, but "decorative", and his art is certainly not what the British public generally will like.' However, under strong pressure from the art establishment – Marsh, Rothenstein, Lawrence Binyon and Eric Maclagan in particular – Buchan gave way: 'I think we will have to send Paul Nash as one of our artists to the Front. There is a tremendous consensus of opinion about his work, with which Maclagan wholly agrees. I DO NOT, but he is a good fellow and understands the front line.' (This half-heartedness may explain the gap of several weeks in communications between the DoI and Nash, during which time he was warned for active service in Egypt and saved only by the last-minute intervention of Buchan.)

Unlike Nevinson and Kennington, both discharged as medically unfit, Nash still held his commission in the Army and the DoI had to obtain his secondment. This was granted on 16 October 1917 – initially for a period of four weeks only, but repeatedly extended, and Nash never went back to active service. Like Nevinson, he was to have two periods of official employment: from 23 October 1917 until the end of April 1918 he worked for the DoI, spending November in France and working on his sketches in England for the rest of the time; then, after a hiatus of roughly a month, he was re-employed by the Ministry of Information until February 1919.

His agreement with the DoI was virtually identical to those signed by Nevinson and Kennington and, like them, he was insistent on his right to sell his works as soon as they were completed (though the Government retained copyright for the duration) – an attitude which reflected his financial position in 1917. Never precisely poor, he had nonetheless never been especially well off; in 1914 he was earning £250 p.a. at a time when the average middle-class professional was earning considerably more. (John Buchan, for example, earned £1000 as Director of Information.)

In the early years of the war Nash was able to declare cheerfully, 'I don't think our happiness depends on more money than will feed and shelter us – pay for my paints and some pretty clothes for Bunty [his wife Margaret].' However, after he accepted his commission he had to meet in addition the expenses of an officer on £3 13s 6d a week, the meagre pay of a 2nd Lieutenant. 'I suppose you can't think of anyone who will buy a drawing,' he wrote to Gordon Bottomley in January 1917, 'because I'm going to be ruined over this commission.'

The DoI appointment proved a blessing. In addition to the soldier's pay he drew from the War Office, he received from Buchan a total of £40 for expenses in France;[29] even after his return he seems to have been paid a 'subsistence allowance' of £3 10s a week over and above his Army pay. (It is not clear whether or not other DoI artists received a similar benefit.) He was also given a room at Wellington House for use as a studio in December and January and thereafter drew 7s a week to rent a studio of his own. He was thus effectively being subsidised both by the War Office and the DoI to work full-time at his peace-time profession, with the right to sell any of the work he produced.

Nash was in Flanders during the last days of Passchendaele (though he reported that he had 'missed the battle'), and he was a witness of its aftermath. His immediate concerns were to find his brother John, a corporal in the Artists' Rifles, (they met 'somewhere in the back areas' and went out to tea), and then to move as far forward as possible. In the first week of November he 'set the machinery of a somewhat reluctant Army headquarters to working on getting me put up at least within gunshot. The truth is that it takes hours getting backwards and forwards through the traffic, which is very heavy and complicated about here.'

Moving closer to the Front, however, brought its own problems: 'they have no accommodation for me in any Mess so I have all meals out.' Nash's dependence on local resources for bed and board resulted in expense claims he feared the DoI would think extravagant, and he felt compelled to justify himself: 'I am in the hands of these bloody robbers the French who for the smallest breakfast with only one egg attatched [sic] charge me 3f because I'm an officer. . . . Chauffers [sic] meals, which I have to pay too, are rather less – he has the same food, but being a different rank & dining in the kitchen gets off lightly.'[30]

By 16 November he had completed '40 [sketches] & I think all good ones – many of which will make paintings', and had moved close enough to the Front to be 'damn near killed – the bosche seems to have got wind of my coming & shelled me most rudely every time I opened my book.' His accommodation problem was, however, solved – 'I am comfortably housed and drive in style with a manservant, chauffer and car. The servant is an ex-valet and cooks amazingly – he has that rare gift of serving army rations in a form, not merely palatable and decorative, but delicious – the chauffer is all that a chauffer should be, alive to all places of interest & the whereabouts of every pretty girl in the zone of the British Army in France.' Unfortunately this happy state of affairs lasted only until 22 November, when he wrote glumly to Masterman, 'My excellent chauffer is leaving and my chef has been precipitated into the windscreen & messed up his mouth. With true spirit & the nice feeling of a faithful servant he only said, "How fortunate it wasn't you, sir!" I was much touched.'

Paul Nash, *After the Battle* (pen and watercolour), $18\frac{1}{4} \times 23\frac{1}{2}$

Nash's work to date had been executed principally in the battlefields around Ypres – Zillebeke, Hill 60, Sanctuary Wood, Gheluvelt and Inverness Copse – and he had made fifty drawings, all of 'muddy places on the Front'. In search of variety he applied for a week's extension of his stay and paid a short visit south to Vimy Ridge. The new area had little to offer him, however, in comparison with Flanders.

It is almost impossible now to conceive what the field of Passchendaele was like at the end of the three-month campaign. The battle was fought on a front of approximately eleven miles, over which the British advanced an average of four miles; by the end of October 1917 devastation was total over an area of some fifty square miles. The intensity of shelling was greater than at any other stage in the war: during the first bombardment the British alone expended four and three-quarter tons of high explosive on each yard of the Front. The land of Flanders is low-lying and in 1917

[55]

had an ancient and delicate drainage system of dykes and ditches; these were all obliterated and in the torrential autumn rains the clay was churned by countless shells into a morass of sucking mud, in which men drowned by the thousand.[31] Nash saw a country totally changed in form, colour and character – a nightmare land of vast dimensions, the graveyard of almost half a million men.

He had not been insensitive to the bleakness of the Salient before the battle, when a relatively small area was affected; on Good Friday 1917 he wrote to his wife, 'Imagine a wide landscape flat and scantily wooded and what trees remain blasted and torn, naked and scarred and riddled. The ground for miles around furrowed into trenches, pitted with yawning holes in which the water lies still and cold or heaped with mounds of earth, tangles of rusty wire, tin plates, stakes, sandbags and all the refuse of war.' But then the desolation was alleviated. It was spring, and 'where I sit now in the reserve line the place is just joyous, the dandelions are bright gold over the parapet and nearby a lilac bush is breaking into bloom.' Nash and his men lived in relative comfort, 'easy, careless, well fed, wrapped up in warm clothes . . . perpetually smoking.'

Thus he was able to view the whole scene primarily as magnificent source material. 'We are all sent out here to glean,' he wrote. 'Painter, poet, musician, sculptor – no one will return empty-handed but bringing his sheaves with him' – and he responded in aesthetic terms of colour, shape and design, exclaiming at 'wonderful ruinous forms . . . toast-rackety roofs and halves of houses here and there among the bright trees'. He confessed to being 'very happy . . . in fact, I believe I am happier in the trenches than anywhere out here. It sounds absurd, but life has a greater meaning here and a new zest, and beauty is more poignant.'

When he returned to the Western Front in November under official auspices, Nash was still expecting 'wonderful things' of the battlefields, but the impact of what he saw transformed him. 'I have just returned, last night, from a visit to Brigade Headquarters up the Line [at Zillebeke], and I shall not forget it as long as I live. I have seen the most frightful nightmare of a country more conceived by Dante or Poe than by nature, unspeakable, utterly indescribable. . . . Evil and the incarnate fiend alone can be master of this war, and no glimmer of God's hand is seen anywhere. Sunset and sunrise are blasphemous, they are mockeries to man, only the black rain out of the bruised and swollen clouds all through the bitter black of night is fit atmosphere in such a land. The rain drives on, the stinking mud becomes more evilly yellow, the shell-holes fill up with green-white water, the roads and tracks are covered in inches of slime, the black dying trees ooze and sweat and the shells never cease. They alone plunge overhead, tearing away the rotting tree stumps, breaking the plank roads, striking down horses and mules, annihilating, maiming, maddening, they plunge into the grave which is this land; one huge grave, and cast up on it the poor dead. It is unspeakable, godless, hopeless. I am no longer an artist interested and curious, I am a messenger who will bring back word from the men who are fighting to those who want the war to go on for ever. Feeble, inarticulate, will be my message, but it will have a bitter truth, and may it burn their lousy souls.'[32]

Nash's official pictures reflect this extraordinary and greatly heightened intensity of feeling – darker colours, more dramatic contrasts of light and shade, a greater sense of outrage and devastation, the consequences not simply of the physical change in

Paul Nash, *The Mule Track* (oil on canvas), 24 × 36

what he saw but also the emotional alteration the scene had wrought in him. It is ironic that when he was a soldier he behaved more like a fascinated onlooker – 'My time in France was very wonderful and I never stopped gaping.' In November, when he had been sent as a bystander, he began to express himself as a participant.

With the breaking down of his objectivity came the crumbling of his belief in the rightness of war. In the spring he had displayed a straightforward patriotism: 'This thing that brings men to fight and suffer together . . . is a very great and healthy force,' he informed his wife. 'No terrors will ever frighten me into regret. What are the closing lines of Tennyson's 'Maud'? – "I have felt I am one with my native land." ' In November he could see 'no glimmer of God's hand', and in this change of heart there is a certain resemblance to Nevinson's gradual recognition of the misery, squalor and futility of war.[33] However, Nash did not focus as Nevinson had done on the sufferings of men, who are conspicuously absent from most of the pictures; his main preoccupation remained the landscape and its violation.

The most significant difference between the spring and autumn pictures, unofficial and official works, is the use of oils in the latter, Nash's first use of the medium – 'a piece of towering audacity', as he put it later. The new medium lent itself to an

Paul Nash, *The Ypres Salient at Night* (oil on canvas), 28 × 36

intensification of expression, but the change seems less likely to have been a spontaneous reaction to the changed conditions of the Salient in autumn than a decision
made well in advance. During the spring visit Nash must have been aware of the
possibilities for an experiment of this sort. Before leaving England in November he
had obtained from Masterman an assurance that he would be given plenty of time
on his return in which to work up the pictures, and the DoI lived up to its promise,
allowing him four months, divided between his Gower Street studio and his parents'
house in Iver Heath, Buckinghamshire, during which work was interrupted only by
circumstances beyond the Department's control: in late January he complained, 'The
deep peace of our country night has been broken by the sound of guns. I hope the
buggers get lost in the fog or run into the moon or hurt themselves somehow'.

    Nash did not rely exclusively on oils: some sketches he worked over with ink and
watercolour, other drawings he did in various mediums fresh from his working notes.
His original sketch of Inverness Copse, for example, was worked up into *Sunrise: Inverness Copse*, itself the basis for the later oil *We Are Making a New World*.

    Though he claims to have felt he had failed in his duty as official artist,[34] the propa-
gandists were perfectly satisfied; the only dissenting voice was that of Colonel Lee,
to whom photographs of the pictures had to be sent for censorship. He returned them

untouched, with the comment – 'Nash's funny pictures . . . cannot possibly give the enemy any information. . . . I cannot help thinking that Nash is having a huge joke with the British public, and lovers of "art" in particular. Is he?'

With Stopford's comment in mind, Masterman put Nash's work to good use: several pictures were reproduced in periodicals such as *Country Life*, and fifteen were issued together as Volume III of *British Artists at the Front*. As Nash had not completed sufficient new pictures in time, some of his earlier 'unofficial' drawings had to be included; Nash made no objection in principle, though he assured Masterman that 'when I have carried out these later drawings you will not want to use the old ones.' The volume contained a biographical essay by 'John Salis' (Jan Gordon) and, as usual, an introduction by C. E. Montague. Under the title 'Strange but True', Montague wrote an inspired essay on the surreal feeling of trench warfare; essentially conservative in his artistic tastes, he felt bound to explain away the non-realistic aspects of Nash's art as reflections of the images seen by men under the intense strain of battle. 'Some fault will be found with what Lieut. Paul Nash has done here. It will be said that no barbed wire ever twirled on this earth in the forms which are taken by his; that some of his men are made of wood and some of his duckboards are not . . . but in drawing strange places so strangely, Mr Nash contrives to bring back to the mind the strange things felt by men who are there, at moments of stress. One does not see with the eyes alone, but with the brain and nerves too, and if these are worked upon in unusual ways, then the messages brought in by the little waves of light that break on delicate shores in the eye are changed – some may say, disturbed or blurred; others may say, refined into an uncommon rightness, not to be had at other times.' Montague's admiration for the pictures was sincere, but his method of defending them exasperated Nash: 'All that talk by Montague in the prevace [sic] is nonsense of course. Wire does and did grow as it is shown here [in *Landscape 1917*], and I was neither mad nor drunk or trying to show an abnormal vision when I drew it.'

Publication of Nash's *British Artists* was timed to coincide, like Nevinson's, with an exhibition of the artist's official work at the Leicester Galleries in May 1918. Nash was delighted with the response from both public and critics. 'It has done a great deal for me in the way of prestige.' Indeed, the work produced during the DoI appointment (and continued during his employment by the Ministry of Information) conclusively established his reputation: by 1919 *The Observer* was commenting, 'The war has been a powerful stimulus to imagination. Paul Nash . . . has now become a regular cult.'

Interestingly Nash himself had reservations about the pictures. 'I am pleased to have done them, but I should have liked to have done them again!' he told Rothenstein in 1919. 'Only a few seem to me (looking back at them from the standard I have reached since) to be adequate aesthetic statements, however telling they may seem at first glance as statements of violent emotional experience.'[35] And later he was inclined to minimise their importance in his development – 'It's a long time ago and I'm painting something else.' Nevertheless his official appointment, quite apart from keeping him out of active service at a time when the life expectancy of a subaltern on the Western Front was brief, played a crucial part in his career in two respects. It sent him to the source of his most powerful inspiration, and it gave him the time in which to work out in a new medium the ideas which resulted.

CHAPTER TWELVE

William Rothenstein

ONE of the most wholehearted supporters of Nash's official appointment
was William Rothenstein, who by his advocacy managed effectively to postpone his
own employment (originally proposed in
June 1917.) It is entirely characteristic
both that Rothenstein's influence as a
patron should have outweighed his own
claims as an artist – this, to his regret, was
the direction his career was increasingly
taking – and that his appointment should
have started on a misunderstanding; it was
to be throughout a saga of hurt feelings and
good intentions thwarted, for Rothenstein's
desire to give his services never met a similar eagerness to receive them.

He was the last of the DoI artists,
appointed on 17 December 1917, on conditions similar to his predecessors – the
most important, in his opinion, being that
the Government had the right to reproduce
his pictures for propaganda purposes. He
saw the job as a form of public service: he
received no military rank, no expenses and
no salary, and neither wished nor expected
to make a profit from the sale of the
pictures.

In some ways Rothenstein was an
improbable war artist. His tendency to ex-
patiate on his own shortcomings provoked
from Robert Ross a malicious reference to
'overweening humility'; but his misgivings
about his prospects in France were
genuine. In 1917 he was forty-five and far
from robust; his experience of the Western
Front was confined to a brief unofficial visit

William Rothenstein

to Belgium in 1915, and he was conscious of being at a disadvantage compared with the soldier-artists who were already familiar with the scene.

Above all he was afraid of 'molestation', the 'discomfort and indignity' of frequent arrest of which Kennington had warned him – and to which he was particularly vulnerable. Although he had been born in Bradford, his parents were German-born and he himself had a perceptible accent. Having worked for many years before the war for the cause of better relations between Britain and Germany,[36] at the outbreak he found it impossible to work up a hatred of Germans – as he told Frances Cornford, 'This wretched war has shown me how much I am a child of my fathers.' (Accordingly in 1916 he refused to anglicise his name to Rutherston with his two brothers.)

He was in fact an English patriot of the most unashamedly romantic kind: he had painted[37] a large symbolic canvas depicting the Chancellor at Oxford conferring a degree on a young soldier, with representatives of Britain's lost youth – Rupert Brooke, Julian Grenfell and Raymond Asquith among them, gowns over their khaki – 'walking up hand in hand, to receive symbolically what could never now be given them'. And he was to write to Edward Marsh in 1918, 'I hope we are fighting for Grantchester: for Grantchester I am willing to squat in a trench or trudge in the desert.' Thus he was deeply wounded by suspicions in his village (Far Oakridge, in Gloucestershire) that he was a German spy, on the grounds that he had been seen drawing a railway tunnel and that his house had a stone terrace ideal for an enemy gun emplacement.

Rothenstein went out to join Kennington on the Somme in mid-December, and some of his forebodings were promptly realised. The winter of 1917–18 was so cold that the paint on his brush often froze before reaching the paper, and he felt under constant pressure of time, intensified by the fact that he could not work from memory and had to paint directly from the model. 'The difficulty lies in the richness of the material,' he wrote, 'where to begin and what to do. . . . I am really obsessed by a sense of the shortness of time given me,' and he begged not to be recalled too soon: 'We should not be treated as boys trying to play truant'.

Nevertheless he worked with enthusiasm (Kennington described him as 'leaping with enjoyment') and dedication. The element of truth in Steer's jibe – 'Will paints much the same as the rest of us, but from higher motives, of course' – is evident in Rothenstein's war work. War art was a subject to which he had given much thought since his early championing of an official scheme, and he had various large-scale plans for systematising the recording of war. He suggested attaching artists to each army specifically to document its activities; with his devotion to things Indian, he was especially anxious that the Indian contribution to the war be recorded; and he proposed that sets of drawings should be made in France which would be of special interest to particular localities in England (as records of the areas in which local regiments had fought, for instance) and which could be hung in local galleries – an interesting extension of his lifelong crusade for local art patronage.

These ideas, though innovative and interesting, fell on singularly stony ground, and they were in any case increasingly submerged by Rothenstein's growing conviction of his own 'sacred task'. He was profoundly affected by the physical beauty of the ruins of Northern France – 'the pink flush of the red bricks, deepening to blood colour where the impact of a shell had made a wound in the wall . . . the worn, attenuated

William Rothenstein, *Talbot House, Ypres* (gouache), 13 × 20

rafters making pitiful shapes against the sky . . . the colours of wallpapers . . . delicate and flower-like'. But this beauty had for him much more than just an aesthetic significance – it had a moral, even mystical meaning. In the catalogue to his wartime exhibition,[38] he explained his feelings: 'Over a battlefield, where the hopes and fears and passions of thousands of men were concentrated, a strange atmosphere of awe seems to hang. Throughout the desolation of war there is woven a pattern of austere beauty, and the human drama associated with war gives to this beauty a religious character. . . . I felt as a pilgrim visiting sacred sites.' He felt it his duty to record and convey this deeper significance before the 'sacred sites' of desolation were in their turn obliterated, or returned to commonplace order.

He was based first with Kennington, some ten miles from Péronne at Montigny Farm near Roisel, where both British and American troops were quartered;[39] he found it 'a desolate spot, where a few tin huts were grouped together in a flat muddy landscape', and preferred to look for subjects in the ruined towns nearby. He acquired a car in which he toured the neighbourhood, often skirting the fighting front and coming under shell-fire. It was during this time that he saw a party of German prisoners being paraded through a wrecked village to be abused and humiliated by its inhabitants – and Kennington found him later, sitting on a heap of rubble in tears.

Rothenstein was next posted to the Jodhpur Lancers at Devise, where to his delight he was given a horse, an Indian orderly, an interpreter, and his first chance to study the Indian warrior class. In his element, he produced large numbers of portraits, despite the unfortunate precedent set by Kennington, one of whose subjects had been killed in the trenches shortly after sitting.

[62]

In January 1918 Rothenstein used private connections to have himself attached to General Gough's Headquarters at Nesle and was with the Fifth Army during the preparations for the German spring offensive. It was a nervous period – 'spy fever' was rife, and for the first time he was subjected to the indignity he had most feared. A. L. Galbraith, then a subaltern with an artillery battery in reserve at Roisel, saw him being escorted to Corps HQ for questioning as a suspected spy, 'a smallish, spectacled man like Mr Pickwick and with the same bland and smiling visage', wedged between two large guards in the back of a car. He later explained how the arrest had come about: 'The men were critical of his work, and adversely too. . . . If his job was to paint war scenes, they said, why didn't he go where war was and not potter about here where we were at peace. They criticised his technique and his execution, his foreign name, and finally decided that he was up to no good. In the officers' mess our standards of art appreciation were *La Vie Parisienne* . . . and we didn't know whether the men were right or wrong – probably right. The Battery Commander solved his doubts by putting him under arrest.'

This account would seem to justify Orpen in remarking unkindly of Rothenstein, 'I can't see him hobnobbing with the Tommies'; he failed to fraternise and was arrested in consequence. But the suggestion that he deliberately avoided the fighting is unjust. Rothenstein was ashamed of the privileges he received – he described the official artist as 'a kind of official parasite with nothing to do but draw and draw' – and found the care taken of him as a non-combatant embarrassing. In the event he did more than enough to demonstrate his readiness to share the dangers and discomforts of the men among whom he lived.

On the day of the German advance, 21 March 1918, he set off, in the fog and confusion, into the teeth of the bombardment, and though he was finally persuaded to turn back, by the time he reached Marchèlepot casualties were pouring in. 'To draw now seemed indecent,' he observed, and it does not seem to have occurred to him to leave. According to a surgeon in charge of a Territorial Medical Unit with the Fifth Army, 'About 4.00 p.m. on 23rd March a figure in shirt-sleeves and an orderly's gown, unshaven and very tired, came to me when visiting the surgical ward for bad cases. It was Rothenstein!. . . The Sister told me that Rothenstein had not left the ward for over forty-eight hours . . . he had done invaluable work.' In a diary entry for the last week of March 1918, C. E. Montague described graphically the kind of casualties with which Rothenstein was dealing – 'Some of the cases mere bundles of cloth, mud, blood, and torn meat. Unpacked carefully by nurses, who despair of nothing still warm.' Rothenstein's first task was to identify the most desperately wounded so that their relatives might be informed; he frequently failed, as 'many were so fearfully mangled, that it was often impossible to find their identity discs'; and he wrote to his wife, 'God bless you all, and keep from the beloved children any such sights as I have to look on while they live.'

By the end of March, when Lee found out where he was and sent him home, Rothenstein had completed one oil, twenty-eight gouaches and forty-two pastels (most of them Indian portraits), and in May he mounted an exhibition at the Goupil Gallery, entitled 'On the Péronne Front'. He considered the opportunity of going to France to have been 'the greatest privilege life has given me', and wanted the resulting pictures to

WHILE DEMOCRACY IS UNCHAINED, TYRANNY IS BOUND & FROM THE TRENCHES IS BROUGHT THE HOPE OF FRUITFUL SERVICE FOR ALL

William Rothenstein, *The Triumph of Democracy* (lithograph in colours), 17×28

serve a national purpose, in public rather than private possession. However, it soon became embarrassingly clear that his zeal was not shared.

As he sadly observed himself, his work was not popular. Since his glittering *fin-de-siècle* career in Paris and Oxford, as a friend of Whistler and Pissarro, Lautrec and Dégas, Verlaine, Wilde and Beerbohm, his attitude to life and to art had become increasingly earnest, a quest for 'probity' above all things, and the character of his painting had altered accordingly. Wyndham Lewis wrote perceptively, 'No trace there of the flashing intelligence. He becomes a humble workman, fumbling almost in his grim sincerity.'

In his anxiety to impart universal truths Rothenstein neglected that sense of the particular which most effectively involves the observer; in the words of one critic, the pictures 'did not convey to me the real atmosphere of France and the war, and the ruined houses might just as well have been at Messina as in France'. Yockney wrote regretfully, 'It is thought that his drawings of the Western Front are scarcely representative of actual warfare, however beautiful they may be as works of art,' and the intended issue of *British Artists at the Front* was abandoned.[40] Of the seventy or so pictures he had completed, the Government bought four. And when the question arose of his further employment under the Ministry of Information there was humiliating confusion over whether or not he still had the status of an official artist, being thereby exempt from military service – a débâcle which ended in his writing to Yockney, 'I believed I could be more use to the country as an artist than as a soldier. You have decided otherwise.'

[64]

CHAPTER THIRTEEN

William Orpen

WILLIAM Orpen had been in France throughout 1917 as Nevinson, Kennington, Nash and Rothenstein in turn came out. Originally included in the official complement of two artists at GHQ, by the end of 1917 he had become the DoI's 'special case'.[41]

After the initial contretemps with Masterman and the censors, Orpen began to find his appointment very much to his liking. His responsibilities to the DoI were light – it had eventually been agreed that he was to send back, until Masterman was 'sick of the sight of them', a minimum of four sketches per month for propaganda use – and his life, with his own car, chauffeur, batman and manager, was relatively comfortable: largely responsible for his own accommodation, he could afford the best hotels available and, as a Major, enjoying the friendship of Haig, Cowans and Sassoon, he had little red tape to contend with.

That he wanted nothing more than to preserve the *status quo* became apparent when Beaverbrook, thwarted in his earlier attempt to commandeer Orpen's services for the Canadian War Memorials Fund,[42] made another approach. The DoI had no objections to second Orpen to the Canadians temporarily (as Masterman pointed out, pictures of Canadian forces would make equally good propaganda for the Allied cause) but Orpen himself resisted strongly – partly because he was reluctant to leave the battle zone for the portrait work the Canadians wanted: 'It is sickening with all these wonders all around to have to sit down and do a 'face' just as if one were in London.' Beaverbrook's efforts (which included a personal attempt at persuasion, over a bottle of champagne in the quayside buffet at Boulogne) drove Orpen to write

Orpen at work in Amiens

to Buchan at the end of October 1917, pleading to be left alone: 'The Canadians have nobbled every artist of distinction in England. . . . I think myself it is a pity that no pictorial record of the war, except illustrations (such as Bone's) are going to remain intact in England. . . . If I were given a free hand to continue to work under my present ideal conditions for the British . . . I am perfectly prepared, & would like, to present to the Government (without pay) all the studies, drawings, portraits and canvases I have done here, & all the future pictures I intend to do from them – provided they are kept intact & not scattered about. . . .' This gift (through no fault of Orpen's) was subsequently to cause a great deal of trouble, but at the time it proved a perfectly effective bribe: though lent occasionally to the Canadians, Orpen remained permanently attached to the British.

His motives were not as entirely disinterested as his letter to Buchan suggests. There was no question of his hoping to profit financially – he wrote to Robert Ross, 'The last thing I want is to make money out of the sights I have seen here,' and the gift of his pictures bears this out. On the contrary, he was considerably the worse off for his official employment: besides the loss of potential earnings for 1917–18 (and in 1916 he had earned £7200 from portraits alone), he paid all expenses for himself and his staff, which by March 1918 already amounted to £1830. What may have impelled him to insist on staying at the Front was the prospect of breaking away from the gradual petrification of his career as a society portraitist, a unique opportunity to find the artistic fulfilment he was increasingly unlikely to achieve in London where he was constrained by the demands of his wealthy clients. Not implausibly, in *Ready to Start* (completed in June 1917) he was not simply adding to the long line of self-portraits he painted throughout his life: he was recording a new beginning as an artist.

Orpen had arrived on the Somme just after the German retrenchment along the Hindenburg line. Six inches of snow had recently fallen and he first saw the battlefields as they are most commonly pictured – freezing, wet and desolate, 'miles and miles of Shell Holes bodies rifles steel Helmets gas Helmets and all kinds of battered clothes German and English, and shells and wire . . . not a living soul anywhere near, a truly terrible peace in the new and terribly modern desert.' From his base at Amiens he drove up and down behind the Line – to Albert, Thiepval, Beaumont-Hamel, Bapaume, La Boiselle, Péronne – watching in horrified fascination the men coming back from the Front: 'some sick; some with trench feet; some on stretchers; some wounded; worn, sad and dirty – all stumbling along in the glare. . . . Their eyes were wide open, the pupils very small . . .'

In June and July he moved up to the Ypres Salient, and returned to the Somme in August to find it transformed into a region of unexpected beauty. 'The dreary, dismal mud was baked white and pure – dazzling white. White daisies, red poppies and a blue flower, great masses of them, stretched for miles and miles. The sky a pure dark blue, and the whole air, up to a height of about forty feet, thick with white butterflies: your clothes were covered with butterflies. It was like an enchanted land; but in the place of fairies there were thousands of little white crosses. . . .'

Against these contrasting backgrounds the subjects he sketched were the same –

OPPOSITE, William Orpen, *Ready to Start* (oil on panel), 24 × 20

[66]

William Orpen, *A Trench, Beaumont Hamel* (pencil with touches of watercolour), $16\frac{1}{2} \times 21$

trenches, craters, graves, wrecked tanks, tangled bodies, men marching, wounded, resting, thinking – but almost never fighting. Orpen did not go up to the front line, nor had he any experience of active service to draw on; and the dearth of front-line subjects was to be the more striking when his work was set against that of Nevinson and Nash. Despite the grimness of the themes, the pictures he eventually produced from his sketches were uniformly decorative (incongruously so, to some critics), and the colours of such oils as *A View from the Old British Trenches* and *German Wire, Thiepval* bright to the point of garishness, possibly the consequence of Orpen's mild colour-blindness.

From the propaganda point of view, the most valuable pictures produced during this period were portraits of Sir Douglas Haig and General Trenchard (commanding the RFC) which were used to great effect in newspapers and magazines at home and abroad. It was Trenchard's ADC, Maurice Baring, who recognised how valuable such publicity could be to the newest branch of the Services, and urged Orpen to paint two of the RFC's leading 'aces'.

Lieutenant A. P. F. Rhys-Davids, DSO, MC, had been Captain of Eton in 1915–16 and was waiting eagerly for the war to end so that he could go up to Oxford; he always carried a volume of Blake's poetry with him on his flights in case he was taken prisoner. When Orpen painted him he had accounted for twenty-two enemy planes; a week later he was shot down, the day before he was due to go home on leave. The DoI immediately recognised the portrait's potential as propaganda – 'a masterly representation of a resolute British hero . . . a symbol of self-confident strength in a good cause' – and it went straight on to the cover of *War Pictorial*.[43]

Lieutenant R. T. C. Hoidge, MC, annoyed Orpen by turning up late for his sitting, but offered an irresistible excuse – that of having narrowly escaped death in a dog-fight some two hours earlier. Orpen quoted his account: 'Let a damned old Bosche get on my tail . . . I was so intent on an old two-seater I was chasing I never noticed the blighter – if old Beaumont hadn't come up and chased the blighter off I was for it – he put one bullet through the box by my head, blew off $\frac{1}{2}$ my tail and cut 3 stays . . . but the morning wasn't wasted I got 4 Bosche afterwards' – and commented, 'Here was this youth the calmest thing in the world drinking his lemon squash. . . .'

Orpen spent October 1917 with 56th Squadron near Cassel. Regrettably he does not appear to have gone up in a plane, but he deeply admired the young pilots, felt accepted by them, and joined happily in their off-duty amusements, taking pride in having beaten at ping-pong McCudden VC, DSO, MC, MM, the most decorated man in the RFC.[44]

In general Orpen seems to have enjoyed on the Western Front a social life no less hectic than in London, alternating between the war zone's two 'rest and recreation'

William Orpen, *Christmas Night, Cassel* (pencil and watercolour), $17 \times 21\frac{1}{2}$

centres. Amiens was the one large town 'that could be reached easily from the Somme front for dinner', crowded with bars, prostitutes and war correspondents. Orpen stayed at the Hôtel de la Paix, where his room was known as 'the Bar' and smelt of 'mud, paint, drink, smoke, and the fumes from the famous "Flamme Bleue" stove'. In Cassel, a small hill town with the 2nd Army Headquarters in the casino at its summit, he lived in the Hôtel Sauvage, whose restaurant had a view of the Line from Nieuport to Armentières and was always packed with 'fighting boys from the Salient', eating, drinking and singing round the piano. According to Philip Gibbs,[45] only officers were admitted (but not those of the RFC, who had proved too rowdy); occasionally Orpen would retreat to the kitchen and create his own 'entertainments' – 'I would stand the drinks, and Howlett (my chauffeur) played the mouth-organ, and Green (my batman) step-danced.'

He paid fairly frequent visits to Paris, principally for portrait work. Much of this was for the Canadians – and Augustus John, out in France at the start of 1918, described dinners given by Beaverbrook for the artists' amusement: prostitutes were provided but at that stage, according to John, Orpen would modestly retire. Nevertheless it would be misleading to accept at face value the statement he made to a reporter – 'I cut my hair short, wear white collars, and have no interesting vices.' The monogram he used to sign one of his wartime letters to Alfred Rich is lewd to a degree, and by the end of 1917 he had acquired a young and exceptionally beautiful mistress.

Yvonne Aubicq, a refugee from Lille, where her father was the mayor, was to model for some of Orpen's most famous pictures. She was a voluntary Red Cross worker and Orpen may have met her in hospital, for at the end of November 1917 he contracted a mysterious ailment which marred his time in France and may permanently have ruined his health. Originally diagnosed as lice, and then as scabies, it was finally identified as 'blood poisoning', with symptoms which Orpen described with the artist's awareness of colour and his own particular eye for the revolting – 'a white hole [in the throat] with a black band round it, and all the flesh for about six inches beyond it a deep scarlet'.

At the end of March 1918, as the German advance gathered momentum, he was called home with the other official artists – to find himself in deep disgrace. The cause was two portraits of Yvonne which, in an attempt to provide 'war interest', he had entitled 'The Spy', explaining to the censors that the subject was a Hungarian refugee caught spying for the Germans and shot by the French.

It is not clear why Orpen persisted with this fiction after the first *frisson* it not unnaturally caused in Intelligence. He may have thought it amusing to insinuate his mistress into official war records; he may primarily have been concerned to provoke Lee (who was at first taken in completely, though he later met Yvonne and the episode became a standing joke). Most probably the story was intended simply to advertise the pictures: it was still circulating a year later on both sides of the Atlantic, with some remarkable frills (including the suggestion that when the rifles of the French firing-squad were trained on her, 'The Spy' let her fur coat slip to the ground and revealed herself naked, in an eleventh-hour attempt to create a diversion).[46] Unfortunately it had the dual effect of portraying the French as monsters of inhumanity and presenting the Germans with a martyr, and Orpen wrote later to Rich, 'The day you

ABOVE, wartime photograph of Yvonne Aubicq – dawn in Rue Dannon, reproduced by kind permission of P. Murray Lee; RIGHT, *The Refugee (b)* (oil on canvas), 30 × 25

saw my family "top hole and full of a rare joy" I was being court-martialled at the War Office!!!!' The pictures were retitled *The Refugee (a)* and *(b)*, and it was to take a skilful use of his connections to get Orpen back to France.

Orpen's considerable output (of over fifty oils and seventy drawings and watercolours) was never published *en bloc*, which must be counted an opportunity missed by the propaganda authorities, the more conspicuous in the light of the exposure they gave to Lavery's generally less effective efforts. There was, however, an exhibition of his war work at Agnew's in May 1918 which attracted a great deal of critical attention and attendances of over 10,000 in five weeks – a considerable success for a show which charged an entrance fee (one shilling). Shortly after the opening Orpen's gift of his pictures to 'the British Nation' was made public, and in the birthday honours list of 3 June he was knighted 'for services in connection with the war'.

The general enthusiasm was not unqualified. Orpen's aim was not simply to record the war but to interpret it – hence his sneer at Bone's 'illustrations' – but one criticism, originally made in *The Times*, gained wide currency, and has often been repeated since. 'His work produced in France', wrote the reviewer, 'adds to our knowledge of himself but nothing to our knowledge of war . . . its psychology . . . its profoundly spiritual or emotional significance, or even healthy humour.'

Undeniably, Orpen was intensely interested in himself. Self-portraits appeared with sufficient regularity – three of them during his stay on the Western Front – to prompt an unkind verse in *Punch*:

> *Bill Orpen's rapier thrust is great;*
> *He'll paint your portrait while you wait;*
> *But, though he doesn't want it known,*
> *He much prefers to paint his own.*

However, there is no reason to question the sincerity of his desire to convey to others both the atmosphere and the significance of what he had seen, and certain of his reactions to war – the fear and revulsion he felt – are expressed as convincingly and as informatively as anyone could wish.

Orpen was not ashamed to admit that he was afraid in France. He wrote to Lavery, 'Of all the blinking funks that ever lived I'm the worst – my stomjack just gets tied up in knots and I get a great longing to dig myself in at once.' He also revealed a keen sensitivity to horrors. Once he found and began to paint the mingled remnants of two soldiers, one British and one German, by the trenches at Thiepval. After a while, oppressed by a growing sense of strangeness, he sat down to rest on the trunk of a blown-up tree. 'Suddenly I was thrown on the back of my head on the ground. My heavy easel was upset, and one of the skulls went through the canvas.'

Orpen portrayed the grotesque side of war on the Western Front more powerfully than any other official artist. One passage from *An Onlooker in France* brings together several of the images that haunted him: 'A hand lying on the duckboards . . . the "Cough-drop" with the stench coming from its watery bottom; the shell-holes with the shapes of bodies faintly showing through the putrid water . . . one could not paint the smell.' The motif of the severed hand recurs throughout the book, and in several of his war pictures (most notably *The Mad Woman of Douai* and, closer to home, one of the self-portraits) a single foot pokes horridly out of the earth. His colours are often disturbing – his landscapes lurid, his corpses the green of putrefaction, his skeletons yellow.

He was both relieved and ashamed to be protected from the miseries endured by the fighting men: 'There I sat in the car, her nose pointing away from danger, and they walked past in the other direction to Hell. . . . They looked at me, but they never uttered a word – yet those looks made me crouch, and in shame cover my eyes with my hands.' Perfectly aware that his position was privileged, he stoutly resisted efforts to erode it – but at the same time he felt an irresistible compulsion to record in evidence the monstrosities of which he was merely an 'onlooker'.

CHAPTER FOURTEEN

Propaganda

IT would not be unfair to say that the DoI valued official war art *only* as propaganda – hence the lack of interest in retaining the pictures. Neither Buchan nor Masterman was anything other than a professional propagandist; they had ambitions neither as patrons of artists nor as collectors of pictures.

On the face of it, the artists appointed by the DoI were (with the obvious exception of Francis Dodd) under no constraints as regards either subject or medium. 'I have always taken the view', Masterman remarked, 'that it is not for a Government department to attempt to regulate artists in their work, art being so largely individual in expression. I have always told the artist to draw whatever he thinks best and to develop his work along his own lines.' One should not take too naïve a view of this apparent freedom: on the basis of the information supplied by his art advisers, Masterman would have been able to gauge with reasonable accuracy the probable outcome of sending a particular artist to a particular location (Kennington to work with the fighting men, for example, or Bone to the ruined villages behind the Front), and the balance and range of subjects achieved suggests the shrewdness of his predictions. In the event of an artist producing work that was unexpected and unwelcome, the DoI could fall back on its ultimate control of the use of the pictures for the duration. Nevertheless, there is no sign that any of the artists felt obliged to compromise his artistic integrity by painting subjects he would not otherwise have painted, in a manner other than his usual one, simply for the sake of propaganda. Some of the artists – Nash and McBey, in particular – seem to have been virtually oblivious of their propaganda function; Nash's reaction was, if anything, anti-war.

But however little propagandist intent the artists themselves may have had, in the hands of the DoI their pictures were unquestionably used to help in the manipulation of public opinion. It is important to realise that in Britain at that time the censors and propagandists between them controlled all the pictures, photographs and films seen by the civilian population. Inevitably the public had only those visual images of the war that it was permitted to have: there was no independent standard of 'truth' by which they could be verified – and war art added materially to the stock of images available for use.

Initially the pictures were used simply to supplement photographs in the DoI's illustrated publications, to provide variety and, it was hoped, an intensification of the messages to be conveyed. Some critics obligingly pointed out the artist's superior ability to select and focus, colour and interpret his material; others considered the official pictures, Bone's in particular, to offer no improvement at all on the 'artist-despised camera'.

Later the pictures were reproduced on postcards, calendars, matchboxes,[47] bookmarks and other ephemera of the type it was hoped would penetrate down to the 'lower deck'. Nor was war art's potential value for moulding *post-war* opinion on the 'lower deck' overlooked: it was suggested to Masterman by one W. M. Meredith that Orpen should be asked to do a series of military portraits for mass circulation after the war. 'When the war is over', Meredith argued, 'and the greater proportion of the new armies go back to work, the most important problems will be social and labour, and it will be of essential importance unostentatiously to keep fresh in the memory of the soldiers the men who have led them and whom they have admired and with whom they have faced death during the war, for this will go far to counteract the evil influences which are likely to be rampant.' Perhaps fortunately, Masterman declined on the grounds that Francis Dodd was already at work.

Though not without popular appeal, war art was soon seen to have limitations as mass propaganda – the Ministry of National Service refusing to use Bone's pictures for recruitment posters, commented bluntly, 'They are really too good for the purpose of appealing to British workmen.' Increasing emphasis was laid instead on its utility as a means of conveying propaganda messages to an educated minority which Wellington House had long considered a vital target: 'It is better to influence those who can influence others than attempt a direct appeal to the mass of the population.'[48] The DoI already had several methods of approaching this influential minority – lectures, books, personal correspondence and contacts, all pitched in a deliberately low key without melodrama, horror stories or jingoism. War art, conveying sentiments far less obvious and overtly emotional than those expressed by popular illustrators, cartoonists and poster artists, was clearly appropriate as part of an 'aesthetic appeal' to an 'aesthetic public'. The muted images of Muirhead Bone were as powerfully propagandist to certain sections of society as the strident cartoons of Louis Raemaekers to a mass public; and an audience which rejected the raped women and bayoneted babies of the popular press as over-sensational and sordid was more likely to react in anger to Nash's devastated landscapes.

The art world itself provided a convenient and effective distribution network for fine art propaganda. Private galleries had their own carefully nurtured clienteles and the art periodicals their regular subscribers – and all were eager both to play a part in the war effort and to take advantage of the commercial appeal of war art. Public galleries, starved of funds during the war, were likewise delighted to receive pre-arranged exhibitions. The propagandists oiled the wheels with a deliberate campaign of social enhancement for war art: public figures opened the official exhibitions and wrote the introductions to catalogues, and royalty made widely reported visits. Moreover, the majority of artists chosen were either eminent figures in society themselves, or currently in vogue in fashionable circles, and the effect was not diluted by the use of obscure or second-rate names. Publication of the artists' work under the banner of *Country Life* set the seal.

War art accounted for only a tiny part of the DoI's annual budget – less than 1% of an approximate £1·3 million. Nevertheless, considerable care and thought went into its use as propaganda, and many of the DoI's favourite themes can be identified in those pictures selected for publication or exhibition. Hatred of the enemy was fanned by giving prominence to pictures demonstrating German brutality and callousness – Nevinson's *A Taube*, for instance, whose centre-piece is the broken figure of a little

C. R. W. Nevinson, *A Taube* (oil on canvas), 25 × 30

boy killed in a German bombing raid, and Bone's *Spite!*, a once attractive cottage on the Somme systematically wrecked. The portraits of Dodd and Orpen were deployed to bolster the prestige of Britain's war leaders, while Kennington's sketches of Indians and Orpen's *Poilu and Tommy* (in which a French soldier carries a wounded British soldier out of No Man's Land) promoted friendship between the Allies. Bone's pictures could be used to fuel belief in our fighting chance to win: his *The Hall of the Million Shells*,[49] for example, carried the message that the shell shortages of 1915 were over; and his shipyard scenes, published in October 1917, with the German submarine campaign still in full force, hinted at inexhaustible naval strength in reserve.

Muting the true horror of war was an essential task to which various types of pictures

Muirhead Bone, *The Hall of the Million Shells* (charcoal and wash), $14\frac{1}{4} \times 21$

lent themselves – those, for instance, which presented the battlefields merely as pictur-esque landscapes with no evidence of casualties. One prime example is Bone's *Panorama from the Scherpenberg*, in which the British bombardment of Wytschaete and Messines appears no doubt exactly as he saw it – as a few puffs of smoke on the horizon. Others were selected to highlight the elements of comradeship and heroism in front-line life – from Kennington's rank and file sharing tea, cigarettes and complaints to Orpen's Old Etonian fliers; and in the face of appalling casualty lists, reassurance was offered by pictures suggesting that the wounded invariably received the best possible care from devoted nurses and grimly determined RAMC doctors such as appeared in Bone's *The VAD Rest Room* and *Waiting for the Wounded*.

When the pictures could be accompanied by a descriptive text, as in the publications, their propagandist potential was greatly enhanced: in Montague's hands, the letter-press was regularly used to turn into propaganda pictures which by themselves con-veyed no message, the link between picture and letterpress often being tenuous in the extreme. *The Western Front* and *British Artists at the Front* were flexible propaganda instruments: although the three-month production process meant that they were rarely very topical, they could effectively focus and play on the more permanent themes. The barbarism of the enemy was evidenced in descriptions of British hospital ships bombed and French country gardens wrecked: 'where [the Germans] had not the time', Montague wrote passionately, 'both to impede the pursuing British army and also to cut down the village priest's half-grown cherry trees, or to prevent some old French cottager from ever sitting in her little yew tree arbour again, then these practitioners of scientific war really seem to have thrown Clausewitz to the winds and concentrated their forces against priest and old woman. Hot blood and foul blood, not cold.' The theme of solidarity with Britain's Allies was a constant, though not always felicitously expressed – 'French girls test, with swift precision, the straightness of British bayonets, on which much depends.'

Through appropriate letterpress the propagandists could further subdue the terrors of war by making the Western Front sound familiar and intelligible and, in consequence, manageable – by likening the scenery and atmosphere to that of England, for example: Montague described the area around Loos as 'a black country, where men of the South Lancashires feel at home and grant that the landscape has some of the points of Wigan' – and by making life at the Front sound as much like normal existence as possible. 'It is always merry travelling up to the Front by day in a train,' wrote Montague. 'During pauses the engine driver is visited and some of his boiling water is diverted . . . from its ordinary propulsive task to the making of tea.'

The war art publications could also sometimes respond to specific claims made by the Germans. To counter their continued assertions that Admiral Beatty's flagship, HMS *Lion*, had been sunk at Jutland, *The Western Front* carried a sketch of the *Lion* safe in dry dock with the letterpress, 'Officially "sunk" by the Germans, she will yet prove a troublesome ghost to them.' The DoI was likewise anxious to end a German campaign of interference with the American supply of horses and mules to the British Army in France. In an attempt to have the export of horses banned, the German-funded Organisation of American Women for Strict Neutrality circulated reports of Belgian fire-brigade horses dying in tragic circumstances: the DoI's response included the reproduction of Bone's tranquil and bucolic scene *Transport Horses in a French Orchard*, and Nevinson's *A Mule Team*, with the caption, 'Those which are not often exposed to enemy fire, the great majority, probably live about as long as they would have done in peacetime, thanks to a pervasive system of general and special veterinary hospitals, rest camps and sick horse halts.'

It is obviously difficult to evaluate the effect of any particular picture, or of war art itself as one aspect of propaganda: the essence of propaganda is that it is a *cumulative* exercise, the constant repetition of simple messages through a multitude of channels. 'It is absurdly difficult to explain . . . why any particular piece of propaganda is desirable,' Masterman remarked ruefully. 'Every little piece of it easily looks ridiculous; it is only by the concentrated effect of all that the result we desire is obtained.' As far as war art is concerned, the numbers of people who can be reckoned actually to have seen the propaganda give an indication (no more) of its likely effectiveness, and in this respect it is worth comparing the various uses to which war art was put.

Press coverage was wide and invaluable in making the pictures known, both by reproducing and by reviewing them: Yockney sent gratis copies of *The Western Front* to 158 London and provincial newspapers and magazines, and to 68 in the Empire and Dominions, and few reviewers missed the opportunity to express their patriotism.

Exhibitions were generally successful – not only in the prestigious West End galleries, where attendances ranged from 250 a week for McBey to 2000 a week for Orpen, but also among a wider public at the municipal galleries in London and the provinces: 43,500 people saw the exhibition of Bone's drawings at the Whitechapel Gallery in London's East End in October and November 1917, and in Rochdale 10,000 people visited the joint Bone and Dodd exhibition in May 1918.

Far less effective, if results are measured against intentions, were the war art publications and reproductions. These were primarily intended for sale – 50% in Britain and 35% in America, with the residual 15% to be given away as a 'pump-priming' exercise. Exact figures are now irretrievable, but the general impression is that sales were poor, although better in the UK than the USA. (There were, of course, exceptions – the *de luxe* edition of Bone's *Tanks*, at 5s, sold in thousands all over the world,[50] its success probably reflecting the novelty value of the subject.) Clearly it did not take the DoI long to acknowledge their failure: by early 1918 over 50% of the Bone publications – 202,900 out of 397,800 – had been distributed free and large stocks still remained; in the USA only one fifth of all *The Western Front* issues were sold.

This should not necessarily be seen as a general reflection on the efficiency of art as propaganda. Public interest as manifested in press coverage and exhibition attendances was, after all, considerable, and the effect of the free copies distributed, which is obviously impossible to measure, may equally have been significant. Rather it should be seen as a commercial failure, due to the DoI's inexperience in the field of art publications. The success Wellington House had achieved in 1915 with the distribution of 15,000 copies of Raemaekers' cartoons seems to have encouraged false hopes of a similar market for war art. With profit margins as high as 50%, even the cheapest of the DoI's publications was, at 2s, four times as expensive as the cartoons. More to the point, they lacked the same power to 'filter through to workmen's homes' which, despite the propagandists' fondness for the 'cultured minority', it was obviously hoped they would somehow do. Irritatingly it was an American publisher who put his finger on the problem, insisting that *The Western Front* was 'far above the heads of the people you need to influence. Its influence is, and must remain, restricted to an educated and artistic class. It stands no comparison with Raemaekers' book which is emotional and dramatic. Muirhead Bone is "precious" – and the public simply won't *feel* his work at all.'

It is interesting to compare the exploitation of the official artists' work with another quite separate exercise in art propaganda – the series of sixty-six lithographs by eighteen leading artists, collectively known as 'Britain's Efforts and Ideals in the Great War'.[51] Little is known about the series, as almost all records except those in Yockney's private possession were destroyed in a fire at HMSO in the 1960s. It was definitely executed under the auspices of the DoI; but though initiated expressly for propaganda purposes, it was unrelated to the scheme for sending official artists to the Front (except inasmuch as previous participation in 'Efforts and Ideals' may have been a factor in the selection of Nevinson, Kennington and Rothenstein).

Charles Ricketts, *Italia Redenta* (lithograph in colour), $27\frac{1}{4} \times 17$

Charles Shannon, *The Rebirth of the Arts* (lithograph in colour), $29\frac{1}{4} \times 19\frac{1}{2}$

There were twelve 'Ideals' – colour lithographs, mostly heavily allegorical, some expressing specific territorial ambitions (George Clausen's *The Reconstruction of Belgium*, for example, Gerald Moira's *The Restoration of Serbia* and Charles Ricketts's *Italia Redenta*), others more general aims (such as Rothenstein's *The Triumph of Democracy* and Charles Shannon's *The Rebirth of the Arts*). The 'Efforts' consisted of nine sets of six lithographs in black and white, each depicting a different aspect of Britain's war effort – women's work by Archibald Hartrick, the training of the Navy by Brangwyn, aircraft production by Nevinson.

The series as a whole was first shown at the Fine Art Society in July 1917; it was widely reproduced in the press and proofs were offered for sale in limited editions of two hundred. Touring exhibitions were also arranged, both in Britain and, simultaneously, in Paris, New York and Los Angeles. Though not mounted with the panache for which Thomas Derrick (who had charge of the series at the DoI) had hoped, they made a considerable impact, particularly in America. 'It is difficult to explain the far-reaching effect of the lithographs,' wrote a British representative in New York, 'but they have been a revelation to American Fifth Avenue art patrons, dealers, critics, etc. We have had more success with them and the *Tank* than anything else except films. They put up British prestige.'[52]

The stated objective of the series was to give 'concerted artistic expression to themes which are of deep and widespread moment in our national life' – but quite what prompted the DoI to embark on this large-scale venture when it did is not certain. The explanation *may* lie in the Government's campaign during 1917 to combat civilian defeatism at home. After the slaughter of the Somme in the late summer of 1916, a growing 'war-weariness' was obvious among the British people, manifested in pacifism at all levels of society and a growing inclination to listen to the German overtures for peace. With his 'Never-Endian' attitude to the war, Lloyd George found this weakening of Britain's war effort unacceptable and, in the spring of 1917, in an attempt to rally public opinion, he set up an all-party parliamentary committee under his own chairmanship – the National War Aims Committee. It is not unlikely that the 'Efforts and Ideals' lithographs were produced by Masterman's department at the direct request of the NWAC as propaganda aimed at the class which was particularly eloquent in its advocacy of an end to the war.

This possible connection between the NWAC and 'Efforts and Ideals' highlights the major anomaly of war art: produced at the instigation and under the auspices of an organisation founded principally to conduct propaganda abroad, it was also used widely as an instrument of propaganda at home.

CHAPTER FIFTEEN

The Ministry of Information

B Y the end of 1917 it was obvious that the DoI had failed to live up to its promise of revolutionising British propaganda. As its staff would have been the first to acknowledge, 'Victories are the best propaganda', and the Allies' bleak military record during 1917 (encompassing the collapse of Russia in the throes of revolution, mutinies in the French Army, and the disasters of Caporetto and Passchendaele), had done little to help. Ironically, the DoI, despite the restraint of its own output, also suffered from the backlash of the world's growing disenchantment with propaganda as practised by the Germans: 'The Department was faced by the expectation that our propaganda would be as valueless and in fact that any statement made under the auspices of any propagandist association would necessarily be untrue.'

Lord Beaverbrook, National Portrait Gallery

John Buchan had not proved an ideal Director of Information. Throughout 1917 he was dogged by personal troubles – an operation for his ulcers which kept him bedbound for the first month of his appointment; the loss of his youngest brother, who died of wounds at Arras in April, leaving him to comfort his extremely demanding mother; and a reverse in his wife's family fortunes, which obliged him to embark again on the lucrative but time-consuming business of writing novels – *Mr Standfast* was started during his appointment as Director.

Unfortunately it was a job which required undivided attention. Despite his efforts, Buchan was never able to establish satisfactory relations between the DoI and other Government departments, which restricted the vital flow of information on which propaganda was based. He lacked the necessary political authority to champion his Department effectively, and had no ready access to Lloyd George or the War Cabinet either for support against other departments or for the day-to-day contact with the policy-makers which is essential to the proper direction and smooth running of a propaganda campaign.

Buchan's experiences proved, rather too late, the wisdom of Robert Donald's suggestion that the Director should be a political figure, and in August 1917 Lloyd George buttressed the DoI's authority by putting Sir Edward Carson, a member of the War

Cabinet, in overall charge of both foreign and home propaganda. Buchan's relief was, however, short-lived: before long Carson was neglecting his new duties to concentrate on his old over-riding interest in the Irish question.

When Carson ultimately resigned at the beginning of 1918, Lloyd George saw the opportunity to kill two birds with one stone – to put propaganda on a satisfactory footing by creating a totally new organisation, this time a full-blown Ministry; and to range the powerful figures of Lords Beaverbrook and Northcliffe on his side. Henceforth he was to be, in the words of a contemporary newspaper report, a 'Faust with two Mephistopheles'.

Beaverbrook had played a crucial role in the sequence of events which brought Lloyd George to power in December 1916, and his appointment as Minister of Information in February 1918 can be seen as the final payment on the debt.[53] As Arnold Bennett later put it, 'The belief widely exists that the Ministry was brought into being for the sake of the Minister.' The appointment of Northcliffe as Director of Propaganda in Enemy Countries was intended to pre-empt the opposition expected from *The Times* and other Northcliffe papers to Lloyd George's plans for displacing some of the top generals, in particular Sir William Robertson (dismissed on the day Northcliffe's appointment was announced).

It remained only to divide responsibility for propaganda. For fear of its abuse, the powerful weapon of home propaganda was kept independent of the new Ministry in the hands of the all-party NWAC.[54] In the sphere of overseas propaganda, the need to accommodate both Beaverbrook and Northcliffe led to a formal split, for the first time, between propaganda in enemy countries and propaganda among Allies and neutrals. Northcliffe, in charge of the former, was technically subordinate to Beaverbrook as Minister in charge of the latter; however, at his own insistence, his organisation at Crewe House, though in close liaison with Beaverbrook's Ministry, had its own separate Vote and was responsible directly to the War Cabinet.

Thus Beaverbrook was left with oversight of propaganda in Allied and neutral countries only. By the end of April 1918 a highly efficient, cost-conscious organisation had been created out of the remains of the DoI, with many of the senior posts filled by Beaverbrook's business contacts. Each geographical target area was put under the control of a 'National' who decided the form propaganda should take in his area, aided by information from the MoI's representative on the spot; there were some talented pairings, including Arnold Bennett as the National for France[55] with Eric Maclagan as his man in Paris.[56] Each National put in requests for the various types of propaganda material (films, photographs, pictures, articles, etc.) to the 'production' departments – among which was numbered Masterman's Literature and Art Department – and expenditure in each area was regulated by specialist Controllers, experienced businessmen such as C. E. Hambro and R. S. Guinness, appointed specifically to advise on cost-effectiveness.

In the new Ministry there was a distinct shift of emphasis in propaganda. The stress was now firmly on news, disseminated abroad by wireless and cable, rather than analysis and comment, and these priorities were reflected by the secondment for the duration of the Managing Director of Reuters, Roderick Jones, to be the MoI's Chief Executive. The main instruments of mass propaganda were films and photographs, and in the

influencing of prominent individuals greater use was made of personal contacts – meetings with senior politicians and military personnel, entertainments, and more numerous conducted visits to the Front.

For Masterman's Department the consequence was a dramatic reduction in size and
importance. Responsibility for official photographs passed to a separate section and
the flow of publications was cut to a trickle. Books and pamphlets were too slow in
production to be suitable vehicles for news; moreover, the worsening paper shortage
made publications too expensive, especially the illustrated papers. Under the watchful
eye of the Controller for Paper – F. W. Bowater – annual paper consumption declined
from 6000 to 2000 tons; and it was principally at the expense of the Literature and
Art Department that Beaverbrook was able to reduce the MoI's estimated budget for
1918 from £1·8 million to £1·2 million. The diminished Department was moved from
its birthplace in Wellington House to a cramped hotel off the Strand, equipped with
only one telephone. The level of esteem in which Beaverbrook was held among the
old Wellington House staff is indicated by a curious document entitled 'A Month of
the Ministry'; anonymous and highly satirical, it is a diary of life under the regime
of 'Lord Burrowmole of Backstairs', including an episode in which all the official artists
are recalled from the Front to paint Lord Burrowmole's portrait on a squadron of Wellington House white elephants.

For Masterman himself, the new Ministry marked yet another step downwards:
already in May 1918 a newspaper was cruelly reflecting, 'Mr Masterman! The name
sounds like an echo from the dead past!' There was bitter irony for him in the manner
in which Beaverbrook had acquired the power to make his changes; he had obtained
his seat in the Cabinet not as Minister of Information, which was not a Cabinet appointment, but through his simultaneous appointment in February 1918 as Chancellor
of the Duchy of Lancaster – until 1915 Masterman's own post.

The consequences for war art of the radical reorganisation could have been disastrous. Under the new system neither Masterman nor Buchan (now heading the MoI's
Intelligence Section) had the power to initiate propaganda; and with the cuts in his
Department's budget (which precipitated the demise of the *War Pictorial* and *British
Artists at the Front*) and the shift of emphasis towards news, Masterman could no longer
justify the employment of artists; the position was not improved by the huge stockpile
of unsold reproductions. Nor is there any evidence that Northcliffe intended to utilise,
or ever did utilise artists in his propaganda campaign against enemy countries. Thus
with the withdrawal of all artists from France in March 1918 in the face of the German
advance, the termination of the scheme would have been a logical step. That it was
not taken, and that war art in fact flourished during 1918, was due solely to Lord
Beaverbrook: the man who initiated the changes that should have put paid to war
art was virtually the only person Lloyd George could have chosen as Minister who
saw a real value in it.

Max Aitken had arrived in England from his native Canada in 1910, a self-made
millionaire at the age of thirty-one through mergers and share transactions in the
unregulated business milieu of Montreal; one newspaper sneered, 'Lord Beaverbrook
is like a German pill-box – made of cast iron and cement.' He plunged enthusiastically
into British politics as the Unionist Member for Ashton-under-Lyne, and quickly

became an intimate of Bonar Law; his knighthood in 1911 was bestowed in anticipation of contributions to party funds. The newspaper empire for which he is perhaps
most famous was founded in 1916, when he acquired the *Daily Express*.

Surprisingly the British found no post for Beaverbrook when war broke out, and
he turned his formidable energies to reporting and recording Canada's share in the
war. As the self-appointed 'Eye Witness' at the Front he brought home – through articles, photographs and films – the sacrifices and successes of the Canadian troops, and
in 1916 he established the Canadian War Record Office in London, to put together
a thorough documentary record.

Then in 1917, with the substantial profits from sales of photographs and film
receipts, Beaverbrook financed as an offshoot of the War Record Office a charity, the
Canadian War Memorials Fund, set up to compile an artistic record of Canada's role
in the war; by the time of his appointment as Minister of Information, a large collection
of important canvases had been commissioned from a wide variety of artists, the majority of them British.

His activities had attracted favourable notice in art circles and, no doubt gratified
by this, Beaverbrook saw in his new appointment an opportunity to repeat his success
for the country of his adoption. Almost his first act as Minister was to set up a special
body, the British War Memorials Committee, with a view to assembling a similar collection of pictures for Britain.

Thus responsibility for war art finally moved away from Masterman's Department:
and the end of the Wellington House era also coincided with a change in the function
of war art. Though later in 1918 Treasury opposition was to compel lip-service to
the notion of using art as propaganda, Beaverbrook's underlying objective throughout
1918 was different – he wanted not merely to exploit the official artists' pictures, but
to collect them, with the aim of building, on the Canadian pattern, both a record and
a memorial of the war in art.

CHAPTER SIXTEEN

The British War Memorials Committee

Arnold Bennett, <small>National Portrait Gallery</small>

B EAVERBROOK appears at first to have seen his two concurrent picture-collecting ventures as complementary, and to have talked in terms of active co-operation – the pooling of artists, cars and other facilities at the Front, and so forth. In the event the BWMC was to borrow several ideas and artists from its Canadian model, and was to have members in common with the CWMF – not only Beaverbrook, but also Lord Rothermere as Chairman and P. G. Konody, the art critic on Rothermere's papers. Nevertheless, after the early meetings in March, which the Secretary of the CWMF attended to offer practical advice, the Committee operated independently and developed its own artistic policy.

The other members gave the British scheme a decided character of its own. Foremost among them were Masterman and Arnold Bennett[57] (who with Beaverbrook and Rothermere formed the executive quorum) – with Alfred Yockney as Secretary to the Committee, and Muirhead Bone and Robert Ross the most active from the penumbra of art advisers.

Arnold Bennett was recognised as a knowledgeable amateur in contemporary art circles, a reputation built in part on his journalism – he was a skilful populariser of modern painting, trading heavily on three years spent on the Bohemian fringes of Paris – and in part on his genuinely discriminating patronage of such young artists as Nevinson, Nash and William Roberts. It would be fair to say, however, that he was appointed principally because of his friendship with Beaverbrook, who greatly admired his writing and appreciated his achievements as a self-made man; for his part, Bennett was fascinated by Beaverbrook's world of money and power – and put his observations to good use in *Lord Raingo*, a novel centred round a millionaire entrepreneur made Minister of Records in wartime. . . .

Bennett took his position on the Committee very seriously, and he was later to claim that he and Masterman had been responsible for all the commissioning of artists – 'a hades of a lot of cerebration'. Unquestionably he did originate several interesting ideas – it was he who first stressed the importance of *Home* Front subjects, and the desirability of a variety of modes of expression, including sculpture, etchings and humorous art. However, he was seriously underrating the contribution made by the expert advisers who besides Konody included Dodgson and Derrick, Robert Ross and Muirhead Bone.

Bone, now largely recovered from his nervous collapse, was drawn in as the main representative of an unofficial artists' committee, whose other members were Tonks and Orpen (though it is not clear how much the latter did to help). Ross, described by Bennett as one of the most *indirectly* creative men he had ever known, was in 1918 an art critic and connoisseur of considerable authority, and a Trustee of the Tate Gallery. His circle of friends and protégés was remarkable – Tonks, McColl, Ricketts and Duncan Grant: Shaw, Beerbohm and George Moore: Sassoon, Graves, Owen and Osbert Sitwell. He was best known, however, to his cost, as Oscar Wilde's most loyal defender; he commissioned Epstein's controversial sculpture for Wilde's tomb in Paris and, as his literary executor, devoted thirteen years to rehabilitating his artistic reputation.

The BWMC's approach to its task was systematic. It had no scruples in telling its artists exactly what to paint: the subject matter came first, and artists were to be chosen to serve it, not vice versa: Derrick in particular warned against assembling 'a series of pictures, more or less relevant to the war, in which the individual artists were allowed merely to run their own individual "stunts"'. (He was thinking in particular of Glyn Philpot, who had suggested for himself the subject of 'A Bathing Parade'. 'I cannot say whether this is a really significant incident in the life of soldiers,' wrote Derrick to Masterman, 'but I will bet anything that Philpot suggested it because it gave him the opportunity of painting the nude.')

As a basis for operations two lists of the subjects to be covered were drawn up – one for the Home Front, compiled by Arnold Bennett, the other for the Western Front, by Bone and Yockney. Bennett felt strongly that the Home Front was 'almost as picturesque and certainly as humanly interesting' as the Western Front, which he had visited briefly in 1915. It also had the advantage of providing subjects not exclusively military, so that both women and older men, excluded from or unwilling to risk the battle zone, could be used.

He made eight careful groupings of potential material – Army, Navy, Air Force, Merchant Marine, Land, Munitions, Clerical & other Work by Women, and Public Manifestations – with brief, persuasive conspectuses that vividly reflected his own interests as a novelist of working life and one-time editor of *Woman* magazine. Of clerical work he wrote – 'It is impossible not to feel the picturesqueness of the life in all the commandeered hotels and the temporary buildings in Parks . . . largely occupied by women who perhaps never before worked outside their own homes. For example, extraordinarily picturesque sights can be seen from the top of an omnibus in the City through the windows of banks and other commercial institutions: vast floors full of figures bending over books under hundreds of little green-shaded lights.'[58]

For the Western Front Bone drew both on his own wide experience and that of others (Montague, Dodd and Nash all offered suggestions) to produce three groups of subjects – 'The Channel Crossing', 'Behind the Front' (the allocation of billets by the Town Majors, for example, and soldiers in billets with their French hosts; labour camps and the coloured troops – Chinese, Indian and Egyptian – who carried out the unpleasant tasks of clearance and salvage on the battlefields; prisoners; cemeteries), and 'The Front' itself.

Simultaneously the Committee considered the question of artists to fit subjects. It had first to accommodate those previously employed. Of the nine existing official artists, four did no work for the MoI: Dodd, whose appointment, by mutual consent, was not renewed; Kennington, whose relationship with the authorities did not survive the arguments over censorship and the price of his pictures; and Lavery and Rothenstein who, though their appointments were extended on the loose basis of their giving the Government first option, in the event produced no work for the Ministry.[59] Nevinson and Nash were signed up, though on terms quite different from their DoI agreements; and the long-term appointments of Bone, McBey and Orpen were assimilated virtually unchanged into the new scheme.

The importance of Bone's role in the choice of further artists cannot be overstated: with his keen interest in and knowledge of modern art he combined enthusiasm and energy which left his colleagues breathless, and the MoI's ultimate selection, made principally from among the British artists on the Canadian list and the lists produced by Bone, was extraordinarily catholic. With a conspicuous freedom from prejudice for the most part, the Committee chose representatives of virtually every school, consciously avoiding only exponents of the studio 'battle-picture', artificial and melodramatic, reconstructed from descriptions.

The Royal Academy was represented, despite Bennett's determination to keep out the 'reactionary mass of RA and ARA muck', by Sargent, Charles Sims and George Clausen (the two last doubtless tolerated because of their declared intention of reforming the Academy from within). Considerable weight was also given to the 'old guard' of the NEAC and the Slade which, with its insistence on technical proficiency, turned out expert draughtsmen ideally equipped as recorders of war and accounted for a remarkable proportion of the war artists.[60] The School's principal teachers (Tonks, Steer and Walter Russell) were all employed, as were several of their more conventional pupils – Alfred Hayward and A. N. Lewis, for example – under which heading should perhaps also be included Augustus John, who by 1918, left behind by the Post-Impressionists, could no longer be called *avant-garde*.

Despite Tonks's efforts to shield his pupils from the contaminating influence of Post-Impressionism, the Slade had also produced many of the leading 'moderns'. These were well represented on the MoI list by Vorticists Wyndham Lewis and William Roberts,[61] Nevinson, Paul Nash, Colin Gill and Stanley Spencer. Other radicals were drawn from outside the Slade: Henry Lamb, Post-Impressionist and intimate of the Bloomsbury Group; Bernard Adeney, a friend of Roger Fry and member of his Omega Workshops, considered 'very Cubist' by Campbell Dodgson; and John Duncan Fergusson, one of the few British Fauvists.[62]

Bennett made a spirited attempt to leaven the mixture by recruiting Max Beerbohm to portray the war's lighter side, but in a letter of typical elegance Beerbohm declined:

'I cannot, without violence to myself, see the war, or anything therewith connected, *comically*; and at the same time I cannot draw in any but a wildly comic manner. . . . My sense of the villainy of what Germany has done, and of the loathsomeness of the age we live in precludes fun; and fun is all I'm good for. . . . I could chaff the German Emperor delightfully – if he weren't the symbol of Germany.' He did nonetheless execute a series of three caricatures, entitled *British Artists at the Front*, of Sargent, John and Orpen (the last a drawing of the artist at work, observed by a group of German prisoners, one of whom is translated as remarking: 'Let us right-well-lengthily discuss how it is that this so cultured artist does not the never-sufficiently-to-be-praised Cubismus adopt').[63]

Not all the artists chosen were immediately available. The Canadians had prior claims on many of them, and a large number were on active service. Whereas

Max Beerbohm, *Sir William Orpen* (reproduced in *Reveille*, 1919)

previously only three of the nine employed – McBey, Orpen and Nash – had needed to be released in order to serve as artists, Beaverbrook now wished to deploy a far greater number, and in mid-March he submitted a request to the War Office for the release of sixteen serving soldier–artists. Among them were several sculptors – Gilbert Ledward, for example, on duty with a siege battery in Italy; and Eric Gill who, having completed the Westminster 'Stations of the Cross', had been conscripted into the RAF to learn 'motor-driving'. (The Committee, on learning that he had been passed Grade I, withdrew its application, in accordance with its post-Passchendaele policy of employing only men unfit for combat – though Bone grumbled, 'I don't understand about his Grade I qualification – because he is a shrimp of a man, very small and undersized'.) Epstein, to his intense displeasure, was a Private in the Royal Fusiliers, called up after what he saw as a 'deliberate conspiracy in the Press', orchestrated by Augustus John. 'I loom too large for our feeble small folk of the brush and chisel.' Whatever the truth of this, Beaverbrook's request for him met with flat refusal; the others, however, were all eventually released.

Given the BWMC's open-minded approach, it is intriguing to consider the artists they did *not* choose. Bloomsbury, for example, was represented only peripherally by Lamb and Adeney; a splendidly prim passage in the BWMC minutes speaks volumes: 'The attainments of Mr Fry were discussed but no recommendations were made.' The Committee's objections are likely to have been artistic rather than political: Duncan Grant and Mark Gertler were both approached despite their well-known moral opposition to the war[64] – Grant at the suggestion of Robert Ross, himself a pacifist. Curiously, both accepted: Gertler graciously expressed himself willing to 'sacrifice a certain amount of my time', and was asked to depict a scene in the London tube during an air-raid. Grant, working on the land as a conscientious objector, turned down Masterman's innocuous suggestion of a landscape of allotments and proposed a decidedly more militaristic subject in an aeroplane factory. Unfortunately the Pelham Committee (which controlled conscientious objectors) refused to release him, despite Yockney's appeal for help to Maynard Keynes, and Beaverbrook's argument that using Grant for this work would release a *fighting* man. (The only artist actually to object on conscientious grounds was Harold Knight: asked to paint seaplanes at Newlyn harbour, he agreed to do so for record purposes, but withdrew when he discovered that the pictures might be used for propaganda.)

Conspicuously few women artists were ultimately selected. Three were chosen – Anna Airy, Dorothy Coke and Flora Lion – but the Ministry never actually acquired any pictures from any of them. Airy's picture, of munition girls leaving work, was rejected as unsatisfactory by the Committee, using for the only time its right to refuse a picture it had commissioned. Bone had suggested, without response, the names of several women artists who have subsequently become much better known – including Dora Carrington, Dorothy Brett, Gwen Raverat and Gwen John – and whose works would now seem a far greater asset than those of some of the men.

It would also have been fascinating to have seen what some of his other rejected nominees would have made of appointments as war artists, given that they ranged from the 'Neo-Pre-Raphaelites' (Ricketts, Shannon and Sturge Moore) to the Cubist Bomberg, via Lucien Pissarro and Art Nouveau in the persons of Gordon Craig and Charles Rennie Mackintosh.

The distinction of being the only painter to refuse the BWMC's invitation *ab initio* fell to Walter Sickert. His reasons are obscure as he is known to have painted war subjects, but the explanation may lie in a personal antipathy to Bennett, whose popular status as an arbiter of taste Sickert resented: 'It is absurd that a Bennett should be referred to for anything except the time of a train, or the cost of a bicycle lamp.'

CHAPTER SEVENTEEN

The Hall of Remembrance

D URING the first month at least the BWMC rushed ahead with the selection and pairing of subjects and artists rather as an intellectual exercise, with little thought as to the use which might be made of the resulting pictures, and with no object more clearly defined than the accumulation of a 'national collection of war pictures', to be displayed somewhere, preferably together, after the war. However, as the scheme got fully under way, the practical implications had to be faced: for instance, what kind of pictures were wanted? large? small? oil? watercolour? allegory? illustration? – and precisely where and how would they be housed?

The original intention, based loosely on the Canadian precedent, was to build up a general collection of pictures which would be of interest primarily as documents of the war, straightforward and informative, centred on a nucleus of more ambitious canvases designed somehow to epitomise the war, to express the artists' feelings about it, and in so doing to commemorate the nation's sacrifice. It was this 'memorial' element which came rapidly to the fore to give the scheme its distinctive character, idealistic and a trifle grandiose.

Robert Ross was the first to focus on the concept of an 'art memorial', with the proposal that the Ministry's collection should be designed to have an unmistakeable unity and identity.[65] The pictures should be of standard sizes, all large enough to have a heroic and 'monumental' character – he suggested as models two of the great battle-pieces of the past, Velasquez' *The Surrender of Breda*, 120×144, and Uccello's *Rout of San Romano* panels, 72×125.

The Committee seized eagerly on the idea of standardisation and decided also that the larger pictures should be uniform in scale – particularly with regard to figures – and should be paired by subject, the latter a suggestion made by the Scottish etcher D. Y. Cameron, ARA. With an eye to the effect they would create when hung, Cameron proposed that landscapes paired in this way should have the same horizon line, being divided in the proportion of two-thirds land to one-third sky. He pointed out, rather regretfully, that the uneventful Flemish landscape, unlike the 'ragged and jagged heights' in which he himself normally specialised, would make this type of uniformity easy to observe. Nevertheless, pairing was not a success. Three combinations were tentatively suggested – William Roberts and John Nash to do battle scenes; George Clausen and Anna Airy, munitions scenes; and Cameron himself and Charles Sims, Western Front landscapes, one in spring, the other autumn – but only Cameron and Sims appear to have made any real effort to co-operate: Roberts and Nash failed even to paint pictures of the same size.

The Committee had some modifications to make to the recommended standard sizes of pictures, resolving that as a general rule the largest 'memorial canvas' should be of the Uccello size, with exceptional provision for a small number of 'super-pictures', larger even than *The Surrender of Breda*. Variety was to be achieved by offering some artists an alternative, squarer shape of 72×86; and for those requiring or required to paint on a smaller scale, the size of 42×60 was adopted.

The Committee then devised three sets of financial conditions – Schemes 1, 2 and 3 – under which artists would be employed to produce this 'memorial' series. Under the first arrangement – Scheme 1 – the artist was to produce a *single* picture in one of the standard 'memorial' sizes, in return for which he would receive a lump sum (£600 for a 'super-picture', £300 for the 72×125 and 72×86 sizes, and £150 for the smaller size – payment being conditional on acceptance by the Committee);[66] expenses for subsistence away from home, materials, models and, at the Committee's discretion, studio rent; facilities at the scene, arranged by the Ministry; and the right to sell any sketches made,[67] provided the BWMC had the first option. The idea of paying Scheme 1 artists a fixed price did not go unchallenged, either on the grounds of equity – painters of higher reputation, it was thought, should receive more than those lesser known; and those in the battle zone, according to Kennington, should be paid more than those at work on 'Arrival in Port' or 'Historic Towns' – or on practical grounds: 'Pictures have their "market value" like any other goods,' spluttered Konody. 'To pay £300 . . . to an artist who would gladly accept £100, seems to me quixotic and wasteful.' Beaverbrook, however, insisted on the fixed price – and his business sense was as usual unerring. Scheme 1 was intended primarily to apply to artists of 'high standing' – in other words, older and better-established artists, who commanded fees just as likely to be *above* the standard price as *below* it.

Under this heading came such figures as George Clausen (aged 66), Steer (58), Tonks (56), Walter Bayes (49)[68] and Charles Holmes (50);[69] but the chief ornaments of Scheme 1 were unquestionably John Singer Sargent and Augustus John. Sargent had been a social lion since the 1890s; his biographer Evan Charteris records a distinguished diplomat's habit of asking, when seated at dinner next to a woman he had not met before, 'How do you like your Sargent drawing?' – a conversational gambit he claimed was successful nine times out of ten. John, at forty, was, according to *The Times*, simply 'the most famous of living painters' – or as Lytton Strachey more sourly put it, 'the darling of the upper classes', who celebrated him in every conceivable manner: the highlight of the entertainment at a garden party in aid of the Nation's Fund for Nurses was 'Living Friezes on the Terrace of St James's Palace – from Shakespeare, Botticelli, Augustus John, Chu Chin Chow, etc. . . .'

Scheme 2 was altogether more speculative: the artist was to make over to the BWMC his total output for a specified period (initially six months), during which he was to do no outside work of any kind,[70] receiving in return a salary of £300 per annum (over and above his military pay, if he was serving in the Forces),[71] plus all expenses. These were less generous terms, especially as 'total output' was in most cases intended to include a picture in one of the memorial sizes, and generally speaking they were offered to artists of more modest reputation, those with no proven ability to execute oil paintings on the large scale, or younger and more experimental painters. Paul and John Nash were both employed on this basis, as were Roberts, Meninsky, Colin Gill, John Wheatley and Henry Rushbury – all of whom were under thirty. (Scheme 2 was offered to Nevinson, but he declined – ostensibly on the grounds of the unacceptable threat the offer posed to his artistic freedom, but also, more truthfully, because 'it might prove a bad business proposition' – and was 'promoted' to Scheme 1.) Scheme 2 also proved the most convenient basis for assimilating Bone and McBey, on whose total output the Government already had a lien.

Scheme 3 was similar to the DoI standard agreement: in return for facilities the artist was to offer the first option on all the work he produced, at a 'reasonable' price (but transferring copyright only if the option was exercised); he would receive neither salary nor expenses. This was, in effect, a 'catch-all' scheme, designed to cover artists who were considered to be worth neither the relatively high outlay of Scheme 1 nor the risk inherent in Scheme 2, but who were nevertheless potentially useful – or men whom the Committee had no wish to offend. Those appointed were a miscellaneous collection: Rothenstein, for example, agreed to give the Committee the option on pictures he would paint in his spare time while working as a lecturer for the Army's educational programme in France;[72] the Fauvist Fergusson was offered Scheme 3 as a kind of probation; and Vorticist Frank Dobson was employed under it, interestingly as a painter, though he was to become far better known for his sculpture.

The Committee realised that while Scheme 1 artists would paint only pictures in the standard sizes to form part of the memorial series, Schemes 2 and 3 would almost certainly produce a number of smaller, non-uniform pictures, whose quality and subjects would be controlled less closely. Whatever value these might have as miscellaneous records of the war, the prospect alarmed Bone, who was anxious not to weaken the impact of the Ministry's collection by diluting it or blurring its outlines. To him the commemoration of the war in art became something of a crusade, and under his prodding the BWMC elaborated still further its plans for an 'art memorial'.[73]

As early as April Ross had insisted that the collection should be displayed in a worthy setting and suggested a special wing of the Tate Gallery. By May the Committee was considering the possibility of a wholly separate show-case – a 'Hall of Remembrance' to be custom-built by the Government after the war as part of a 'plan of Reconstruction'. It would consist of 'a beautiful homogeneous set of Galleries' – small rooms for home, naval and air subjects, centred on a main gallery for the biggest pictures of 'fighting subjects' (the Uccello-sized canvases and the super-pictures, of which four were now contemplated, each on the theme of co-operation between allies – American, French, Italian and Colonial troops standing shoulder to shoulder with the British).

Ross had advised that the pictures should harmonise with their surroundings, should perhaps even be let into the walls with wooden panelling rather than merely hung on them. The Committee now aimed higher: the Hall itself was to be an integrated whole, in which architecture and sculpture would play almost as important a part as the pictures themselves. At Bone's instigation the project was entrusted to Charles Holden, an architect with an outstanding record of interest in contemporary art, and especially in the unity of art and architecture. (It was Holden's firm which in 1908 had commissioned the young Jacob Epstein to carve eighteen figures for the exterior of the British Medical Association building in the Strand, stoutly defending the sculptures as an integral part of the design throughout the storm of controversy they provoked.) The Committee had him recalled from France, where he was working for the Imperial War Graves Commission, and instructed him to draw up blueprints.

Sculpture was a more intractable problem. Ross followed his proposals for standardising the pictures with similar suggestions for a uniform and unified sculptural scheme: random collecting, he believed, should be eschewed, for fear of accumulating 'war-genre pieces possessing only ephemeral interest and possibly nauseating to the next generation if not to the present'. The number of sculptors employed should be limited – there were, in his opinion, very few in England of any distinction at all, or even many 'ordinary competent image-makers' – and they should be set to work together in the same mode, and with the same materials, on carefully chosen subjects. Bas-relief was the mode he recommended, in preference to sculpture in the round which he felt too often tended towards the waxwork in the hands of contemporary carvers; and, given the English climate, which made all sculpture look 'depressing', he advocated the use of alabaster, possibly discreetly coloured, rather than marble or bronze.

The sculptures, like the pictures, were to be *memorials* of events, not illustrations of them. War, Ross felt, lent itself badly to naturalistic representation: too many of its trappings – guns, bayonets, uniforms, helmets – looked absurd rendered into stone, and it would be necessary to exclude the sculptor's principal subject, 'the nude, without which modern sculpture . . . becomes merely fashionable and ephemeral'. The themes represented should be abstract – 'Physical Force opposed to or united to Thought', 'Patriotism', 'Domination', 'Nationality', and so forth. The Committee, with some reservations, accepted his proposals and considered various names – among them Gilbert Ledward, Charles Jagger, Havard Thomas, Derwent Wood and John Tweed.

It is not easy to gauge how much faith the administrators – Masterman, Bennett and Beaverbrook – had in the fulfilment of the plans for the 'Hall of Remembrance': Beaverbrook in particular seems to have seen the separate housing of the collection as a subsidiary issue, and an ambition which he was perfectly prepared to sacrifice in order to preserve the collection intact. But for Ross and Bone, loyally supported by Yockney, the Hall of Remembrance was what made the war art scheme worthwhile. 'Our dreams . . . ought to be as clear and concrete to us', Bone wrote, 'as their Heaven was to the Primitive Church.' In his mind's eye he saw 'a kind of Pavilion' breathing 'a choice modest beauty of conception', set in its own garden – he suggested a site on Richmond Hill; in one of the small galleries music would play, and the main gallery would end in an oratory with a single decoration representing '"the coming Brotherhood of Man", for which we all pray'. The Hall would house only pictures of 'a serious and noble character', expressing both the age's reflections on war and its finest achievements in art; Bone believed sincerely in the importance of including the ideas, on both war and art, of the generation which had borne the brunt of the battle, and urged that space be left for artists now fighting, to be filled after the war. 'We must be careful lest they find no place for them just where they have every right to be employed.'

He saw the scheme not simply as an interesting experiment in art patronage, as it was later to be represented, but as a mission to convey to posterity the real meaning of the Great War. 'Before the better knowledge of our descendants,' he wrote, 'our present political ideals may seem remote, but if we enshrine our feelings expressed by our artists in terms of beauty, we speak to succeeding generations in a voice which never grows unintelligible or stale. . . . the power of Art . . . is as clear and telling as the "moral voice within us" – let us help to make it speak nobly.'

CHAPTER EIGHTEEN

The 'Super-pictures' and the Western Front

T HE BWMC's intention was that its variegated team of artists should cover every theatre of operations and every aspect of war. Nevertheless, the Western Front was until the end the main focus for war art. The 'fighting subjects' to be seen at the Front were to be at the heart of the Hall of Remembrance, and at the heart of the fighting subjects was the group of 'super-pictures', an idea which may have originated in the Committee's anticipation of the needs of Augustus John.

When John was first being considered by the BWMC, Robert Ross counselled, 'You must allow for him doing [his picture] or *not* doing it, in his own way' – a warning all too prophetic. John had originally applied to the DoI for an official appointment in mid-June 1917;[74] but the DoI offer (which did not carry a salary) left him, with eight children and two houses to support, singularly unimpressed and he was lured away by a promise from the Canadians of a Major's commission with full pay.

He went to France for the CWMF in January 1918, to the area around Vimy, and appears to have made an indelible impression as the only bearded officer in the Imperial Army besides the King – for whom he was regularly mistaken, his appearance being enough to make every ordinary private 'start saluting a mile off'. To Tonks he wrote that he was 'overjoyed to be out here', but he survived only two months before being sent home in disgrace for

Max Beerbohm, *Major Augustus John* (reproduced in *Reveille*, 1918)

knocking out a fellow officer, one Captain Peter Wright – a gesture, he claimed, 'with only an indirect relation to my cod-piece'.

Taking advantage of the débâcle, the BWMC approached him at the end of March with a specific commission. In view of his fondness for large canvases and his 'synthetic' approach to composition, pulling together into one design a multitude of incidents and details observed at different times, he was invited to summarise his ideas on 'The Junction of Our Lines with the French' in a picture nine feet high by twenty feet wide.

In September 1917 Campbell Dodgson had remarked hopefully, 'I am of the opinion that it might be the making of John to be brought into contact with reality and the hard facts of warfare, instead of doing things entirely out of his own head as he does at present.' It seems, however, to have been too late to halt the slide into self-indulgence. By this time John was drinking heavily, subject to fits of melancholy, and the 'hard facts of warfare' failed to stimulate any genuine response. 'When out at the front,' he wrote, 'I admire things unreasonably and conduct myself with the instinctive tact which is the mark of a moral traitor.' Beerbohm's caricature has a cruel point: John is portrayed amidst the débris of war, sketch-book at the ready, peering into a field dotted with French peasant women in statuesque Johnian poses – 'Ah, now *there* really is a subject.'

He seems never to have begun the British super-picture, and never passed the cartoon stage for his Canadian commission *Pageant of War*.[75] It perhaps sums up his lack of aptitude as a war artist that the only canvas the MoI received from him was *Fraternity* ($93\frac{1}{2} \times 57$) – a name coined by Yockney – which depicts a group of soldiers sharing a light for their cigarettes, and is a straight copy of a mass-circulation postcard made from the *Daily Mail*'s Official War Pictures, Series 2 No. 11 – 'A "Fag" after a Fight'.[76]

postcard, *Daily Mail Official War Pictures, Series 2 No. 11 – 'A "Fag" after a Fight'*

OPPOSITE, Augustus John, *Fraternity* (oil on canvas), $93\frac{1}{2} \times 57$

With the second super-picture the Committee had more success. As an American, Sargent was a natural choice for the subject of co-operation between Britain and her most powerful ally – and the potential value of the picture in the furthering of harmonious Anglo-American relations, quite apart from his own eminence, may explain the reverence with which Sargent was handled. His formal invitation from the BWMC was followed by a personal letter from Lloyd George, and the greatest care was taken to ensure his 'VIP' treatment in France.

He arrived at the beginning of July and was billeted at Berles-au-Bois on the Somme, where he spent some time with the Guards Division. There was a faint air of unreality about the first weeks of his stay; a bulky and unwarlike figure with bushy beard and florid visage, he had no grasp of military matters at all and is reported to have asked whether there was fighting on Sundays. He sketched by day in the shade of a large white umbrella (which the Americans later made him camouflage, though the British took no exception to it), and on one of his days off went joy-riding in a tank with Philip Sassoon, a friend of long standing – 'up and down slopes, and over trenches and looping the loop generally'.

But any cushioning of his life at the Front was not at his own instigation. Before leaving he had expressed a desire to see 'the more rugged side of the war', and Lee reported in some perplexity, 'Sargent has taken up his abode in a German Prisoner

sargent looks rather the worse for wear.

William Orpen, *John Singer Sargent* (ink), reproduced by kind permission of P. Murray Lee

[98]

of War cage . . . [and] reports that he is very happy and that bombs are coming from all directions, which is "just what he likes". That particular type of amusement does not appeal to all of us.'

Sargent did not find his commission easy, largely because his methods were the antithesis of John's: he worked most often directly from life[77] – and it was almost impossible to find British and American troops actually working together. 'Though historically and sentimentally the thing happens, the naked eye cannot catch it in the act,' he complained, 'nor have I, so far, forged the Vulcan's net in which the act can be imprisoned. . . . How can there be anything flagrant enough for a picture when Mars and Venus are miles apart whether in camps or front trenches. And the further forward one goes the more scattered and meagre everything is. . . . The MoI expects an epic – and how can one do an epic without masses of men?' It occurred to him to depict a road with American troops and British artillery going up to the Line on one side, and British wounded coming down on the other – but he dismissed it as too much of an 'illustrated paper kind of subject' to be done on the large scale, with the distinct risk of it looking like 'going to the Derby'.

Nor was he happy with the proposed size of the canvas (again selected, it would appear, with John in mind), describing $9' \times 20'$ as 'an awfully long strip of a picture' and objecting in particular to the requirement that figures should be life-size, with 'a lot of life-size buttons and buckles and boots'. Yockney began to worry about the design of the Hall of Remembrance: it had already been decided that Sargent's picture should be flanked by the matched landscapes of Cameron and Sims, and now he wrote anxiously to Bone, 'The keystone of the arch has moved a little. Do you think you can push it back into place?' Sargent was persuaded to retain the 'super' dimensions, with figures half-life-size. However, despite moving up to stay with the American Division at Ypres, he was still unable to find his Anglo-American subject and eventually abandoned the idea, choosing instead to paint a scene witnessed earlier at le-Bac-du-Sud, on the Arras-Doullens Road. He had come upon a dressing-station into which were shuffling hundreds of victims of mustard-gas, whose main effect was a painful swelling of the conjunctiva and eyelids. These symptoms, appearing some eight hours after the attack, were not permanent, but while they lasted the sufferers were blinded, and Sargent watched orderlies steering helpless files of soldiers, each with his hands on the shoulders of the man in front, through the sprawled figures of other victims. Fascinated, he made detailed studies[78] of the scene, and the painting he subsequently completed – *Gassed* (90×240)* – was to be one of the most famous of all First World War pictures; for the next twenty years it was to be widely reproduced, both as a tribute to the endurance of the fighting man and as anti-war propaganda.[79]

Nevertheless, it was hardly what the BWMC had asked for, and the scheme for celebrating the co-operation of the Allies cannot be described as a success. Orpen remarked unkindly, 'One thing I think you must have learnt by now & that is – don't tell an artist what to do . . . instead of "America & France" you have *Gassed* by J.S.S. & *Query* by Aug. E.J. So much for ordering artists about.' To add injury to insult, he was writing to disassociate himself entirely from the proposal that *he* might be persuaded to do 'an elephant like 20ft × 10ft'. In July 1918 he countered the attempt to send him to Italy in search of an Anglo-Italian subject by having himself made supernumerary batman to a general and decamping back to the Western Front for the duration.[80]

The first artist to go to France to do a canvas in the 'Uccello' size was Henry Tonks, selected under Scheme 1 for his unique suitability to record the work of the medical services. He had trained, qualified and, until the age of thirty, practised as a surgeon[81] – but always with aspirations to art. While a demonstrator in anatomy at the London Hospital he made hundreds of drawings of the dissected bodies he used in his class; if he wanted whole models he would bribe a porter to leave a corpse on the post-mortem table. In 1887 he started attending Fred Brown's evening classes at the Westminster School of Art; and in 1892, when Brown was made Professor at the Slade, Tonks was appointed his Assistant and gave up medicine as a career.

During the war he used both skills, working briefly in 1915 as a civilian doctor on the Marne and in Italy. In 1916 he joined the RAMC and worked at Sidcup with Sir Harold Gillies, one of the pioneers of plastic surgery; with a series of 'before' and 'after' pastel drawings, he became 'the historian of facial war injuries'.[82] Early in 1917 Tonks had been invited to record the activities of the RAMC for the DoI's 'Efforts and Ideals' series; the time offered, however, was far too short for a man of his perfectionism, and he declined. The MoI was equally anxious for him to make artistic capital out of his experiences and employed him to paint, at a more leisurely pace, a single large picture of an advanced dressing-station, the 'half-way house' between emergency treatment on the field and the casualty clearing-stations outside the firing line.

He went out at the beginning of July to join Sargent on the Somme. The two had

John Singer Sargent, *Henry Tonks* (pencil and ink), Fitzwilliam Museum, Cambridge

Henry Tonks, *An Advanced Dressing-Station in France, 1918* (oil on canvas), 72 × 86

been friends since the early days of the NEAC; now Tonks found himself part of Sargent's triumphal progress and enjoyed it. 'Sargent is worshipped here,' he wrote to Ross, 'and I pass well as his ADC. . . . We dine out rather more than we should in London.' However, his picture presented problems: though victory was in the air, the fighting was still intense and conditions for painting near-impossible. 'You can imagine the difficulty', he wrote to Yockney, 'when I tell you that a peculiarly vicious gun very near makes my canvas give a great jump every time it fires which it does about every three minutes.' He had nowhere private to sleep, let alone a room in which to work, and his horror of criticism made him acutely nervous of painting in public. 'I may as well confess', he wrote, 'that anybody less suited to be a special artist probably does not exist. If everything is exactly right, place, light, model, material, and in my own time, I may do a passable drawing . . . many times I have not made a sketch of something which it was most important to have, because someone was standing near the place from which I wanted to do it.'

In addition, while as a medical man he had found modern war surgery absorbing, as an artist he was distracted by more promising subjects elsewhere. He confided to

Ross: 'I have tried to see the real thing and have industriously regarded wounded, though the landscape and ruined houses interest me much more.' Nevertheless, in an advanced dressing-station near Bailleument he found the setting for his picture, which he peopled with the casualties he had seen at stations up and down the Front.[83]

The Committee had intended that Tonks should be followed in France by Alfred Munnings, the renowned painter of equestrian subjects whom they had appointed under Scheme 2 in the hope that he might produce a cavalry series equal to the one he had executed for the Canadians. However, at the last minute Munnings, who had already lost one eye and a finger, injured his knee falling off a bus and the visit was cancelled.

A further mishap delayed the departure of Charles Sims: the car Tonks was using was badly shelled at Arras, and no other transport was available. Sims eventually set out at the end of October to gather material for his autumnal Western Front landscape, *The Old German Front Line, Arras, 1916* (72 × 125) – Lee later remembered him during this visit as 'nice, quiet, but rather strange', inclined to fuss about the cold and the fact that his chauffeur had run out of wash-leathers.[84]

Sims was joined in Arras at the beginning of November by Colin Gill, who had been sent to paint a large artillery subject as part of his total output. Having enlisted in the Royal Garrison Artillery in 1914, Gill had been seconded to the Royal Engineers in 1916 as a camouflage officer, and requested the visit to France in order to 'revive his impressions' of heavy guns; he eventually chose as his subject *Heavy Artillery* (72 × 125),* a camouflaged battery of 9·2 inch howitzers, the gun known familiarly to the troops as 'Mother'.

The last artist to go out to the Western Front was Cameron, engaged under Scheme 1 to portray 'The Road to the Front'. After 'much searching and motoring' on the road between Ypres and Menin he had compiled enough notes to produce a composite picture which he entitled *The Battlefield of Ypres* (72 × 125), with the remark, 'It is not a portrait of any one spot – photographers can do that.'

CHAPTER NINETEEN

The MoI Artists – The Soldier-Artists

OF all the artists mentioned in the preceding chapter, Colin Gill was the only one to have seen active service; the older men needed their visits to France in order to find their subjects. Of the younger artists commissioned to execute 'fighting subjects', the majority had seen more than enough of the Western Front and were happy to dispense with the proffered facilities.

The agreement Paul Nash had signed with the DoI terminated at the end of April 1918 with his exhibition at the Leicester Galleries. After a month's respite from war pictures, he was appointed by the MoI under Scheme 2, his output to include a large picture of 'A Flanders Battlefield'. Like Cameron he chose the Menin Road, 'a tract of country near Gheluvelt village . . . perhaps the most dread and disasterous [sic] locality of any area in any of the theatres of war'.

He worked on it throughout the summer at Tubb's Farm, Chalfont St Peter, in a studio which Chalfont locals described as 'a shop for touching up old War Pictures'. Previously used as a herb-drying shed, it had huge windows and wooden walls, and Nash and his wife furnished it with an oil stove, a frying pan and a piano; here he was more than ever sensitive to the contrast with the life he had known as a soldier – 'France and the trenches would be a mere dream if our minds were not perpetually bent upon those scenes. And yet how difficult it is folded as we are in the luxuriant green country, to put it aside and brood on those wastes in Flanders, the torments, the cruelty and terror of this war. Well it is on these I brood for it seems the only justification of what I do now – if I can help to rob war of the last shred of glory, the last shine of glamour.'

Nash was working on several pictures – the oils *A Howitzer Firing*, *The Mule Track* and *Spring in the Trenches*, *Ridge Wood*, *1917*, and a series of large watercolours; but most of his energies were absorbed by *The Menin Road* (72 × 125)*. 'I feel very serious about this big picture,' he told Gordon Bottomley. 'It's going to have all I can muster . . . I pray I may carry it through.' By

Paul and John Nash (*right* and *left*),
Tate Gallery

October it was well enough advanced for him to turn down the offer of a 'refresher' visit to France.

He then experienced, however, a sequence of 'every sort of interruption, dissappoint-ment[*sic*] and delay'. Evicted from the herb-drying shed, he worked on the picture first in a bungalow, then in a studio (in Gower Street) so small that, in order to view the canvas from a distance, he had to climb out of the window on to the lead roof of the bay window below. There is also a tantalising and unexplained reference in the notes for his unfinished autobiography to '"The Menin Road" and the burning van'. Nevertheless, by the time it was finished in May 1919, Nash was describing it as 'by far the best thing I have yet done'.

For most of the summer of 1918 Nash's sojourn at Tubb's Farm had been shared by his younger brother John, whose appointment under Scheme 2 he had canvassed vigorously and achieved in April.[85] John Nash's total output consisted of six oils, six finished drawings (in pencil, pen, chalk and watercolour), and a quantity of studies. His contribution to the memorial series was the large oil *Oppy Wood* (72×84), depicting two soldiers at the edge of the shattered wood, sheltering in a trench which a VC with experience of the Oppy Wood action described as 'far too clean – no bully beef tins or débris generally'.

Even more remarkable, however, was his *'Over the Top'* ($31\frac{1}{4} \times 42\frac{1}{4}$),* one of the very few pictures in the Ministry's collection to depict a specific action – in this case, the last Nash had seen on active service. *'Over the Top'* records a scene early in the morning of 30 December 1917 at Welsh Ridge, Marcoing, just south-west of Cambrai. The First Battalion of the Artists' Rifles, having just withdrawn to the support trenches, were recalled to the Line to repel a German attack and made their way back laboriously in the freezing cold, through trenches shelled and blocked by casualties. Nash's 'B' Company (in which he had charge of the fourteen men of a bomber section) arriving at zero hour had to go straight 'over the top' to act as a diversion for a bombing raid on their left. The action was disastrous, with 68 of the 80 officers and men killed or wounded. Nash recalled, 'It was in fact pure murder and I was lucky to escape untouched. . . . It was bitterly cold and we were easy targets against the snow and in daylight. . . . I think the vivid memory of the occasion helped me when I painted the picture and provoked whatever intensity of feeling may be found in it.'

Like his brother, John Nash rejected as unnecessary a return to the Front. One artist who was anxious to arrange such a visit was Nevinson, commissioned in August under Scheme 1; in line with his new preoccupations he requested as his subject a dressing-station scene – 'It is this side that interests and moves me the most.' Surprisingly, in view of Tonks' appointment, the Committee agreed – hoping, perhaps, for another *La Patrie*.

Unfortunately Nevinson refused to accept the honorary commission as 2nd Lieuten-ant which alone would have guaranteed his freedom of movement at the Front, con-vinced that to take it would be to forfeit his exemption and render himself liable once more to service in the trenches. In consequence he went out to France as a visitor again, but this time the trip was a fiasco: he was tormented by 'the maddening distrac-tion of constant conversation' from his conducting officer and was, he claimed, kept well away from the dressing-stations. Thus he painted instead *walking* wounded mak-

C. R. W. Nevinson, *The Harvest of Battle* (oil on canvas), 72×125

ing their way to the rear after a dawn offensive – a *Harvest of Battle* (72×125) which was to be described enthusiastically by the *Daily Express* as 'a combination of the Deluge, the Last Day, Dante's Inferno, and the "Sea Giving up its Dead"'.

During the same period, the summer and autumn of 1918, William Roberts was working simultaneously for the CWMF and the MoI, on half-pay to both organisations. He had been serving as a gunner with the Royal Field Artillery in France when, at the end of December 1917, he was told of fellow-Vorticist Wyndham Lewis's appointment as an official artist for the Canadians. This prompted him to make a hasty drawing on a sheet of newspaper and send it to the Canadian committee – which accepted him with the stricture that 'Cubist work is inadmissible'. (David Bomberg had received a similar warning which he chose to ignore – with the result that the original version of his *Sappers at Work: A Canadian Tunnelling Company* was rejected and he was compelled to paint the subject again in a more naturalistic style.)

The MoI, appointing Roberts under Scheme 2, imposed no such restrictions and were rewarded with more characteristic and impressive work. Intrigued by the lines of communication used to transport rations, materials and ammunition to the Front, he chose as the subject of his big picture *A Shell Dump, France* (72×125)[86] – for which he did not require to return to the Front, making his studies instead at training camps in England and from photographs of the various types of shell. He also produced a quantity of watercolour drawings of trench life, with such titles as *Tommies filling their*

William Roberts, *A Shell Dump, France* (oil on canvas) 72 × 125

Water Bottles with Rain from a Shell Hole, *An Attack* (the capture of Delville Wood), *Signallers* and *The Gas Chamber*.

For something less than £300, this represented excellent value for the MoI; and that the benefit was mutual is shown by his plight after his appointment ceased in January 1919, when he relapsed into the dire poverty of the early war years, writing pathetically to Yockney, 'I am in such a turmoil over money matters as not to know what I am doing at times.'

Wyndham Lewis was another soldier-artist who worked simultaneously for both of Beaverbrook's picture-collecting agencies. He had joined up, somewhat resentfully, in March 1916, at a time when he had, in his opinion, been on the verge of extreme success as both an artist and a writer. In May 1917 he had been posted as a 2nd Lieutenant to the 6th Howitzer Battery near Bailleul; he found life in the Salient (which he described as 'all scooped-out and very El Greco') an unattractive mixture of tedium and acute danger,[87] and after six months he took steps to 'save' himself with an appointment as an artist.

In his first autobiography, *Blasting and Bombardiering*, Lewis claimed that his appetite was whetted by a meeting with Orpen, a fellow-student at the Slade, but not one he admired. Orpen had already been 'blasted' in the war number of *Blast* in July 1915: now he offered Lewis whisky from Haig's own mess and irritated him with insistent and, in Lewis's opinion, affected references to life in the Salient as Hell (which he pronounced 'Hail'). 'The glimpse, frankly, that I got', snarled Lewis, 'of this posh portraitist living on the fat of the land at Cassel made my mouth water.' He had an entrée to the Canadian scheme through Konody ('blessed' in *Blast* No. 1), and though he waxed satirical on the subject of Canadians as patrons of art – 'We do not associate the land of the "Mounties" and of Montcalm with the fine arts' – he was quite happy for the CWMF to extract him from active service. (Like Nash, however, he felt twinges of guilt at leaving others to bear the sufferings he would now be spared. 'Half my mind was elated at the congenial prospect of twirling my brush once more and bringing to life upon the canvas a painted battery. . . . But half my mind was forlorn as I said goodbye to my untidy little batman. I was like the heartless young squire bidding a last farewell to the simple young village maid he has betrayed beside the cottage gate.')

The CWMF sent him to Vimy Ridge, but during his stay (January–March 1918) the area was very quiet and he claimed to have seen fighting only when he and Augustus John, searching for another artist, Ian Strang,[88] drove, after a good lunch, straight into the front line at Béthune. Nevertheless, he made the necessary sketches to carry

William Roberts, *'Feeds Round': Stable-time in the wagon-lines, France* (oil on canvas), 20 × 24,
Bone Fund

[107]

out his commission – 'the unnecessary sketches, I should perhaps say, as I could draw a gun with my eyes shut of course'.

Perhaps with this facility in mind, the BWMC lost no time in commissioning from him, as soon as he returned from France, a large picture of siege artillery, to be completed as soon as the Canadians released him. In fact, no sooner had he completed his Canadian commission (*A Canadian Gunpit*) than he plunged into preparations for his first (unofficial) one-man show – a series of drawings depicting the gunner's progress from his arrival at the Dépôt to his life in the Line, exhibited in January 1919 at the Goupil Gallery under the title 'Guns'. Flu and pneumonia further distracted him and he did not start work on the MoI commission until April 1919.

Lewis chose as his subject *A Battery Shelled* (72×125).* In *Blasting and Bombardiering* he has described the curious remoteness and detachment of a siege gunner's life: 'A gunner does not fight. He merely

P. Wyndham Lewis, National Portrait Gallery

shells and is shelled. He discharges a large metal cylinder, aiming it by means of a delicately-adjusted mechanism, to fall at a certain spot which he cannot see, in the hope that he may kill somebody he hopes is there. . . . [He is] a very dangerous type of spectator.' His picture portrays three of these spectators[89] calmly observing the effects of a barrage – 'every type of projectile, groaning, panting, bumbling, whistling and wheezing overhead'. In his introduction to the catalogue for 'Guns' he set out his attitude to war pictures, in order to explain his perceptible (and much remarked upon) retreat from extreme abstraction: 'I have attempted here only one thing: that is in a direct, ready formula to give an interpretation of what I took part in in France. . . . Experimentation is waived: I have tried to do with the pencil and brush what storytellers like Chekhov or Stendhal did in their books.'

Augustus John rudely paraphrased this as 'striving to reduce his "Vorticism" to the level of Canadian intelligibility' – and *A Canadian Gunpit* is certainly more naturalistic than his pre-war painting. Nevertheless, *A Battery Shelled* was to be, with Roberts's *Shell Dump*, one of the most controversial pictures to come out of the First World War.

CHAPTER TWENTY

Other Fronts: Home and Abroad

A WAY from the Western Front, coverage of the war was far from being as systematic as the Committee had intended. No artists were sent, for example, to Italy:[90]
Tonks was persuaded against looking for a dressing-station subject there on the
grounds that in July 1918 'nothing was going on'; Alfred Hayward had hoped for
the chance to go, but Bone pressed for someone better; unfortunately the Committee's
choice was Orpen, and the remaining months of opportunity were wasted in the effort
to winkle him out of France.

With the exception of James McBey, whose appointment was inherited from the
DoI, the Ministry also failed to get anyone to Egypt, Palestine, Mesopotamia or Salonica
during the war; several important canvases were, however, acquired after the war,
the majority painted from memory by soldier-artists from these areas.[91]

Henry Lamb, having originally given up medical training to become an artist, had,
like Tonks, returned to medicine at the outbreak of war: on qualifying he joined the
RAMC and was posted first to Macedonia in 1916–17 (where he won the Military
Cross) and subsequently to Palestine in 1917–18. The War Office was understandably
reluctant to release him during the Palestine campaign, and his transfer to the Western
Front in September 1918 put his secondment out of the question: then just before
the Armistice he was badly gassed. Thus despite the MoI's best efforts he was not free
to start on a memorial canvas until March 1919, when he was asked for a Palestine
subject, and painted *Irish Troops in the Judaean Hills Surprised by a Turkish Bombardment*
(72 × 86)* – a picture which did much to make his name, but one which might more
accurately be called 'dossers surprised in the Vale of Health'. Having had great difficulty
in finding models Lamb asked Yockney to supply three Irish soldiers, *other* than Irish
Guards, as he wanted his sitters 'to look as little spick and span as they dare be seen'.
Guardsmen were all Yockney could find in London: in the military hospital near Lamb's
Hampstead studio he could unearth only 'a few Australians' and eventually settled,
with misgivings, for three men from a Salvation Army hostel in the Euston Road.

The MoI's sole memorial of the Expeditionary Force in Egypt was also provided after
the war, by Gilbert Spencer. He was young and inexperienced, and was employed
with the right of refusal heavily stressed; in the event, his picture, *New Arrivals*
(72 × 86)*, in a military hospital at Mahemdia, Sinai (painted from a study made at
the time of the attack on Gaza in April 1917) was received without enthusiasm –
Konody wrote rudely of it that the soldier perched at the end of a bed looked like the
ventriloquist's 'Little Nipper' – and it took all Bone's persuasive power to get it accepted.

The Ministry could contrive to send no artists to Mesopotamia,[92] but in Macedonia
it was more fortunate. William Wood, as a Corporal in the RFC on the Salonica Front,
had been responsible for making panoramic drawings of enemy-held territory from
balloons and observation posts, for use by artillery spotters. He had painted similar

scenes in his spare time, and in late 1917 his C-in-C sent him home with the idea of using his pictures to impress on both the public and the War Office the uniquely difficult conditions of climate, terrain and disease which British troops were facing on this unglamorous front. The MoI at least was sufficiently struck by the pictures to employ Wood under Scheme 2: his Salonica sketches were exhibited under official auspices at the Leicester Galleries in June 1918, and he painted for the memorial series a large canvas of *The Doiran Front* (42 × 60).

At the same time the Committee made repeated requests for two artists still serving in Macedonia – Slade contemporaries Darsie Japp and Stanley Spencer. By mid-1918, however, Japp was a Major commanding an artillery battery and could not be spared; his canvas *The Royal Field Artillery in Macedonia* (72 × 125) was painted after the war. Bone, who was to be a lifelong patron of Spencer, suggested that he be invited to depict 'A Religious Service at the Front': he obviously had in mind the religious pictures of 1912–14 (one of which, *Zacharias and Elizabeth*, he had himself acquired). The proposal had the full support of Tonks, who was very attached to his former pupil and deplored his detention by the War Office: 'Spencer is, I should think, not much good as a private soldier though I am sure very willing, a genius pitched in the mud.' (His guess was shrewd: Spencer was, by his own account, a liability – 'During the time when the Bulgars were going back I was told by a Sergeant that I was a Confounded Nuisance. I had somehow let a coil of ribbon wire slip off my shoulder and had become entangled,[93] we were in a hurry at the time. This is only one of the many outstanding features of my army career.')

Spencer had done little drawing during his two and a half years in Macedonia. Nevertheless, he saw his war years increasingly as a time of preparation, not of waste – a period 'not of degeneration but of being in the "refiner's fire"'. In the hilly area around Kalinova, a ruined village forty-five miles north of Salonica, he found inspiration as potent as that which his home village, Cookham, had held for him in peacetime: to his sister Florence he wrote, 'A little space of ground will be as it used to be to me, a universe.' His feelings were ultimately to find their fullest expression in the murals he painted for the Oratory of All Souls, Burghclere, but the work he did there is clearly foreshadowed, both in factual and emotional content, in his MoI picture: what he wrote of his official appointment in 1918 applies equally to the paintings he did between 1926 and 1932: 'If I get this job, I shall be able to show God in the bare "real" things, in a limber wagon, in ravines, in fouling mule lines.'

Application for his release was made to GHQ Salonica in May 1918 and again at regular intervals until November, but the MoI received no reply to its letters; this may be explained by poor communications, but there is also the suggestion that, for reasons which are not clear, the letters were deliberately suppressed. It was not until Spencer was invalided home with malaria in December 1918 that he could take up the appointment: in January 1919, after a pause to complete *Swan Upping at Cookham*, which he had left half-finished when he enlisted in 1915, he began *Travoys Arriving with Wounded at a Dressing-Station at Smol, Macedonia, September 1916* (72 × 86).*

The inspiration for the painting was a scene at an old Greek church used as a dressing-station for casualties after an attack by 22nd Division on Machine Gun Hill in the Doiran-Varda sector. Spencer, with customary candour, declared on handing over the work in August 1919, 'This picture is not in any material or practical sense a truthful representation of the scene it is supposed to depict.' Even so, it was deeply rooted in his own experience. Before transferring to a fighting regiment (the Royal Berkshires) in 1917, he had worked with the RAMC Field Ambulance units, where he spent much of his time bringing in the wounded from the Line to field hospitals on mule-drawn stretchers or travoys, a task complicated by the mules' tendency to sink in somnolence to the ground, with Spencer, whom even his father described as 'a midget', struggling to hold the casualties on to the travoys as they tilted.

The period following Spencer's return to Cookham was an intensely happy one: in January he wrote to Yockney, 'I feel very hopeful. . . . And feeling hopeful makes me feel strong and able like Benvenuto Cellini.' *Travoys* reflects this optimism: though he had rejected Bone's suggestion of a straightforward 'religious' subject, he had observed the overwhelming sense of peace, of release in the dressing-station – 'the calm way the wounded men spoke to each other – about some cabbages they had been trying to grow for instance' – and he invested *Travoys* with much of the atmosphere of his more explicitly 'spiritual' works. He regarded the subject not as 'a scene of horror but a scene of redemption from it', and wrote later, 'I was as right in making it a happy picture as the early painters were right in making the Crucifixion a happy painting.'

Spencer's enthusiasm, however, faded quickly. He was technically employed under Scheme 2, and hopes were expressed that he would do some smaller Macedonian pictures as part of his total output – but with no notes to work from (he had mislaid his sketchbook in the bath-house at Smol), he became discouraged and wrote to Yockney in July: 'Somehow I seem to have lost the thread of my "Balkanish feelings".' He had not given up on his war service – 'I still have hope in the next few years to do something good out of my Balkan experiences,' he wrote, but in 1919 he was not to be rushed. 'It's off Mr Yockney . . . the thing is this Mr Yockney, as artists we can do just what we like (that sounds very nice) BUT WE MUST NOT DO WOT WE DONT LIKE, woe unto us if we break this law'; and it was to be seven years before he recaptured at Burghclere his feelings about Macedonia.

On the Home Front, too, coverage was less comprehensive than the BWMC, with its careful lists of subjects, had intended. As far as the Navy was concerned, a string of artists was deployed along the South Coast during the summer of 1918. Philip Wilson Steer journeyed to Dover, and the BWMC eagerly awaited his picture of the harbour under wartime conditions, hoping, such was his prestige in the art world, for a 'great national possession'. They could not have anticipated, however, the difficulties he would encounter. Philip Connard, a member of Steer's Chelsea circle, is reported to have listed Steer's requirements while painting as, in order of importance – 1) shelter from the wind (Steer's own secretary claimed he used to put his hat on to go from room to room, for fear of draughts); 2) proximity to a lavatory; 3) shade from the sun; 4) protection from children; and 5) a suitable subject. Steer, accommodated at a hotel he found 'both depressing and rather sloppy', at once saw 'great difficulties ahead. . . . the place is so vast, for instance the Admiralty Pier is a mile and a half . . . and then when one gets there it is almost impossible to get shelter from the wind.'

Moreover, whenever he *did* settle down to sketch, 'Some blighter comes up and wants to see my permits, which is very upsetting just in the middle of laying in a wash.' After a taxing month he had sufficient material to complete a canvas 42×60[94] but his troubles were not over: 'Ships and boats are very obstinate customers to deal with,' he complained, 'and after spending much time and labour in putting one in, one finds one has got it in the wrong place.'

John Fergusson was provisionally involved under Scheme 3 to paint dockyard scenes at Portsmouth, but though he found there an inspiration 'which I have not had before in my work', none of his pictures was acquired.[95] At Southampton Thomas Derrick spent six months anxiously wrestling with a small canvas (28×36) depicting *American Troops at Southampton Embarking for France*.* 'Such subjects are frightfully *intricate*,' he fussed, 'and I have literally hundreds of figures, all of which I am more or less individualising . . . one has to be careful not to put too many heads than there are cubic feet of deck space to accommodate the legs and feet of!'

John Wheatley, another protégé of Bone and Tonks, was initially posted to Rosyth. However, he was a frail young man, and, handicapped by his lack of rank or uniform, suffered acutely at the hands of the naval authorities until finally sent packing from the Grand Fleet. 'I was as polite as possible to the Chief of Staff,' he wrote miserably, 'but he said for no reason at all "The MoI was as naught to him". . . . I hope he will feel better tomorrow.' Posted instead to Southampton to record the work of the Salvage Service he settled in happily, appearing to relish the occasional dramas of salvage work: 'Yesterday I was present at a land-mine going up. Too near to be nice, so I did a drawing and then went to see the poor fellows who were in it.' He was loth to be disturbed – 'We are on short notice at present so I do not think it is safe to come to town because I might miss a good wreck' – and with a total output of over forty paintings and drawings he was the most prolific of the artists employed under Scheme 2; he also contributed to the memorial series *Divers at Work Repairing a Torpedoed Ship* (42×60).

In Devon Walter Bayes spent the summer painting his *Landing Survivors from a Torpedoed Ship*[96],* subsequently claiming expenses for 'certain researches into the behaviour of waves and so forth'. He wanted to do *Landing Survivors* on the same scale as his earlier success, *The Underworld* (100×216), and was disappointed to be allowed only 72×125: 'One parts reluctantly with the dream of hypnotising a crowd with a dramatic design on a scale a crowd can see.'

By comparison, the Army in England was meagrely represented: Bernard Adeney alone was employed, working at the 'Tankodrome', the experimental tank ground at Dollis Hill, drawing the various types of tank – 'Whippet', 'Tadpole', and the 'Mark V' in its 'male' and 'female' manifestations.

Munitions subjects were little better served. Clausen returned to Woolwich Arsenal, where he had made studies for the 'Efforts and Ideals' series, and produced one large oil – *In the Gun Factory at Woolwich Arsenal, 1918* (72×125). Charles Holmes made studies in Sheffield for *A Two-Year-Old Steel Works, 1918* (42×60), the aim of which was to demonstrate the expansion of munitions manufacturing capacity in the latter stages of the war under the leadership of Lloyd George. (Ironically, the completion of the picture was delayed by Holmes' inability to obtain the materials he needed, in particular Flake White paint: this incorporated white lead, whose issue was strictly controlled.)

Randolph Schwabe was the only artist detailed to cover work on the land, including the various activities of the Women's Land Army: thatching, tree-felling, shepherding, hoeing, milking and ploughing. Sensitive on the subject of his own un-English-sounding name, he appears to have bitterly resented the fact that decent English girls were assisted in their labours by 'those blighters', the German prisoners of war. In August he made studies of the flax harvest (a crop revived during the war especially to meet the needs of aeroplane manufacture) for his big picture *Voluntary Workers in a Flax Field, Podington, Northamptonshire* (42 × 60).*

The subject perhaps best represented was London life in wartime – the coming and going of troops and wounded, the transport of food, the city's defences, its public gatherings. Henry Rushbury, a pupil of Francis Dodd, was used as a 'general utility artist', sent wherever a subject needed covering, rather like an illustrator for a newspaper. He recorded the preparations against air attack – the night-watch in the Dome of St Paul's, the sand-bags round the Egyptian treasures in the British Museum and the tomb of Edward the Confessor in Westminster Abbey. He depicted special events such as the Anglo-Saxon celebration at Central Hall, Westminster, on Independence Day 1918, when Churchill made his pronouncement, 'Germany must be beaten, must know she is beaten, must feel she is beaten.' He captured vignettes of scenes that it was thought would never be repeated – *Kensington Palace and Allotments, Captured German Guns in the Mall, 1918*, and pictures of the captured U-boat *Deutschland* in St Katharine's Dock. His memorial canvas was *The War Refugees' Camp, Earls Court 1918* (42 × 60), about which Yockney commented, 'So far as the public is concerned, I feel sure that the picture will be a satisfactory antidote to the more violent pictorial expressions of the war. It will be like Holbein after Nevinson.'

The comings and goings of troops were permissibly emotive subjects. Bernard Meninsky painted *The Arrival of a Leave Train, Victoria Station, 1918* (42 × 60), and Alfred Hayward the more painful departure – *The Staff Train at Charing Cross Station, 1918* (42 × 60), 'Whatever the strain of war,' wrote General Charteris, 'for the individual the greatest strain was those periodic partings at the termination of the brief periods of leave we spent at home. The whole tragic poignancy of war was condensed daily in the departure of the leave train from London.'

CHAPTER TWENTY-ONE

Transition

A S an artistic endeavour the MoI scheme proved a considerable success, assembling under its aegis some of the best art to appear during the war. However, the corollary – that the pictures should remain a separate and independent collection, a unique memorial and record of the Great War – was not to be achieved, and must be counted one of Beaverbrook's rare failures.

From the start the new Minister of Information was determined that the collection should survive the dissolution of his Ministry which was inevitable at, or shortly after, the end of the war. His first move towards this end, in March 1918, was to apply to register a charity (with four members of the BWMC as Trustees) under the War Charities Act 1916, bearing the name 'British War Memorials Fund', with the intention of creating a legal entity separate from the MoI which would have an autonomous existence, protected by law like any other charity, after the Ministry's demise. He then set about making the new body, like its model the Canadian War Memorials Fund, self-financing and obtained from the Chancellor of the Exchequer (fortuitously his closest friend in politics, Bonar Law) permission to direct to 'war charities' the proceeds of any exhibition the MoI might organise – apparently without mentioning that he was in the process of forming his own 'captive' charity.

At the time the consent was given, the MoI's exhibition income was small, consisting only of the modest proceeds of art and photographic exhibitions. Beaverbrook, however, was Chairman of the British War Office Cinematograph Committee, whose income from the exhibition of films during 1917–18 was £65,923 19s 7d, and he lost no time in persuading the War Office that it would be in everyone's best interests for the complex business of making and distributing films to be taken over by the propaganda experts, who would bear all the expenses – and, naturally, retain the profits. It remained only to obtain the consent of the National War Aims Committee to this encroachment into the field of home propaganda – and this was readily given.

His colleagues, however, would appear to have been uneasy. On 15 May 1918, the day after the registration of the BWMF, Bennett and Masterman, both official Trustees of the new charity, held a private meeting with Beaverbrook and Rothermere, which resulted in the two press barons offering the BWMF their personal guarantees of £10,000 each. The implication must be that Bennett and Masterman were afraid of their personal liability, in the event of Beaverbrook's scheme being called into question – and this they had good reason to fear.

The most obvious objection to his arrangements was that he had no right to subsidise what was in effect his own private charity – linked to the MoI by no more than the fact that some, not all, of its Trustees were Ministry employees – with money raised by the exhibition of Government property. Nor, incidentally, was it ethical for him to persuade artists to work for 'the nation' at reduced fees if their work was to go to a private enterprise. Doubts were in any case already being cast on the BWMF's charitable status: its objects, as stated on the application for registration, were now deemed (unofficially, at least) unlikely to constitute it a genuine war charity.

It is not inconceivable that Beaverbrook might have ignored these obstacles and proceeded with his scheme simply on the basis of the personal guarantees, had it not been for the fact that the Select Committee on Public Expenditure, an investigative parliamentary body of considerable power, had the MoI as its next target.[97] At this crucial juncture the Ministry acquired a new Acting Secretary, R. W. Needham, who, with several years of experience at the Treasury behind him, readily appreciated the flaws in Beaverbrook's scheme and suggested two alternative solutions.

The BWMF could, he argued, be maintained as a charity, but only as a body explicitly independent of Ministry and Government, which would appeal, like other charities, directly to the public for funds. Alternatively the charitable aspect could be abandoned, and the war art scheme brought firmly within the Ministry – in which case it could properly be paid for out of the Ministry's normal allocation. Beaverbrook chose to adopt the latter course and it was really at this stage that his hopes for a wholly independent art memorial died; henceforth he was to have two main aims – to advance the collection (paid for out of the MoI's Vote) to a point where its existence was a *fait accompli* which could not later be undone; and to find it a safe home after the war.

Needham had made it quite clear that for the scheme to receive Treasury approval as a facet of MoI activities, its connection with propaganda, the Ministry's sole *raison d'être*, must be established. So at a time when the use of pictures as propaganda had been greatly diminished, and Ross and Bone's plans for the Hall of Remembrance were taking their most fully-blown form, Beaverbrook set in train an elaborate piece of window-dressing for the Treasury's benefit.

As a first step the BWMC was reconstituted as a departmental committee, with its name suitably altered as a declaration of its new objectives: as the 'Pictorial Propaganda Committee' it met for the first time on 24 July 1918. To allay further any suspicion that this was a picture-collecting body, the expert art advisers were excluded from its meetings. This was doubly convenient for Beaverbrook, following personal attacks on Konody and, more particularly, on Ross, whose pacifism had subjected him to police harassment and whose association with Oscar Wilde had once more been raked up in the furore surrounding the Pemberton Billings case.[98] In an extraordinary outburst to Beaverbrook, Arnold Bennett deplored the decision to dismiss Ross,[99] describing him as 'an entirely honest man. He stuck to Oscar when Oscar was ruined, and without reward of any kind he has put Oscar's family on its feet. He is not a sodomist, never was, and never defends sodomist doctrines. He merely has a weakness for looking after people in adversity'; but Beaverbrook feared questions in Parliament, and the protest went unheeded.

To justify the Committee's new title, art exhibitions were arranged for propaganda purposes. Most significantly, a large exhibition of official war art was assembled for display in the USA. Throughout August Yockney worked frenetically to put together almost three hundred pictures, including 103 Orpens, the nucleus of the show.

These were despatched in September and October for display in the major East Coast cities, including Washington and New York. By the time the exhibition opened the war was over; nevertheless, with an eye to Anglo-American relations after the Armistice, the Ministry could count it one of its more striking propaganda successes. Billed as an advertisement for the concept of 'the two great Anglo-Saxon democracies standing shoulder to shoulder in the ever momentous and historic struggle for freedom', the show broke all records in Washington, where attendances reached 6500 a day, and it was described by one critic as 'perhaps the greatest tribute that has been paid to art in modern times', on the perverse reasoning that it recognised the practical value of art in furthering the cause of war.

Under cover of these largely cosmetic changes, the commissioning of artists proceeded virtually unchecked. However, the Committee's new approach did claim two important casualties. The first was the scheme for sculpture. Ross's series of alabaster bas-reliefs on abstract themes had by this time become, in Bone's more practical hands, a 'sculptured history of the war', a kind of lateral Trajan's Column, a factual counterpoint to the memorial pictures. The punctilious Needham pointed out that sculpture of this sort, commissioned explicitly as an integral part of a memorial gallery and still somewhat rarefied in theme, could have very little demonstrable value as wartime propaganda. He proposed instead the commissioning of propagandist pieces along traditional lines – marble soldiers, guns and tanks, free-standing for ease of exhibition – but, as anticipated, the Committee balked. 'What you can do, you will not do,' Needham concluded, 'and what you would like to do, you may not do.'

This impasse may explain why, despite grandiose plans, only two of the sculptors initially considered were actually employed. In a valiant attempt to reconcile the original plans with the demands of propaganda, Gilbert Ledward was appointed to portray events from the invasion of Belgium to the Battle of the Marne in an enormous frieze 40 feet long and $7\frac{1}{2}$ feet high – but was asked to begin by producing only a plaster fragment (114×96) for exhibition purposes. (The full frieze was never completed.) Similarly Charles Jagger was required to produce for immediate use a single panel (96×154) representing the First Battle of Ypres.[100]

The other casualty, perhaps inevitably, was the Hall of Remembrance itself. By the autumn of 1918 the need for propaganda was declining as the Allied advance gathered speed, and the demise of the MoI was in sight. To ensure the Treasury's sanction for outstanding commissions it was imperative both to establish the long-term value of the collection as a record of the war, and to associate it convincingly with a national institution that had a secure future. The Imperial War Museum, whose official terms of reference specifically included the collecting of pictures (something it had been doing independently since 1917), was an obvious answer: Beaverbrook turned to its representatives as allies in the battle with the Treasury and seems tacitly to have replaced the Hall of Remembrance with the IWM as the collection's ultimate resting-place.

That this was not his original intention is clear. Relations between the Ministry and the Museum had not always been smooth, and there is the suggestion of an acrimonious personal rivalry between Beaverbrook and Sir Alfred Mond, the Museum's Chairman, originating in Beaverbrook's proposal, in the early days of the MoI, that the Ministry should in fact buy out the Museum's art collection. Despite the presence of the Museum's representatives, Mond and Director-General Sir Martin Conway, on the PPC, no explicit commitment was ever made to hand over the Ministry's pictures.

Charles Sergeant Jagger, *The Battle of Ypres, 1914* (plaster relief), 96 × 154

Nevertheless, Mond and Conway were alive to the possibility of a major gain to the Museum, and throughout the autumn they played a valuable part in convincing the Treasury of the utility of Beaverbrook's scheme. By October they were declaring themselves to be relying on the MoI for 'some pictures of historic importance', and at the end of that month Mond stated categorically that 'should any of the arrangements made now by the PPC be questioned by the Treasury the responsibility could be transferred to the IWM.'

It had already become quite clear that the Ministry's days were numbered and when the war ended its dissolution was almost instantaneous.[101] But this now made little difference to the future of war art. In the first week of November, the Treasury was formally notified that the IWM wished to 'utilise the organisation of the Ministry for acquiring pictures'. On 29 November the Lords of the Treasury finally gave their sanction for 'existing irreversible commitments' (to the tune of £6000 on Scheme 1, £7000 on Scheme 2, and £1000 on Scheme 3) to be charged retrospectively to the MoI Vote, and provided that any further expenditure on the scheme was to be the responsibility of the IWM. The artists, generally speaking, continued to work as if nothing had happened, and on 1 January 1919 Yockney was transferred to the IWM to carry the erstwhile MoI art memorial scheme to its conclusion.

CHAPTER TWENTY-TWO

The Imperial War Museum

IN default of the Hall of Remembrance, the Imperial War Museum[102] was not an unsuitable home for the Ministry's collection. Since its inception in March 1917 the acquisition of pictures had been an important part of the Museum's work. By the end of the war it had accumulated through purchases and commissions some 850 pictures of its own, and as an employer of artists the IWM was, quantitatively at least, the equal of the propaganda organisations, though with different objects in view; where the DoI was concerned principally with the value of the pictures as propaganda, and the MoI with their use as a memorial to effort and sacrifice, the Museum saw them simply as another type of record to set beside the trophies, posters, medals, maps, books and photographs which comprised the rest of its collection.

Sir Alfred Mond, National Portrait Gallery

The initial suggestion for a war museum seems to have come almost simultaneously from Lieutenant Charles ffoulkes, RNVR,[103] the Curator of the Armoury at the Tower of London, and from MP Ian Malcolm; both published articles in *The Times* in February 1917, coincidentally on consecutive days. The idea was taken up by Sir Alfred Mond, then First Commissioner of Works, and placed before the War Cabinet. On 5 March 1917 Mond was instructed to form a committee for the purpose of establishing the new museum; in retrospect the date of the museum's inception is significant, coinciding both with the formation of the NWAC and with the establishment of the DoI – all, it might seem, elements in Lloyd George's reorganisation of propaganda and his effort to combat war-weariness. A war museum is an obvious focus for patriotism, and the IWM was to organise touring exhibitions of trophies, pictures and photographs, which by the end of 1918 had been seen by two million people in a hundred towns and which, in addition to their own intrinsic propaganda value, provided a platform for other government organisations, including the NWAC, to deliver their messages.[104]

Mond appointed two permanent administrative staff (Sir Martin Conway as Director-General and Charles ffoulkes as Curator and Secretary) and established a General Committee under his own chairmanship, comprising, besides Conway and ffoulkes, representatives of the Admiralty, the War Office, the Ministry of Munitions, the RAF (after

Maurice Codner, *Charles ffoulkes, CB, CBE, 1868–1947* (oil on canvas), 46 × 34

April 1918), and various unpaid honorary members responsible for more specialised areas of interest, including Ian Malcolm, for art, and (also after April 1918) Priscilla Lady Norman, for women's work.

This Committee met for the first time on 29 March 1917 and defined two principal objectives: the formulation of proposals as to the ultimate size and scope of the Museum and, more urgently, an immediate start to the collection of exhibits and records of the earlier war years while they were still accessible. The representatives of the Services then formed specialist sub-committees, each to assemble its own exhibits and determine the scope of its section.

By the end of August 1917 the General Committee had delivered an ambitious report to the War Cabinet, proposing a magnificent site in Hyde Park (opposite Lancaster Gate) and a budget of £750,000 for a museum which was to have a dual function as both a complete record of the war and the National War Memorial. With the carnage of Passchendaele at its height, the War Cabinet was in no mood to approve this grandiose scheme; Curzon in particular objected to a museum devoted to a war 'which we have not yet won and which it is quite conceivable that in the future we might desire as far as possible to forget'. The Cabinet temporised and a Committee was appointed under Lord Crawford and Balcarres to investigate the proposals. Mond was a member, and traces of a rearguard action are apparent in the Crawford Report, delivered on 14 April 1918, which recommended that the IWM be built on a site of $3\frac{1}{2}$ acres, on the south bank of the Thames opposite Westminster, at a cost of £665,000. This time the War Cabinet, preoccupied with the German advance, simply shelved the Report for the duration. In the aftermath of savage post-war cuts in public spending, the IWM was eventually to be housed in part of the old Crystal Palace; it was a much more modest establishment that opened its doors to the public for the first time on 9 June 1920.

This, however, could not have been forecast by the General Committee in 1917. The general belief (which the Crawford recommendations did nothing to dispel) was that the IWM would be a vast enterprise: the Services sub-committees were encouraged both to overestimate the size of their sections and to disregard budgets, indulging an optimism which was to prove disastrous when the inevitable clamp-down came. The consequences for IWM art were serious: only those sections which had started buying and commissioning pictures early were represented even half as fully as they had planned, and the collection's imbalance is clear.

The administrators cannot be blamed for failing to curb the enthusiasm of the sub-committees; the Museum as a whole in its formative years depended on the goodwill of the Navy, the Army, the RAF and the various wartime ministries to provide – free – the essential exhibits, and in the absence of directions from the Cabinet the initiative rested during the collecting period with the sub-committees themselves. The administrators can, however, be criticised for omitting to lay down a coherent overall policy with regard to the acquisition of pictures and the commissioning of artists – the more so as each could claim some interest in art, whereas the Services members, by and large, were sadly lacking in expertise in matters artistic.

Mond was not only a successful (if unpopular) politician, but an exceedingly wealthy industrialist and an avid collector with many connections in London's art world. Conway, besides his attainments as an explorer and mountaineer (in 1898 he had climbed the highest mountain in the Andes, the 23,000-foot Mt Aconcagua, and was later the first man to explore the glaciers of Tierra del Fuego), had also been Slade Professor of Art at Cambridge from 1901–4. Even ffoulkes had once had aspirations as an artist; he had studied in Paris and had exhibited at the Royal Academy before concluding that he was fundamentally lacking in the artistic temperament: 'It seemed to me that to produce a picture of whatever one may choose to call it and surround it by a frame led one nowhere and was not necessarily Art unless one were sufficiently skilled to become a Master.'

The urgent need to secure exhibits while the war lasted engendered throughout 1917 'magpie' collecting, as obvious in the field of art as everywhere else; and it was perhaps with a view to rationalising acquisitions that Robert Ross was appointed Honorary Art Adviser in December 1917. On his suggestion the IWM acquired some of the best of its pictures.

Even after Ross's appointment, however, the IWM's art policy showed a lack of direction, partly perhaps because Mond and Conway were uncertain as to whether they could plan on receiving the pictures being accumulated by the propaganda authorities. That they were entertaining such hopes is perhaps suggested by the fact that the two collections complement each other to a degree unlikely to be entirely coincidental: in the area where the DoI/MoI collection was strongest – Western Front subjects – the IWM appears to have made least effort to acquire pictures of its own; and where the MoI in particular was weak – on Grand Fleet and RAF subjects – the IWM appointed the majority of its artists. Nevertheless, to have taken the pictures' acquisition for granted would have been foolhardy.

Certainly in the days of the DoI the Museum's expectations had been high. In May 1917 Mond tried to secure the output of Bone, Dodd and McBey (at the expense of the British Museum) with an appeal to Lloyd George to direct that their work be handed over to the IWM: 'It would be a great pity that these drawings specially made to illustrate the war should not find a home in the Museum specially created to commemorate the War, and that they should be lost in the masses of drawings at the British Museum with which they have no organic connection, except as works of art.' Although this appeal was unsuccessful, some understanding seems to have been reached with the DoI about later pictures: the problematic clauses in the contracts signed by Nevinson and Kennington, giving the IWM first option on their work at a concessionary price, would seem to be evidence of an agreement of some sort, and in August 1917 Conway reported to the General Committee that he had met John Buchan and 'an undertaking would be given that all works of artists working officially would eventually come to the National War Museum'.

However, relations between the IWM and DoI were amicable largely because the DoI was not a collecting body. With the appointment of Lord Beaverbrook – who made his acquisitive intent manifest with his much-resented offer to buy out the IWM's art collection – the situation changed. Beaverbrook and Mond had much in common: both were ambitious, ruthless and fond of the large-scale plan; both were protégés of Lloyd George – and their appointments to the Cabinet had been greeted with an equal lack of public enthusiasm. They may well have seen each other as rivals in the fashionable role of recorder of war; and it is not inconceivable that Mond regarded the IWM as England's answer to the Canadian War Records Office.

The inevitable confrontation came over the 'Orpen Gift', Orpen's proposal in October

1917 to give all his war paintings – over a hundred of them, worth then at least £20,000 – *en bloc* to 'the Government'. Though the offer was actually delivered to the DoI, it followed hard on the heels of an attempt to buy his pictures by the IWM – which not unnaturally chose to interpret 'the Government' as referring to itself. In February 1918 Orpen wrote to Robert Ross (at this stage employed only by the IWM, though his position was to become increasingly invidious after his appointment as adviser to the BWMC in March 1918), explicitly offering his pictures to the Museum. Furious, Beaverbrook badgered Orpen (by now an unresisting pawn) into retracting the offer and making over his pictures to the 'British Nation' with the MoI as 'Trustees for the time being'. Beaverbrook later entrenched his position by sending the entire Orpen collection to America as the centre-piece of the MoI's touring exhibition.

Needless to say, these manoeuvres were regarded at the IWM as 'evidence of a state of declared opposition between Lord Beaverbrook and the War Museum'. Nevertheless, as the BWMC foundered and the hopes for a separate home for the pictures faded, it became apparent that a *rapprochement* was in everyone's best interests. In accepting the invitation to sit on the Pictorial Propaganda Committee Mond may have been allowing Beaverbrook to manipulate him into precisely the position he wished to occupy, close to the control of the MoI collection.

In the meantime, with the fate of the Ministry's pictures still undecided, Ian Malcolm was complaining that 'up to the present, we have bought and selected [pictures] somewhat irregularly', and he proposed that a separate Art sub-committee be formed 'to recommend to the General Committee the purchase of Pictures, Sculptures, drawings, prints etc'. Under his chairmanship the new sub-committee met for the first time on 8 August 1918, with representatives from all the other sub-committees which were already collecting art, and a specialist art adviser in Herbert Cook. Oddly, Robert Ross was not invited: it was at about this time that he was also dropped from the MoI scheme.[105]

The policy of the Art sub-committee illuminates the art policy of the IWM as a whole during the war years. That it concerned itself solely with purchases underlines the freedom of the Services sub-committees in commissioning their own artists. And the character of the collection which grew under its auspices is suggested by its stated intention of acquiring only those pictures which 'are essentially of the nature of records .... though [the members of the Committee] consider artistic merit a most desirable accompaniment of such records, they prefer the accurate representation of an incident to a more artistic and equally more imaginary composition'. The stamp of conventional military taste is evident in the IWM's art collecting, and until as late as March 1919 – the end of the museum's second financial year and the day of reckoning – the story of official art at the IWM is broadly the story of the Services sub-committees' pursuit of their individual objectives and the attempts of the administrators and Art sub-committee in the background to cover the remaining ground through additional purchases and commissions.

CHAPTER TWENTY-THREE

Medical, Munitions, and the Western Front

I N its somewhat random programme of art purchases, the IWM adhered firmly to one guiding principle – that of buying (or even accepting as gifts) only those pictures 'produced by artists actually present at the event depicted'.

Into this category obviously fell the work of the DoI artists, and on the Museum's behalf Ross attended all the official exhibitions and bought a large number of Western Front scenes, including Kennington's *The Cup Bearer*, Nevinson's *Paths of Glory*, and Paul Nash's *Sunrise: Inverness Copse*. Unofficial exhibitions yielded a more diverse selection of subjects away from the battle zone, from Walter Bayes' massive shelter scene *The Underworld* to a series of tempera paintings made by Nico Jungman as an internee in Ruhleben Camp.

Another unique eye-witness record was presented to the Museum by Herbert Olivier, who as an unofficial observer had painted the Supreme War Council in session at Versailles in the autumn of 1918; he presented at the same time an early example of political art – Lloyd George's blotting-pad, complete with the ferocious doodles, deeply scored in red pencil, he had made during the Council's discussion of the Armistice terms in November 1918.

In an attempt to cover the Middle Eastern fronts the Museum gave an acquisition grant of £500 to General Marshall in Baghdad, who took a keen interest in the pictures produced by soldiers under his command; others were presented by J. D. Revel, the Principal of the Chelsea School of Art, then serving in the ranks in Mesopotamia but permitted by private arrangement to paint full-time on service pay.

One group of purchases was especially valuable for record purposes – a set of water-colour drawings illustrating the work of the Royal Army Veterinary Corps. Made by Edwin Noble, a Corporal at No. 8 Veterinary Hospital in France, these pictures present a vivid vet's-eye view of the misfortunes of horses on active service – the horrible effects of mustard gas and mange parasites on the skin; the damage caused by loose nails and 'crows' feet' deliberately scattered on the roads by the retreating Germans; and K-gas poisoning, which afflicted men and horses with exactly the same symptoms. (An equine gas-mask was devised by the British Veterinary Service and later adopted by the other Allies.)

Records of veterinary work on other fronts – Mesopotamia, Palestine and the Balkans – were provided by Revel and T. C. Dugdale, who contributed such titles as *Shoeing Under Difficulties, Jordan Valley*. (Dugdale also painted the only cavalry action subject in the official war art collection, the *Charge of the 2nd Lancers at El Afuli, Palestine*. He later recalled how the Turks, surprised at dawn in the Valley of Armageddon, had

Edwin Noble, *A case of mustard-gas poisoning* (charcoal and watercolour), $23\frac{1}{4} \times 17\frac{1}{2}$

desperately taken up firing lines with machine-guns assisting; 'but the 2nd Lancers each chose a Turk and tent-pegged him as he lay firing'.)

The first artist actually to be commissioned by the IWM was Adrian Hill. With Haig's

Adrian Hill, *Road Menders* (ink and watercolour), $14\frac{1}{2} \times 20\frac{3}{4}$

personal approval, a War Trophies Section had been hurriedly set up in France in May 1917 to start collecting exhibits, and in November the Section was put on a formal footing with the appointment of Major-General C. G. Donald as Inspector of War Trophies. Until August 1917 Hill had been a private in the Honourable Artillery Company in France, encouraged to sketch by his commanding officer who intended to use the results to illustrate the regimental history. On being invalided home he took the opportunity to show ffoulkes some of the sketches he had made under fire, as a scout and sniper; and on 27 December 1917 Hill was commissioned 2nd Lieutenant and transferred to the War Trophies Section to work exclusively as an artist for the IWM on Army pay and allowances.

As a WTS officer he had a car and driver, and a permit covering the whole Front – French, Italian and Portuguese sectors included. His brief from ffoulkes was correspondingly wide-ranging: 'towns and localities behind the lines which are specially identified with the British Army . . . points of juncture between our line and the line

Adrian Hill, '*A Penny all the Way*' (pen and ink and watercolour), $12\frac{1}{4} \times 17\frac{1}{4}$

occupied by French, American, Belgian and Portuguese, so as to show the different nationalities side by side . . . labour and engineering work by Coloured Battalions, which would show the distinct dress of the Chinese etc., and especially some sketches of Tanks HQ showing repairing and the like'.

The IWM's preoccupation with the documentary aspect of war art is manifest in ffoulkes's specific request for 'more uninteresting technical drawings' such as the interior design of pill-boxes and dug-outs. Nevertheless, Hill's large output, 187 pictures in all, is a vivid, journalistic record of life in the war zone – its 'types', its notable buildings and its activities: pictures like *Sketch at the Messenger Dogs' Camp, Étaples, 7th October 1918*, '*A Penny all the Way*': *London Motor Buses on the Amiens Road*, and *The Chief Actors in the 'Pageant of the Dragon', Performed by the Chinese Labour Corps, Dannes* complemented well the more sombre and anonymous Western Front work of Bone – and it is quite possible that this was ffoulkes's intention. Hill was also the only official artist left in France between April and July 1918 during the German advance, and his careful records of its immediate aftermath – St John's Hospital, Étaples, in ruins after the air-raid on Whit Sunday, and the church at Albert, with the statue of the Virgin finally toppled – fill a significant gap.

It had been agreed when the WTS was first established that it should, if desired, appoint *two* artists, giving it parity with the DoI. The IWM's second choice was Jacob Epstein. This was a bold decision: through his British Medical Association statues and the monument for Wilde's tomb, Epstein had achieved a notoriety which had deterred many public bodies from employing him. However, he had loyal supporters at the IWM in Conway, who had written to *The Times* in 1908 deprecating the furore over the BMA statues as merely 'one of those periodical outbursts of rage against the nude in sculpture which lovers of art have to endure from time to time', and Ross, who had actually commissioned the Wilde monument.

They were further encouraged by the triumph in 1917 of Epstein's war sculpture, *The Tin Hat*, acclaimed as the epitome of the British soldier; in the hope of a similar success Conway proposed that he should sculpt 'type-heads of the many groups of men employed in the war . . . Jews, Turks, infidels, heretics, and all the rest'. Epstein himself badly wanted the appointment and tried to rally support. He wrote to George Bernard Shaw, 'I could be commissioned to go out and make records for them such as my *Tin Hat* . . . or a bust of Sir Douglas Haig . . . I would be doing better for England, the world and myself than by the forming of fours and marching round a square.' Unfortunately Shaw did not open the letter until some three months later, when he passed it to the IWM with the remark, 'Epstein wants to make a bust of Haig. But he would make a bust of the devil to get back to his proper work.'

Epstein's release from the Army was approved by Haig on 31 December 1917; like Hill, he was to be given a commission and attached to the WTS. Then suddenly permission was withdrawn, after the receipt of a letter from sculptor and Academician Sir George Frampton. The contents of this letter will never be known; ffoulkes extracted it from the file in 1919 and it was not seen again. Of the various counts on which Epstein could have been objectionable to Frampton, none are particularly likely to have prompted the letter: the success of *The Tin Hat* might be thought to have outweighed the outrage his pre-war work had provoked; with Mond at the head of the IWM, an anti-semitic outburst would have been singularly ill-advised; and despite his reluctance to be drafted, Epstein was not a pacifist. Possibly Frampton had heard about Epstein's controversial *Risen Christ*, which he had started in 1917 (though it was not exhibited until 1920). Many considered it appallingly blasphemous, and this might have been used to persuade Haig, a devout Christian, of Epstein's unworthiness for a prestigious appointment.

Whatever Frampton's motives, his letter had serious consequences. It killed the IWM commission stone dead and doubtless contributed to the War Office's refusal to release Epstein to the MoI in March 1918; despite Lady Randolph Churchill's offer of 'Winston's help', Epstein never became an official artist in the First World War.

There was a further curious sequel in 1919 when the *Dundee Advertiser* made the seemingly innocuous suggestion that the IWM had commissioned Epstein to do a *bas-relief* of the Moeuvres Incident, in which Sergeant D. F. Hunter of the Highland Light Infantry had won his VC. The commission came, in fact, from Muirhead Bone, who intended to present the work to the IWM, and the Museum saw fit to issue in the national press a hasty and somewhat hysterical denial of any connection with Epstein – a response which now seems out of all proportion to the event.[106]

After this débâcle no further artists were nominated for the WTS, and the supply of pictures from the Western Front was thus restricted to purchases and gifts, the work of Adrian Hill, and the few pictures resulting from an official appeal to soldier-artists in every unit in France. This appeal, made by Donald in July 1918, was prompted by the success of a similar request made to RAMC units by the head of the IWM Army Medical Section, Lieutenant-Colonel F. S. Brereton. Earlier in the war the War Office and the RAMC, with the aim of founding a medical museum on the lines of the Museé Val de Grâce in Paris, had initiated a Committee for the Medical History of the War, of which Brereton was chairman; when the IWM was founded, Brereton was asked to provide it with a representative medical collection. Pictures were an integral part of both his schemes and besides his wartime appeal he also assembled after the war a team of thirteen artists with medical experience and set them to work in a studio in the Fulham Road on paintings, sculpture and models. The most distinguished of his artists was perhaps Austin Spare, something of a prodigy in his day, having first exhibited at the Royal Academy at the age of seventeen.[107]

The pictures produced ranged from exact anatomical drawings to portraits of leading figures in the medical world; the majority were scenes of places associated with the RAMC, in France and elsewhere, and typical RAMC activities both behind the lines and under fire. 161 of the less technical and more illustrative pictures came to the IWM, a valuable record of a period during which great advances were made, of necessity, in medicine; the remainder were distributed among the Army medical and hygiene schools when it became obvious that Brereton's medical museum would never be built.

The Royal Navy's Medical Section representative, Surgeon-Commander Montague H. Knapp, trusted more to the camera and acquired the work of only three artists – Oswald Moser and Oscar Parkes, both of whom painted on board hospital ships at Gallipoli, and G. F. 'Jan' Gordon, who in 1914 had joined his wife as a member of a medical unit bound for Serbia. There he recorded the Royal Naval Armoured Car Squadron at work, transporting wounded soldiers on sledges through the snow and mud of the Turkish Front in winter.

The other branch of the IWM to take an interest in art was the Munitions sub-committee which, perhaps recognising the important part played by women in the wartime munitions industry, employed one of the first official British women artists, Anna Airy. Airy, a contemporary of Orpen and Augustus John, was a talented draughtsperson in the Academic manner and one of England's most successful women artists. Nevertheless the Munitions sub-committee, possibly doubting the reliability of someone who was both an artist *and* a woman, drew up for her an agreement with terms more stringent than those imposed on any other artist, including the right of rejection without payment and a penalty clause more appropriate to a commercial manufacturing contract, imposing a 5% diminution in price for each month's delay.

Airy was to paint four large canvases (72×84) at £280 each, representative of typical scenes at munitions works – a shell forge, a shell-filling department, a gun forge and an aircraft assembly shop.

The difficult working conditions caused her no trouble: a widely reported spirit of adventure had led her as a student into East End vice-dens in search of her subjects – her picture *The Gambling Club* captures the moment before a gambler was stabbed to death in front of her – and in contrast she took the painting of shells at Hackney Marshes as light relief: 'I've never felt such heat! The floor got "black hot". I burnt a pair of shoes right off my feet! . . . You have to paint these red-hot shells so very fast because of the colour changing; so glancing rapidly up and down from a glowing shell to my canvas, I would suddenly catch sight of a black object apparently fallen on to the shell . . . a kipper being cooked to provide an impromptu meal! Munition-makers specially liked kippers – they liked to eat one about every fifteen minutes! You put one on a red-hot shell – up goes the back in flames – and you eat piping hot and half raw whatever kipper remains!'

CHAPTER TWENTY-FOUR

IWM – the Admiralty Artists

H ONOURS for the best-organised and most comprehensive art collection within the IWM scheme belong to the Admiralty sub-committee – its success due to the fact that these Service representatives had, for once, a genuine interest in art.

Rear-Admiral Sir Douglas Brownrigg had no formal connection with the Museum, but as Chief Naval Censor he was responsible both for censoring the pictures and for obtaining facilities for the artists with the Fleet. He was an elderly man who had been retired for several years before the war necessitated the recall of such experienced officers as himself, and he was proudly conscious of the Navy's artistic tradition. With an eye to posterity he was determined that the Admiralty section of the new war museum should excel, and in this aim he was backed wholeheartedly by Commander Colpoys Walcott, the first chairman of the IWM's Admiralty sub-committee, in day-to-day control of the Admiralty art scheme. Both Brownrigg and Walcott had been closely involved with the naval side of the DoI scheme, Brownrigg in his capacity as Censor, and Walcott as Admiralty Liaison Officer; and by the end of 1917, when the IWM scheme started, they had some insight into the practical difficulties of official art.

Their aim was to have represented 'every Branch of the British Navy with regard to types of ships, bases and areas involved in naval operations', and this they achieved in two stages: by deploying an initial team of eight artists, selected in December 1917, to cover home subjects generally; and by supplementing this team throughout 1918 and after on an *ad hoc* basis as new subjects arose, most of them the activities of the Navy in foreign waters.

The Admiralty sub-committee was conspicuous within the IWM for its concern with the artistic merits of its pictures. The choice of artists was made after consultation with several art experts – among them Clifford Smith at the Victoria and Albert Museum, Charles Aitken at the Tate, D. S. McColl at the Wallace Collection, and Charles Holmes at the National Gallery; and on 6 December 1917, Walcott invited to lunch at his club the first eight artists – Geoffrey Allfree, Philip Connard, Nelson Dawson, John Lavery,[108] Ambrose McEvoy, Charles Pears, Glyn Philpot and Norman Wilkinson – to discuss the allocation of subjects and to offer them, with rare good sense, 'a free hand in dealing with these subjects', urging that the finished pictures should be 'in every way representative and worthy as sea pictures to hand down to posterity, both as regards subject and quality of the art'.[109]

Fees, unlike those offered by the propaganda organisations, were not standard – McEvoy, Philpot, Wilkinson and Lavery were to receive an agreed amount per canvas,[110] and the others were salaried at varying rates.[111] Brownrigg arranged honorary commissions in the Royal Marines for those who otherwise held no military rank,[112] there was an allowance for uniforms, and a flat rate of £1 per week for materials was paid to the salaried artists. The Fleet was given formal notice of the appointments in an

Admiralty Weekly Order, and in January the necessary permits were issued for work to begin.

Regardless of Dodd's recent efforts for the DoI, the Admiralty sub-committee set its heart on a further series of portraits – in oils rather than charcoal and watercolour – of the senior Admirals, and another of the Navy's VCs. Admirals were the province of Glyn Philpot, who generously offered to paint each canvas for £100, one sixth of his usual fee. He encountered many of the same problems as Dodd with busy sitters and cramped working conditions, complicated by the more cumbersome medium of oils, and in despair he took Walcott to lunch at the Ritz to beg that the Admirals should present themselves for sittings at his studio. Unfortunately the bribe bore no fruit and ultimately only four portraits were completed – Tyrwhitt, Sturdee, Keyes and Jellicoe.

The task of depicting the VCs fell to McEvoy, a fashionable society artist, described by one critic as 'a magician of light and colour'. By 1917 he had moved away from the 'restful interiors with figures, and poetical landscapes' of his early career to concentrate on portraiture; his official appointment for the IWM, during which he completed nineteen male portraits, was an uncharacteristic episode in a career devoted increasingly to the celebration of beautiful women. The correspondence shows no reluctance to undertake the work, but equally there is no evidence that he found it engrossing. Part of his brief was the reconstruction of likenesses of posthumous VCs from photographs; to a man for whom colour and atmosphere were of the utmost importance, the task of creating a portrait from a blurry, tinted studio print was extremely uncongenial and though McEvoy started several, he finished none.

He completed seven living VCs without complaint, however, and in the men and work of the Royal Naval Division and the Royal Marines on the Somme, where he was sent in August 1918, he found a subject of real excitement. Unfortunately he translated little of this inspiration into paint, completing only three pictures which were not portraits.

With the exception of Norman Wilkinson, the remaining artists were used flexibly to cover the home bases. Nelson Dawson was sent to record the vital work of the Dover Patrol, a motley collection of vessels responsible for guarding the transport ships which ferried men and munitions to France, and for maintaining an illuminated strip across the Channel to prevent enemy ships slipping through undetected at night. At Portsmouth Geoffrey Allfree, a young 2nd Lieutenant in command of a motor launch, was in his spare time to depict the diverse work of motor launches and coastal motor boats – mine-sweeping, patrols and torpedo-running. Unfortunately, neither venture was wholly successful: the exigencies of active service prevented Allfree, to his distress, from doing any work he considered adequate; and Dawson, though keen and conscientious, was, in the opinion of Admiral Keyes (Commander-in-Chief, Dover Patrol), 'without exception, *the* most helpless and ignorant person of the kind I have ever come across'. At the end of April 1918, when all work in progress was inspected, both appointments were terminated.

Lavery, with his DoI experience behind him and a wife whom Brownrigg surmised had 'done some spade work on her own account up in the north', fared better. In January he was sent up to Scapa Flow in the Orkneys, a daunting prospect in midwinter even for a much younger man; in an effort to combat the cold he acquired an electrified suit taken off a German airman, but it stood no chance against the bitter wind of Scapa and he lasted only four days – producing, however, a quartet of canvases fully expressive of the impossible conditions endured by the men of the Grand Fleet.

During the rest of 1918 Lavery visited other naval bases and docks – Richborough, Southampton, London and Rosyth, where he painted the 6th American Battle Squadron at anchor in the Firth of Forth. In August he was at East Fortune, the base for British airships of the North Sea Patrol. He later cited his experiences there as evidence of his remoteness from the real war: 'Escorting convoys and painting from "blimps" ... I felt nothing of the stark reality, losing sight of my fellow men being blown to pieces in submarines or slowly choking to death in mud. I saw only new beauties of colour and design as seen from above, and the excitement of getting ready to bomb a submarine, which as often as not was a whale coming up to blow.'

Charles Pears was also given a roving commission: in January he was at Rosyth where, despite 30 degrees of frost, he found the subject matter uplifting: 'I am very conscious', he wrote, 'of the smallness of the personal pronoun and the largeness of the possibilities of the northern bases.' Where Lavery's brief had been seascapes, Pears – a noted contributor of marine subjects to the illustrated press – was instructed principally to make detailed drawings of ships; he was a conscientious worker, using photographs to ensure total veracity of detail – rigging, wireless equipment, camouflage and other markings – and compiled meticulous records of such unique vessels as HMS *Furious*, the prototype 'Aerodrome Ship'. Posted to Harwich he witnessed the remarkable scene on 11 August 1918 when a tiny ship-launched aircraft brought down a Zeppelin over the North Sea: as the airship fell in flames the flagship signalled 'See Hymn 224. Verse 7'. ('Oh happy band of pilgrims/ Look upward to the skies/ Where such a light affliction/ Shall win so great a prize.')

Also at Harwich was Philip Connard, a prominent figure in the NEAC and a friend of Steer and Tonks. Previously a Captain in the Royal Artillery, Connard was a poor sailor and his sojourn with the cruiser squadron was uncomfortable; 'he was admired', wrote Brownrigg, 'for the plucky way in which he stuck to his work in all weathers. ... He made frequent journeys to the ship's side to "discharge cargo" but always went back to his work.' By way of contrast he was posted in August to the Grand Fleet at Rosyth to make studies of life on board the heavy ships. But here he seems to have fallen victim to the same insularity which had baffled John Wheatley; unlike Wheatley he did not wait to be sent away but, after two or three days, simply packed and left. (It is worth noting that, with the possible exception of Bone, no official artist was able to live and work successfully on board the battleships. Suspicion of civilians, especially artists, was particularly acute in the Navy; Allfree recorded an example of caution taken to ludicrous lengths – a civilian arrested in Portsmouth for carrying a blank canvas through the streets.)

Walcott, disappointed but not particularly surprised, sent Connard instead to Constantinople to record the surrender of the Turkish ships and the opening of the Dardanelles – an event of particular significance to the Navy in redeeming the fiasco at Gallipoli in 1915. The Gallipoli engagements themselves are commemorated in the IWM collection chiefly by the work of marine painter Norman Wilkinson, who had been

Philip Connard, *The Guns of HMS Caesar* (oil on canvas), 20 × 24

at the landing at Suvla Bay on 7 August 1915 and painted a series of watercolours shortly afterwards. These the Admiralty sub-committee wanted him to duplicate in oils, and he eventually completed six. In his autobiography, *A Brush With Life*, written at the age of ninety-one, Wilkinson described his experiences at Suvla: 'By climbing into the foretop of the vessel, it was possible to watch the living cinema of battle.... The troops marching in open order across the salt lake formed a most stirring picture as they crossed the unbroken surface of silver white. Overhead shrapnel burst unceasingly, leaving small crumpled forms on the ground, one or more of which would slowly rise ... others lay where they fell.'

Wilkinson was also commissioned to illustrate the effects of dazzle-painting, a form of naval camouflage he had himself invented. 'Dazzle' – the application of strongly contrasting blocks of colour in a carefully devised pattern designed to alter perspective and form – was not intended to make vessels invisible at sea, but so to distort the outline and general shape of a ship that a U-boat commander (dazzle-painting was solely concerned with submarine attacks) would have difficulty in estimating the vessel's course and speed and thus in making a successful torpedo attack. It was particularly effective in moonlight, when pale colours were enhanced.[113]

The IWM was not as scrupulous in its commissions as in its purchases in employing only artists who had been present at the events they depicted. Where eyewitness artists like Wilkinson were available the Admiralty sub-committee was happy to use them; in this way they commissioned paintings of Jutland from Able Seaman Robert Smith and, from Frank Mason, scenes on the Suez Canal in 1915. However, where events called for commemoration and no eyewitnesses presented themselves, Brownrigg and Walcott unashamedly resorted to sending painters on 'fact-finding' trips after the war. Mason was sent to Malta and the Dardanelles, Cecil King to the Baltic, and Montague Dawson to Gibraltar, for much this purpose; but the most blatant example was that of Donald Maxwell, one of the *Graphic*'s longest-serving illustrators. He was sent to the Middle East to recreate the naval operations along the coast of Palestine and the Lebanon in support of Allenby's push to the north, and the 1915 Mesopotamian campaigns on the Tigris and Euphrates, sketching the settings and reconstructing the incidents themselves from verbal descriptions in the true spirit of the illustrator.

Two artists who in December 1917 had fallen outside the Admiralty sub-committee's purview were later used to good effect – Francis Dodd and Muirhead Bone. Dodd was sent to Harwich to record life on board submarines, and his sketches below decks provide a unique record of the primitive marine technology of the First World War. Bone was a personal friend of Brownrigg, who whetted his appetite for a return to work[114] by packing him off to Dover to draw HMS *Vindictive* receiving a hero's welcome after the Zeebrugge Raid on St George's Day. Bone's next assignment was similarly therapeutic – a four-month sketching tour of merchant marine ports with his merchant captain brother David, which resulted in a thorough record of an otherwise rather neglected aspect of Britain's naval efforts.[115]

Thus refreshed, Bone was ready to take advantage of the chance to record the Navy's supreme moment – the surrender of the Kaiser's High Seas Fleet. He was not the only artist favoured: Brownrigg was particularly anxious that every stage in the drama should be recorded and obtained special permission from the First Lord of the Admiralty, Sir Eric Geddes, for John Lavery to be present when the terms of the surrender were discussed. On 15 November Lavery was aboard Beatty's flagship, HMS *Queen Elizabeth* at Rosyth, to witness the arrival of the German delegates, led by Konter-Admiral Hugo Maurer. It was dark and foggy when they came on to the foredeck and Lavery, standing concealed on the far side of the 'group lamps', made rapid sketches; he then hurried down to Beatty's cabin and, dressed as a Post-Captain, took up position in a corner behind the German delegates where he proceeded surreptitiously to paint the scene. 'Most people would have been all ears,' Lavery wrote later, 'but I was all eyes,' concentrating furiously on the German representatives, from whom, needless to say, he could get no further sittings. As a historical document the

Henry Lamb, *Irish Troops in the Judaean Hills surprised by a Turkish Bombardment* (oil on canvas),
72 × 86

Stanley Spencer, *Travoys arriving with Wounded at a Dressing-Station at Smol, Macedonia, September, 1916* (oil on canvas), 72 × 86.

OPPOSITE ABOVE, Walter Bayes, *Landing Survivors from a Torpedoed Ship* (oil on canvas), 28 × 36.
BELOW, Thomas Derrick, *American Troops at Southampton embarking for France* (oil on canvas), 28 × 36

Austin Spare, *Dressing the Wounded during a Gas Attack* (pastel), $40 \times 29\frac{3}{4}$

OPPOSITE ABOVE, Randolph Schwabe, *Voluntary Land Workers in a Flax-Field, Podington, Northamptonshire* (oil on canvas), 42×60. BELOW, Bernard Meninsky, *The Arrival* (oil on canvas), 30×40

John Lavery, *A Convoy, North Sea, 1918. From NS7* (oil on canvas), 68 × 78

Sydney Carline, *The Destruction of the Turkish Transport* (oil on canvas), 48 × 48

John Lavery, *The End* (oil on canvas), 87 × 109

OPPOSITE ABOVE, Richard Carline, *Jerusalem and the Dead Sea from an Aeroplane* (oil on canvas), $48\frac{1}{2} × 51\frac{1}{2}$. BELOW, Henry Tonks, *The Surrender of Pujos Gora, 1919* (oil on canvas), $28\frac{1}{2} × 40$

picture is one of the most valuable in the national collection.

However, it was Bone who witnessed and recorded most vividly the actual delivery of the German Fleet at Inchkeith on 21 November 1918. Up in the foretop of the *Queen Elizabeth*, drawing all day from dawn till sunset, 'refusing to come down for food or drink or billiards', he described the scene: 'Out of the grey dawn came the first of the Hun ships with our little *Cardiff* leading them. Then our tremendous line "the sufficient force" which we had promised the Hun would meet and escort him, made a great turn – a wheel round and moved along with him. A great day. . . .'

But there was no one present to record the scene some seven months later when, in a last gesture of defiance, the entire German Fleet scuttled itself at Scapa Flow.

CHAPTER TWENTY-FIVE

The RAF Artists

I N 1918 aerial flight was a profoundly romantic subject: 'Now is the time', wrote Montague, 'while flying is young, to look at aircraft and to draw them, it being our luck to have seen man make himself free of the air in our day; in this navigation, at least, we are in the age of Columbus. . . .' Yet the air services were thinly represented in art under the propaganda authorities, with a mere handful of pictures from Nevinson, Lavery and Bone – and more of aircraft manufacture than of flight itself.

Quantitatively the IWM compensated for this deficiency but the difficulties inherent in the subject resulted in some of the worst examples of official art (though, in the work of Richard and Sydney Carline, the RAF sub-committee was responsible for some of the most interesting pictures produced under the auspices of the IWM).

The Air Services sub-section had been set up as early as November 1917, comprised of representatives of the Royal Flying Corps and the Royal Naval Air Services under the chairmanship of Lieutenant-Colonel A. C. MacLean, Commander-in-Chief of the Armaments School at Uxbridge. However, no artists were commissioned until after the RAF had been founded as a separate service in April 1918, and MacLean consequently promoted to the General Committee of the IWM.

He was all too conscious that in art collecting the RAF had 'considerable leeway to make up compared with the Navy'; and there were other disadvantages. Without a tradition of aeronautical art to look to, MacLean had no guide except his own inclinations, foremost among which were a passion for technical accuracy and the desire to further the prestige of the newest service. His choice of artists was dictated, and drastically curtailed, by a determination to appoint only those actually serving in the RAF – 'There is an excellent opportunity for some artists to make a little money,' he wrote, 'and I am keen to keep it in the family.' He had no time for 'modern art' nor, it seems, for art experts, and he chose to entrust the task of determining the scope and direction of RAF art to Richard Carline – a twenty-one-year-old 2nd Lieutenant in the RAF, the youngest of all the official war artists and one who, having joined up when he was nineteen, had not even completed his formal art education.

Richard Carline could be said to have initiated RAF art by presenting Conway and Robert Ross with a sheaf of 'curious maps for instructional purposes . . . very pretty things' (in fact aerial views of Vimy Ridge for the guidance of airborne artillery observers), in the hope that the IWM might employ him to do something similar for record purposes. MacLean not only approved his employment, but also ordered him to draw up an overall scheme of subjects and artists as a methodical basis for the building of an RAF art collection.

At this time Carline had two main concerns – to explore the possibilities of landscapes painted from the air and, more urgently, to save his elder brother Sydney (already an established artist) from further active service as a fighter pilot; having survived

Norman Arnold, *The Last Fight of Captain Ball, VC, DSO, MC, 17th May, 1917* (watercolour), 24 × 36

being shot down once over the Somme, Sydney, now recovered from his wounds, had been posted in February 1918 to the Italian Front. Richard seized his chance and drew up a 'family tree' of subjects to be covered, dividing them neatly among three artists – himself, Sydney and Norman Arnold (head of the studios at the Armaments School). His own responsibility was to be landscapes of the various fronts as seen from the air; Sydney's was to be operations in the air on every front; and to Arnold was left a miscellaneous category labelled 'technical', which included types of aircraft, methods of flying and fighting, and representations of 'famous incidents', such as *The Last Fight of Captain Ball, VC, DSO, MC, 17th May 1917*.

MacLean accepted the suggestions but on his own initiative expanded the 'technical' side considerably, commissioning several more artists on an *ad hoc* basis. His choices reflect a greater interest in aeroplanes than in art: he passed over Eric Gill, Henry Rushbury, Keith Henderson and William Wood, all in the RAF, in favour of men on whom he could rely for detailed and literal representations of the RAF's history and personalities.

A scheme of portraits was started which was to include all the flying VCs, living and dead; but very few were completed. Of the two portraitists appointed, Corporal Cowan Dobson and Captain Edward Newling, only the latter would willingly work from photographs to paint the dead men; and the living heroes, almost to a man, ignored orders to attend sittings. For the senior RAF officers sculpture seemed more appropriate, and MacLean employed Louis Frederick Roslyn to make portrait busts of Brancker, Salmond, Paine and Sykes.

G. H. Davis, who had instituted the aerial manoeuvre diagrams used in training, was commissioned to paint scenes illustrative of two of these manoeuvres – *Closing Up* and *Putting Out His Eyes*; Louis Weirter contributed a representation of William Bishop winning his VC, an incident Weirter had himself witnessed from a kite balloon; Stuart Reid, on active service in the Middle East, was detailed to recreate individual acts of heroism in that theatre of war; and C. R. Fleming-Williams had the good fortune to have approved in its entirety a proposal for sixty watercolours depicting the RAF's work 'over the sea'.

By the beginning of 1919 the work of these artists clearly demonstrated the direction RAF art was taking – and the emphasis on technical accuracy and reconstructed 'action' pictures brought MacLean into conflict with the Art sub-committee, whose artistic backbone had been stiffened by Yockney's arrival at the IWM. The first (and last) trial of strength came over the Fleming-Williams series. After inspecting the first eleven, which included such titles as *Exploding Enemy Mines by Machine-Gun Fire from the Air*, Yockney wrote firmly to ffoulkes: 'Whatever use these drawings may have as illustrations they have little artistic merit'; and he forced a showdown by rejecting two of the next batch. MacLean refused to be 'dictated to', and persuaded the General Committee to pass a resolution setting Yockney straight. 'It was generally considered that while the advice of the Art Committee was considered to be very useful with respect to the artistic value of paintings, the opinion of Officers in HM Forces, with respect to the value of such pictures as records, must be held to have the precedence.' The two pictures were accepted and MacLean's assistant reported: 'I think the battle has been won . . . although there may be a little difficulty when the question of hanging arises. Most probably they will want to hang the artist beside the pictures.'

MacLean further made his point by selecting his own art adviser, Harold Wyllie, a Lieutenant-Colonel in the RAF and a painter of the representational school. The campaign for photographic accuracy gathered momentum. Even Fleming-Williams was ordered to make his boats 'float better' – but it was the few moderns in the RAF team who suffered most. Vorticist Frank Dobson had been asked to paint the balloon barrage defences put up at sunset over Canvey Island. His work was inspected by Wyllie and Yockney wrote apologetically to Dobson, 'As regards the unfinished *Balloon Apron* I am asked to suggest that . . . it would be desirable to concentrate on the Apron and its work and to subordinate the landscape and atmospheric effects. The smoke and sky seemed to worry the Committee and if these effects could be subdued they would be glad.'

Fortunately, by this time the lynchpins of the RAF scheme – Richard and Sydney Carline, who with discernible Post-Impressionist sympathies were far more acceptable to Yockney than to Wyllie or MacLean – were well clear, touring the Middle East with a view to recording the scenes of RAF activity there and reconstructing the principal operations.

This trip – which at times resembled a package tour of the Holy Land – they had earned by first proving themselves as war artists under fire in Europe. Richard had arrived in France on 27 July 1918, after taking a course in aerial gunnery to equip himself for flying over enemy lines. He was billeted at the RAF Guest House, near Hesdin, and spent his time being flown over the battlefields in a Bristol two-seater. Sydney remained in Italy, but from August 1918 onwards as an artist rather than an operational pilot; he found a studio in the museum at Vicenza and was supplied with a Sopwith Camel for sketching flights. He had in fact been sketching unofficially since February, and from one of these studies painted *The Destruction of an Austrian Machine in the Gorge of the Brenta Valley*. A letter home records the incident: 'On patrol with two others we saw a Hun two-seater taking photos 5000 feet below us (we at 10,000) and on our side of the Line, we dived on him. He put up no show, the pilot was shot, and the observer leaning over tried to dive for home but he was shot and the machine crashed into the river.'

Sketching from the open cockpit of a Sopwith – awkward at the best of times with the shuddering of the plane and the wind threatening to snatch the paper away – became increasingly difficult as the autumn approached: 'This morning I have been . . . making sketches for the new picture of Bristol Fighters in Archie bursts over the Alps. It was so cold up high that my paint froze almost before I could put it on the paper, with the result that the sketches are very blotchy, where lumps of iced paint have thawed.'

Throughout their official appointment the Carlines' relationship with the IWM was ambivalent: although Mond championed them consistently, ffoulkes seems slightly to have mistrusted them as men who were apparently fit but not fighting. Moreover, Sydney was reputed to be 'a little inclined to take life easily – in art at any rate', with a lamentable tendency in his aerial subjects to display more interest in the landscapes than the flying. Until December, when both returned to England, MacLean chivvied them constantly: 'Put your back into the work as the IWM is a business institution, and they require a return for the employment of all their Staff.'

To their frustration, the Carlines had little time to work up their studies before Mac-Lean rushed them out to the Middle East, afraid that the squadrons would disperse and the opportunity of recording operations in the area be lost. With a brief which now included Palestine, Mesopotamia and Salonica, the Carlines arrived at Port Said on 18 January 1919 and travelled to Ramleh, their base in Palestine. It was also the home of 1st Squadron, Australian Flying Corps, whom Richard and Sydney found rather inclined 'to make a fetish of their roughness' – though preferable in every way to the Arabs – 'such a horrible, untrustworthy, deceitful, money-grubbing, filthy lot of people, that the whole British Army appears to be *unanimous* in its preference to fight them any day rather than the Germans or Turks!'

Their plan was to tour Palestine and the Lebanon by train and car to survey the terrain, returning later to make flights over the chosen areas, and they began by travelling slowly north to Jerusalem, via the Jordan Valley and the Dead Sea. At Wadi Fara Sydney made studies for *The Destruction of the Turkish Transport*;* here the RAF had intercepted part of the Turkish Army as it retreated before the advance of Allenby's troops. 'The road ran along the side of a steep gorge', wrote Sydney, 'with precipitous drops down to the Wady running below. All along were the débris of overturned carts and motors, and lying everywhere were the skeletons of horses and even men, their bones having been cleaned white by the jackals. It was a dreary tortuous place and the Turkish Army trying to escape down it was easily stopped and massacred by aeroplanes.'

The Governor of Nazareth loaned them his car and chauffeur to visit the Sea of Galilee. After four drab years of war they found their surroundings intoxicating: 'We seem to spend most of our time studying the archaeological and historical scenes of interest' – and their letters home form a fascinating period guide to the Holy Land (Jordan, Jericho, Magdala, Nazareth, Galilee, Tiberias, Damascus), in sharp contrast to their dutiful weekly reports to MacLean. Only in one place, near Aleppo, did they actually see the remains of war, the wrecked aerodrome of Rayak, bombed by the RAF, the ground littered with 'Turkish machines burnt into queer contortions'.

Concluding the land tour with a short visit to Beirut, they returned to Ramleh to make the necessary flights – Sydney over the Wadi Fara and the Sea of Galilee, Richard over Gaza and Jerusalem (where he completed the sketches for one of his best known early paintings – *Jerusalem and the Dead Sea From an Aeroplane*)[116]* After an uneasy stay in Cairo amidst Moslem agitation against the delivery of Palestine to the Jews, they moved on to Mesopotamia, which, in the heat of mid-summer, they found less appealing. Based at Baghdad, they travelled only locally until mid-July when they went up to Mosul to participate in a punitive bombing raid against the Kurds. Their intention was then to press on through the mountains of Persia to the Black Sea, and from there by ship to Constantinople and Salonica. But to their eternal regret, the journey was cut short by their urgent recall for demobilisation – 'and so disappeared for ever the idea of seeing the real capital of the Moslem world, whose domains we have been spending the year in traversing'.

The Carlines had had unique opportunities – of which the IWM was unable to take full advantage. They arrived home in November 1919, with sketches and notes for twenty-five large canvases between them, only to find that MacLean's victory over the Art sub-committee earlier in the year had proved pyrrhic. His optimistic attitude to budgets, engendered by the General Committee's aspirations for the Museum, had led him drastically to exceed the sum (£1000) he had been allotted by the Committee – Fleming–Williams' series alone would have cost £2000 – and as early as April 1919 he had been forced to instruct artists to restrict themselves to work actually in progress. By November he had left the RAF and his successor, Air Commodore Lambe, took the only possible course – sharing out the little money remaining among the artists who still had work in hand, and axeing the rest, a disastrous truncation of the scheme which left the RAF only modestly represented in art in the First World War.

With *no* work in progress, merely the raw material for pictures, the Carlines were something of a special case, and Lambe compromised by cutting the proposed twenty-five canvases to seven – three from Richard and four from Sydney, a meagre result for almost a year's work. Worse, the brothers were pressurised by Wyllie, who considered their work 'not of a standard which warrants the unlimited expenditure of public money'; their polite intransigence ultimately provoked a stern letter informing

Richard Carline, *Mount Hermon and Mount Sannin above the Clouds* (oil on canvas), $42\frac{1}{2} \times 54\frac{1}{2}$

them that the RAF Section was 'not prepared to exhibit, in the Museum, pictures showing any extreme forms of art' (it being essential to remember that 'the impression of one individual may seriously clash with the impression of others').

But as compensation for the cuts, they were allowed to retain most of their three hundred sketches from the Middle East; and with them they put on a joint exhibition at the Goupil Gallery in March 1920, which brought public recognition on a scale undreamed of before their official appointments.

CHAPTER TWENTY-SIX

1919 – Post-War Collecting

T HE shortage of money which sabotaged the RAF Section's scheme was ultimately to bring art collecting throughout the IWM to a halt; by the end of 1919 the attention of the administrators was focused less on further acquisition than on the display of the pictures they had already assembled. Fortunately, between Christmas 1918, when the Museum took charge of the MoI pictures, and Christmas 1919 when the official British war art collection was unveiled at the Royal Academy, there was time for some notable additions to be made.

One important gap was filled when the Women's Work Section belatedly awoke to the usefulness of paintings as records. This Section was decidedly the Museum's 'poor relation'; when estimates of the floor space required for the IWM were first drawn up for the approval of the War Cabinet, Women's Work received a miserly 5000 square feet as compared with the 127,000 square feet allocated to the Admiralty. In its leader, Priscilla Lady Norman, it had, however, a considerable asset. Daughter of Lord Aberconway and wife of Sir Hugh Norman MP, she was prominent among the younger society matrons – 'somewhat fragile in appearance, with grey eyes and quantities of soft brown hair and a delicate complexion'. She was also one of the few society women to possess the coveted 1914 medal, for running a hospital in France in the first months of the war; and she was determined to ensure that the emergence of women in society as a result of the war was properly documented.

She had initially been inclined to concentrate on the collection of documents, photographs and models.[117] She felt that there were too many paintings at exhibitions of women's work in France, and she adopted an independent stance over portraits despite the fact that they were an important aspect of IWM art strategy: 'Women have distinguished themselves in so many forms of war that we feel it is a little invidious to select some and not others.'

Nevertheless, it was this Section, appropriately enough, which appointed the first official British woman war artist. In May 1918 (a month before Anna Airy signed for the Munitions sub-committee) Lady Norman sent Victoria Monkhouse, a young Cambridge graduate who had attracted attention with her caricatures of academic life, to make a series of sketches of women in the new and unfamiliar roles in which war had cast them – as Royal Mail van-drivers, bus conductresses, telegraph girls, railway ticket collectors and carriage cleaners, postwomen and window-cleaners. (After her first efforts Monkhouse was admonished to make her women 'smarter and neater' – of the window-cleaners she was advised, 'They have some very picturesque ones at Harrods.')

Yockney's accession to the Art sub-committee on 31 December 1918 appears to have galvanised the Section into further picture-collecting. His suggestion – made in the knowledge that Lady Norman was concerned primarily with *records* – that she

Victoria Monkhouse, *A Woman Window-Cleaner* (pencil and watercolour), $18\frac{1}{2} \times 12\frac{1}{2}$

should confine her pictorial acquisitions to enlarged photographs stung her to the extent
that she obtained a ruling from the Director-General that the Women's Work Section
'had power to follow their own judgement in the purchase of paintings and drawings

irrespective of the Art Committee'. She pressed ahead with a campaign designed to display women's work to the best possible effect with the dwindling funds available; in the process she and her honorary staff employed methods which were less than a good advertisement for the emancipated woman – coaxing, wheedling, half-truths, and, where necessary, moral blackmail. Nellie Isaac was instructed to paint six water-colours of social life at the aero-engine factory in which she worked, for one guinea each – raised to two guineas when she explained that they were taking her longer than expected because of acute neurasthenia. (One might contrast this with the fees paid to the male artists employed, none of whom worked for less than £100.)[118] Ursula Wood was told that her fee (somewhere in the region of £25) for five sketches of girls in timber-felling camps could not be met in full, as the Art sub-committee 'consisting of men' had reported against them; there is no record of such a resolution in the minutes. Lucy Kemp-Welch, commissioned to paint *The Ladies Army Remount Depot, Russley Park, Wiltshire* for £150, was badgered into presenting free a second, far larger picture, *The Straw Ride* (72×156), which Lady Norman had seen and preferred at a private exhibition (where it had been priced at £1000). The Newlyn painter Stanhope Forbes, mortified by Lady Norman's invocation of disinterested patriotism, was blud-geoned into quartering his £400 fee for *WRNS Ratings Sail-making* as his painfully abject letters show: 'I was quite unaware that artists were painting these pictures mainly for the honour of being represented in the National Collection . . . I am only too anxious not to be behindhand in any such object.'

Only Lavery was proof against bullying, going no further than to halve his fee for twelve pictures to 1250 guineas, and to wait a year for payment. His commission (carried out in May and June 1919) was the single most important in the Women's Work collection, a series recording the work of women in France – in hospitals and hospital ships; in Queen Mary's Army Auxiliary Corps, serving in canteens and tending graves; at 'the picturesque Archbishop's Palace [in Rouen] where women deal with the clerical work involved in connection with the deaths and effects of men'; in the RAF repair shops; and in the Army Bakery at Dieppe, then the largest bakery in the world. He had detailed instructions as to the type of women he should depict – the VAD Motor Convoy at Étaples, for example: 'They do all the ambulance driving for a large district and contain some of the finest golfing and sporting women among the personnel' – and was exhorted to emphasise 'their companionship with the men, which is officially encouraged as tending to lessen the unrest on the part of the Tommies since the Armistice'. He declined, however, the invitation to paint them footballing together at Dieppe.

The Art sub-committee, circumvented by the Admiralty and generally worsted in its bouts with the other sub-committees, did however make its own contribution to the artistic standard of the collection. In June 1919, Tonks was sent to join the BEF attempting to assist the White Russians against the Bolsheviks on the Murman Coast. A more unlikely adventurer than Tonks it would be hard to imagine – in later years he was to refuse to go abroad for fear of syphilitic infection from the hands that would rummage in his luggage at the customs. He travelled first to Murmansk on a troop ship, then on to Archangel in a small steamer, with six young women from the Ameri-can YWCA intent on teaching juvenile Russia temperance and baseball, and a young

Stanhope Forbes *WRNS Ratings Sail-Making* (oil on canvas), 42 × 54

VC who sat in the stern fishing and reading poetry – all of them living off a hamper which the prudent Tonks had brought.

At Archangel the climate was intolerable – 87 degrees in the shade and so humid that he could work only at night, with the sweat still pouring from him. War subjects were virtually non-existent and he wrote, not without amusement, 'The two subjects I have seen that have interested me have been girls bathing in the Dwina, which I am happy to say they do stark naked. . . . Ladies of Archangel bathing under the protection of British guns would make a nice subject. I assure you it's charming.' To fulfil his commission he was obliged to accompany an expeditionary force comprised of the 11th North Russian Rifles under Colonel Kruglyakov in its attack on Pujos Gora, a small town in a strategic position on Lake Onega, occupied by the 'Bolos'; his Slade students would doubtless have been astonished to see him on forced route march through the Russian forest, sleeping out, riding painfully in a farm cart or flat on his face under fire in the bottom of a rowing boat. Unfortunately he found the taking of Pujos Gora 'a very boring battle', (possibly because he was left behind with the baggage); but he did paint the formal *Surrender of Pujos Gora 1919** and has the distinction of being the only official[119] British artist to have recorded the war in Russia (a feat accomplished for less than the price of keeping Steer for a month in a hotel in Dover).

The Art sub-committee's other major commission was one it had inherited involuntarily from the MoI scheme. Shortly before the Ministry was closed down Orpen had been approached to record the signing of peace at Versailles, in the expectation that under the terms of his gift to the nation he would work unpaid, in exchange for facilities. By 1919, however, he was feeling less generous. As early as February 1918 he had written to William Rothenstein – 'I am very happy; but am slowly losing all the money I ever made, so I expect a rough time after the war'; and in post-war Paris during the Peace Conference, the cost of living was astronomical. 'Can you let me have a couple of thousand pounds on account? I'm starving,' he wrote to Yockney – and he doubtless also complained to his more influential friends, among them Sir George Riddell, an intimate of Lloyd George and the founder of the *News of the World*. In February 1919 Mond received a letter from Lloyd George's private secretary informing him that as the Prime Minister felt that 'the Peace Conference ought not to be allowed to pass without some suitable and permanent memento having been made of these gatherings', it had been arranged by Riddell for 'two of the most famous of British artists', Orpen and Augustus John, to oblige – at a cost of £3000 each for one large canvas, plus expenses of £3 per day, for all of which the IWM was responsible.

However, Lloyd George and Riddell had misjudged their men: from John they got precisely nothing and from Orpen no 'suitable memento', but three separate expressions of his own somewhat jaundiced view of the Conference.[120] In France Orpen had conceived a sincere, if sentimental, reverence for the 'fighting man', the unsung hero whom he feared would be forgotten when the war ended. Now in Paris, depressed and enfeebled by a recurrence of his blood-poisoning, he was disgusted by what he saw as the greed, vanity and pettiness of the statesmen, jockeying for position as they re-drew the map of Europe: 'All these "frocks" seemed to me very small personalities in comparison with the fighting men,' he wrote. 'It was all like an *opéra bouffe. . .*'

The first two of his official pictures, *A Peace Conference at the Quai d'Orsay* and *The Signing of Peace in the Hall of Mirrors, Versailles, 28th June 1919*, merely hint at his mood – the 'frocks' in each case dwarfed by their surroundings, dingy intrusions into glittering set-piece interiors. In the third picture, completed three years later, he indulged himself to the full. A third formal group had originally been intended – 'thirty-six soldiers, sailors, politicians, Presidents etc.', posed in the Hall of Peace leading to the Hall of Mirrors – and he worked for nine months on the picture. But only weeks after his first visit to the Peace Conference Orpen had complained that it was 'deadly matter to work with'; and this time he could not carry the picture through. 'It all seemed so unimportant somehow,' he explained later to the press; 'I kept thinking of the soldiers who remain in France for ever.' (At the time he told ffoulkes that he found the figures ruined both the colour scheme and the composition – rather more practical objections.) In any event, he painted over his painstaking portraiture and substituted 'a coffin covered with the Union Jack and two semi-nude soldiers guarding

William Orpen, *The Signing of Peace in the Hall of Mirrors, Versailles, 28th June, 1919* (oil on canvas), 60 × 50

it and two cherubs in the air above' and gave it the title *To the Unknown British Soldier in France* – the idea being that 'after all the negotiations and discussions, the Armistice and Peace, the only tangible result is the ragged unemployed soldier and the Dead.'[121]

Exhibited at the Royal Academy's summer exhibition in 1923, *To the Unknown British Soldier* was voted, by public ballot, picture of the year; and it roused extremes of press response. 'A magnificent allegorical tribute to the men who really won the war,' wrote the Socialist *Daily Herald*; but to the *Patriot* it was 'a joke and a bad joke

William Orpen, *'To the Unknown British Soldier in France'* (oil on canvas), $60 \times 50\frac{1}{2}$, as altered

at that. . . . The English people are not quite so stupid as some of the Irish who live among us suppose. . . . If these are their feelings, why do they not go and live in their own country? Certainly to artists who have a turn for the grotesque and the fantastic desolation of war, there are excellent subjects ready to hand in Southern Ireland.'

The Trustees of the IWM (who included both Haig and Beatty) inspected the picture at a private view and, as Orpen expected, rejected it, remarking with restraint, 'It is not on the subject designated. . . . It does not show what we wished shown.' They

[148]

remained unperturbed by the derision of more radical organs: 'Orpen declines to paint the floors of hell with the colours of paradise,' intoned the *Liverpool Echo*, 'to pander to the pompous heroics of the red tab brigade. The IWM may reject the picture, but the shadow legions of the dead sleeping out and far will applaud it with Homeric hush.'[122]

Orpen's pictures, though not unfortunately his expenses, were to be paid for by a special grant from the Treasury, over and above the IWM's allocation for 1919–20. By mid-July the allocation (which at £6000 was less than half that made for the previous year) had already been exceeded. By October Ian Malcolm was advising a moratorium on art expenditure of all kinds, except portraiture. The IWM had intended as one of its principal contributions to war art a portrait series of every military leader and every fighting hero the war had produced, both as a record and a memorial. Each Section drew up a list of nominees and Yockney spent long hours matching subjects to artists.[123] But the series was nowhere near completion when the IWM art budget for 1920–21 was announced: a mere £850, it was immediately absorbed, indeed exceeded, by Orpen's expenses in Paris, and the portrait scheme petered out – a victim, perhaps, of the politicians' craving for immortality at the hands of John and Orpen.

Yockney had similar stringencies to face in bringing the MoI scheme to its conclusion. With little prospect of help from the IWM's coffers, in order to keep costs within the limits set by the Treasury in November 1918 he was obliged to cancel those commissions on which work had not yet started[124] and to reduce the salaries of Scheme 2 artists. He contrived, however, to make one or two useful additions to the series – Ian Strang's *The Outskirts of Lens* in the Uccello size, and Leon Underwood's *Erecting a Camouflage Tree* (42×60)[125] – before devoting his energies to assembling the completed pictures for exhibition at Burlington House.

Yockney's championing of the MoI scheme (to which his contribution had been crucial, though unobtrusive – George Clausen wrote to him in 1920, 'Few people outside artistic circles realise how much the collection owes to your intelligence, sympathy and zeal') made his position at the IWM somewhat equivocal. The division between the MoI and IWM collections is blurred now, but to Yockney then it was extremely significant. 'The IWM contribution', he wrote, 'grew from many centres, with Pictorial Record as the guiding principle. Art "happened", as Whistler said, in some cases. . . . The MoI contribution . . . had Art as its motive. Record, in the accepted sense, was not desired, though in many cases it occurred.'

He feared works of genuine artistic merit sinking without trace amidst a mass of less distinguished pictorial records, displayed amidst tanks, guns, medals, models and uniforms. In this he was warmly supported by Bone, who had already made efforts of his own to raise the standards of the official art collection. At the end of 1918 he had subscribed £2000[126] to form the 'Bone Fund' for the acquisition of new works – to be chosen, most decidedly, by himself.[127]

Out of this Fund he added to the IWM collection not only further works by Sargent, Steer, Tonks, Bayes, Wyndham Lewis, Roberts and Gilbert Spencer, but also works by artists otherwise unrepresented – Bomberg, McColl, Rupert Lee and Elliott Seabrooke. John's *Fraternity* and Epstein's *The Tin Hat*, *Sergeant Hunter VC* and *An American Soldier* were all paid for out of the Bone Fund. Bone also contributed in William

Rothenstein's *Watch on the Rhine* one of the few artistic records of the British Army of Occupation in post-war Germany. Rothenstein, working in Bonn for the Canadians, had persuaded the military authorities to place a single howitzer on the embankment of the Rhine, 'symbolic of our unboastful share in the final downfall of the German military power'.

A last chance of having the art memorial separately housed appeared to present itself in the proposal that an exhibition of the official pictures should be mounted at the Royal Academy at the end of 1919.[128] Responsibility for its organisation rested initially with the Art sub-committee; but with Malcolm absent at the Peace Conference, Yockney was able to engineer the transfer of day-to-day administration to a Hanging Committee headed by Bone and heavily weighted with past participants in, and supporters of, the MoI scheme – Tonks, Holmes, Cameron and Sims, plus partisans Francis Dodd and Charles Aitken.

Meeting for the first time on 20 May, this body declared its objective to be 'an Art exhibition . . . to convince the public that provision must be made for an important Picture Gallery', and it went on to frame selection criteria likely to exclude a large proportion of IWM art: 'The collection to be selected on merit . . . the Hangers to have full powers to eliminate the pictorial records which were collected not from an art motive but to explain the work of various sections of the Museum.' This clear challenge prompted a stern response from Conway, who insisted that all sections of the Museum be properly represented, and the Committee was forced to concede what Yockney described as 'a Chamber of Horrors'. Nevertheless, the great majority of the 925 pictures and sculptures finally displayed at the Academy were MoI or Bone Fund acquisitions, and the stage was set for judgement to be pronounced on the national war art collection.[129]

The exhibition opened on 13 December 1919, not without incident. Stanley Spencer was turned away from the private view by an attendant who refused to believe that so small and scruffy a figure could be an exhibitor; and Nevinson, finding that *Harvest of Battle* was not hung in the main room, conducted over several weeks a campaign of hysterical abuse against the 'cabals' and 'coteries' he discerned at work in the IWM, headed, as ever, by Tonks. Though the episode was not without its comic side, its effects on Nevinson were disastrous; he never recovered a true perspective on his war work and its critical reception, and twenty years later was to write a sorry epitaph on what many considered his finest achievement: 'The very mention of war pictures revives such feelings in me that I prefer never to think of them.'

In commercial terms too the RA exhibition was only a moderate success – it was visited by far fewer people than the Canadian exhibition of official pictures (also at the Royal Academy) earlier in the year, which had to some extent satisfied public curiosity about war art, or the IWM's own 'Sea Power' exhibition (which had included trophies and photographs as well). And far from provoking a unanimous public outcry for the pictures to be accorded national memorial status, the show generated an extraordinary diversity of opinion in the press.

From art critics, who appreciated both the remarkable catholicity of the collection

OPPOSITE, Colin Gill, *Evening after a Push* (oil on canvas), 30 × 20

and the inevitable harshness of the subject, the reaction was generally favourable (though few went as far as Hanging Committee member Charles Holmes in the *Manchester Guardian* in heralding 'the arrival of a new artistic movement, as novel and startling as that which began some sixty years ago, when the first works of the Pre-Raphaelite Brotherhood stung a drowsy world into fury').

From the popular press, on the other hand, came a chorus of righteous wrath, generated largely by the work of the 'moderns' in the MoI series – Lewis, Roberts, Japp, Colin Gill, John Nash and Gilbert Spencer in particular. The work of the *avant-garde* was an unfamiliar sight in the galleries of the Royal Academy, and the Hanging Committee had offered no compromise, giving pride of place in the main gallery to Roberts's *Shell Dump in France*, one of the most 'advanced' pictures in the collection. Extremism in art was readily equated with subversion[130] – one paper referred darkly to 'Bolshevism in Art' – and particular exception was taken to pictures deemed unworthy of the fighting man (most notably John Nash's '*Over the Top*' and Gilbert Spencer's *New Arrivals*): 'The fine men who fought in the great war are represented, either wilfully or through ineptitude, as clockwork manikins. Respect for the gallant fellows ... should have made such pictures impossible. ... They suggest caricatures "made in Germany,"' said the *Morning Post*; and the *Manchester Evening News* ran a headline 'Heroes Made To Look Like Clowns'. As for the *Daily Mirror*: 'When I got into the next gallery I knew what they meant by the horrors of war – it's the pictures.'

The most consistently savage attack was launched by the *Daily Graphic*, one of the most successful of the illustrated newspapers, which throughout the war had relied on the spurious and sentimental heroics of the popular illustrators and resented their exclusion from the official scheme. The *Graphic* deplored the absence of 'battle scenes' (where, it asked superfluously, was the Battle of Mons?), and an excess of Home Front subjects, 'records of the trivial and ephemeral' exemplifying nothing more than the organisers' determination to 'keep artists from the firing zone during active operations'. It conducted an Australian Sergeant-Major round the exhibition and recorded his comments (of Stanley Spencer's *Travoys* he opined, 'His eyesight needs attention,' and of the 'modernist' pictures he concluded triumphantly, 'They'll never dare send them to Australia!'); and, describing the work of the moderns as 'riding a hobby horse over the bones of dead heroes', it cast grave doubts on the wisdom of housing the pictures anywhere at all, let alone in their own special gallery.

More serious for the IWM was the fact that questions were asked in Parliament about the 'freak' pictures[131] and the Museum's expenditure thereon. Mond's reaction was to declare that inasmuch as the pictures in question had been commissioned by Lord Beaverbrook's Ministry, he personally was 'in no way responsible either for their ordering or their acquisition'; and he added, 'I have observed myself with some astonishment that most of the art critics consider them very fine works of art' – an answer which, in its bluff mistrust of aesthetic extremism, was a clear pointer to the exhibitions policy of the IWM in the inter-war years with regard to official war art.

PART II

THE SECOND WORLD WAR

Leslie Cole, *Men of the Royal Berkshire Regiment form the spearhead of a patrol, cutting through the jungle on the Toungoo–Manchi road* (oil on canvas), 35 × 27

[154]

CHAPTER TWENTY-SEVEN

Between the Wars

Kenneth Clark (reproduced by kind permission of the BBC)

T HE general unadventurousness of the IWM's art policy between the wars was dictated partly by factors beyond its control: a minimal purchase grant for pictures, which virtually restricted acquisitions to such gifts as the Museum was offered,[132] and an acute lack of space in which to display the existing collection. The Crystal Palace rapidly proved unsuitable as an art gallery in every respect – it was alternately too hot and too cold, with a roof which let in both sunlight and rain in excessive quantities – and it was succeeded by the Western Galleries of the Imperial Institute in South Kensington, with wall space for only a tiny proportion of the pictures. The element of choice in hanging was further complicated by the need to respect and display both the Orpen and Lavery Gifts, and as many as possible of the unwieldy memorial canvases, incontestably among the most important in the collection. When in 1936 the IWM moved with relief to its present home in the old Bethlem Royal Hospital at Southwark, the Art staff had just enough time to unpack and settle the pictures before being required to recrate them in the autumn of 1939.

It would nevertheless have been reasonable to expect the IWM at the outbreak of war to seek to extend their involvement with the tradition of war art and to become the principal focus of any official scheme. However, the Museum played little part in proceedings until 1946, when it once again became the main recipient of the pictures collected by others. This may be explained by the lack of dynamic personality on the Masterman or Beaverbrook scale within the IWM to set a scheme in motion. Perhaps more to the point, the Museum was hamstrung by the uncertainty of its status as a potential repository for relics of the Second World War, with separate museums for the Services being mooted.

But though the IWM itself was not in the forefront, the fact of its already existing war art collection did much to fuel the widespread pressure during 1939, in intellectual circles at least, for full use to be made of artists at a time when once again their livelihood was severely threatened. Several of the old voices were silent. Masterman had

[155]

died in 1927, unfulfilled and profoundly unhappy, tormented by fears of bankruptcy and destitution for his family. Bennett died two years later of typhoid contracted in France; and Beaverbrook was preoccupied by the problems associated with his appointment as Minister of Aircraft Production and, later, of Supply. John Buchan was by now Governor-General of Canada – one of his first acts being to sign the Dominion's declaration of war.

But Rothenstein (now Sir William) was still crusading: 'The Empire is concentrating all its moral . . . forces against the powers of evil: in this the arts have their part to play.' Yockney, now on the staff of the Art Exhibitions Bureau, urged the despatch of artists with this new BEF, pointing to the propaganda value of their pictures, and Nevinson called for 'an artistic mobilisation with a general in charge who is himself an artist'.

Much pointed reference was made in the press both to the First World War schemes, and to the more recent efforts made in America, as part of the 'New Deal', to relieve artists hit by the Depression by employing them on the decoration of public buildings.

As in the First World War, the pressure was diffuse – but it nevertheless proved effective, and by the end of 1939 a number of organisations had come into existence. Some aimed only to procure a livelihood for artists: the Central Institute of Art and Design and, on a less ambitious scale, the Arts Bureau set up in Oxford by Paul Nash were in effect employment agencies (though the former also proved a useful focus for ideas and protests from bodies like the Artists International Association).[133] Others sought to utilise artists' skills specifically for the furtherance of the war effort: the Ministry of Labour and National Service formed both a 'Publicity Artists' Committee' whose brief was to compile a register of artists suitable for propaganda work (on posters, pamphlets, etc.), and a separate list of artists for camouflage work. The Pilgrim Trust was dedicated, more generally, to keeping alive a tradition of cultural activity in Britain: its *Domesday Book* project provided for the recording by artists of Britain's threatened landscape and architectural heritage. The Trust also helped to fund a new venture – the Council for the Encouragement of Music and the Arts – which, after the war, was to become the principal source of patronage for the arts, the Arts Council.

In all these enterprises, a single hand was at work – that of Sir Kenneth Clark (later Lord Clark).[134] 1939 was the height of what he has described sardonically as 'the Great Clark Boom'. At the age of thirty-six, Clark was Surveyor of the King's Pictures at Windsor, a Fellow of Magdalen College, Oxford, had been Ryerson Lecturer at Yale in 1936, and Director of the National Gallery for the past seven years. Not surprisingly, he and his wife Jane were lionised in society, treated almost as mascots by fashionable hostesses such as Emerald Cunard and Sybil Colefax, and his influence as a connoisseur, critic and patron of young artists was considerable on both sides of the Atlantic.

Evidence of his efforts on behalf of artists is widespread – Carel Weight, for example, wrote in December 1939 to express his 'sincere thanks for your wholehearted championship of artists and the arts during these wretched times. Being on the Central Committee of the Artists International Association, I have an opportunity of seeing how much you have done.' The achievement in which Clark later took most pride, however, was the successful attempt to mobilise the Ministry of Information in the campaign for the employment of artists.

Several features made this second MoI an obvious target, not least the appointment as the first Minister of Lord Macmillan (a leading figure in the Pilgrim Trust, later the first chairman of CEMA) and Clark's own employment as Head of Films, a strong foothold from which to conduct operations. Furthermore, the Ministry was the easier to manipulate for being a relatively recent and inchoate organisation.

As prospects for a lasting peace receded with Hitler's consolidation of power, the British began to make plans for a future war;[135] among the preparatory measures was a report submitted in July 1936 to the Committee of Imperial Defence, laying the foundations of a propaganda organisation to be activated at short notice. This shadow Ministry was to be charged with the control and dissemination of information in the interests of 'presenting the national case' both abroad and (a responsibility denied to its First World War predecessor) at home. In marked contrast with its Nazi counterpart under Goebbels, it was a half-hearted and amateurish part-time organisation; and when war broke out and the Ministry was formally constituted, there was no magical transformation. Caught between the demands of the press for more information and the insistence of the Services that they be given less, and failing totally to understand the mood of the public in the early days of the war, the MoI rapidly developed an unrivalled reputation for irresolution and inefficiency.

One consequence of its lack of direction was, however, the scope it left for the forceful individual within it. Clark wrote, 'In this undirected orchestra it was necessary for each man to blow his own trumpet as loudly as he could.' His personal clarion call during the war was 'simply to keep artists at work on any pretext, and, as far as possible, to prevent them from being killed', and it was through the MoI, in pursuit of this end, that he was to initiate the rebirth of official war art.

There was a price to be paid. Like its predecessor, the MoI was essentially a propaganda organisation, and in adopting and financing official war art it had propaganda ends in view. Clark's priorities may have been elsewhere, but he had at least to pay lip-service to his employers' *raison d'être* and in 1940, in the attempt to justify the scheme to the Treasury, he wrote, 'We believed that we should be able to use the work produced as propaganda.'

The MoI's use of fine art in this way should not be seen in isolation. Efforts to exploit the persuasive power of painting had not ceased with the Armistice in 1918. The IWM's pictures, for example, were reproduced as illustrations for the spate of war books published at the end of the 1920s, and they were lent for exhibition both abroad and at home – most significantly perhaps as part of Portsmouth's Navy Week in August 1936. 'In response to recent events abroad',[136] a display of the pictures of the Admiralty artists was mounted to revive public interest in a Service which felt that since 1919 it had been allowed dangerously to decline, as a result of the widespread belief that the safety of the Empire would henceforth depend on air strength.

Fine art was also among the tools to be used, according to Sir Stephen Tallents (head of the Empire Marketing Board, 1928–30), in the development of a new art – 'the art of national projection', whose object was 'to throw a fitting presentation of England upon the world's screen', to bolster her political prestige and improve her trading position. Tallents's campaign, initiated in 1932 by the publication *The Projection of England*, contributed significantly to the establishment of the British Council in 1934.

[157]

The British Council was conceived to operate in a world at peace, but interestingly its Director, while emphasising that 'political propaganda' did not come within its sphere, nevertheless put his Fine Arts Committee at Macmillan's service in 1939, considering it better qualified than any other body to advise the MoI on the employment of artists: 'The British Council was formed to deal with cultural propaganda and . . . Fine Arts could not possibly be included under any other heading.' Macmillan preferred, however, the scheme already put to him by Kenneth Clark.

CHAPTER TWENTY-EIGHT

The War Artists' Advisory Committee

C LARK's intention was to produce a pictorial record of the war, to which as many artists as possible would contribute – an idea consciously derived from what he knew of the First World War schemes[137] – and on 29 August 1939 he approached the MoI with the suggestion that it appoint a committee to advise on the employment of artists to record the war. His contact within the Ministry was a man who was to prove a most effective ally in the effort to revive official war art, and a second Yockney in its subsequent administration: E. M. O'Rourke Dickey, a serious painter in his own right,[138] had been Professor of Fine Art at Durham for five years before becoming Staff Inspector of Art at the Board of Education in 1931 – acquiring invaluable insight into the civil service mind and a firm grasp of the niceties of bureaucratic procedure.

Even more fortuitously, when Clark's proposal reached the MoI's higher echelons, there to receive and foster it was Raymond Needham, erstwhile Secretary to Beaverbrook's MoI in the First World War, now serving briefly in this new MoI before being spirited away again to assist Beaverbrook at the Ministry of Aircraft Production.[139]

At the end of September, Needham and Clark met to discuss the scheme – by which time Clark was himself an employee of the MoI.[140] The proposal prospered and on 7 November Lord Macmillan gave his formal consent to the scheme. Opposition to the MoI's plans came, however, from the War Office and the Admiralty – each of which was cherishing independent ambitions. Unbeknownst to the MoI, both these Services had formulated plans of their own for employing artists – the Admiralty with a view to accumulating records, it was supposed, for the National Maritime Museum, and the War Office as part of its general programme of public relations.

At this point the initiative passed out of Clark's hands and into the realm of political rivalry between the new MoI and the old-established Services. Sensing an attempt to trespass on MoI preserves – 'Painting of war scenes is publicity and not news, and it ought therefore to be our responsibility and not that of the Service departments' – the Ministry's senior staff set out to persuade the Treasury (which fortunately had not as yet sanctioned any of the rival proposals) to give their approval only to a scheme which centralised the control of war art in the MoI.

The Treasury was inclined to consent, but in the face of stout resistance from both Services to a totally centralised scheme, a compromise was reached which was to prove fundamental to the shape and scope of the Second World War official war art collection. Each Service was to have attached to it the artists it had requested – four for the War Office and one for the Admiralty – and to pay their salaries.[141] However, Clark's committee was to have some say in their selection and in the direction of their work, and full control of the pictures and their ultimate destination. In addition, Clark's committee was to have a budget of £5000 of its own for its first year of operations.

The War Artists' Advisory Committee[142] met for the first time on 23 November 1939,

Sir Muirhead Bone aboard *HMS Victory*

with Clark in the chair and Dickey as its Secretary.[143] All three Services were represented[144] and, in addition, those wartime Ministries whose activities might reasonably be recorded in pictures – Supply, Home Security and War Transport. The Services representatives and the high-ranking civil servants were indispensable in providing facilities for artists at the scene of their assignments; and through them the WAAC was also on occasion made aware, on a purely informal basis,[145] of forthcoming events which might merit recording. However, the Committee's public image was shaped principally by its artist-members, to whose selection Clark had given careful thought; well aware of the jealousies his Government-funded Committee might inspire, he was anxious that its members should represent the widest possible spectrum of taste.

The first artist invited was Muirhead Bone,[146] an old friend whom Clark considered 'one of the most honest, warm-hearted and unselfish men I have ever known', and whose appointment served several purposes. Bone had not relaxed his efforts on behalf of other artists – working in the late '30s principally for refugees from Nazi Germany – and his tastes in art remained remarkably eclectic. In addition, he supplied the most obvious link possible with the First World War scheme; and his presence on the WAAC went far towards mollifying the IWM, which tended to resent its position on the periphery and welcomed the opportunity of expressing its views through Bone, who had been a Trustee since 1920.

P. H. Jowett, Sir William Rothenstein's successor as Principal of the Royal College of Art, was another obvious choice – a 'modest and liberal-minded man' who took an enthusiastic interest in the work of younger artists. The RCA was to stand in much the same relation to the second war art scheme as the Slade had done to the first, supplying from among its staff and pupils a remarkable proportion of the official artists. (Interestingly the IWM collection was located very close to the RCA for several years, whilst at the Imperial Institute.)

The Slade was, however, represented by its Professor, Tonks's successor, Randolph Schwabe (also a former war artist), after the evacuation of the RCA to Ambleside made Jowett's appearances unavoidably rare.

Both Clark and Dickey were anxious that the Royal Academy – 'a touchy body of old gentlemen', according to one senior member of the MoI – should be represented, if at all, on a purely individual, rather than an institutional basis, and Sir Walter Russell was approached – the Keeper of the Academy, but a mild and elderly man most unlikely to fight for the interests of its more aggressively reactionary members.[147]

Clark's success in creating the impression of a genuine diversity of opinion among his advisers is evident from the equally wide range of critical reaction to his Committee – the *Glasgow Herald* was anxious lest it confine itself exclusively to academic art, while *The Tatler* considered it 'so unequivocally advanced that it seems doubtful whether any painter whose technique and vision combine to interest, please, or inspire ordinary people will be chosen. . . . The real danger lies in its leaning towards the abstract school, familiarly called the upside down boys.'

The WAAC was, however, less entirely at liberty to indulge personal tastes than its critics suggested (and continue to suggest). Its terms of reference drawn up by the MoI were: 'To draw up a list of artists qualified to record the war at home and abroad. In co-operation with the Services Departments, and other Government Departments, as may be desirable, to advise on the selection of artists from this list for War purposes and on the arrangements for their employment. To advise on such questions as copyright, disposal and exhibition of works and the publication of reproductions.'

This emphasis on records effectively prevented the inclusion of much sculpture, whose function the Committee saw as largely memorial and, as such, more properly left until after the war. The members remained unconvinced by spirited representations from the Royal Society of British Sculptors, the Central Institute of Art and Design and from the individual sculptors,[148] as to the value of statuettes as records of uniform and equipment – 'Sculptors have tried to prove that they can make miniature groups of men round a gun etc., but the result is like toy soldiers which have not the advantage of being moveable' – and concluded, 'The only sculptured record which is appropriate to the moment is that of the portrait bust.' Commissions were accordingly offered to only a limited number of sculptors, including Epstein, Frank Dobson, John Skeaping, Charles Wheeler, William McMillan and C. W. Dyson Smith.

The Committee's terms of reference also helped, *The Tatler*'s apprehension notwithstanding, to discourage the use of artists whose work was wholly or largely non-representational, and these remained one of the few groups to be somewhat neglected in the Second World War scheme.

Clark made no secret of this fact, clearly setting out the Committee's position in an article in the *Studio*: 'The War Artists collection cannot be completely representative of modern English art, because it cannot include those pure painters who are interested solely in putting down their feelings about shapes and colours, and not in facts, drama, and human emotions generally. For this reason it contains no work by such distinguished painters as Matthew Smith, Frances Hodgkins, Ethel Walker, Ivon Hitchens, Ben Nicholson[149] and Victor Pasmore. It would be a pleasure to see the names of these fine painters among those of the War Artists, but it is very doubtful if they would do as good work on war subjects as they are continuing to do on the subjects which they have made their own.' Nor would such artists necessarily have been willing to abandon these subjects for war art: Henry Moore has remarked of those abstract artists he knew best, 'They didn't want to do it – why should they? They didn't want to connect their work with the war; their objective was to be *pure* artists, to be above emotion – once you begin to connect, then you're not pure.'

Moore was himself a borderline case, like Graham Sutherland, both being artists who before the war 'were producing work which departed very far from ordinary visual experiences, and so it seemed unlikely that they would make records which could be interpreted by posterity'. Clark considered their appointment 'the War Artists' Committee's boldest stroke'.

Few would quarrel with the success of the risks the Committee did take, but there has been criticism of its apparent unwillingness to give certain other more abstract and experimental artists the same opportunities – David Bomberg being the example most frequently cited. Bomberg's relationship with the WAAC was coloured by his extreme poverty during the war:[150] his first application in 1939 was one of literally hundreds he was to make to potential employers.[151] It is possible that the members were deterred by the non-representational aspects of his work (though Clark personally regretted the move away from his far more overtly abstract First World War style), but equally likely that they found his brand of expressionism unattractively violent, even incoherent. In any event, for over two years Bomberg received no commission, and relieved his feelings with a furious letter, ending: 'If I am forced out of my profession into either destitution or acceptance of dilutee labour . . . the responsibility for this must rest with the Artists' Advisory Committee in general and my professional colleagues on that Committee in particular.'

He was promptly offered a commission for 25 guineas to paint activities in an underground bomb store, and travelled to Burton-on-Trent at the beginning of April 1942. The subject he found 'rich with possibilities', and he was eager to pay tribute to 'the heroism of that kind of labour' in a large memorial panel, 120×144. However, not only was his proposal turned down but the commissioned oil was rejected as 'of inferior quality', the WAAC taking instead only three of the preliminary drawings.

This may show a lack of discernment on the Committee's part – in which case it was a failing that was widely shared, as Bomberg's later work is only now being favourably reappraised. Equally the members may have been alienated by his apparent assumption that he was owed a livelihood; even Bone, a supporter for over twenty years, seems to have lost patience: 'I'm afraid your Bomb Store work was unfortunate . . . the Committee seemed disappointed . . . a tough 51-year-old man like yourself should be able to get employment of some sort in these days!'

In its first sixteen weeks the Committee considered almost eight hundred names (many, though by no means all, put forward by the artists themselves), including all those artists employed under the First World War scheme. The majority of these veterans were rejected, or listed for employment but never used – among them Airy, Adeney, Cameron, Colin Gill, Japp, McBey, Noble, Spare and W. T. Wood, Lavery, Clausen and Stanhope Forbes, and virtually all the artists who had been employed by the RAF sub-committee – not only Wyllie, G. H. Davis and C. R. Fleming-Williams, but also Richard Carline, whom this time the Committee felt should not be taken away from his work in camouflage.

The saddest omission was perhaps Nevinson, who had continued to paint after the First World War in a more realistic and increasingly less inspired manner. An unfortunate, and extremely public, passing reference by Clark[152] to this decline prompted a vigorous response in the old style – Nevinson dismissing the remark as 'a judgment insulting, callous . . . unasked for, based on petty personality and ignorance of some Benighted Clerk'; the Committee rejected, nevertheless, the three pictures he submitted to it. He was profoundly and audibly mortified, and it was with some relief that the members found themselves able to purchase his record of the fire-bombing of the City at the end of 1940, *The Fire of London, December 29th – An historic record*. His feelings were further smoothed by an independent commission from the RAF[153] to cover the embarkation for the raid on Dieppe in August 1942. But further exchanges with the

David Bomberg, *An Underground Bomb Store* (charcoal), 21 × 26

Committee were forestalled by a severe stroke, doubtless precipitated by his insistence on serving, as in the First World War, as a stretcher-bearer.

Nevinson was determined against all odds to carry on. Pathetically, he applied for a minor clerical job as assistant to the WAAC Secretary, writing about other people's war art: 'Though an eye is lost,' he wrote, 'my hand is not and there is every hope of getting it right back.' The hopes were unfounded, however, and he learned to paint with his left hand; but in October 1946, protesting to the end, he died at the age of fifty-seven.

CHAPTER TWENTY-NINE

The Phoney War

THE compromise agreement reached between Treasury, Admiralty, War Office and WAAC at the end of 1939 provided the official war art scheme with its skeleton, in the shape of the full-time salaried artists attached to the two senior Services, plus the two subsequently allocated to the RAF. These artists could not be expected to produce anything other than Service subjects, in reasonably limited quantities; the WAAC's principal task was thus, within its separate budget, to flesh out the skeleton, both by supplementing the records of military life and by ensuring that non-military subjects were also covered.

From the beginning the Committee had three distinct methods of acquiring pictures. To a minority of artists – those who, in Eric Newton's[154] words, 'can be relied upon to do a workmanlike job under almost any conditions' – it offered the equivalent of a salaried post, commandeering their entire output on a variety of subjects over a fixed period in return for a fixed sum. To others – of the type of artist 'whose personality so strongly colours his work that it is important that his theme should be chosen for him from time to time' – the Committee gave separate commissions for specific subjects. Finally, it encouraged submissions from artists, professional or amateur, serving[155] or civilian, thus giving itself the opportunity of purchasing work by the artist 'who can only paint a war picture when he feels moved to do so'.

The members had in addition hoped to acquire works by means of invitations extended to the most eminent painters of the day, Sickert and John, on their own terms: respectful letters asked for 'any work you would like to carry out. . . .' They had, however, little more success with these artists than their First World War predecessors, one of whom, Lord Beaverbrook, warned them what to expect, from John at least – 'I cannot tell you what benefits I did not bestow on him. And do you know what work I got out of John? – Not a damned thing.'

Though Bone loyally persisted in bringing John's name before the Committee, as each successive attempt to pin him down failed the members concluded regretfully that he was 'so unreliable that they did not quite like the idea of commissioning him'. Sickert, now eighty, simply omitted to reply to the letter.

The fees the Committee offered were low – £300 was the maximum paid for a particularly large oil,[156] £150 or £200 more usual, 50 or 75 guineas for portraits, and prices of less than £10 not at all uncommon for watercolours or drawings. Such money as it had, the Committee wished to spread among as many artists as possible, and as evenly as possible: Bone was once again insistent on the importance of parity of treatment between old and young, famous and relatively obscure, and where practicable no exaggerated financial distinctions were made.

In its early days, the Committee approached its task by sorting the artists considered most eligible for employment according to the subject matter they seemed best qualified to depict.[157] These were, however, the most general of categories – 'figures in action at the front', 'subjects involving complicated technical draughtsmanship', and so on – and specific subjects proved rather more difficult to find in the period between the fall of Poland and the fall of France, known as the 'Phoney War' or 'Sitzkrieg'.

Perhaps for this reason, the first two artists to be commissioned from the WAAC's own funds were detailed to make portraits of military leaders, at home and in France – as safe a start as any, and valuable publicity. Neither assignment was conspicuously successful. Eric Kennington was commissioned in December 1939 for eight portraits, at 25 guineas a head, of 'the chiefs of the fighting Services' (partly, it would seem, with the precedent of Dodd's *Admirals and Generals* in mind, and with an eye to their mass reproduction as postcards). However, he failed to secure a sitting from Lord Gort, the BEF's C-in-C, and his portrait of the First Sea Lord, Sir Dudley Pound, was suppressed, at the request of the Admiralty, as 'not thought to be a sufficiently good likeness.' It was not until he was sent to Plymouth, where he found HMS *Exeter* in port, home from the River Plate, that he rediscovered what he considered his true *métier* – 'I'm a young warriors' artist' – and produced some of his best wartime portraits, pastel drawings of naval ratings.

The WAAC's second nominee had, like Kennington, largely established his reputation as a portraitist by his work for T. E. Lawrence on *The Seven Pillars of Wisdom*. William Roberts was commissioned to do six drawings of Corps Commanders, at 10 guineas each, and after finishing his picture of the Canadian Major-General McNaughton he should have gone to France to complete the set. However, after an unscheduled and miserably uncomfortable overnight delay in dock at Folkestone, he made the unilateral decision to abandon both ship and project, and went home. The War Office representative was very angry, afraid that Roberts's action would prejudice the chances for further artists in France, and the offender was sent off in disgrace to draw civilians – two workmen at Woolwich Arsenal, and the Minister of Labour, Ernest Bevin.[158]

In other areas the Committee's start was slow as it laboured to evolve an administrative routine, drawing up greatly extended lists of 'recommended' and 'reserve' artists, and casting around for subjects to give them. At home, during the Sitzkrieg, attention was largely focused on the preparations already made for passive defence against the devastating air attacks which military planners believed would open the war. One of the most obvious and emotive of these precautions was the evacuation of children from potential target areas, and the Committee sent lithographer Ethel Gabain to draw East End evacuees both at the railway stations and in their new rural homes.[159]

The work of the Air-Raid Precaution

R. V. Pitchforth (photograph reproduced by kind permission of Gerald Pitchforth)

Ethel Gabain, *The evacuation of children from Southend, Sunday, 2nd June, 1940* (lithograph), $12\frac{7}{8} \times 20\frac{1}{8}$

services in London was entrusted principally to Roland Vivian Pitchforth[160] – not without some apprehension, as Pitchforth, a graduate of the RCA and a member of the London Artists' Association, had been stone deaf since his service with the Wakefield Battery of the Royal Garrison Artillery in the First World War. However, once suitable precautions had been taken 'to prevent a good artist from being shot by an over-zealous sentry', Pitchforth's work, on ARP and a variety of other subjects, was one of the successes of the scheme, invariably received by the Committee with 'acclamation'. Such pictures as *A.F.S. Practice with a Trailer-Pump on the banks of the Serpentine* and *Anti-Aircraft Guns Under Construction* admirably captured the uneasy atmosphere of shadow-boxing before Dunkirk.

ARP activities in the provinces[161] seemed a suitable subject to offer Robert Medley[162] (himself an ARP warden) when, to the WAAC's intense embarrassment, MI5 refused him permission to go to France to depict the BEF's 'disembarkation points and base camps'. The reason given was unambiguous: the investigators alleged Medley to have been 'closely associated with subversive Communist doctrines for the last eight or ten years'. That this was clearly a case of mistaken identity made no difference, as MI5, despite being pressed by Clark, was not prepared to admit the error; the interview in which Dickey had to explain to Medley (without mentioning MI5) his sudden diversion to Grimsby was traumatic enough to ensure that all future names were submitted for vetting before appointment letters were issued.

One other obvious feature of the Phoney War was the rapid increase in munitions production, and the Committee sent Henry Rushbury, now one of the more vigorous RAs, to record the construction of new factories and the building of a naval gun – from the pouring of the ingot to the mounting of the finished weapon on the turret of a battleship. Having chosen him carefully for his skill in handling scenes of bustling activity, the Committee was dashed by Rushbury's dissatisfaction with the factory-building project: 'One of the things we particularly don't want to do is to give an artist a job that *doesn't* give him a pictorial chance.'

Meanwhile the Services had filled their salaried posts – and the first official artist in action, in this war as the last, was Muirhead Bone (who as full-time Artist to the Admiralty finally achieved the coveted crowns of an Honorary Major, RM). Bone had lost none of his eye for the compelling image, and his first drawing of HMS *Victory* in Portsmouth Yard was nicely gauged to appeal to popular sentiment – 'Nelson's Flagship stands as a symbol of the greatness of the Royal Navy.' Panoramas of the celebrations in honour of the Battle of the River Plate – the officers and men of HMS *Exeter* and HMS *Ajax* on parade at Whitehall and at the following Victory Luncheon in the Guildhall – were similarly stirring. He ran into trouble, however, with his pictures of the SS *Highlander*, a tiny merchant vessel which had somehow, with a light and hastily erected armament, brought down two German planes, one actually crashing in flames on her deck. Bone described the drawings as 'very good propaganda indeed' – but the wide publicity they received aroused real fears of direct reprisals against the ship, and at the Admiralty's request her name was changed.

At the beginning of June, Bone recorded the end of the Phoney War in *Dawn from the Signal Station, Dover* and *The Return from Dunkirk*. It was also the end of an expedition which, for all its frustrations and inactivity, had been given full coverage by the War Office, which chose to send to France all four of its salaried artists – Edward Ardizzone, Edward Bawden, Reginald Eves and Barnett Freedman.

Of the four, three were best known as illustrators, recommended to the War Office by the Committee perhaps with an eye to the obligation to ensure an intelligible commentary on proceedings. The exception was Eves: a Slade contemporary of Orpen and a protégé of Sargent, by 1939 he was their natural successor as one of the most successful of society portraitists. At sixty-four, he was an RA and, in the eyes of the *Daily Telegraph*, 'the doyen of the BEF artists', whose salary of £650 per annum was less than his peacetime fee for one canvas.

Freedman was from an altogether different background, a Polish Jewish immigrant's son, whose impoverished childhood in the East End was complicated by four years in hospital with a weak heart. Extreme determination, and the timely intervention of William Rothenstein, took him on a scholarship to the RCA; the period immediately afterwards he described in *Who's Who* as a time of starvation, but by the 1930s he had begun to make a name through his work on posters and promotional booklets for Shell and the GPO, and through his winning design for the George V Jubilee stamp. By 1939 he had achieved his greatest success as an illustrator, expert in both line drawing and colour lithography, with such publications as Sassoon's *Memoirs of an Infantry Officer* (1931), Borrow's *Lavengro* (1936) and Tolstoy's *War and Peace* (1938) to his credit; his painting was perhaps the least known aspect of his work.

Ardizzone had made a late start as an artist, taking up the profession full-time only in 1926 at the age of twenty-six, after six years as a statistics clerk for a telegraph company. By 1939 his work was familiar to a wide public, mainly through his drawings for the *Radio Times* and books for children which he both wrote and illustrated.[163]

Bawden was slightly younger than the others, born in 1903, the *annus mirabilis* of twentieth-century British art (his coevals including Richard Eurich, Thomas Hennell, Barbara Hepworth, Robert Medley, John Piper, Eric Ravilious, Ceri Richards and Graham Sutherland). He had begun to establish himself while still at the RCA (where he studied calligraphy and book illustration) with poster commissions for Shell and London Transport; and the murals, commissioned in 1928 by Morley College, which he executed in collaboration with Eric Ravilious, were widely admired.[164] In 1932 he moved to Great Bardfield, Essex, and developed as a watercolourist of rural landscapes; but he continued to experiment with various forms of applied art – most notably wallpaper design – and at the outbreak of war his reputation was primarily that of a distinguished designer and illustrator, and stalwart of the Curwen Press.

For Eves, the Phoney War in France provided ideal conditions, as his sitters – Alanbrooke, Auchinleck, Alexander and even Gort – had little else to do at the outset and were happy to present themselves for painting in his hotel room at Arras, home of the British Headquarters in France. However, the stalemate had nothing to offer the other three artists: their guided tour of First World War trenches ('to induce the right mood for the occasion') was a clear sign both that the PR staff (to whom the war artists were attached) had little idea what to do with them, and that there was perhaps some uncertainty about the nature of the forthcoming conflict.

Certainly Freedman and Bawden were both sent to record defensive preparations which in the event proved entirely futile. Freedman travelled to Thélus, thirty miles north of Arras, to record the construction of a runway, and Bawden to Halluin to watch the 5th Manchester Regiment hastily erecting blockhouses on the Belgian border. Ardizzone attached himself to a fighting unit, as was to be his wont, and found slightly more promising material in the routine life of ordinary soldiers; with the 300th Highland Artillery battery at Merris, near Bailleul, he produced such pictures as *Pulling Off the Padre's Boots* and *GHQ Has a Nice Taste in Forage Caps*.

These three, the first artists to be faced with the problem of identifying their subjects on a fighting front, found themselves in limbo, exposed by their nondescript General Service badges to constant challenge, even arrest by the Army ('I was terrified of being shot as a 5th columnist,' protested Freedman), and automatically equated with press photographers, hustled round to see 'news' events singularly lacking in pictorial scope. Their dissatisfaction was expressed most forcibly to the WAAC by Freedman – too forcibly perhaps for the good of the cause. Freedman's friends describe him with great affection as sympathetic, funny and stimulating, with 'an enormous voice, a fund of good stories, the cheek of the devil and a great charm of manner': they accepted, even admired, as part of the whole his undoubted belligerence. The War Office representative was, however, much less ready to be amused.

[168]

Reginald Eves, *General the Viscount Gort, VC, GCB, CBE, DSO, MVO, MC* (oil on canvas), 20 × 16

The complaints finally became superfluous on 10 May when the Germans invaded Belgium and Luxemburg. The war artists ceased to be a source of perplexity and became a positive nuisance, bundled from one unit to another and finally left to fend for themselves. Of the three,[165] Ardizzone was the most closely in contact with events as British forces advanced into Belgium to meet the threat:[166] he accompanied the triumphal progress into Brussels through crowds weeping with relief and piling the jeeps with

Edward Ardizzone, *The bombing of GHQ, Boulogne, May 1940* (watercolour), $14\frac{1}{2} \times 22$

lilac blossom. Then, as the BEF retreated in a desperate attempt to get out of the trap which had been set for it, he and the other war artists made their separate ways with difficulty to the coast.

Ardizzone and Freedman found themselves in Boulogne on the night that GHQ was bombed; Ardizzone recorded the scene on the sea-front, with the bodies being carried out of the shattered building by the mingled light of the moon and a burning car, to lie grotesquely on the steps of a small bandstand. Two days later he was on his way home in an overcrowded and antiquated cross-Channel steamer – Freedman following two hours behind in an ammunition boat, having gone back to the hotel at the last moment to rescue the one oil he had done with the BEF.[167] His last meal in France, according to Ardizzone, consisted of 'three bottles of champagne and one tin of bully-beef taken sitting by himself on the railway lines at the quayside.'

Further up the coast at Dunkirk, Bawden, marching in with the troops, had to run the gauntlet of French soldiers lining the roads to jeer. Once in the town he made not for the beaches but for the docks, where he stayed for two eventful days, gathering impressions and making notes of the confused and extraordinary scenes as thousands of troops embarked under constant shell-fire and strafing.[168] Urged to embark himself, he refused: 'I didn't feel it was time for me to buzz off yet. . . . Most of the time I spent lying down under privet bushes in a small park, or dodging about. I remember feeling curiously calm, probably because I react rather slowly – my flashpoint is a high one.' Forced to abandon everything else, he preserved intact the drawings he had made in France: 'Like a soldier, I had to keep my only weapon.'

CHAPTER THIRTY

The War in the Air

RELATIONS between the art administrators and the Services were generally smooth during the Second World War; such problems as there were came mainly, as in the First World War, from the RAF or its civilian representatives in the Air Ministry. Here there were no pretensions to artistic expertise, and unlike their counterparts in the War Office and Admiralty, the Air Ministry made no moves to appoint its own artists. Nevertheless, the RAF had the clearest possible ideas of what it wanted out of the war art scheme once established; of the three Services it was by far the most avid for the kind of publicity the pictures might bring.

Between the wars, its independent existence as the junior Service had been consistently challenged by its seniors, and functional Commands – Fighter, Bomber and Coastal – had been established only in 1936.[169] It now had, besides its operational goals, two main aims – to bolster internal morale and esprit de corps (partly to compensate for undeniable deficiencies in organisation and training) and, apparently in this order, to make the RAF known to the general public.

Thus in its art priority was given to individual portraits, often of a kind that the Committee as a whole eschewed, much stress being laid on the 'gentlemanliness' of a force which had regularly been described by the other Services as 'motor mechanics in uniform'.[170] The Air Ministry displayed a fondness for the dramatic reconstruction, and insisted on technical accuracy – and to these ends it was prepared, as the Committee was not, to utilise commercial artists and more or less gifted amateurs within the RAF's ranks.

The divergence between the RAF and the WAAC was demonstrated clearly and immediately in the fate of the first two RAF artists appointed on the Committee's recommmendation – Keith Henderson and Paul Nash. Henderson, a Scot, was sent to Leuchars to cover Scottish Coastal Command, but found on arrival that he had been preempted. William Rothenstein at sixty-seven had a serious heart condition and his work was, in the Committee's opinion at least, no longer of the standard required for an official appointment. However, his enthusiasm and courage were undimmed and earned him personal invitations from station commanders: at the beginning of December 1939 he set off on a prolonged tour of aerodromes throughout Britain. Rothenstein produced an inordinate number of portrait drawings of both officers and men – with the result that Henderson, in April, found most of his intended subjects already covered, apparently with the Air Ministry's blessing. He felt compelled to concentrate largely on 'views' and hangar scenes (*Petrol Bowsers*, *Ascent of the Met Balloon*, and so on); the Air Ministry were 'disappointed', and his appointment was terminated after six months. Henderson was a modest and genial man, and he was able to take this rebuff lightheartedly; not so Paul Nash, who was going through perhaps the least happy period of his life.

Keith Henderson, *An improvised test of an under-carriage* (oil on canvas), 30 × 40

Nash was chronically ill with bronchial asthma – exacerbated by anxiety about money – and his demands on the Committee were incessant. His illness and perhaps his financial position confined him largely to a ground-floor flat in Oxford – 'this Rip van Winkle paradise' – which bored and depressed him. An observer of war at the closest possible range in 1917 and 1918, he was now forced to construct his first pictures for the WAAC principally from photographs,[171] assisted occasionally by visits to aerodromes but never by actual experience of flight. Being a long-time champion of photography as an aid and complement to contemporary art,[172] he saw nothing untoward in this – and certainly the Committee were delighted by the pictures which resulted, 'the best work sent in so far by any artist'.

    The first pictures, submitted in August 1940, were a series of watercolours entitled 'Raiders', crashed German planes, each against a characteristic Nash setting – the beaches at Swanage and Dymchurch, the slopes beneath Silbury Hill, and so on. These were designed to emphasise the incongruity of the alien machines, helpless out of their element, in the idyllic English landscape[173] – a device which provoked from John Piper the comment: 'For a long time his ideal pictorial topic has been the object in the wrong box, that in some way turned out to be the inevitable box.'

'Raiders' were followed in September 1940 by a series of 'Aerial Creatures', the working-out in watercolour of Nash's theories on the personality of planes.[174] Machines and not men, he claimed, were the real protagonists in this war – machines which, once activated, had virtually an independent life, with moods of their own, and the characteristics of the living creatures which they resembled – the long-nosed Blenheim a shark, the Hampden a pterodactyl, the Wellington a whale ('jolly . . . on the plump side'), the Whitley a 'dove of death'; and he painted what he described as 'portraits' of them in their 'lairs', 'sunning', 'watching the skies', 'at play'.[175]

This combination of whimsy and an unsporting tendency to gloat over the fallen enemy appealed to the Air Ministry very little at a time when the Battle of Britain pilots were the nation's heroes.[176] The RAF had come, quite deservedly, to the forefront, and it was felt that Nash, with an avowed lack of interest in either the men operating the planes or the actual structure of the planes themselves, was hardly the man to turn such celebrity to advantage. The termination of his appointment in October 1940 hurt Nash's pride, threatened his finances, and frustrated his sincere patriotism.

His selection had been, in Eric Newton's words, 'rather like asking T. S. Eliot to write

Paul Nash, *The Messerschmitt in Windsor Great Park* (pencil, chalks and watercolour), $15\frac{3}{4} \times 22\frac{3}{4}$, (Tate Gallery)

a report on the Louis-Farr fight', and Clark, though contemptuous of the Air Ministry's decision, was not surprised by it; henceforth any attempt to impose advanced tastes upon the RAF was abandoned. The proposal that its art budget should be devoted to a plurality of small commissions, easier to control than a salaried appointment, was resisted; but succeeding salaried artists were far more to the Air Ministry's liking.

Of the two artists on salary to the RAF at any one time, one was always to be a portraitist; and the first of these, Eric Kennington, with his apparently irresistible compulsion to portray the heroic fighting man,[177] gave the RAF precisely what it wanted. He considered many of the early pictures by other war artists 'little pretty pretties . . . by children for children', and he supplied instead a constant stream of over-life-size pastels – of bomber pilots, fighter pilots (including both Douglas Bader and Richard Hillary), parachutists and glider personnel, depicted with an unbridled admiration which, though it was in tune with the popular mood, some critics found positively sinister: 'The violence of Mr Kennington's style', wrote Raymond Mortimer, 'seems to me as hysterical as the eloquence of Hitler.'[178]

Kennington's portraits (many of whose sitters were dead before the Committee received their likenesses) were circulated by way of a moral tonic to RAF messes; his portraits of Allied pilots, including the American volunteers of the Eagle Squadrons, were exhibited in their sitters' countries – but there was no wider publicity, despite Kennington's demands, and in September 1942 he resigned in protest.

Curiously, he was replaced by A. R. Thomson, a portraitist whose skills were not in doubt, but whose disability – he was deaf-mute – had in 1940 been considered to disqualify him. Now, without any explanation of the change of heart, he was sent to paint bomber crews, and achieved a large number of portraits – his most distinctive contribution being a series of West Indian aircrew – before the Air Ministry found itself once again 'disappointed'.[179]

Thomson's successor was William Dring, an exceptionally hard worker, who was nonetheless slightly overwhelmed by 'what appear to be several acres of heroic young men', both with the 2nd Tactical Air Force and the Rocket Typhoon Wing in France and Belgium after the Normandy invasion.[180]

To depict the machines, the Air Ministry replaced Paul Nash with Charles Cundall. Cundall served as an RAF salaried artist from the beginning of 1941 until the end of the war,[181] and his pictures record the rearming of Bomber Command – the twin-engined Hampdens and Whitleys being gradually supplanted in his paintings by the heavier four-engined Short Stirlings, and, subsequently, Lancasters. He was a conscientious, accurate and accomplished recorder upon whom the Air Ministry could depend to portray RAF activities in an acceptable manner, and he was used flexibly – to document the US Air Station in Windsor Great Park[182] and the RAF Morse School at Blackpool; the arrival of American Flying Fortresses and Liberators in Northern Ireland, and of airborne casualties from France after D-Day. Cundall had been known before the war as a chronicler of national events, and he delighted the Air Ministry with his painting of the Battle of Britain parade in front of Buckingham Palace in 1943.

The work of the RAF salaried artists was supplemented by specific commissions made by the WAAC – for pictures of aircraft manufacture by Raymond McGrath and John Ensor; of maintenance and test flights by Vivian Pitchforth; of aerodrome buildings

Eric Kennington, *Squadron-Leader D. R. S. Bader, DSO, DFC,* (pastel), $24\frac{3}{4} \times 17\frac{1}{4}$

Alan Sorrell, *Up in the morning early: RAF Camp, 1941* (tempera on paper), $13\frac{3}{4} \times 15$, (Tate Gallery)

and life in the rapidly mushrooming hutted camps by Alan Sorrell; of aeroplanes in flight – *Southern England 1944: Spitfires attacking flying bombs, Fighter Affiliation* and so forth – by Thomas Monnington, RA.

Especial pains were taken to compile a record of the balloon barrage which protected important ground targets against low-level attack. Several paintings were bought from the exhibition held at the National Portrait Gallery by artists working in Balloon Command,[183] and in November 1941 and February 1942 the Committee made what the Air Ministry considered two of its most felicitous commissions. By 1940, Dame Laura Knight was 'one of the most publicised artists of the first half of the century'; she was also among the very best of the realists, painting 'jolly subjects in a fine fresh hefty way'. For the Air Ministry she painted *In for Repairs* – WAAFs at work on a partially inflated balloon 'like a great silver toad with a pulse in all its sides' – and *A Balloon Site, Coventry*. She considered these pictures, which were done for a fraction of her usual fee, two of her best, and they were among the most popular of the war. (*In for Repairs* even received the accolade of a parody in the *Daily Express*.)[184]

In its pursuit of a fitting artistic record, the Air Ministry also acquired works outside the official scheme – to the irritation of Kenneth Clark, who wrote to Nash: 'The Services are supposed to buy their pictures through us. . . . The only Service to break this rule is the Air Force, which thinks that our taste is too modern and likes to go off on its own.' There is evidence of at least two RAF art ventures over which the WAAC had no influence: a fund of £2000 was privately subscribed from which pictures were purchased for officers' messes in the new Air Ministry buildings; and several serving airmen artists – among them H. W. Hailstone, Julius Stafford-Baker and Frank Wootton – appear to have been transferred from their ordinary duties to draw and paint full-time. Their pictures were realistic, often dramatic, always technically correct, and several were purchased by the Committee to bridge gaps in its pictorial history of the war.[185]

Meanwhile Paul Nash, now employed (at Clark's instigation) to work for the WAAC under the auspices of the MoI,[186] was producing what are generally considered the best aerial paintings of the war, comparable, in Clark's view at least, with the major commemorative pictures of the First World War. Ironically he had very much the same end in view as that of his erstwhile employers – 'to strike a blow on behalf of the RAF, apart from any triumph of art for its own sake.' Nash was one of the foremost advocates of the use of fine art as propaganda[187] – 'appealing to the eye quickly, striking and leaving an impression before any power can prevent the impact.' He carried out a

W. T. Monnington, *Southern England, 1944: Spitfires attacking flying-bombs* (oil on canvas), $40\frac{1}{2} \times 55\frac{1}{2}$

number of overtly propagandist works for the MoI's General Production Division –
among them the three 'Follow the Fuehrer' collages (*Above the Clouds*, *Under the Water*
and *Over the Snows*)[188] and a series of photo-montages entitled 'Evil Growths',[189]
designed for use in Latin-American shop windows. However, he was equally anxious
for the paintings he executed for the WAAC to be deployed in the national interest
– 'I would get *inside* this business and frighten someone or bust!'

His intentions were quite obvious in his first large oil, *'Totes meer'* (*Dead Sea*)*,[190]
which he worked up from photographs of crashed German planes after visits at night
to the Cowley dump. By the light of the waning moon the contours of the heaped
wreckage had been briefly metamorphosed into a metallic inundation, 'a vast tide moving across the fields, the breakers rearing up and crashing on the plain', before freezing
again into a lifeless sea of scrap iron. 'The only moving creature is the white owl flying
low over the bodies of the other predatory creatures, raking the shadows for rats and
voles.' *'Totes meer'* was also a 'sea of death', death of both the aerial creatures and
their pilots, and Nash urged that its message of victory over the invader be broadcast
as widely as possible – 'Don't you think it would make a good reproduction for depressing the Nazis?' – accompanied by running totals of the enemy planes brought down.
He also made a photo-montage out of *'Totes meer'*, superimposing the images of a corpse
and the head of Hitler.[191]

Nash took seriously his status as one of the leaders of a British school of painting;
he may also have felt obliged to emulate his own success as an artist in the First World
War. In any event his approach to the recording of the war in the air was both systematic and ambitious. Almost his first act in the employ of the RAF had been to order
a huge canvas, 120×180, in which to encapsulate the Service's activities.[192] He seems
also to have intended from the start to complete one large oil and one or more series
of watercolours of each of the RAF Commands and of their antagonists.[193]

With *'Totes meer'* and the two series, 'Raiders' and 'Marching against England', Nash
had disposed of the enemy. Now he turned to Fighter Command, and in *Battle of Britain,
August–October, 1940*[194] presented 'an epitome' of the previous summer's struggle
– RAF fighters sweeping along the Channel to break up an advancing Luftwaffe formation, in a hot summer sky festooned with vapour trails and parachutes.[195] His aim
was an imaginative rather than a literal summing up – 'Facts here, both of science
and nature are . . . respected only in so far as they suggest symbols for the picture
plan' – and Clark, in entire sympathy, congratulated him on his success: 'It is impossible to paint great events without allegory. . . . You have discovered a way of making
the symbols out of the events themselves.'

To symbolise the activities of Coastal Command, Nash chose a Sunderland flying-
boat sinking a U-boat off the Dorset coast, where 'white Portland stone is quarried
to rebuild what the Luftwaffe have tried to destroy of Albion'. In *Defence of Albion*[196]
the 'personality of planes' motif made its final appearance; as the emblem of defensive
attack, the Sunderland (popularly known as the 'Flying Porcupine' because of its bristling armament) was, for Nash, 'a beast as important as the Lion or the Unicorn in
relation to Britain'. He was hampered by having seen neither Sunderland nor U-boat
in life (having been prevented from making a special journey to the coast by a bad
bronchial attack), and he wrote a little pathetically to Eric Ravilious in January 1942

asking him to describe 'the colour of a Sunderland against a dark background with a low sun shining across the sea against a cliff'.

Nevertheless the incident he was attempting to depict excited him – 'It's the *Boy's Own Paper* all right!' – and in the finished picture he felt he had achieved something – 'There is a good deal of *volume*. The "goings on" as it were of *Battle of Britain* are equivalent to a lightweight activity . . . compared with *Defence of Albion*, which is decidedly *cruiserweight* . . . [a] regular dust up.'

Nash's final oil – a synthesis of Bomber Command activity over Germany – was painted 'under positively excruciatingly exasperating circumstances'. His health was rapidly deteriorating, and he was unable to glean from photographs the documentary evidence he needed to fuel his imagination. He was obliged to rely instead upon verbal descriptions, studying official reports closely and asking to be put in touch with 'some intelligent airman' experienced in night bombing; arguably the far greater degree of abstraction evident in *Battle of Germany*[*197] is, in part at least, the result of this dearth of pictorial material.

This final picture was the product of much reflection: deprived of the necessary working conditions Nash had 'painted it in my mind a dozen times'. Explaining it to Clark, he wrote, 'The moment of the picture is when the city, lying under the uncertain light of the moon, awaits the blow at her heart. In the background a gigantic column of smoke rises . . . these two objects, pillar and moon, seem to threaten the city no less than the flights of bombers even now towering in the red sky. . . . The other half of the picture shows the opening of the bombardment. . . . Here forms are used quite arbitrarily and colours by a kind of chromatic percussion with one purpose, to suggest explosion and detonation.'

In September 1942 Nash said of *Battle of Germany*, 'If it comes off it might be the best thing I have done of any kind.' Less than six months later he was describing it as 'that painting which no one save its author and a few of the very young seem to care for'. After *Battle of Britain* the Committee's reception of his work would seem progressively to have cooled.[198] In *Defence of Albion*, in order to express the 'more than mechanical' character of the Sunderland and emphasise its quasi-animal individuality he had distorted its true shape, giving it an exaggeratedly large tail-fin. Clark quite correctly anticipated opposition from the Air Ministry: 'People are used to artists changing the proportion of landscape and even figures, but there is something sacred about the nicely calculated proportions of an aircraft.' But much to his own chagrin and that of Nash, it was Clark himself who objected to *Battle of Germany* for 'the (to my eye) different planes of reality in which it is painted. . . . Alas, I can't understand it . . . it is sad to find oneself so little able to appreciate what is new. . . . I am a natural blimp, must grow accustomed to my moustache.'

Nash, tired and disappointed, turned his attention entirely to other occupants of the inhabited sky – sun, moon, and aerial flowers. In February 1945, pressed by the MoI to account for the expenditure of some £6 on the transit of *Battle of Germany* he burst out, 'There isn't time left in my life to explain.' On the night of 10 July 1946 he died peacefully in his sleep. He left behind him an essay, 'Aerial Flowers',[199] which ended with the words, 'Death, I believe, is the only solution to this problem of how to fly. Personally I feel that if death can give us that, death will be good.'

CHAPTER THIRTY-ONE

Blitz and Baedeker

O N the evening of 7 September 1940, the Luftwaffe switched its attack from the battered airfields of the RAF to the major centres of civilian population, and the Blitz began. Sustained and heavy bombing continued, day and night, until May 1941 when the bombers were diverted to the Russian Front; however, raids were to persist at intervals until very nearly the end of the war.

One effect of the Blitz was to render less meaningful the distinction obvious in the First World War between 'artists at the front' and 'artists at home'; John Nash has recalled the sense of superiority felt in 1918 by the soldier-artists over those who had been left behind to record 'the knitting of woolly garments'. Now every artist in the cities of Britain was exposed daily to scenes of violent death and the devastation of property, experiences which could be equally a menace or a stimulus to his art.

Several of the official artists found themselves without studios, among them Henry Moore, Henry Carr and Carel Weight (who in addition lost all his early work). Frank Dobson's portrait bust of the C-in-C, Portsmouth, left overnight in the ballroom of the old Admiralty building where he was working on it, was reduced to the semblance of 'a deflated football'; and all trace of Mervyn Peake's first published work was obliterated when the entire edition of *Captain Slaughterboard Drops Anchor* was destroyed in

Auxiliary Firemen: Bernard Hailstone and Leonard Rosoman to the left

a warehouse fire. Ardizzone's home in Maida Vale received 'a near hit', and Freedman, bereft of the top floor of his Kensington house, begged the WAAC to procure him an Anderson shelter so that he could work at night in his basement with an untroubled mind. Francis Dodd, south of the river, recorded the worst alarums: 'Fritz dropped a lot of turnips about last night and one landed just *outside* my studio . . . his new dodge of parachute bombs is the v. devil for they are silent and v. v. large – one 8ft high not $\frac{1}{2}$ mile from here. . . .'

A large number of painters were actively involved in combatting the consequences of the bombing – like Nevinson, as stretcher-bearers, or in other branches of civil defence. Wherever possible they recorded their first-hand experiences, and at exhibitions of work by Firemen Artists and Civil Defence Artists the WAAC purchased

[180]

Matvyn Wright, *A parachute bomb* (oil on canvas), 20 × 30

pictures and took note of names for future employment – among them Bernard Hailstone,[200] Norman Hepple, Matvyn Wright and Leonard Rosoman. Rosoman's painting
A House Collapsing on Two Firemen, Shoe Lane, London EC4, purchased in August 1941,
became particularly well-known and widely praised; it depicts two of his colleagues
in the shadow of a falling wall, the moment before they were crushed and killed by
the red-hot rubble, a death which he himself barely escaped. He now dislikes the picture
intensely, criticising it as 'sentimental and superficial' in its uncontrolled emotion. In
his later work for the WAAC, Rosoman was much preoccupied with the machinery
and equipment of warfare – a reaction perhaps against the vulnerability of the human
protagonists.

'The background to this war, corresponding to the Western Front in the last war,
is the bombed city,' wrote Stephen Spender. On every side extraordinary subjects, from
the sublime to the grotesque, presented themselves for painting, prompting a wave
of submissions to the WAAC for purchase; and the Committee made its own more
systematic arrangements for recording the phenomenon of the Blitz.

The first weeks of raids had produced a remarkable crop of civilian heroes – firemen,
policemen, tanker drivers, ARP wardens, and nurses – and the Committee detailed
several artists to make portraits of those decorated for valour. Among them A. R.
Thomson, ARA, revelled most obviously in the work, finding in his sitters, often shy
and overawed, an inspiration all too often lacking in his peacetime models. Of the
sixteen-year-old despatch rider, Charity Bick, GM, he wrote, 'That Grace Darling . . .
shone as she sat. . . . Next time I would go anywhere to paint another one.' Anthony
Devas, one of the most successful of the WAAC's portraitists, was equally enthusiastic

A. R. Thomson, *Miss Charity Bick, GM, of West Bromwich, the youngest woman Civil Defence worker to be decorated with the George Medal, 1941* (oil on canvas), 36×28

OPPOSITE, John Armstrong, *Coggeshall Church, Essex* (tempera on wood), $22\frac{1}{2} \times 15$, (Tate Gallery)

about his rather more formidable subject, the Matron of Charing Cross Hospital, *Miss M. S. Cochrane, RRC, SRN*, 'the sort of woman who goes on down the ages – one can imagine her painted by Rembrandt, Hals or Goya'.[201]

Unbeknown to the WAAC, among their civil defence portraits they acquired a memorial to one of the architects of official war art – Wellington House's Chief Executive Ernest Gowers, now Sir Ernest Gowers KCB, KBE, Senior Regional Commissioner for Civil Defence in the London Region. The picture, by Meredith Frampton, was made into a group portrait (the first Frampton had painted for twenty years) after Gowers pointed out, with characteristic modesty, the absurdity of his appearing to run London's civil defence on his own; it captures, in detail so immaculate as to be faintly surreal, the atmosphere and paraphernalia of the Regional Control Room, half underground in the space between the Geological and Natural History Museums in Exhibition Road.[202]

Inevitably, some elements are absent from the WAAC's record of the Blitz. There

Meredith Frampton, *Sir Ernest Gowers, KCB, KBE, Lieutenant-Colonel A. J. Child, OBE, MC, and K. A. L. Parker, in the ARP Control Room* (oil on canvas), $58\frac{1}{8} \times 66\frac{1}{4}$

OPPOSITE, Sir Muirhead Bone, *St Bride's and the City after the Fire, 29th December, 1940* (chalk and pen), $77\frac{7}{8} \times 44\frac{1}{8}$

are no pictures of looting or riots, of the mass trekking away from the bombed areas, or of the displays of anti-Semitism not uncommon in the shelters. (There is, perhaps, a whiff of the controversial in Feliks Topolski's *A West End Luxury Hotel, October 1940*, with its fat, befurred figures repairing to comparative comfort underground, in marked contrast to his *The Salvation Army in the East End of London*.)[203] Corpses are occasionally apparent, but no shock cases, and panic among civilians was not considered a fit subject for acquisition. Carel Weight's much praised picture of a trolley-bus threatened by a swooping Messerschmitt, its passengers (the artist among them) not unnaturally scurrying for cover, was found 'unacceptable' by the Committee; Weight was, however, encouraged to recreate, in a series of four vignettes, the flight of a panic-stricken zebra from the Zoo.[204]

In compiling its record of the charred and twisted buildings of Britain's bombed cities, the WAAC's main concern was to hurry artists to the scenes of devastation before the clearance and salvage workers had a chance to spoil the aesthetic effect: 'It is our experience that damage by bombing is most spectacular when seen soon after the event.' Muirhead Bone was summoned from the west coast of Scotland to depict the ruins of the City after the catastrophic incendiary raid of 29 December 1940.[205] The resulting drawing, *St Bride's and the City after the Fire*, is one of the principal *tours de force* of the Second World War scheme – an enormous ($77\frac{7}{8} \times 44\frac{1}{8}$) and microscopically accurate perspective in pen and chalk, with St Paul's Cathedral its focal point – 'the kind of document one would produce as evidence before a commission on bomb damage'. The Cathedral also proved an irresistible subject for Duncan Grant. 'I know you have painted St Paul's a great many times,' encouraged Clark, 'but . . . I don't think it has ever looked more beautiful rising out of this sort of Pompeii in the foreground.'

Pitchforth, one of the most versatile of the WAAC's artists, proved so successful in documenting air-raid damage (in pictures such as *Demolition Workers, Oxford Street, London W1* and *Sunday Morning, Great Titchfield Street, London W1*), that in December 1940 he was given a six-month salaried MoI appointment specifically to cover subjects for the Ministries of Home Security and Supply. One of his first subjects was the havoc wrought at the headquarters of the GPO and the surrounding area of the City. In March 1941 he wrote that work on these topics was proceeding smoothly, but that he wanted to do 'a much larger drawing of "lift shafts" sprawling across the City. They look like dead prehistoric animals lying over the jagged walls. I met Sutherland and Moore scouting round last week, very excited, so I hope they will soon bring you something very good.'[206]

Pitchforth did his 'lift shaft' picture – but it was to be Sutherland who made the subject his own. In 1940 he was thirty-seven, self-described as an 'etcher and painter', and at this time a guest of Kenneth Clark at his house in Gloucestershire. His name was added to the WAAC's list of recommended artists in February 1940,[207] but because he was working towards a one-man show at the Leicester Galleries, he received no commission until 5 June 1940.

This was originally for two drawings, at 25 guineas, of the 'transport by rail of armaments and aeroplanes under net', but it was not met to the letter, the Committee being satisfied instead by *Breech-blocks in the shop at gun-testing range* (based on material

R. V. Pitchforth, *Post Office buildings: the Telephone Exchange* (watercolour), $21\frac{1}{2} \times 30$

from an earlier visit to a site in Melton Mowbray) and *Picketed Aircraft No 1*.[208]

His second commission, dated 3 August 1940, was more auspicious, being simply an instruction on behalf of the Ministry of Home Security to 'stand by to make pictures of debris and damage caused by air-raids', sporadic bombing, mainly of industrial targets, having already started in the provinces.[209] This commission was for 50 guineas, and Sutherland enquired how much work would be expected in return. Dickey's response reveals one of the traits which made the WAAC attractive in most artists' eyes – its flexibility: 'Our plan has been to leave it more or less to the artists to produce what they think is fair ... and to get the work done at the pace which suits them best.' (This arrangement also had the advantage, by putting artists effectively on their honour, of extracting far more work from them than could have been procured by a more straightforward commercial transaction.)

Sutherland was to go to Cardiff and Llantwit Major – for which he was provided, exceptionally, with petrol coupons, in response to his plea that, 'Trains and other public vehicles are liable to give me a mild form of claustrophobia, irritating enough to put me in a fuss from a work point of view.' By 4 September Sutherland had abandoned Cardiff as 'the damage there was slight' and worked his way along the South Wales coast as far as Swansea. He eventually delivered seven gouaches, a folio of studies and one oil painting (for which the Committee paid an extra £35) commenting, 'The subjects cover a wide range – Farm House, Masonic Hall, Hospital, Private House, Workers' Houses, plus some drawings of individual and domestic elements of debris. Some of the final drawings . . . I have completed within reach of the "motif" as the complexity of the subject necessitated constant reference. . . . Doing the scenes of devastation I have found most absorbing.'

The beginning of the Blitz over London was to give Sutherland virtually unlimited material of this kind on an immeasurably grander scale. With effect from 1 January 1941, he was made an MoI salaried artist at £325 for six months,[210] a period spent, despite the original intention that he should work equally on Supply subjects, entirely in the City and the East End.

Sutherland saw the devastation of London when the first onslaught was over and the second had not begun, in the lull that followed the great fire-raid on the City, when the brunt of the assault was being borne by provincial centres. In the first few weeks of his appointment he spent occasional nights in the capital – with friends, at hotels, and once or twice at the heart of the devastated area, with the firewatchers in St Paul's, sleeping fitfully in one of the deckchairs ranged round the Gallery at the base of the Dome.

In 1971 he reconstructed his impressions of the scene for the poet Edwin Mullins: 'Those extraordinary first encounters: the silence, the absolute dead silence, except every now and again a thin tinkle of falling glass. . . . Everywhere there was a terrible stench – perhaps of burnt dirt; and always the silence. . . . Very occasionally there would be the crash of a building collapsing of its own volition.'

Against this eerie background, the shapes assumed by the towering office buildings in their fall made a deep impression on Sutherland. Like Pitchforth, he saw animal features in the contorted lift shafts: 'Their movements were animal movements. One shaft in particular . . . suggested a wounded tiger in a painting by Delacroix.' Inside one of the shattered buildings, a factory for ladies' coats, looking up he saw the machines: 'their entrails hanging through the floors . . . looking extraordinarily beautiful'.

He found the City, above all else, exciting; in the East End and the docks the atmosphere became 'much more tragic'. 'In the City one didn't think of the destruction of life. All the destroyed buildings were office buildings and people weren't in them at night. But in the East End one did think of the hurt to people. . . . Even a mattress that had been blown out of a house into the middle of the street looked more like a body. . . . From butchers' shops which had been hit the meat spewed onto the road.' Here it was the skeletons of whole streets which haunted him, 'the shells of long terraces of houses . . . great – surprisingly wide – perspectives of destruction seeming to recede into infinity, the windowless blocks were like sightless eyes.'

The East End also alerted him to the understandable hostility of blitz victims towards sightseers, and he wrote to Dickey asking for a different pass: 'I would like to take some photographs as supplementary material. . . . It would be a great help as it is difficult to draw in some places without rousing a sense of resentment in the people.'

Sutherland was not the only Blitz artist to find himself in this predicament. John Piper was a similarly uncomfortable spectator, aware of a feeling among the inhabitants of wrecked buildings that war artists were somehow 'cashing in' on their misfortunes, and he too used a camera for discretion's sake.

Piper had not sought appointment as a war artist; having at an early stage volunteered and been accepted by the RAF, he was only prevented from spending the war as a member of a photographic interpretation unit by the intervention of Kenneth Clark. He was one of the leading figures of the younger generation of artists much admired by Clark, and he had the best qualifications of any to make records of bombed buildings. Since his childhood he had been interested in local archaeology and architecture, in the detail and personality of buildings in every state of preservation and decay, and though in the mid-30s his painting had been exclusively abstract, towards the end of the decade he had made the decision to return to a more representational style, signalling his intentions by such projects as *The Shell Guide to Oxfordshire* on which he collaborated with John Betjeman.

Echoes of Piper's abstract days are still to be seen, however, in the two oils of ARP control-rooms which formed part of his first commission from the WAAC. The dotted lines, asymmetric geometrical forms and blocks of pure colour of *The passage to the control-room at S W Regional Headquarters, Bristol** are strongly reminiscent, for example, of his 1936 *Forms on Dark Blue*; and he now sees the ARP pictures as an important stage in the transition – 'the first step on the non-abstract ladder'.

After these two oils, Piper felt that he had exhausted the artistic possibilities of ARP control-rooms, and he asked for 'an opportunity to paint transport subjects' in fulfilment of his 100-guinea commission. But war transport proved another pictorial dead-end at that stage, and though he started several canvases he finished none of them: 'There were times', he wrote, 'when I felt I had met my Waterloo.' Clark came to his rescue by suggesting that he earn out the fee with 'pictures of bombed churches', among them Newport Pagnell; and the Committee, enthusiastic, issued a supplementary commission for 50 guineas on 7 November 1940.

Piper was in effect on stand-by, and a few days later a brief holiday was interrupted by the request that he go at once to paint the ruins of Coventry Cathedral, bombed the previous night and still smoking.[211] On his arrival, the ugly mood of the crowd watching bodies being dug from the rubble persuaded him to seek a discreet vantage point in a nearby office building, and he made the notes for his painting of the shell of the cathedral from the window of a solicitor's office (an environment familiar from five misspent years in articles).

He hurried to finish the picture,[212] and sped it to London via John Betjeman (then an MoI employee), in the knowledge that the WAAC was anxious to reproduce it as a postcard. He was not aware, perhaps, of the verse which the Committee intended to append: 'Thank God for war and fire, To burn the silly objects of desire, That from the ruin of a church thrown down, We see God clear and high above the town' (Anna Wickham).[213]

Piper's first bomb-damage commission was completed in January 1941 with three paintings of blitzed churches in Bristol – *St Mary Le Port, Bristol*, *The Temple Church, Bristol* and *Church of the Holy Nativity, (Knowle), near Bristol* and one in London, *Christ Church Newgate Street, January 1st, 1941*. In retrospect he recalls feeling no particularly intense emotion at the spectacle of their destruction – a surprising lack of reaction which he attributes partly to the deadening effect of the months of anticipation, and partly to the much more violent impression made on him as a small boy by the Zeppelin raids over London. He was perhaps most interested in the contrast between these 'instant ruins' and the scenes of natural architectural decay which had preoccupied him immediately before the war: 'If you see a building that's gone bonk in the night, it's quite different from one that's fallen down gradually, with weeds and whiskers of grass sprouting. . . .'

His third commission, issued on 26 March 1941, was more open – 'subjects by arrangement' to the value of £50. The Committee unsuccessfully attempted to interest him in an underground aircraft factory, and in the event the commission was fulfilled by the delivery of *Council Chamber, House of Commons, 1941*. Piper, like Betjeman, was a specialist in the architecture of the Gothic Revival, and he painted a further picture of the Parliament buildings, seriously damaged by bombing on 10 May 1941 – *Aye Lobby, House of Commons, 1941*. Remarkably, neither these, nor Pitchforth's series on the same subject, were stopped by the censors, whose First World War counterpart, Colonel Lee, would unquestionably have frowned on them for offering, like Nevinson's *Group of Soldiers*, succour to the enemy.

In the spring of 1942, after almost a year of relative calm, intensive bombing began again with the so-called Baedeker raids, launched against Britain's most beautiful and historic towns in retaliation for the British bombing of Lübeck, Cologne and Rostock. The WAAC made some attempt at systematic coverage – purchasing, for example, drawings by Dennis Flanders of *Exeter, the Great Crater* and *Canterbury Cathedral 1941* – but once again Piper was the mainstay. On 29 April 1942 he was commissioned to paint three watercolours of bomb damage in Bath – paintings which in Betjeman's view were his best war work. 'When the bombs fell, when the city churches crashed, when the classic and Perpendicular glory of England was burnt and stark, he produced a series of oil paintings, using his theory of colour to keep the drama of a newly fallen bomb alive. He was probably never better than at Bath, because there is no city to which he is more attached.'

By the end of November 1943, Piper had moved on to the subject of shelter experiments. In an old brickfield near Woburn he observed the Ministry of Home Security's efforts to improve the resistance to blast of 'igloos', and huts of various descriptions.[214] These small surface shelters were, however, hardly typical of the phenomenon which, after bomb damage, supplied the most compelling pictorial material of the Blitz.

Almost from the moment the bombs began to fall, a large number of London's inhabitants took refuge, in defiance of Government orders, in the Underground. The WAAC was naturally anxious to secure records of the curious colonies springing up at night

OPPOSITE ABOVE, Feliks Topolski, *The Tube, October, 1940* (wash), $13\frac{3}{4} \times 18\frac{5}{8}$ BELOW, John Piper, *All Saints' Chapel, Bath* (watercolour and black ink), $16\frac{3}{4} \times 22$, (Tate Gallery)

along the platforms, and by October 1940 had commissioned pictures from both Ardizzone and Topolski.[215] Between them they captured vividly the humour, the squalor and the tedium of existence underground, but it was not until some three months later that the Committee received work which suggested that there was in shelter life any element of the mysterious, the dignified, or the fearful.

At the beginning of December 1940 Kenneth Clark informed the WAAC of certain drawings of shelterers which he considered 'outstandingly good' – the work of Henry Moore, already one of Britain's leading sculptors, with a growing international reputation. Moore had been approached long before by Clark to work as a war artist, but his service in the previous war had inured him to the sight of soldiers in khaki and the other incidental emblems of a country at war, and he could find nothing in the situation to move or inspire him. Then, shortly after the start of the Blitz, having been out to dinner with friends in the West End he was forced, unusually, to travel back to Hampstead on the tube; and he had his first sight of the sleepers.

He was struck simultaneously by the nightmarish quality of the scene – the sprawled figures arranged in a confined space 'like so many slaves chained in the hold of a ship' – and its essential humanity: on the dirty, crowded platforms families were doing their best to behave exactly as though they were at home, eating, knitting, undressing their children for bed. He also saw in the shelters, as he has since recalled, the embodiment of his major artistic preoccupations – the reclining figure, hundreds of them stretched along the platforms; the mother and child motif; and in the tunnel walls encircling the huddled sleeping mass of figures, the interior/exterior forms.

Throughout the autumn and winter of 1940–41, Moore made regular nightly visits to underground stations all over London, taking a ticket in the evening and emerging in the early hours of the next day when the sleepers were settled and still. He took only a small sketchbook and collected his material surreptitiously; the shelter dwellers had evolved their own code of behaviour to deal with discomfort and lack of privacy, and Moore remembers, 'I had to behave as though I wasn't trying to look; they were undressing, after all. . . . I would have been chased out if I'd been caught sketching.'

From verbal notes and hasty sketches made out of sight in the stairwells, Moore would work up drawings in a larger sketchbook the next day, while the images were still fresh in his mind: from these he would select one or two subjects for elaboration into fuller, more finished pictures. It was one of the large sketchbooks which prompted Clark to tell Moore, 'Now *surely* you are ready to be a war artist.' On 1 January 1941 the WAAC bought for 32 guineas four of the drawings he had already finished, and gave him a commission for 50 guineas to continue the series under official auspices.[216]

Moore now feels that his experience of life in the shelters made itself felt in several ways in his later work, both drawing and sculpture. It encouraged him to reaffirm his 'humanist side' which he had temporarily subordinated in the experimental sculptural drawings and geometrical string sculptures of the late 1930s, then his most severely abstract work. 'Without the war, which directed one's attention to life itself, I think I would have been a far less sensitive and responsible person.'

From the swaddled forms of the sleepers, untidily wrapped in blankets and coats, evolved later draped sculptures: 'What I began to learn then about its function as form gave me the intention . . . to use drapery in sculpture in a more realistic way.'

Henry Moore, *Tube shelter perspective* (pen, chalk, watercolour and gouache), $19 \times 17\frac{1}{4}$, (Tate Gallery)

The 'family group' made its first appearance as a significant motif in 1944. And in his *Three Standing Figures* (1947–8) in Battersea Park, he embodied his most powerful memory of the shelters, 'The group sense of communion in apprehension.'

CHAPTER THIRTY-TWO

The Home Front – Production and Transport

D ESPITE the occasional valiant flourish on the 'We Can Take It' theme, the WAAC's Blitz pictures generally depicted the disruption of normal existence and the British people on the defensive. The Committee was anxious also to record the more positive side of life on the Home Front – the endeavour to carry on some semblance of the peacetime routine and, more constructively, the invaluable contributions made by civilians to the war effort. This was a war in which civilians were far more closely involved – by the threat of invasion, the reality of aerial attack, the shortage of essential supplies and, perhaps, a more vivid conviction of the necessity to fight – and the official pictures reflect this, including home subjects in far greater number and variety than the First World War collection.

Largely through purchases, the WAAC assembled a mosaic of life in wartime Britain – pictures of rationing, austerity and the British Restaurants;[217] of the black-out;[218] of knitting parties, evacuees and 'Digging for Victory'.[219] It showed on occasion a lack of the 'common touch' in its perception of what was important to ordinary people in their daily wartime lives. The BBC, which, with ITMA and Vera Lynn as much as with its broadcasts of Churchill's speeches, had an incalculable effect in maintaining public morale, complained that its activities had been wholly neglected,[220] and Churchill himself went unrepresented until after the war. In 1943 the Committee rejected as 'not sufficiently connected with the later stages of the war' Topolski's drawing of the Prime Minister speaking in the Commons, and Epstein's famous bust was commissioned in September 1945, well after Churchill's election defeat. Nor did the Committee defer to keen public interest in Royal activities; Walter Bayes' painting of a German aircrew baling out after an unsuccessful attempt to bomb Buckingham Palace was perhaps a small concession to popular taste.

In its commissions the Committee concentrated on two major facets of civilian effort – work on the land and the production of armaments. In both areas it took pains to emphasise the increasing participation of women, partly at the prompting of Lady Norman (now a Trustee of the IWM) and partly in response to the introduction of conscription for women. Ethel Gabain's lithographs of women employed in traditionally male occupations – as lumberjacks, ferry pilots and manual labourers, filling sandbags, clearing debris and sorting bricks for salvage – were instructive. The more genteel activities of the Women's Voluntary Services were recorded by such artists as Ruskin Spear (*A WVS Canteen at the Docks*), Evelyn Dunbar (*A canning demonstration*) and Erlund Hudson (*WVS Bandage-making*).

Dunbar also captured well the savour of the girls' boarding-school in the life of the Women's Land Army, travelling all over the country for potato-sorting in Berwick, pruning in Sussex, animal husbandry on the Hampshire Downs and *Milking Practice*

Evelyn Dunbar, *A canning demonstration* (oil on canvas), 20 × 24

with Artificial Udders near Winchester. Of the other artists detailed to record agricultural work, James Bateman, RA, had early been set to depicting piggeries and silos, Mona Moore to Land Girls carting oats and the Committee later acquired drawings of cabbages being cultivated (by Archibald Hartrick) and the de-seeding of flax (by Nora Lavrin).

In 1941 the Committee employed for the first time an artist whose work was to be among the scheme's greatest successes – Thomas Hennell, the son of a Kentish parson, and himself very much a countryman, both practitioner and recorder of surviving country crafts.[221] A gentle and unaffected man, he grew cherries, kept bees, and by 1939 had written and illustrated several works of poetry and prose on the changing face of rural England. Dressed in stout tweeds and corduroys with poacher pockets for sketchbook and sandwiches, he would set off for drawing trips on his father's antiquated bicycle. For the WAAC he painted the record harvest of 1941 – threshing, gleaning, stooking wheat and baling straw.

However, as Kenneth Clark remarked, 'The trouble about war pictures of agriculture is that they are rather hard to distinguish from peace pictures,' and the Committee maintained polite resistance to the Ministry of Agriculture's pressure for more acreage of canvas,[222] preferring to publicise Britain's more obviously warlike preparations in mine, factory and shipyard.

The recorders of the 'underground army' were Henry Moore and Graham Sutherland, and their individual responses to the comparable stimuli of coal- and tin-mining are in striking contrast. With official acceptance of the use of the Underground and the consequent regimentation of the shelterers (by the installation and allocation of bunks and so on), shelter scenes lost both their pleasingly anarchic air and their pictorial variety, and Moore's interest faded rapidly.[223] It was then that coal-mining was suggested to him as a possible subject by Herbert Read. The idea of perpetuating the theme of life underground in this particular way appealed to Moore, not least because, although he came from a mining town, Castleford, and both his father and (briefly) eldest brother had been miners, he himself had never been down a coal-mine.

On 29 August 1941 the Committee issued a commission for 25 guineas[224] and, at Moore's request, arranged facilities at the Wheldale Colliery in Castleford. 'My idea is to stay at Castleford for about a week,' he wrote, 'getting a general idea of what strikes me most, and then come back . . . for a week or so to make drawing notes of these first impressions; and then go back to Yorkshire a second time . . . for a longer stay and with more definite objectives in my mind.'

Moore's attitude to the mines was a mundane one. He knew the work was unpleasant and arduous, a belief fully confirmed by his first day in the stifling heat, dust and din at the coal-face. But he also knew that it was within the bounds of normal human capacity – men could, and did, work as miners all their lives. There was no element of the unique or abnormal behaviour that had attracted him in the shelters, and though interesting and stimulating, the mines did not make a strong emotional impact on him. It was the technical difficulties they presented which concerned him most.

As an artist, Moore's main preoccupation since his student days had been with the female form and, as a sculptor, with the static form rather than the form in motion. Now he was confronted exclusively with the male form in motion – though he was helped at the coal-face at least by the cramped conditions which restricted movement largely to the upper part of the body – the figure of the miner on his knees hewing coal being 'stuck, as it were, to the pedestal'.

He was also faced with the challenge of conveying the impression of forms emerging from darkness, relying largely in this on his knowledge of Seurat's drawing. In conscious imitation of another master, he placed special emphasis on the whiteness of the miners' eyes against their blackened

Henry Moore, still from '*Out of Chaos*',
(courtesy of Henry Moore)

Henry Moore, *A miner at work* (ink and chalk), $19\frac{1}{2} \times 19\frac{1}{2}$

faces. 'Giotto and people before him, they made no difference in a face between the whites of the eyes and the rest of the face. But Masaccio – I noticed one day . . . the whites of the eyes were the lightest part of the whole face easily and that this gave a strangely human but dramatic – Greek drama – sense. And I've used that a little bit in the coalmine drawings.' The absence of colour underground – other than the yellow of the miners' lamps feebly piercing the dust – was a further problem, one he had not encountered in the shelters, where the dim light had often had the effect of enhancing colours, the bright hues of blankets, coats and dresses, causing them to stand out more sharply than in daylight.

Sutherland's approach to mining subjects was very different, at once more literary and more emotional: he found in the tin-mines of Cornwall[225] 'a world of such beauty and such mystery that I shall never forget it'.

Graham Sutherland, *Waiting miner at the meeting of the tunnels* (gouache, wax crayon, ink on hardboard) $37\frac{1}{2} \times 19\frac{1}{2}$. (City Art Gallery, Wakefield)

He was sent to the Geevor Mine near Pendeen in June 1942, having already spent much of the previous summer working for the Ministry of Supply at the steel works of Dowlais and Port Talbot.[226] Though the bullet-like descent to 1300 feet in the 'bucket' had its own terrors, Sutherland does not seem to have suffered from the claustrophobia which 'fussed' him on trains and buses. He was wholly absorbed by the new environment – the almost tangible sense of remoteness in the tunnels, with the sounds of work on other levels faintly audible, the smell of acetylene, and the water dripping constantly from the walls – finding in it, perhaps, 'the element of daily enthralment' he sensed in the attitude of the workers themselves.

These men – 'grand, handsome da Vinci types . . . ennobled underground and with an added stature which above ground they lacked' – attracted him as subjects no less than their surroundings. This was a development by which Clark and the WAAC may well have been surprised. In the drawings Sutherland had made of the blast furnaces of South Wales, he had included ancillary groups of figures – ethereal shapes transfixed at significant moments in the rite of steel production, the first figures to appear in his work. In the tin-mines he drew his human subjects almost naturalistically. This apparent progression of an interest in the human form and face encouraged several of his friends and critics to insist, perhaps too strongly, on an organic unity

OPPOSITE ABOVE, Paul Nash, *Battle of Britain, August-October, 1940* (oil on canvas), 48 × 72
BELOW, Paul Nash, *Battle of Germany* (oil on canvas), 48 × 72

ABOVE, Paul Nash, *'Totes Meer' (Dead Sea)* (oil on canvas),
40 × 60, (Tate Gallery)

RIGHT, John Piper, *The passage to the control-room at S. W. Regional
Headquarters, Bristol* (oil on panel), 30 × 20

OPPOSITE ABOVE, John Piper, *Somerset Place, Bath* (watercolour
and black ink), $19\frac{1}{4} \times 30$, (Tate Gallery). BELOW, Graham Sutherland,
Devastation, 1941: an East End Street (ink and gouache),
$25\frac{1}{2} \times 44\frac{3}{4}$, (Tate Gallery)

Evelyn Dunbar, *A Land Girl and the bail bull* (oil on canvas), 36 × 72, (Tate Gallery)

Stanley Spencer, detail from *Shipbuilding on the Clyde: bending the keel plate* (oil on canvas)

Thomas Hennell, *A threshing-team* (watercolour), $13\frac{1}{2} \times 18\frac{1}{2}$

Stanley Spencer, detail from *Shipbuilding on the Clyde: riveters* (oil on canvas)

William Roberts, *Women railway porters in war-time* (watercolour), $14\frac{1}{8} \times 20\frac{3}{8}$

Henry Moore, *Pink and green sleepers* (pen, wash and gouache), 15×22, (Tate Gallery)

Robert Colquhoun, Study for 'Weaving Army Cloth, Drawing Warp Threads' (coloured crayon and wash), $20 \times 16\frac{3}{4}$

Ceri Richards, *Rollerman at bosh with doubler and furnace man* (watercolour), 15 × 22 (National Museum of Wales, Cardiff)

in his work. In 1943 Edward Sackville-West reasoned, 'These [mining] portraits – for that is what they are – are a new point of departure for Sutherland; they represent an ability until now latent in his art. Latent but always I think there: the hand that drew the oak tree, in the etching *Pastoral* [1930] is clearly the same as that which now delineates another kind of worn, hard bitten feature.' There are some who now extend Sackville-West's argument to explain Sutherland's later preoccupation with the faces of the rich, the famous and the old, establishing a chain of connections between his pre-war plant personalities and his post-war portraits. Arguably, however,

OPPOSITE ABOVE, Eric Ravilious, *RNAS sick bay, Dundee* (watercolour), $19\frac{1}{4} \times 21\frac{3}{8}$. BELOW, Eric Ravilious, *Midnight Sun* (watercolour), $18\frac{1}{2} \times 23\frac{1}{4}$, (Tate Gallery)

Michael Ayrton, *Chainmakers* (gouache, crayon and ink) $18 \times 21\frac{1}{2}$

to draw out the possibly tenuous 1943 link between Pembroke and Geevor to encompass Cap d'Ail does Sutherland a major disservice by associating the post-war portraits inextricably with the mainstream of his work.

It was perhaps in the documenting of wartime production that the WAAC used the widest variety of artists – their heterogeneous records the more valuable, as Cecil Beaton pointed out, for being of subjects largely beyond the scope of the cameras of the time. 'In those vulcan forges . . . our eyes become attuned, unlike the camera lens, to the nuances of darkness amid a strange world that is spasmodically suffused by flashes of green, magenta, puce and golden light . . . [a] world of molten metals, of glowing furnaces, soot and firework sparks, that only the painter can interpret.' As records of the working of tin into tin-plate the Committee selected, appropriately enough, the drawings of Ceri Richards,[227] a past colleague of Sutherland's at the Chelsea School of Art; and Michael Ayrton, another artist much influenced by neo-Romanticism, recorded work at one of the few remaining factories where heavy chains were still made by hand.

Ayrton's friend Robert Colquhoun[228] was ultimately employed to draw the weaving of army cloth – but not before the Committee had received two letters from Colquhoun's life-long companion Robert MacBryde, expressing fears for his mental health should he be exposed any longer to service in the RAMC emptying latrine buckets and scrubbing floors, deprived of the opportunity to paint. 'The sickness of soul this lad has experienced begins to manifest itself in his body and anything that can be done for this lad must be done quickly.' It was to be four years before Colquhoun received the textile commission for 25 guineas – to be executed not, as he suggested, in the Western Isles, but in a factory at Peebles.

At the other end of the stylistic spectrum, Francis Dodd drew Tom Bearley, the Wilkinson Sword Company's master sword-maker at work; and another ancient trade, charcoal-burning, revived during the war, was recorded in watercolour by Vincent Lines. More contemporary armaments – tanks, shells, bombs and bombers – fell to artists as diverse as Charles Ginner, Terence Cuneo, Leslie Cole, Vivian Pitchforth, John Armstrong, Ethel Gabain and John Ensor.

Some of the most compelling images among the production subjects came from Mervyn Peake, already established at the age of twenty-eight as an outstanding draughtsman and a teacher of life drawing at Westminster School of Art, with his first one-man London exhibition behind him. The war dislocated this career, and his experiences were subsequently to find expression less in painting than in the poetry and novels (notably the *Gormenghast* trilogy) on which his present reputation largely rests.

Peake was called up in 1940 and quickly forced the Army to the conclusion that he was 'quite unsuited to soldiering'. A series of despairing Commanding Officers – responsible for directing his efforts as, successively, an anti-aircraft gunner, a driving instructor, a bomb-disposal aide, and a theodolite trainee – left him largely to his own devices, with the result that during his period of service he was able virtually to complete *Titus Groan* and to supplement his army pay by book illustration.

However, army life bore down on Peake and brought him to the verge of nervous collapse, which the WAAC seems inadvertently to have had a hand in precipitating. He had badly wanted to be an official war artist and had applied, with a reference from Augustus John, in the early months, when his name was placed on the reserve list. In April 1940 he suggested drawing prisoners of war before they were shipped to Canada, but the Committee refused permission. He sent in six drawings of army life, and none were bought. In October 1941 his current CO fervently supported his application, but again he was turned down, with the comment, 'It was felt most important that the Committee should not, in such cases, allow themselves to be influenced by the fact that the artist might wish to get out of the Army.' His hopes were raised in March 1942 when the possibility of his drawing miners in the Rhondda

Mervyn Peake (photograph courtesy of Mrs Maeve Peake)

Mervyn Peake, *The evolution of the cathode ray (radiolocation) tube* (oil on canvas), $33\frac{1}{2} \times 43\frac{1}{2}$

Valley seems seriously to have been considered. 'I feel keyed up', he wrote, 'to do what I am sure will be the best and most significant work I have produced so far.' A month later, however, the project was abandoned. No explanation was given – though the commission already offered to Moore was doubtless a factor. This disappointment seems to have been the final straw: Peake, in the throes of a nervous breakdown, went absent without leave and was later despatched to the Army Military Hospital at Southport whence, after an extended period of sick leave, he was invalided out of the Army in May 1943.

Six months after his breakdown, the MoI employed Peake as a propaganda artist,[229] and the WAAC itself made belated amends with a 35-guinea commission on 31 January 1943 for a 'picture and drawings of a glass factory' where cathode ray tubes were blown. So successful were his first efforts that on 13 May he was given a three-month salaried post to continue with the subject.[230] Peake was bewitched by the factory where the glass was blown – 'a world upon its own, a place of roaring fires and monstrous shadows' – and translated his feelings into both paintings and poetry:

> *It is the ballet of gold sweat. It is*
> *The hidden ballet of the heavy feet*
> *And flickering hands: the dance of men unconscious*
> *Of dancing and the golden wizardries.*
> *Rough clothed, rough headed, drenched with sweat, they are*
> *As poised as floodlit acrobats in air,*
> *They twist the throbbing fire-globes over water*
> *And whirl the ripe chameleon pears, whose fire*
> *Threatens to loll like a breast, or a tongue or a serpent,*
> *Over the breath rod and the surly trough. . . .*
> (*The Glassblowers*, 1950)

For a more mundane vision of factory life the Committee looked to the likes of L. S. Lowry and Ruskin Spear. Lowry's subject was *Going to Work*[231] at a Manchester factory, one of his very few paintings to include, amongst the scurrying figures, a motor vehicle – or rather two, double-decker buses included at the suggestion of his housekeeper. At the other end of the day, Spear's picture *Scene in an Underground Train, 1943* showed sleeping workers returning from the night-shift; and vignettes of the factory worker's daily routine, on and off duty, were contributed by Pitchforth (*Snack Time in a Factory*), Kenneth Rowntree (*CEMA Canteen Concert, Isle of Dogs, London, E14, 1941*) and Frank Dobson, whose *An Escalator in an Underground Factory* furrowed brows at the Ministry of Supply: 'Why do you have to give factory girls enormous legs in the same way as in your statuettes? I feel sure they could balance on the escalators just as well with natural figures.'

An obvious and important corollary of production was the transport both of raw materials and of the finished goods, and the *nouveau* Ministry of War Transport was eager for its share of immortality. A War Transport representative, Fleetwood Pritchard, joined the WAAC in 1943, and the Treasury was persuaded to sanction the appointment of two full-time salaried artists – John Platt and fireman-artist Bernard Hailstone.

Hailstone was to travel to the Mediterranean and North Africa to record the work of the mercantile marine, in paintings such as *Convoy at Augusta*.[232] Platt (who earlier in the war had been given special facilities by the Committee to paint coastal subjects, including convoys, and wartime traffic on the Thames) had the more modest assignment of transport at home, principally docks and railways. At the end of May 1944 he was transferred to work for the WAAC on individually commissioned war transport subjects, and his place was taken by John Piper.

Piper's service as a salaried war transport artist (which ran from July 1944 until September 1945) was, at this late stage of the war, largely uneventful, consisting principally of recording 'coastwise shipping, loading of unusual cargoes, etc.' up and down the southern coasts from Cardiff to Southampton. Locals in South Wales made life more

John Piper, *A Ministry of War Transport crane unloading armoured cars and lorries from American ships, Cardiff* (watercolour), $21\frac{1}{2} \times 16\frac{7}{8}$

interesting by refusing, quite correctly, to direct him to the storage site where he had been instructed to observe and record obsolete engines from the Canadian Pacific Railway, shipped over to be melted down for shells. A skilled topographer, he eventually located them in a remote valley, some fifty or sixty of them 'with cow-catchers on the front, and those lovely chimneys'. In Cardiff events took an even more bizarre turn when he went to make studies for a panorama of the docks from the top floor of a large refrigerated warehouse, 'a rather sinister place . . . 18 storeys of nothing but meat, all covered with icicles. . . . One knew one was alone with all these thousands and thousands of frozen carcases – very Kafka-esque: Francis Bacon might have made something of it, but it didn't appeal to me.'

One other major area of production remained – and to Stanley Spencer was entrusted the task of recording the huge expansion in merchant shipbuilding to meet the appalling losses of the Battle of the Atlantic.

At the end of 1939 Spencer's life was in perhaps its most serious state of disorder. The critical approval extended to him after the Burghclere series had largely been withdrawn. In the words of his dealer, he was 'terribly in debt all round', and obliged to devote much of his time to landscapes, leaving little energy for the expression of his own obsessions, religious and sexual. He was also, after the failure of his first marriage and the fiasco of the second, in an emotional turmoil, his health so precarious that the WAAC was, exceptionally, to pay for him to travel first-class, considering him too small and delicate to risk anything less comfortable.

It was Spencer's dealer, Dudley Tooth, who suggested his appointment to Kenneth Clark, as a partial solution to his financial plight. Interestingly, in the decision to commission him, the Committee seems to have been influenced less by the Burghclere series, which would have indicated a front-line subject, than by five panels on the theme of *Industry and Peace*[233] which had since March 1939 been on display at the Tate Gallery. In response to Spencer's suggestion that he might execute 'a great picture of the Crucifixion with a predella which would contain scenes connected with the present war such as the overrunning of Poland', the Committee proposed, more modestly, two 50-guinea commissions for 'a painting of shipbuilding and a painting of an aerodrome'.

Perhaps not surprisingly, nothing came of the latter; but the shipbuilding subject struck a chord. In 1935, entering a design for Cunard's competition to find a decorative panel for the ballroom of the *Queen Mary*, Spencer had, somewhat incongruously, chosen a shipbuilding subject. Now, within a fortnight of the Committee's approach, before any arrangements had been made for him to visit a shipyard, the Admiralty representative reported that Spencer, having already made studies of shipbuilding (presumably those worked up from photographs in 1935), had 'an ambitious project' in mind.

He made his first visit to the yards – Lithgow's, at Port Glasgow – in May 1940,[234] and when the resulting sketches were shown to the WAAC, it was agreed that 'it should be suggested to the artist that he might carry out for a fee of £300, a set of pictures to form a related series showing different aspects of shipbuilding.' Whether or not this was precisely Spencer's 'ambitious project' is not clear, but his enthusiasm for the idea of a series is manifest in innumerable plans and diagrams scattered throughout his writings of the period. The most extensive of these is drawn on the first page of a notebook headed 'Epsom 1941' and shows the four walls of a room hung with sixty-eight separate panels, including a double predella on two walls and a single predella on the other two.

The tangle of ideas and profusion of plans, many of the most grandiose never fulfilled, has had the unfortunate effect of partially obscuring the reality of what Spencer *did* achieve – an extended composition embracing most of the principal trades to be found in a shipyard (welding, riveting, plumbing and so on), covering a series of fourteen canvases averaging two feet in height and aggregating roughly 137 feet in length.

Spencer saw the pictures as a unity in which he could reproduce 'the impression one gets in the shipyard itself . . . in wandering about among the varied happenings': just as one activity in the yards merged into the next, so the subjects of his pictures would overflow from one canvas to the next – 'These transitional parts or joinings are very important.' In August 1944 he supplied the Committee with a 'hanging plan', the order being (from left to right): *Burners* (triptych[235] 20×80, 42×60, 20×80); *Riveters* (single canvas 30×228)*, and, directly above *Riveters*, *The Riggers* (two canvases – a main panel $20 \times 194\frac{1}{2}$ and centred above this a small panel $12 \times 32\frac{1}{2}$); *The*

Furnaces (single canvas $61\frac{1}{2} \times 44\frac{3}{4}$); *Bending the Keel Plate* (single canvas 30×228)*
and, directly above this, *Plumbers* (again two canvases – a main panel 20×194 [*sic*]
and centred above this a small panel 12×35); and *Welders* (triptych 20×80, 42×60,
20×80).[236] Spencer completed one further canvas as part of the series – *The Template*
(single canvas 20×228) – which was the first section of a predella intended to run
the length of the principal canvases, drawing together after the fashion of Italian
Renaissance altar-pieces more minor incidents and themes which did not warrant
inclusion in the canvases above.

Spencer's notebooks and letters contain an extraordinary multiplicity of ideas and
suggestions as to what attracted him in the shipyards. His major preoccupations of
the '30s were not unnaturally present: 'Everything I see is manifestly religious and
sexual. . . . It is not that coils of rope suggest Haloes; it is that all these items . . . have
a hallowing capacity of their own. . . . When I went into the room where the big pieces
of stiff material were being sewn . . . there was a woman standing with her back to
me. She was working at a table and at her left side was a great Camouflaged Tarpaulin
heaped up and heaping up as it emerged from her side like some sort of spawn coming
from her.'

However, far more important to him at the start of the shipbuilding series was his
sense of the 'homeliness' of the yards. 'I am interested in the relationship between
many of the shipbuilding activities and domestic activities,' he wrote. 'Many of the
places and corners of Lithgow's factory moved me in much the same way as I was
by the rooms of my childhood.' He felt completely at ease with the shipbuilders. At
the yards, after an initial flurry of curiosity (prompted partly by his ineffably scruffy
appearance, pyjamas protruding above his collar and his feet through his shoes), they
left him to get on with his work as they got on with theirs; and outside the yards
they made him welcome – he was put up for much of his time in Port Glasgow by
one of the workers, greatly appreciating the bed provided for him, 'in a deep fitting
recess in the wall, a great dark place'.

Spencer demonstrated his feeling of belonging by including himself in at least two
of the pictures (*Burners* and *Welders*), making himself part of the team effort around
him. The yards, like the few other places where he had been happy, reminded him
sharply of Cookham: he described them to Gilbert Spencer as 'dark and cosy and full
of mysterious places and happenings, like a vast Cookham's blacksmith's shop interior'.
After the break-up of his second marriage, Spencer had moved away from the village
in October 1938 'in a mood of depression',[237] and it is not improbable that for a period
he found in the shipyards a surrogate home, where he could shelter from both his
emotional and financial problems. 'I like a homely atmosphere,' he wrote, 'and look
for some kind of home, no matter what I may be experiencing. Or it may be a certain
atmosphere which I feel a need for in myself, and it is the privilege of the spirit that
it can find what it needs anywhere.'

However, in January 1942 Spencer moved back to Cookham to his old studio, his
finances were taken in hand by Dudley Tooth – and his need for the close-knit society
of the shipyards diminished accordingly. It is interesting to note that of all the pictures
completed, only one (*Plumbers*, arguably the least spontaneous composition) has no
roots in the period before Spencer's return to Cookham. *Burners* had been delivered

Stanley Spencer, *Shipbuilding on the Clyde: the furnaces* (oil on canvas), $61\frac{1}{2} \times 44\frac{3}{4}$

in October 1940, *Welders* in March 1941 and *Riveters* in September 1941; and although the remaining pictures were delivered after January 1942,[238] they had each been conceived before. The WAAC was informed in June 1941 that the design for the predella (*The Template*) had been discussed with the Admiralty representative; Spencer was 'still "experimenting" ' with *Bending the Keel Plate* . . . 'only this time on the canvas itself' in November 1941; the verbal description of the riggers' loft was in Spencer's Epsom notebook (covering the period May–December 1941), *The Riggers* itself drawn on to the canvas in March 1942, and *The Furnaces* was completed from a study made in 1940.

This makes all the more remarkable the fact that after his return to Cookham, between 1942 and 1946, he delivered on average only one composition every twelve months. For Spencer this rate of output was abnormally slow, and it seems likely that he protracted the shipbuilding series quite deliberately in order to keep open his access to Port Glasgow and the yards which, in wartime, would otherwise have been denied.

These facilities had now become doubly essential to Spencer, for by the end of 1942, perhaps in consequence of his return to Cookham – the reestablishing of old patterns of thought and the picking up of previous threads – he had conceived another in his series of resurrection subjects, this one peopled by shipyard workers and their families.

By his own account the 'Port Glasgow Resurrection' series was stimulated by a visionary experience he had whilst on Clydeside, and there is a suggestion in the official correspondence that it occurred during his visit of September 1942, when he begged the Committee (with an enthusiasm that did not manifest itself in a torrent of shipyard canvases) for 'a few days more. It would be difficult to crowd into a month all I shall need for what I hope to do. My days are very full and I am delighted with the pleasure and privilege of being given the opportunity of making these drawings.'

Quite when the Committee realised that its commission was no longer Spencer's main priority is not clear; it is to the members' credit that when light dawned they made no attempt to terminate the contract, contenting themselves with paying from March 1945 onwards only half of Spencer's living expenses in Glasgow. The WAAC was, however, determined that he should bring the official project to a reasonable state of completion. *The Furnaces*, the work's centrepiece and the pivot of the hanging plan, was not started until the autumn of 1945, and appears to have been completed only as a result of pressure from Bone and Schwabe. The Committee has been criticised for rushing Spencer, thus inducing him to skimp the painting – he later wrote, 'I wish I had done a better and bigger central picture than I did.' One might equally argue that without official intervention the composition as a whole would have been immeasurably the weaker for being without a focal point, and Spencer's achievement that much the less.

The achievement, in any case, left one observer unimpressed. In December, it was reported to the Committee that Sir James Lithgow, Director of Merchant Shipbuilding and Spencer's host for the past two years, 'was anxious to get a factual record of merchant shipbuilding on the Clyde or elsewhere'. A discreet veil had apparently been drawn in the managerial mind over what already constituted some fifty-eight feet of pictorial record, and Henry Rushbury was duly commissioned for 100 guineas to do three large and blameless drawings of shipbuilding on the Clyde.

CHAPTER THIRTY-THREE

The War at Sea

IN addition to galvanising Stanley Spencer into action, Muirhead Bone made various visits to the shipyards on his own account during the war. One of his most famous wartime drawings, *Torpedoed oil tanker*, depicted the buckled and gaping wreckage of precisely the type of vessel whose construction Spencer was recording.

Bone was the first and most senior of the Admiralty's artists, and arrangements were made to give the *Illustrated London News* first option on all his drawings, ensuring that his work was the most widely reproduced of all official war art. His style had changed little between the wars, but he showed a preference now for larger and more highly finished drawings which proved invaluable to the Committee both as testaments of ceremonial occasions (a banquet in *The Painted Hall, Greenwich*, for instance) and as detailed documents of individual vessels – the battleship *George V*, the aircraft-carrier *Illustrious* and the submarine *Tradewind* among them. The series he made of mine-laying aboard HMS *Southern Prince* included one of his rare oils, *Winter Mine-Laying off Iceland* – a picture with which, however, he had inordinate difficulty, working on it at intervals for almost a year.

In the spring of 1943 Bone's younger son, Gavin, died of tuberculosis, and although Bone remained a member of the WAAC until 1946, he took six months' leave from his Admiralty post in May 1943 and never returned to it. The family connection was, however, maintained through the work of his older son Stephen, an ex-Slade pupil and a prolific painter in oils of both landscape and figure subjects in a forceful, literal style. During the early part of the war he worked as a camouflage officer, a position from which the Committee was unable to obtain his release; but he was nonetheless useful to the scheme, as his job took him all over the country, and he suggested a wide range of topics for other artists to record – among them 'the two young men who spent an afternoon flying an aeroplane into a balloon cable to see if the wings came off'; acid-factory workers in their sinister protective clothing; and 'macabre blast experiments on goats and apes'. When finally appointed by the WAAC in June 1943 he was encouraged to paint rather more run-of-the-mill subjects in his first year of employment – air-sea rescue, tank landing craft, midget submarines, and so on – and compiled a comprehensive record of life on board an escort carrier, HMS *Pursuer*.[239]

In order to maintain parity between the Admiralty, with its one salaried artist,[240] and the War Office with its four, the WAAC itself appointed two salaried artists to devote themselves entirely to naval subjects. Its first choice was a man who might fairly be described as the least enthusiastic of the official war artists – John Nash.

In 1940 Nash was forty-seven and had since the First World War established a modest but secure reputation as a landscape painter and an illustrator, especially of botanical works. He had been teaching in the School of Design at the RCA for six years, and himself experimenting with wood engraving and lithography. Appointed

Sir Muirhead Bone, *Torpedoed oil tanker* (charcoal, chalk, pen and wash) $23 \times 35\frac{1}{2}$, (Tate Gallery)

by the WAAC on 24 January 1940 for a six-month period, he did not start work until 1 March as he had to finish work on a prior commission for the MoI's General Production Division, a poster on a convoy theme.

It was with considerable reluctance that Nash returned to service as a war artist. No admirer of 'the horrid Hun', he was anxious instead to play as active a part in this war as he had in the last, and applied for various military posts throughout 1940 (a process he described as 'making sundry dashes like an animal in a field towards being as I thought more patriotically employed'). In the circumstances, his first posting was particularly unfortunate. He arrived in Plymouth at the height of a spy scare, to be harassed persistently by the police while sketching in restricted areas, his rank as Honorary Captain, RM, merely adding to his troubles – 'The military discipline, as implying a constant raising of the elbow, is really most oppressive.'

The visit produced a certain amount of material – on flying boats, submarines, dredgers, scrap metal and timber – which he worked up both in watercolour and oils. He insisted nevertheless on rejoining the Observer Corps which he had had to leave at the start of his appointment, explaining to Dickey, 'Yes, dear boy, I feel a bit more useful now. I Paint for the Admiralty, Dig for Victory, and Observe for the Air Ministry.' To his brother he was to complain, 'This war is the wrong kind of war, it does not come to us very much yet and we can't seem to get at it;'[241] and after the first week of his second assignment, this time in Swansea, he wrote to the WAAC, 'Unless I strike something very inspiring here, certain last shreds of honesty compel the feeling that I should not continue in this job.'

He was promptly rewarded by an air-raid during which the ship on which he was based was hit and set ablaze. 'The amount of ducking and throwing oneself flat in the wet was tiring and did not improve the old uniform. I might do a picture of these operations [*A Dockyard Fire*] as it was a really vivid experience while it lasted but I can't say it would be good propaganda except for the enemy.'

This excitement, however, was not enough. Convinced that his appointment had not been a success, Nash 'made a strong plea that the work he had so far done should not be considered equivalent to full-time production', and continued after his contract had expired to send in further drawings, unpaid. In March 1941 he won his way at last into the Royal Marines with some kind of military intelligence post attached to the Commander-in-Chief's staff in Rosyth, writing gleefully to his brother, 'It's a good joke getting right into the Marines by the back door of official war art. No questions were asked about fitness and when they saw me as an honorary Capt. it seemed as if they were sort of hypnotised.' He added, 'I must learn to be a silent if not a strong and silent man' – in which he would seem to have succeeded as Paul was henceforth to refer to him sarcastically as 'John Hushmarine No. 1'.

The WAAC's other artist for Admiralty subjects was Eric Ravilious, a colleague of John Nash on the teaching staff at the RCA, where from 1922–5 he had studied in the Design School under Paul Nash, his fellow-students including his life-long friend Edward Bawden, Douglas Percy Bliss, Barnett Freedman, Raymond Coxon and Henry

Moore. Ravilious was one of the prime movers in the revival of wood engraving in the late 1920s; he also worked throughout the '30s in a remarkable variety of other media – as a mural painter, lithographer, book illustrator[242] and designer of furniture, glass, pottery and china (including the Wedgwood Coronation Mug for Edward VIII). He considered himself, however, first and foremost a watercolourist of rural landscapes, principally those of the Sussex Downs.

Freedman, John Nash and Ravilious (photograph reproduced by permission of the Ravilious children)

Ravilious was appointed by the WAAC on 10 February 1940 to work for six months in the Nore Command, while John Nash covered the Western Approaches. Like Nash he was commissioned an Honorary Captain, RM. He travelled first to Chatham where, again like Nash, he found such naval life as was visible both uneventful and dominated by protocol. 'Naval and Mess etiquette occupies a lot of my spare time . . . a new recruit has to be on the alert the whole time in order not to make devastating mistakes.'

Sheerness, in prohibitively bad weather, was little richer in material, and it was not until he reached Grimsby that he found subjects which excited him – notably an *RMS Party* tackling a magnetic mine on the Whitstable oyster beds. ('RMS is one of these irresistible abbreviations for Rendering Mines Safe.') He was also able for the first time to go to sea in conditions fit for working; in April 1940 he was sent on two trips on a destroyer to the coast of Norway where a British Expeditionary Force was earning the unkind sobriquet reported by Harold Nicolson – 'Back Every Fortnight' – in a short and abortive campaign to oust the newly installed German invaders. The watercolours Ravilious completed are his most famous of the war – among them *Norway, 1940*, *HMS Ark Royal in Action*, and *HMS Glorious in the Arctic*.

It seems that he had then been intended to return to Chatham; but when the Committee learned that 'Sir Plunket ERNLE-ERLE-DRAX, Commander-in-Chief of the Nore, did not appreciate Captain Ravilious's pictures', a new area of operations was quickly found. On 19 July Ravilious arrived at Portsmouth, 'which is almost overwhelming in size and variety. I feel like an earwig setting out to draw Buckingham Palace.' In August he moved to the submarine base, HMS *Dolphin*, at Gosport, and put to sea in submarines. 'It is awfully hot below when they dive and every compartment small and full of people at work. However, this is a change from destroyers and . . . there is no roll or movement at all. . . . The scene is extraordinarily good in a gloomy way. There are small coloured lights about the place and the complexity of a Swiss clock.'

The following month he was in Newhaven making records of the country's coastal defences against invasion, with the Battle of Britain raging above him. 'It is marvellous on the cliffs in this weather, though the wind blows a bit, and bombs fall every afternoon, and sometimes planes.' Perhaps predictably, several of these drawings were impounded by a nervous censor.

Ravilious's next six-month commission was then postponed for almost a year, because he had wanted since January 1940 to execute a series of war lithographs – and in his submarine experience at Gosport he had found his theme. The WAAC was enthusiastic – Ravilious being one of the few lithographers it encouraged during the war – and with the permission of the Vice-Admiral Submarines he made his designs.[243] During this break in official work (when he also accepted a commission for textile designs from the Cotton Board), the Ministry of Home Security was able to inveigle him to record Home Security Control-Rooms, paying him for the drawings (which included *Room 29, Home Security Control Room*, *Wall Maps* and *The Teleprinter Room*) the equivalent of one month's salary, £54 3s 4d.

On 14 July 1941 Ravilious returned to Admiralty subjects at Dover, where he produced a series of thirteen drawings including further coastal defence subjects, scenes of cross-Channel shelling (a feature of wartime life in South-East England which has tended to be forgotten), and his most human subject *The Guard Room*. He enjoyed Dover

Eric Ravilious, *Submarines in dry dock* (watercolour), $17 \times 22\frac{1}{2}$, (Tate Gallery)

very little, again subjected to constant interruption by weather and security forces; he may have mentioned this to John Nash, as his next posting was to Dunfermline where he stayed with Nash and his wife, travelling to naval centres round about to work on a programme mapped out for him by Nash.

At May Island, Methil and Pitcavie, Ravilious painted convoys, from both shore and sea (aboard the SS *Empire Raleigh* in Largo Bay); and in late November and early December he was in Dundee at Royal Naval Air Station HMS *Ambrose*, revelling in the novelty of the subject. 'I spend my time drawing seaplanes,' he wrote, 'and now and again they take me up, this morning rather uncomfortably in the tail, but it was worth it for the view [recorded in *View from the Rear Hatch of a Walrus*]. I do so very much enjoy drawing these queer flying machines and hope to produce a set of aircraft paintings. I hope that Paul N[ash] hasn't already painted Walruses – what I like about them is that they are comic things with a strong personality like a duck, and designed to go slow. You put your head out of the window and it is no more windy than a train.'

His enthusiasm for aeroplanes – manifested in such pictures as *Walrus Aircraft on the Slipway*, *Morning on the Tarmac*, and *RNAS sick bay, Dundee* (the title disguising a portrait of Walruses seen through the window of the sick bay) – was promptly turned to advantage by the WAAC, which in a resolution calling for 'more and better air pictures' agreed to switch Ravilious to RAF subjects for his third six-month commission, starting on 22 February 1942. The new RAF representative, Lord Willoughby de Broke, gave Ravilious 'a wonderful lunch at Boodles of game pie and cake', and they made plans. In the last week of February he went to York to paint Lysanders, and followed this with visits to Debden in April (Tiger Moths) and Sawbridgeworth in May. He was, however, side-tracked from his RAF work in June, when the Committee was informed of efforts to camouflage England's chalk figures and chalk railway cuttings by spraying them with green ink – a subject to which Ravilious, who had been working on watercolours of chalk figures when war was declared, was obviously suited. Regrettably, before he had a chance to start drawing, the figures proved to have been most effectively turfed instead.

In July, Ravilious (earlier thwarted in a desire to go to Russia) mooted the idea of a visit to Iceland, an important staging post for the Atlantic convoys, and arrangements were accordingly made. He had time before leaving to join in the festivities to mark Dickey's retirement as Secretary of the WAAC[244] – 'What fun and what a holiday your dinner party was the other day. I did enjoy it: and went on with a small party to drinks at the Hollybush, and then more drinks at the Clarks, returning at a late hour with Barnett, Harry Moore and Sutherland in high spirits – your going away is unanimously regretted. Nobody likes the idea at all.'

At the end of August 1942, Ravilious set off for Iceland. On 2 September he went on an operational flight in a plane which did not return.[245] His premature death, at the age of thirty-nine, makes the assessment of his war work difficult, because it was so clearly incomplete. Throughout his three commissions, under the obligation to produce work regularly, he was confronted with a bewildering variety of new sights, shapes and experiences; and in making sense of his impressions he seems to have concentrated perhaps a little too intently on the element of design in what he saw. Edward Bawden has written of his later work that it was more *consciously* designed – 'colour and textural effects carefully calculated, everything being carried out with intentional completeness. Design has permeated the whole painting and conditioned its treatment.' It is possible that, given more time, Ravilious might well have progressed beyond his obvious fascination with the novel artefacts of war to produce work that contained, besides sheer beauty and refinement, a real emotional vigour.

The WAAC's record of naval subjects can broadly be divided into three groups of pictures – straightforward documents of naval life both ashore and at sea, made by eyewitnesses; reconstructions of outstanding actions after the event; and naval portraits. The work of Ravilious, Nash and the two Bones obviously falls into the first category, and two further artists might best be described as eyewitnesses – John Worsley, appointed official Admiralty artist in the Mediterranean in July 1943,[246] and Bar-

nett Freedman, who was also to be one of the Admiralty's most successful, if unortho-
dox, portraitists.

Freedman's return from France in May 1940 did not signal the end of his complaints
about his treatment. Frustrated in an attempt to return to Dunkirk to paint, he bela-
boured the War Office for failing to provide him with subjects at home, finally exasperating Coote beyond endurance: 'I can see no alternative to dismissing so cantankerous
a fellow. . . . I have failed to make him understand that a reforming, expanding, and
hectically busy army cannot be expected to welcome any kind of extraneous matter.
It is really more important to keep out the Germans than to take in Mr Barnett
Freedman.'

Freedman's dismissal was not immediate, and in the interim he was sent to record
the defences of the Thames and Medway against invasion, the results being a large
oil, *Coast Defence Battery*, and a watercolour of the same subject, and a composite 'album' of small portraits of the *Royal Artillery Commander and Officers of the Fixed Defences*.
He then suggested making a similar album on board a battleship, 'from the stoker
to the Captain', a proposal received with enthusiasm by the Admiralty representative.
Thus when Freedman's dismissal by the War Office finally came on 10 March 1941,
arrangements were made for him to join HMS *Repulse* in July.

He found the Navy considerably more to his liking – 'Nothing could have been laid
on more perfectly, had I been a high official of the [MoI] even,' – and during his month
aboard *Repulse* he gathered the material for two of his most successful wartime pictures,
15-Inch Gun Turret, HMS Repulse and the album of portraits of the officers and men.
These became the more valuable as records some four months later when on 10
December 1941 HMS *Repulse* and HMS *Prince of Wales* were sunk by Japanese air
strikes off the coast of Malaya.[247]

Freedman's albums were by now extremely popular with the Committee, and he
was borrowed briefly by the Ministry of Supply in December 1942 to pay a similar
compliment to the staff of Parnall's aircraft factory at Bristol. The Admiralty retrieved
him in June 1943 and sent him to join HM Submarine *Tribune*, to make a large drawing
of the control-room and the now familiar album of the crew. Here Freedman was if
anything happier than aboard the *Repulse*. To the crew of *Tribune* he was known as
'Mike', short for Michelangelo (when he was not being nicknamed 'Soc', short for Soc-
rates, in deference to his fondness for protracted argument); Armide Oppé, who as
deputy to the WAAC's Admiralty representative had much to do with him at this
time, has remarked, 'The Navy cannot do without its mascots – and Barnett was their
mascot.'[248]

Freedman's album portraits were, strictly speaking, executed on the WAAC's behalf:
although working primarily on Admiralty subjects, he was in fact on salary to the
MoI. It was the realisation of this fact which brought the Admiralty representative
to the conclusion that the Navy was falling behind the other Services in the accumulation of portraits; for after Kennington's efforts in the early months of the war, few
portraits – other than various sketches of sailors in typical shipboard activities, purchased from John Worsley – had been acquired.

In his attempt to remedy the situation, Gleadowe displayed traces of the competitive
spirit amidst which the WAAC had been set up, writing privately to the Treasury to

Barnett Freedman, *Interior of a submarine* (pen, ink and watercolour), $23\frac{5}{8} \times 37$, (Tate Gallery)

ask for a special grant of £650 for Admiralty portraits. The Treasury had no hesitation in passing this letter straight to the WAAC (an action considered 'ungentlemanly' by the Admiralty) and, in granting a £500 allowance for portraits, placed financial control with the Committee.

The grant, renewed annually, was spent mainly on one-off commissions, from artists including Henry Lamb and Rodrigo Moynihan. To the Admiralty's credit, it was also they who commissioned the majority of the sculptors employed by the Committee – Frank Dobson, John Skeaping, Charles Wheeler and C. W. Dyson-Smith. In November 1940 the WAAC tried to commission Epstein for two heads of naval subjects, but he was too busy and refused. In 1945 the members at last persuaded him to sculpt a sailor – Sir Andrew Cunningham, First Sea Lord – but this time the sitter refused, on grounds of ill health.[249]

Many of the most senior naval officers were not in fact painted until 1945 – Lord Mountbatten (Supreme Allied Commander, South-East Asia Command) by Bernard Hailstone, for example, and Admiral Sir John Cunningham (Commander-in-Chief,

Mediterranean Fleet 1943–6) by John Worsley. The Navy does, however, have an extensive record of more junior officers and men through the efforts of Dennis William Dring. Dring had taken first prize for portraiture at the Slade, where he studied from 1922–5. He came to the WAAC's notice in May 1941 when his *Portrait of a Sailor* was purchased from the Royal Academy Summer Exhibition, and from then on he was employed as a salaried MoI artist until September 1945, working at different times for each of the Services (for the Admiralty between June 1942 and March 1943), and on various one-off commissions ranging from the Directors of Combined Operations to 'the farmer and two ladies who had been decorated for gallantry in carrying on with work on the land [at Dover] during the Battle of Britain'.

Dring worked rapidly, usually in pastels, taking roughly an hour for each portrait – a worthy successor to Francis Dodd. The Committee regarded him as 'outstanding', though they were moved to complain once: of one of his very few female sitters, Dickey wrote – 'The Committee thought her figure tapered in descending and it is suggested that when next you are in London you cut a few inches from the bottom of the picture or add a few ditto to ditto of the lady.'

Dring also contributed to the WAAC's collection of reconstructed battle pictures – *HMS Kelly Limping Home from the Skagerrak*. Reconstructions, though artistically suspect in the eyes of certain members of the WAAC, were undeniably essential in the compiling of a full record of the Navy's activities. The Admiralty artists only rarely witnessed actual combat, and when they did, they could rarely count on seeing enough to make a painting. For detailed pictures of sea battles it was necessary to find artists willing to reconstruct the action from photographs, descriptions and a greater or lesser degree of imagination. Many of the most reliable records of this type were supplied by two veterans of the First World War scheme, Charles Pears and Norman Wilkinson.

Pears was sixty-seven when his first picture was acquired in 1940,[250] the founder and first President of the Royal Society of Marine Painters. He worked with enormous enthusiasm and the same meticulous regard for detail on pictures of many of the most important British successes of the war – including *Convoy led by Admiral Vian fighting its way through to Malta* and *Sinking of the Scharnhorst* – as well as one of the Navy's most glorious losses, the self-sacrifice of the armed merchantman HMS *Jervis Bay* on the guns of the pocket battleship *Admiral Scheer*, which enabled her convoy to scatter virtually unscathed, and won her Captain a posthumous VC.

Norman Wilkinson was until 1942 a camouflage adviser to the RAF, and then resigned in order to paint a series of pictures in which he 'attempted to show every phase of the work of the Royal Navy, Coastal Command and the Merchant Marine'. In two and a half years he completed fifty-four canvases, collectively titled 'The War at Sea', and in 1944 presented them 'to the Nation', by way of the WAAC – one of the very few gifts it accepted.[251]

It was, however, Charles Cundall who supplied the WAAC with its most famous reconstruction – *The withdrawal from Dunkirk, June 1940** – which he finished and submitted to the Committee for purchase in July 1940.[252] A second reconstruction of the BEF's rescue brought almost overnight fame to Richard Eurich – perhaps the most successful of all the Admiralty artists.

Born in 1903, Eurich studied under Tonks at the Slade from 1924–7 in the company of Rex Whistler, William Coldstream and Claude Rogers. In his final year he exhibited at the NEAC, in 1929 held his first one-man show at the Goupil Gallery, and exhibited at the Royal Academy for the first time in 1937.[253] From the time when he first began to draw and paint, Eurich's principal passion was the seascape – 'the great Atlantic breakers . . . the passing light and shadow'. From Christopher Wood, an artist he very much admired, he learned 'how vital it is to paint what you love regardless of fashion', and in the 1930s he spent much of his time in the smaller ports of the south coast, making his home in 1934 near Hythe and Southampton Water.

Eurich expressed himself eager that 'the traditional sea painting of Van der Velde and Turner should be carried on to enrich our heritage', and between 1940 and 1945 the WAAC acquired from him thirty-four oils on naval subjects (including one triptych of the Normandy landings)[254] and one drawing, *Three U-Boats in Portland Dockyard* – initially by purchase of specific commission, although after February 1941 he was an MoI salaried artist.

Eurich's pictures fall roughly into four groups according to the degree of reconstruction involved. Some were made directly from life – *Fishing boats at Whitby in wartime*, for example, or *A motor boat of the British Power Boat Company*. Others were wholly the product of imagination – among them *Survivors from a torpedoed ship**, which Churchill considered 'one of the best paintings to come out of the war'. Freely inspired by a newspaper paragraph, this depicted three sailors on an upturned boat, two unconscious and being kept afloat by a Jamaican shipmate; so powerful was its impact when first exhibited that the WAAC hastily withdrew it, fearing for its discouraging effect on the recruitment of merchant seamen.

Eurich was fascinated by the subject of survival amidst catastrophe: another of his pictures on the same theme falls into the third and largest group of pictures – those in which he recreated actions from eyewitness accounts and his own studies of the vessels involved,[255] to be placed in settings with which he was already familiar. *Rescue of the only survivor of a torpedoed merchant ship* was set around the Lizard, where the sailor, trapped against a rock, exhausted and only moments from drowning, was spotted by evacuees playing on the beach and rescued by a farmer's boy who lassooed him and dragged him ashore. Other south coast haunts were similarly used – in *Night raid, 1941 (an incendiary raid on Portsmouth)*, *Night attack over Southampton Water* and, most explicitly, *Air Fight over Portland*, of which he wrote, 'The scene is Portland (considerably telescoped so as to give the general layout of the place) and the time some day in September 1940 when over fifty German planes were brought down in quite a short action – one *ear* witness said it seemed only to last about quarter of an hour.'

In his paintings of convoys – the most spectacular the WAAC received of this crucial subject – Eurich's method was slightly different. The details of the ships he took from photographs, and he acquired valuable first-hand experience of convoy travel from trips on destroyers through the Straits of Dover. (These were regularly shelled, and he recalls the standing joke – 'Will you have your coffee before the bombardment or after?') In the mid-ocean settings, however, he naturally had complete freedom of expression to paint in his peacetime manner.

Least convincing, perhaps, were the handful of reconstructions in which he had seen neither the incident nor the setting in life, but was obliged nevertheless to aim

Richard Eurich, *Air-fight over Portland* (oil on canvas), 30 × 40

at veracity of detail and photographic realism. Under this heading would fall his versions of the Commando raids on Vaagso, Bruneval and finally Dieppe. (He was at least able to experience vicariously some of the atmosphere of the Dieppe Raid from the Combined Operations control-room, with its model of the town built from Spitfire reconnaissance photographs, following the action by radio through to its bloody conclusion.)

Ironically, this type of picture was required of him as a direct consequence of the enormous success of *The Withdrawal from Dunkerque* – the unrecognised difference being that in the summer of 1939 Eurich had made a sketching trip to Dunkirk and, with his notes and exceedingly acute memory for the detail of seascape, had an intimate working knowledge of the beaches.

The success of his naval work earned him, immediately after the war, three important ceremonial portrait commissions; having completed them, he turned his back on the safe but uninspiring career they opened up. This independence of mind may partly explain why Eurich has never received the acclaim which many critics believe he deserves.

CHAPTER THIRTY-FOUR

The Army in England

A FTER Dunkirk the War Office artists found their area of operations severely restricted – limited enough, in fact, to prompt the suggestion from the Treasury (stoutly resisted) that their appointments might be abolished. Two main theatres of army activity remained open to them – the Middle East, where tension was mounting, and the home base.

At home the focus was on training – a subject on which the WAAC had already made a start before the return of the BEF, with the appointment of Anthony Gross in March 1940 to record life at the Guards Barracks at Caterham. In 1940 Gross was best known as an etcher. After the Slade he had trained in Paris, and he spent much of the late 1920s and 30s in France where the failure of the etching boom had largely been disregarded; in 1930 he married the French painter Marcelle Marguerite Florenty.

During the 1930s he worked on animated films with the American Hector Hoppin – *La Joie de Vivre* in 1933 and *The Fox Hunt*[256] in 1936 – and when the war broke out he was working on *Round the World in 80 Days*. This, and a letter of recommendation from Eric Kennington, brought him to the attention of Kenneth Clark, then Head of Films at the MoI. A proposal for a film on barrage balloons came to nothing after protests against the MoI's 'arty' cinematic output, and Gross was offered instead a month's commission for army training subjects.

At Caterham, Gross outlined the very first stages – the uneasy wait in the reception area, the sight tests, the issue of army clothing – and traced the recruits' drill-dominated daily routine. Then, at Catterick, with the 56th Army Training Regiment, he drew aspects of more specialised training – in signalling, tanks, artillery and engineering.

Later, after his appointment as one of the four salaried War Office artists,[257] he turned to women's training at the ATS centres in Shoeburyness and Camberley. A sprinkling of 'domestic' subjects was perhaps inevitable (*Members of the ATS Cooking with Outdoor Ovens Built from Air Raid Debris* is one example) but Gross took pains to depict the areas in which women were receiving the same training as men – as anti-aircraft observers, calculating the velocity and position of shells, height finding, and so on.

Among the other artists recording army training in 1940 was William Conor, selected as a representative of Northern Ireland and at seventy-eight the oldest official war artist, who provided engaging chalk pictures of Bren gun and bombing practice at Ballykinlar Camp, County Down.

Raymond Coxon, a friend and contemporary of Henry Moore, was commissioned to paint two oils of 'military subjects' for £50. He optimistically suggested 'Orgy in the Mess', but was directed instead to the Horse Guards' Riding School and, having served in a cavalry unit in Palestine in the First World War, was well pleased: 'I wonder if some of your Committee who may not think the subject very apropos of 1940 know that cavalry is still . . . being manufactured. There is many a sore bottom at Windsor.'

For a more contemporary view of mobile warfare, Henry Lamb was detailed to cover tank subjects in South-East Command at Ashdown Forest, and with the Canadians. The material – 'sketches of chaps with their monsters' – was inexhaustible, but he found his concentration impaired by the unrelenting din of the Forces programme on the radio – '14 hours a day, full-bat and non-stop from the mess just the other side of the wall'.

He was not the only artist to chafe at the lack of privacy and the other indignities of army life. These were naturally felt more acutely from the inside. Rodrigo Moynihan, recently a member of the Euston Road School, found himself hopelessly miscast as a gunner in a signal-training regiment. 'I have misgivings', he wrote, 'in my ability to cope with the Morse Code and the inside of motorcycles. . . . It is all supposed to do me an immense amount of good, only really I prefer to be bad.'[258] Carel Weight, similarly unmechanically minded, spent a miserable winter in a Tank Regiment – his training consisting of digging the machines out of snowdrifts. He deeply resented the gratuitous humiliation of recruits by raucous SMs and indifferent MOs and disliked the grossness of the nights in the pub, which constituted the principal entertainment available. He sought and was given the opportunity by the WAAC to pour out his feelings in a Hogarthian series of four paintings entitled *Recruit's Progress*.

From a rather different perspective, Keith Vaughan, serving as a conscientious

Carel Weight, *Recruit's Progress:* The medical inspection (oil on canvas), 20×32
(one of a series of four paintings)

Keith Vaughan, *A barrack-room – sleep* (watercolour), $9\frac{5}{8} \times 12\frac{7}{8}$

objector in a non-combatant unit of the Pioneer Corps (subject nevertheless to military discipline), depicted the curious combination of loneliness and claustrophobia in barrack existence.[259] Miles Chance, a Lieutenant in the Royal Artillery, exposed the more ludicrous side of army training in his *Battle Camp: crawling in Wales*. For another less than serious look at the country's defences, the WAAC turned to the Home Guard.

There were in fact several artists serving in the Home Guard (including Henry Moore, Graham Sutherland, Eric Kennington and Gilbert Spencer), and the choice of Edward Ardizzone, safely outside the organisation and almost guaranteed to take a humorous approach, may well have been a sign of a slightly condescending attitude.[260] The Committee was rewarded by such pictures as *The War in Maida Vale: 'There is life in the old dogs yet'* and *West Country Manoeuvres: We are held up by ferocious Home Guards*, peopled with pudgy belligerents in baggy uniforms, ineffectually garnished with twigs

Miles Chance, *Battle camp: crawling in Wales* (watercolour), $9\frac{7}{8} \times 13\frac{3}{4}$

for camouflage – very much the image of the Home Guard which has been propagated by *Dad's Army*.

For the huge number of soldiers based at home, the period after Dunkirk was frequently as tedious as the Phoney War, and this is reflected in the relative dearth of subjects, other than training, for the War Office artists at home. While the threat of invasion was real, in the summer and autumn of 1940, coastal defences were the object of understandable interest – Gross drew Bren gun-posts at Dover, Freedman heavy batteries on the Isle of Sheppey, and Ravilious searchlights at Newhaven – but this interest waned as the threat receded. When foreign troops – Free French, Polish, and American – first arrived in Britain, their presence was well registered by Feliks Topolski, the Official Artist to the Polish Forces in England, who was used to record the life of Polish soldiers in Blackpool – and in such pictures as Leila Faithfull's *American Soldiers Playing Baseball in Hyde Park* – but again the novelty soon faded. Thus in some of the WAAC's more recherché commissions – Robin Guthrie's *Cutting Bread at the Army School of Cookery, Aldershot* or his *Private B Stockdale, Pastry Section No 2, Mandora Barracks, Aldershot – Shifting Oven Pans* – there is a slight air of desperation.

CHAPTER THIRTY-FIVE

The Middle East

A FTER the fall of France, the only War Office artist to escape in 1940 from 'Fortress Britain' was Edward Bawden. He had made no secret of his lack of interest in the Home Front,[261] and was correspondingly delighted to be instructed to proceed to the Middle East.

Middle East Command stretched from Iran to the Sudan; in July 1940, when Bawden sailed for Cairo, the main focus of activity was East Africa. After Italy's entry into the war in June 1940, her forces had begun to push out of Italian East Africa (Eritrea, Ethiopia and Italian Somaliland) into British possessions – the Sudan, Kenya and British Somaliland; and between September 1940 and August 1941 Bawden spent most of his time travelling south and east in the wake of the campaign to drive them back and out of Africa altogether.

He moved first down the Nile to Khartoum and Omdurman, where the 112° heat forced him indoors to concentrate on portraits, in pen and ink, of native troops, mostly men of the Sudan Defence Force. A little unfortunately, it was Ramadan, and his models had been fasting: 'after they'd been posing for about an hour they began to wilt.'

Then, when the first British offensive was launched into Ethiopia, Bawden went with it, accompanying the 1st Battalion, Essex Regiment, to Gallabat on the Sudanese border, where he painted the artillery attack on Italian positions across the border in Metemma. He was living in a 'birry' of boughs and grass which he enjoyed, but found the so-called virgin jungle a sad disappointment – 'It resembles the barer part of Epping Forest,' he wrote to his wife. His journey was interrupted, nonetheless, by a severe attack of malaria. He was extracted from the local hospital, its first ever white patient, by the District Commissioner of Roseires, who took him on his first foray into the mountains of Ethiopia. Undeterred by ants, termites, scorpions, lizards and bats, or by meals of peanut soup and gazelle's liver, Bawden made a second expedition without his European escort, marching ahead with bamboo pastoral staff and a knapsack containing bullybeef and Robert Bridges's *Testament of Beauty*, while a bearer followed with rifle and sketching bag.

A full-scale trek followed, over the mountains and across the Blue Nile into the heart of Ethiopia. Bawden remembers three parallel columns advancing towards Addis Ababa on the heels of the Italian retreat: the first, Orde Wingate and Haile Selassie and their entourage; the second, an expedition led by Laurens van der Post;[262] and finally his own party, consisting of an English colonel on a white horse, several officers and sergeants, a levy of eighty Ethiopian cadets, a camel train with Sudanese drivers and himself, travelling now with the officers, now with the camels. The Colonel spent his spare time bird-watching, Bawden (a keen gardener) collecting flower seeds, and the Sudanese quarrelling with the Ethiopians. 'There was generally an uproar in which the camels joined, of course. Oh, a most enjoyable experience.'

Edward Bawden, *The Catholic Church, Addis Ababa* (watercolour), $18 \times 22\frac{3}{4}$, (Tate Gallery)

Bawden arrived in Addis shortly after the reinstating of Haile Selassie on 5 May 1941, five years to the day after the surrender to the Italians. He had already painted the Lion of Judah (known familiarly as 'Tiger Tim') in Khartoum: sittings were silent as Selassie spoke no English and Bawden no French – 'but we made I hope courteous gestures'. In July he was billeted briefly in a disused wing of one of Selassie's palaces, sleeping in the corridor surrounding the central audience chamber. 'At night when I walk with a hurricane lamp from an adjoining building . . . large bats flitter in the darkness overhead and rays from the lamp pass and illumine obscure corners of the empty audience chamber. . . . Between the rolling of the thunder comes the evil cry of hyenas, now far off & again close by.' His large watercolour *Menelik's Palace (The*

Old Gebbi) is one of the most famous and atmospheric of his wartime pictures.

He then went north into Eritrea to make portraits of Ethiopian troops of different tribes, relishing the technical challenge: 'When the model is the colour of a grape it is difficult to disassociate form and colour, more especially in the region of the cheek & cheek bone, a rounded expanse of fat with no geographical features & impossible to map with accuracy.'

Bawden left Ethiopia in September 1941 with a mixture of regret and relief. It was the most beautiful country he had ever seen, but he had been ill for most of his stay with a combination of malaria and altitude sickness, and he was now eager to turn to the Western Desert where cooler weather presaged a renewal of operations. In March 1941 Rommel had pushed the British east out of Cyrenaica, leaving only a foothold at Tobruk; and two attempts (Operations 'Brevity' and 'Battleaxe') to relieve the garrison in May and June had failed. In the lull before a renewed British offensive, Bawden set off with a jeep and driver over the Western Desert to seek the Long Range Desert Group at the Siwa Oasis, where he made several topographical drawings;[263] then, after Operation 'Crusader' had forced the Germans back to El Agheila, he embarked on a trip to Benghazi – only to retreat hastily via Tobruk, Bardia and Mersa Matruh as Rommel pushed east again to Gazala.

The trips into the Western Desert were not a success. Bawden found it both like and unlike the popular conception of the desert – muffled in a continuous sandstorm, but so cold that tea leaves turned out of the pot rapidly became a solid lump. Nor did he appreciate the company: 'For glamour read Herodotus, for romance Shakespeare, do not come to the East expecting either. . . . Do not travel with journalists unless you like their attitude, conversation, and manners: for myself I do not care for that type of shit.'

This partly explains his delight at finding, on his return, Anthony Gross installed in Cairo:[264] 'He's an awfully nice fellow. . . . He was interested in my attempts at portraiture: the morning passed rapidly while we talked of Rothenstein and Kennington,

Edward Bawden, *The artist's tent, Mersa Matruh* (watercolour), $10\frac{3}{4} \times 23\frac{1}{4}$

h. 168 – Cairo – Flood time near Pyramids.

Anthony Gross and Edward Bawden (photograph reproduced by kind permission of Anthony Gross)

and of their method which can always guarantee a minimum success. . . . You would not conceive how exciting it is after nearly twenty months to talk openly about painters and painting, or what it has been like working without that stimulus: I tell you that I look at any postcard reproduction of a painting as I would look at green fields.'

Early in 1942 they set off together north into Palestine and the Lebanon. During 1941 there had been decisive military activity throughout the northern section of Middle East Command. In March 1941 the pro-German Raschid Ali became Prime Minister in Iraq and appealed to the Axis for help in evicting the British forces based there.[265] The German attack on the British air base at Habbaniya in May was, however, defeated, and the pro-British regent reinstated. The British were thus encouraged to move, in alliance with the Free French, against the Vichy French in the former French colony of Syria: by July 1941 they had won the right to occupy Syria for the duration. This left Iran as the focus of attention. The entry of Russia into the war in June 1941 had made Iran and the Caucasus crucial as a supply route between Russia and the other Allies; in August 1941 British and Soviet troops invaded to enforce the expulsion of German agents, and in January 1942 Iran signed a treaty of neutrality.

Gross's own brief, such as it was, was to travel through Syria and Iraq to Iran to become official war artist to the 9th Army supposedly being formed there, and then, the timing depending on the fate of the German advance against the Russians, to proceed with the 9th Army through the Caucasus and into Russia. His progress was, however, erratic and highly-coloured.

Bawden and Gross became, and have remained, firm friends, but they had very different approaches to travel. Bawden was a shy man, 'not in the least bit pushful'; of all the opportunities his appointment gave him, he appreciated most the chances of solitary and arduous journeys – 'trekking & camping or a long march gives immense pleasure'. He had little sympathy with the army mentality, or with colonial administrators who showed signs of expecting 'amusing' drawings 'having the flavour of caricature (nasty little wogs & all that, you know)!' He preferred and sought out the company of the native inhabitants: 'For choice I would far rather be with Africans, Indians or living alone in a reed hut in the heavy, steamy malarial heat of sheikhdom than in the improvised unprofessional discomfort of an English troop camp, where our ridiculous sense of humour and too frequent use of a common expletive are needed in order to put up with conditions which with a little care and thought could be easily improved. Natives without exception have better manners.'[266]

Gross was naturally gregarious and, after twenty years in France, something of a bon viveur; his travel diary[267] plots a trail of 'piss ups' and 'beanfeasts'. He was particularly drawn by the French atmosphere of Syria – the gendarmes sipping aperitifs in the shade, the vineyards, the older women dressed all in black, grey shutters, old Renaults jogging along – and after a visit to Trans-Jordan with the Arab Legion and British Druze Cavalry and Camel Force, he appears to have attached himself to the French forces and in the spring of 1942 travelled round recording their various duties with a zest worthy of the maker of *Joie de Vivre*. At Tripoli he drew Fighting French Marines on the Mina, before going to drink arak and smoke a hookah in the Phoenician town of Tartūs, looking out over the 'pirate island' of Arwad. From Selemiya, he struck off into the desert with the intention of recording the attempts of French Meharistes camel corps to separate warring nomad and sedentary tribes: he was, however, thwarted by a truck whose petrol tank sprang a leak (plugged inadequately with a date) and by a French colonel convinced that he was a member of the secret service, on account of his uncanny ability, as an Englishman, to speak French.

Hearing of the migration of the Fedaan across the Euphrates, Gross hastened to Deir es Zōr in an American ambulance full of Arab patients, one of whom was sick all over his portfolio. After laborious and unpleasant repairs, he spent five days drawing the extraordinary scenes as the tribes poured across a narrow swaying suspension bridge with innumerable sheep, goats and donkeys, and camels laden with baggage, bedding, mountains of filthy rugs, and children and dogs in their side-packs. (The aim of the French and British forces had been, in the confusion, to recover loot the Fedaan had pilfered in recent months – which included trucks, armoured cars, several cannon and a tank; in this they were entirely unsuccessful.)

Then, in his bid to reach the Caucasus, Gross moved swiftly to Iran and settled comfortably in the Romanian Legation in Teheran, 'the Paris of the East'. Meanwhile, Bawden in his turn had found congenial surroundings amidst the Marsh Arabs of the Muntafiq, the area of swamp and date garden on the Euphrates between Basra and Nāsirūyah. He had been unimpressed by the artistic potential of military installations in Baghdad – 'similar in every respect (with the addition of a palm & numerous winged pests) to what you enjoy in England' – and the Muntafiq fascinated him both as artist and explorer. 'No one has – so far as I know – attempted to penetrate this wild region with a paint brush.'

His visit was not without some political advantage: 'I am doing the Political Officer

Anthony Gross, *Meharistes resting among Roman ruins, Palmyra, Syria*, pen and wash, $15\frac{1}{8} \times 22$,
(Ashmolean Museum, Oxford)

a small & useful service as the Sheikhs are flattered to receive what they conceive
to be an honour conferred by HM Govt' in return for their support during the fighting
in 1941. But it was, as he acknowledged, a trifle outside his brief: '"We sent you
out to make a record of Army life," you will exclaim, "and you choose to get yourself
in an area banned to troops." How true that is.' And in August he was informed that
he was to be replaced by Edward Ardizzone, and recalled. This he accepted, in his
own words, 'sedately': 'It is good that someone else should do some work literally
with the sweat of his brow & return later a more emaciated and healthier man. I
am glad your choice has fallen on one who can willingly spare some fat in the service
of his country . . . [but] why do you wish to recall me when to the present moment
I have not had the opportunity to contract dysentery, bilhartzia or hookworm!'

He was on his way home when, six hundred miles off Lagos, the ship in which
he was travelling, SS *Laconia*, was torpedoed: Bawden spent five days adrift in a lifeboat
before being picked up by a Vichy French destroyer and interned at Mediouna Camp

outside Casablanca, where he remained for two months until finally liberated by the Americans, after Operation 'Torch'. The worst aspect of this mishap – apart from the irritations of two months of the uncongenial company of his French captors, a diet of cabbage soup, and the necessity of wearing Foreign Legion uniform – was the loss of all his pictures of the Muntafiq. He was determined to return – and in September 1943 was sent back to Iraq, this time under the auspices of the MoI.

It was to take him some time to return to the Marsh Arabs. After a prohibitively uncomfortable trip to Kurdistan (in a car used by General Ritchie in the Western Desert), he retreated to Baghdad and concentrated on portraits of 'quite unimportant Iraqis in British Government service'. Looking back now, Bawden feels that it was during the war years that he 'really learned to draw'. Previously he had rarely ventured on figures bigger than matchstick size: now, with outdoor subjects virtually impossible in the heat amidst swarms of flies and children, he was faced with the necessity of doing portraits at close range. Having taken this step, he proceeded to experiment, progressing from line and heelball to watercolour portraits. 'I cannot altogether dispense with the pen but colour takes the place of black ink, naturally too colour predominates over line – so that I am justified in describing them as paintings & not tinted drawings: also the colour helps to give a sensation of solidity . . . an effect I couldn't achieve while using ingenious cross hatchings & heelball. I think I'm on the track of something which at least for me is new.'

In February 1944 Bawden was offered the chance to accompany the Middle East Anti-Locust Unit – British, Sudanese and Palestinian locust experts – on an expedition across Saudi Arabia from the Red Sea to the Persian Gulf. This was part of an international campaign to forestall the swarm expected in 1944, which threatened food supplies in the Middle East, and to ensure 'perhaps even a surplus which will be badly needed in liberated Europe' by locating the breeding grounds and destroying the young 'hoppers' with poisoned bait. He returned from this adventure with mixed feelings. He cared very little for the British administrators en route who disapproved of his appearance at dinner improperly dressed in a lounge suit (from which, be it said, 'wartime moths had removed the flies'); nor for the Bedouin way of life, excessively communal and slow-moving. 'Like Mr Eliot's Gumbie cat one just sits & sits & sits & sits until the European arse is sore.' He was also cast down by the lack of locusts: 'I like insects and didn't see enough of them.' But around the mission camp at Hail, where most of his drawings were done, the landscape was extraordinary – 'grim, desolate & forbidding as though a great fire had in a past age burnt up every sign of life, leaving the piled rocks blackened by smoke or scorched to redness, but with veins of more vivid colour where the heat remained. . . . The volcanic reds and blacks, austerely rich by juxtaposition, had the dim fiery glow of a Russian ikon. . . . The skyline . . . was always as unexpected in contour as the red line of a seismograph.' The pictures he sent home were among those the Committee most admired.

Then at last Bawden returned to his Marsh Arabs, and spent an extraordinary month, in the steam heat of 120°, exploring the creeks of the Muntafiq in a Middle Eastern version of the gondola, down tunnels of palms, with flooded date gardens on either side, and deep silence broken only by the occasional splash of strange birds fishing and basking terrapins diving to safety. He stayed in the *mudhifs*, or reed guest-

Edward Bawden, *Three armed Muntafiq women* (watercolour), $15\frac{1}{2} \times 20$

houses, of the various sheikhs and, in return for the compliment of his portraits, was regaled with enormous banquets of entire boiled sheep laid out amidst five hundred smaller dishes, the whole eaten by torchlight: 'By touch you have to distinguish a blancmange or a gravy or soft-boiled cucumber.'

Bawden just had time for a trip into Iran to record the movement of supplies to Russia – still the main focus of British activity in the area – when he was recalled in August 1944. By the end, he was distinctly tired of travelling: 'Once I get home,' he wrote to his wife, 'I'll never travel again – except for a holiday with you.' But he had had what he now recalls as a remarkable 'Cook's Tour . . . very happily separated from offices and control. . . . One simply sneaked about with a clean eye – I mean, what an opportunity.'

CHAPTER THIRTY-SIX

The Western Desert and Sicily

T HE last Bawden had seen of Anthony Gross was in April 1942 when at Gross's
instigation the two had jointly taken Bawden's Sudanese servant boating in Beirut
harbour to cure his homesickness; it was from there that Gross had set off on the
travels which landed him in June in Teheran. It did not take him long to realise that
the Russians – at a time when the second German offensive into the Soviet Union
was just being launched – had no intention of letting him into the Caucasus, and
his attention was diverted by what his travel diary succinctly describes as 'The Flap'
in the Western Desert.

In May 1942 Rommel had resumed his eastward offensive, and by mid-June the
Gazala Line was crumbling. Tobruk fell on 21 June, and by the end of the month
the British and German armies were racing for Cairo, one backwards, the other forwards; on the train bringing Gross from Palestine, there was much speculation among
the passengers as to who would be holding Cairo when they reached it. But on 1
July the 8th Army turned to check the German advance in the natural bottleneck
of the Alamein Line, fifty miles west of Alexandria. Though a month's hard fighting
resulted in stale-mate, in the battle of First Alamein the landslide had been halted
and time won for British resupply and reorganisation.

Gross's first act on reaching Cairo had been to look up a doctor he had met on
the troopship coming out, who was now running a hospital outside Alexandria; with
him he meandered about the Delta on a hospital train, helping to pick up the wounded
streaming away from Alamein. Then, hitching a lift with an ammunition convoy,
he proceeded from one medical base to another towards the Front, recording transfu-
sions, operations and, increasingly, deaths. He seems to have ended up at the 2nd
Armoured Brigade's main dressing-station on the night of 21 July, when the Brigade
was involved in an unsuccessful attack on Rommel's front along Ruweisât Ridge. Gross
painted the tanks going up to the ridge, the New Zealand infantry and artillery preparing to advance – and later pouring back as casualties, so many that doctors were operating on two cases at once and the wounded overflowed out of the tents into the open,
where shade was provided by groundsheets pitched from trucks.[268]

On a brief excursion to El Alamein itself, Gross found conditions for painting in the
desert not unfavourable; under the canvas canopy stretched over the control post the
light was fine and diffused, and sand mixed into watercolour he found gave it body
and created pleasant textural effects, while a bomb made an excellent seat. However,
a sojourn with the RAF Desert Force persuaded him to leave the Western Desert. The
pilots, their early 'Hurribombers' at a crippling disadvantage against the faster Italian
fighters, were badly demoralised and reluctant to be painted for fear of a jinx. Censorship prevented Gross from disclosing this state of affairs in any degree of detail; and,
distressed by the number of pilots who failed to return, he decided to go back to Cairo.

[232]

Anthony Gross, *The Battle of Egypt, 1942: bombing-up* (pen and wash), $14\frac{5}{8} \times 21\frac{3}{4}$

He was there instructed by the PR staff to paint a reconstruction of one of the previous year's more heroic feats – the so-called 'Garrett Landing'. When Crete fell at the end of May 1941, Major Garrett was ordered to disband his battalion of Royal Marines, which had reached Sphakia too late to be taken off, and surrender to the Germans. He declined and, in the words of the official War Office account, 'walked through the village shouting, "Who goes home?"' With 140 Royal Marines and an Australian engineer, he set off on the 180-mile voyage to North Africa in a decrepit motor-lighter with no instruments, a small-scale map of the Eastern Mediterranean in a school atlas, and enough food for one-and-a-half square inches of bully beef and a ship's biscuit per head per day; he arrived at Sidi Barrani on 6 June 1941 with the loss of only two men.

While working on his reconstruction, Gross shared a studio with Edward Ardizzone, who had arrived to replace Bawden in the middle of 1942. While Bawden was languishing at Casablanca, Ardizzone was recording the British Eighth Army's breakthrough under Montgomery at the second battle of El Alamein. Montgomery's plan was for his infantry to clear corridors for the tanks through the minefields laid by Rommel. The attack was launched on 23 October; then, after ten days of indecisive pushes, there came a new offensive, concentrated in the northern sector of the Alamein Line. Further south, near Ruweisât Ridge, Ardizzone recorded his impressions: 'All day in a white sandy plain. The signals truck half buried in a hole like a burrowing beetle. Ahead two tanks in pink and black and blue and grey. Beyond them our screen of anti-tank guns looking like partridges in the stubble of an immense field. Beyond

Edward Ardizzone, *Behind Ruweisât Ridge* (watercolour), $14\frac{1}{4} \times 22$

them again more tanks almost invisible in the haze. On the horizon columns of black smoke from burning tanks. A curious and ominous sense of stillness, no movement except for the MO's jeep which, with its Red Cross flag flying, scuttled across the plain like St John's Ambulance at a football match. Tracer shot from the enemy bounding in great arcs across the plain. Air bursts like black notes in the sky. . . . We are shelled considerably all day.'

He found the featureless immensity of the scene very difficult to translate into pictures. Much later he remembered, 'It was all so much like a naval battle . . . all so far apart. . . . I used to sometimes wish I was at the Battle of Waterloo . . . to do a picture which was paintable of troops in line charging.' But by 4 November 1942, when the line of minefields was finally breached, he was right at the Front nonetheless (as his drawing *A battle seen from Battalion HQ* records), acutely aware of taking part in a historic victory. Thirty-five years later he still had vivid memories of 'that night, dawn arising and you saw our own tanks going forward over the minefields. . . . At the end everybody knew, every soldier was smiling, it was a most remarkable and exciting moment.'

Ardizzone was then to follow the British advance all the way across North Africa into Tunisia.[269] On the road outside Alamein he had his first sight of large-scale destruction and death. A convoy of Italian trucks had been blown up and over a huge area the ground was 'speckled with dead bodies. And then right in front of us was a truck which had obviously had some officer's baggage on it, and you know what one's driver was like – mad for loot, mad for loot. . . . He was like a terrier going head first into the truck scattering everything about to try and find something valuable. And lying beside him was a naked leg which had been blown off. . . . It was like a marble leg, it was rather beautiful really, but it was a strange sight.'

Ardizzone's appreciation of the macabre in what he saw was generally subordinated in his pictures of the triumphal progress across Libya and on through Tripoli, which fell on 23 January 1943, exactly three months and 1400 miles after the attack at Alamein. The titles reveal the type of scene he chose to highlight – *Arabs bartering eggs for tea near Sirte, Jocks in the museum at Leptis Magna, Laying out the pasta at our Albergo in Tripoli.* But as another drawing makes clear, he did not lose sight of the cost of the success – *On the road to Tripoli: a cup of tea for the burial party.*

By this time two separate Allied forces were attempting to sweep the Germans out of North Africa. On 8 November 1942 Operation 'Torch' had landed three task forces at Casablanca, Oran and Algiers, and while Montgomery pushed across from the east, these troops, the British First Army and the US II Corps, were converging from the west on Central Tunisia. In February Ardizzone seems to have left the Eighth Army to join the First, witnessing with the 1st Brigade of Guards the end of the battle at the Kasserine Pass. He watched the German counter-attack pushing down into the plain with conflicting emotions: 'We had bedded down for the night among the spring

Edward Ardizzone, *On the road to Tripoli: a cup of tea for the burial party*
(watercolour), $8\frac{1}{2} \times 11\frac{1}{4}$

[235]

flowers. I'll never forget the scent of them, wild mignonette, all out of a sterile desert. . . .
It was a fine dawn and far away hearing the bugles. . . . We could see them coming
down the roads from the mountains, and we shot them up – fascinating. Why it should
be fascinating to see poor men being killed I don't know, but still. . . . And there we
were amongst flowers; it was very moving.'

One crucial long-term factor in the Axis failure in North Africa was the extraordinarily stubborn defence of Malta. The island was a vital naval and air base for the control
of the Eastern Mediterranean and thus of Axis supply routes between Italy and Africa,
and it was under incessant German air attack from June 1940 until the end of 1942.
A peak was reached in April 1942, when the Luftwaffe virtually closed the sea lanes
and cut off supplies;[270] but so great was the courage and determination showed by
the civilian population in resisting and surviving the siege that George VI awarded
the whole Maltese people the George Cross. By May, reinforcements of fighter planes
were reaching Malta; and Rommel himself ascribed his subsequent weakness at Alamein to their depredations on Axis convoys.

It was in July 1942, when the worst of the crisis was past, that it was first proposed
to send an artist to Malta. By August the WAAC had decided to send Leslie Cole, an
ex-RCA student who was now an art teacher at Hull College of Art. The members
had been much impressed by pictures he had submitted on his own initiative – 'one
of the few artists whose work we have seen who can make a vigorous drawing of
figures in action' – and they bought a large number.[271] Now they proposed to employ
him on salary to the MoI, to cover the work of all three Services in Malta.

The appointment was greatly delayed, partly by the difficulty of securing transport,
partly by efforts to guarantee compensation for Cole's wife in the event of his death
– this was considered a particularly hazardous assignment. When he finally arrived
in May 1943, he concentrated largely on civilian subjects, in honour of the contribution ordinary people had made: the defences tunnelled into the soft limestone of the
island (*Malta. The dormitory under St Augustine's, Valetta: people beginning to gather in
the evening; A Malta dockyard: the underground church with Rear-Admiral Kenneth Mackenzie, Mrs Mackenzie, two children and sailors*), and the desperate expedients contrived
against the siege – one subject which particularly appealed was a camouflaged gunpit
with vegetables growing tightly round the base of the gun.

Cole's pictures greatly impressed Lord Gort, Malta's Commander-in-Chief, who personally requested the extension of his appointment; but Cole then managed dexterously
to avoid the kind of pictures Gort wanted – mostly reconstructions of heroic incidents
(such as the building of Krendi aerodrome during the darkest days of the siege 'which
he would entitle Confidence'), preferring to devote his limited time to recording events
as they happened. He wrote excitedly of being allowed to accompany the successful
expedition on June 11–12 to reduce the islands of Pantelleria and Lampedusa used
by the Italians as E-boat bases: 'Admiral Harcourt went into battle wearing a panama
and grey flannel bags. I had all the gear on that the navy offered and must have looked
comical. I lost three pencils, my tin hat and my peace of mind at the first broadside.'

The taking of Pantelleria was an essential preliminary to the Allies' first step back
into Europe – Operation 'Husky', the landing on the south-east corner of Sicily on
10 July 1943. During the spring of 1943 Ardizzone had spent much time in North

Africa with the 50th Division; now he heard of the proposed landing, and contrived to go on to the beach at Avola with them – 'As usual I fell into the water, got soaked.' He preserved his sketchbook, however: 'I'd wrapped that up in a French letter.'

This sketchbook-cum-diary was the start of a new system. Ardizzone hated drawing in public, and never worked from life; nor at this stage of the war did he habitually make sketches to be worked up as more elaborate drawings later.[272] Instead he made *verbal* notes, from which he would reconstruct pictures later, rather as before the war he would have supplied illustrations for a book text – the difference being that this text was his own, drawn from his own experience, and the pictures were built from memory, not imagination. He might make sketches of the more elaborate details – of architecture, perhaps – which he would need for the settings of his chosen scenes; but he was primarily interested in the human element, and the figures themselves were drawn from verbal descriptions.[273]

The diary documents Ardizzone's growing awareness that this was a different kind of war, characterised by close country fighting, all 'round the corner stuff', claustro-phobic and nerve-racking, and acted out against a setting which made the brutality the more appalling. The scenery was extraordinarily lush and beautiful after North Africa, and the living, for British officers at least, comfortable, even lavish at times. The diary gives much detail of food – tomatoes picked from a field near Syracuse, 'salt fresh milk cheese' near Raddusa, fresh figs near Lentini – and of endless 'bibulous' evenings; the entry for 9 September 1943 is fairly typical – 'Have a grand time, lots of liquor and I dance with everybody.'[274]

But even a man of Ardizzone's apparently buoyant temperament could not ignore the bloodiness of the battle when at every turn he was brought face to face with its aftermath. 'We drink a bottle of . . . champagne. Heaven. Brought to earth by the smell of dead bodies hidden somewhere, a smell that haunts one everywhere.' At Primasole Bridge he was confronted with the debris of some of the bitterest fighting in the campaign: 'Bodies disembowelled, stripped of their clothes, blackened, legs and arms gone and even one blown in half. . . . Must try and make some drawings of the horrors but don't want to.' A few days later he forced himself to draw a scene even more hideous for the beauty of its surroundings – tanks burning and blowing up, the ground littered with casualties, twisted and maimed. Ardizzone and his driver picked up a man with his hand blown off – 'quite euphoric, laughing like anything'. *A battle in an orchard of almond trees in Sicily* is one of the most explicit of all Second World War pictures as a record of death and mutilation, doubly horrific for being painted without any variation from Ardizzone's usual style.

As light relief came the ludicrous episode of the surrender of Taormina. When the battalion to which they were attached

Edward Ardizzone

[237]

Edward Ardizzone, *A battle in an orchard of almond trees in Sicily* (watercolour), $14\frac{3}{4} \times 21\frac{1}{4}$

halted for a rest before entering the town, Ardizzone and his friend Geoffrey Keating[275] advanced alone – straight into a large number of startled Italian infantry. 'I waved my stick and obviously dear Geoffrey looked more imposing than I did, because the whole company surrendered to us, complete with machine-guns,' delighted and relieved to find themselves in English rather than German hands. Finding that their camp was outside a particularly attractive hotel, Ardizzone and Keating entered and ordered 'a cracking fine lunch', sending a demand meanwhile to the Commanding Officer that he and the rest of his force of four hundred should surrender. 'My God, I've never been so frightened in all my life. But in fact they did . . . a most extraordinary thing.' The pair then sped away on borrowed bicycles, notifying the forward troops of the town's capture as they passed – 'and they were very angry, of course, they got absolute stick from Monty.' Unfortunately modesty forbade the incorporation of these details in Ardizzone's picture *On the road south to Taormina with some Italian prisoners in the foreground.*

[238]

CHAPTER THIRTY-SEVEN

Italy

ON 3 September Ardizzone was offered and seized the chance to cross the Straits of Messina in the wake of Operation 'Baytown', the Allied invasion of Italy.

He landed at Reggio, which, as he noted in his diary, struck him as 'a wretched town . . . a desolation of twisted shutters and broken wire. Only the riff-raff left and they, with the soldiers, looting the town. The soldier with two dozen coat hangers and two alarm clocks. . . .' Looting was a phenomenon Ardizzone appears to have found peculiarly distasteful and he made several penetrating drawings of the troops in flagrante.[276] His soldiers should not be seen purely as figures of fun. He did have a natural tendency to see the comic side of any scene and, when working entirely for himself, he concentrated on optimistic subjects, showing at worst the more sympathetic human foibles, most evident in the pubs and tarts of Maida Vale which feature largely in his work of the 1930s. But he took his responsibilities as a war artist very

Edward Ardizzone, *Troops and civilians looting in the town of Reggio, Italy, on the day of its occupation, 3rd September, 1943* (watercolour), $11\frac{3}{4} \times 16$

seriously and did not, generally speaking, try to gloss over the unattractive or shameful aspects of victory any more than the horrors of defeat and death; to lay too much stress on the humorous side of his war work is to depreciate it, and to obscure the fact that few other Second World War artists depicted more greed, dishonesty or bloodshed.

Ardizzone's knack of making friends – both within the Army and with the press – enabled him to keep well up to the Front when he wanted to,[277] and he was in the vanguard for much of the Allied advance through Italy – a campaign which was covered in depth, both by him and by others.

Also present at Operation 'Baytown' had been John Worsley,[278] who had joined an LCF (Landing Craft Flat) to go in with the first assault at Reggio, lie off, and give cover for the craft following. 'I felt I was on the touchline as an onlooker watching, and therefore was somehow immune from danger. I set up my board and paints close to two A.A. guns by the bridge and got a nice little wash going, and then, of course, we were divebombed by an Italian aeroplane and everything went for six . . . painting, drawing-boards, paints, etc. . . . So from then on I used just a drawing-pad.' Worsley later joined HMS *Roberts* for the landings at Salerno, sailing from Bizerta with the invasion fleet, and remaining with the landing operation for the first four days.

Ardizzone meanwhile had been pursuing a zig-zag course from toe to heel and back, to enter Naples on the day it fell. 'The people go crazy, mob our jeep as we go ahead,' he wrote. 'They try to lever off the top of our ration box with a bayonet and steal our rations.' After twenty-four hours the squalor and misery of 'bloody Napoli' – bedbugs in the hotel, people begging in the streets ('women will lie with you for a packet of biscuits'), and a 'Goyaesque' scene of headless, armless, naked corpses blackening in the hospital – drove him away, though not before he had involuntarily assimilated the material for some of his most powerful drawings.

His next major series was made with the 8th Army on the Sangro during the campaign to break through the Germans' winter Front on the Gustav Line. He was then intended to cover the other wing of the Allied advance on Rome, and arrangements were made for him to travel to Anzio and Nettuno where landings were scheduled for 22 January 1944. But on 20 January he was in hospital with an ailment he was later convinced was 'a bronchitis of fear' – and he visited the shattered towns only in mid-February, a missed opportunity he later regretted.

When his long-overdue leave was finally granted, Ardizzone spent it in Cairo – and here, in the first week of March 1944, he met William Coldstream; they explored the city together and by the end of the month, perhaps at Ardizzone's prompting, Coldstream had put in a request to go to Italy.

Coldstream, one of the founders in 1937 of the Euston Road School,[279] had first been considered by the WAAC at the beginning of 1941, but he had volunteered for military service immediately after the fall of France[280] and was unable to find the time – he was, and remains, a slow and infinitely painstaking worker – to paint for the Committee until finally appointed a full-time war artist two years later. After a curious month devoted to a portrait of General von Thoma, one of the most illustrious German PoWs in Britain,[281] he sailed in July 1943 for North Africa in the War Office's employ as Official Portrait Artist to the Middle East Forces – an appointment specifically requested by General Alexander.

However, by the time he arrived in Algiers many potential sitters – including Eisenhower, Admiral Sir Andrew Cunningham, and Air Chief Marshal Sir Arthur Tedder (C-in-Cs respectively of the Allied Forces in North Africa, the Mediterranean Fleet, and the Air Forces in the Mediterranean), General Giraud (C-in-C Civil and Military, French North Africa) and Alexander himself – had already been painted by Henry Carr,[282] and Coldstream continued the long trek east to Cairo.

Official war artists in the Middle East were, to their pleasure and relief, under the lightest of controls, Army PR staff being generally more interested in American journalists. Transport in particular was left very much to the artists' initiative. Coldstream has described his travels round North Africa and Italy as 'assisted hitchhiking', and this journey from Algiers to Cairo incorporated an extended trip in a cattle truck across Algeria and Tunisia during which Coldstream, as the thinnest and

William Coldstream

most heat-resistant member of the party, did all the cooking, and a moonlight voyage across the Gulf of Gabes from Sfax to Alexandria, which Coldstream remembers for the pleasantly surrealistic moment when, while on submarine watch, he found a flurry of white rabbits bustling round his feet – fugitives from the French crew who kept them as pets.

Nor when he reached Cairo did he execute the 'official' portraits that might have been expected by the WAAC. Partly, perhaps, to get rid of him, partly because they could find no 'important' sitters who would allow him the time he required (thirty sittings of one and a half hours were not unusual), the PR staff despatched him to paint Indian troops at No II Indian Reinforcement Camp. In the oven-heat of a corrugated hut six kilometres from the pyramids, Coldstream painted some of his most admired portraits[283] – *Subedar Jagat Singh, Havildar Ajmer Singh (Sikh)*, Rifleman Mangal Singh* and *Havildar Kulbir Thapa* – sitters chosen because 'they disliked doing it least . . . I think it got them off various duties.'

Now in the spring of 1944, the Committee decided that Coldstream should go to the devastated area round Cassino where the Allied advance had ground to a halt.[284] His first base was at Capua where, from the roof of a half-finished block of flats, he completed his first subject landscape *Casualty Reception Station at Capua*, fascinated by the contrast between the stillness of the shattered town and the battle he knew to be raging some forty miles away at Monte Cassino. This was followed by *Capua*

Henry Carr painting the portrait of General Dwight D. Eisenhower

Cathedral, a view from the Bishop's Palace, and, in the autumn of 1944. *The Bailey Bridge built by Royal Engineers over the Volturno River, Italy* – this latter subject carefully staged by Coldstream, who asked for a tank to be driven out on to the bridge and posed there for half an hour until its image was firmly in place on the canvas.

Coldstream was not convinced of his aptitude as a war artist: 'I had, as they [the WAAC] knew, really no illustrative gifts – my work really consisted of painting chosen subjects rather carefully and taking a long time. I did feel slightly guilty inasmuch as I felt that my work had absolutely no relevance to the war:[285] but I was only too glad to get on with my painting.' However, his pictures delighted the Committee as some of the most beautiful of the war, and the only complaint was that there were not more of them.

Coldstream was to encounter Ardizzone again, this time in Rome,[286] in November 1944, where they were joined by Edward Bawden. He was hoping to go on to Yugoslavia to join the partisans, but in the meantime the three spent a happy week's sightseeing. 'Guiding Ted is like persuading a large bluebottle to take a certain course across a window pane,' Bawden informed his wife, 'but Coldstream comes very quietly at heel. . . . He is appreciative of almost everything but Ted sometimes jibs, he gives a wild stare, pulls himself up with a start, stares again in a defiant manner and declares that he doesn't really like it. . . . Both of them are delightfully amusing companions. . . .'[287]

This was the prelude to a grim winter on the Gothic Line. Bawden, at his own request, spent Christmas outside Ravenna drawing the men of a Basuto Pioneer Company (*Cesena: the Barrack-Room of a Basuto Pioneer Company under winter conditions*, and *Cesena: Cooks of a Basuto Pioneer Company preparing the midday dinner on Christmas Day 1944*). Subsequently, finding little material at the fighting Front – 'rather less of pictorial interest than an English country lane during manoeuvres' – he turned his attention to the activity of the Italian partisans in the Romagna fen behind the enemy lines, an increasing irritant to the Germans which contributed significantly to the ultimate Allied success in Northern Italy.

'Not a man but a memory', wrote Bawden, 'inspires the fighting brigades which take their names from Garibaldi'; and in February, perched on the roof of a municipal building in Ravenna, he recorded the presentation of the Medaglio d'Oro to the town's partisan leader Bulow in the Piazza Garibaldi. 'Most of the square was clasped in shadow, only a few houses at one end and Garibaldi raised high on a pedestal caught the light, and his figure in white stone dominated the scene. . . . For the occasion . . . a standard uniform was issued: khaki pants, peagreen battledress blouse & cow pat cap. The red scarf around the neck links memories of Garibaldi to more recent ones of the hammer & sickle.'

Edward Bawden, *Ravenna – return of the Garibaldi spirit – Lieutenant-General Sir Richard McCreery decorates Bulow, the partisan leader, with the Medaglio d'Oro for conspicuous personal bravery* (watercolour), $22\frac{3}{8} \times 30\frac{7}{8}$

His main complaint throughout his stay in Italy was the cold, far more trying than the sweltering heat and humidity of the Middle East. 'All the drawings you will receive have been done with cold fingers. Sometimes, as I may have told you, I pee'd into my enamelled mug & then cupped my hands around it to try & receive back some of the heat I had lost. To work under uncomfortably cold conditions does not I fear confer any merit on the work itself, nor excuse any deficiencies, though if the former could be claimed then Thomas Hennell deserves the pot, as he tells me that on one occasion he painted an especially lovely sky in Iceland with his own water.'

Ardizzone meanwhile was facing even less forgiving conditions with the British troops in the mountains beyond Florence – 'spectacular but bloody,' he confided to Bawden – finding wastes of snow as intractable pictorially as he had found the wastes of North African sand. He had more success when he in his turn focused on partisan subjects – but by this time he was conscious of something of an 'end-of-term feeling', and was soon chafing to return to the spearhead of the Allied advance, now with the forces on the Rhine.

He was replaced in Italy by Carel Weight, who left England in May 1945, his brief being to record 'some of the famous buildings which had been damaged or destroyed or changed by the War'.[288] Weight started with those which had been changed. Once his traumatic training period was over, he had been transferred to the Army Education Corps as a Sergeant-Instructor in Art, organising art activities for troops all over the Home Counties; he was now interested to observe and record the work of the Army Education Corps in Italy – at Perugia, where it had its headquarters in the University, and at Florence, where it was running an art school. He took as his theme the classes of burly soldiers in khaki shorts dwarfed amidst the ornate splendour of the university buildings.

He considered less lightheartedly the buildings destroyed. To some extent, where monuments had no strategic importance, they had been marked with yellow flags and their immunity respected by both sides. But in Florence and Verona all the bridges (except the Ponte Vecchio, too narrow for armoured transport) had been blown by the retreating Germans, and Weight recorded the devastation – the Bailey bridge in place of the Ponte S. Niccolo, the wrecked approaches to the Ponte Vecchio, and so on. In Rimini he painted the ruins of the Temple of Malatesta, which he considered 'the finest example of an early Renaissance church in Italy . . . one of the great losses of the war' – but 'not perhaps the most tactful thing I could have painted because I believe that it lost its roof to a bomb dropped by an American plane.'

Weight, like Bawden and Coldstream, was profoundly grateful to the WAAC for his employment. The war had greatly disrupted his painting, and he has since concluded that it took him three or four years after the war to recover his artistic equilibrium. He was much helped in this recovery by his official war work in 1945–6: the WAAC provided materials which were otherwise virtually unobtainable, and he found the experience of *having* to confront a subject and adapt to its demands in a severely limited time to be an invaluable discipline in later years. 'It was a sort of scholarship from the Army.'

Carel Weight, *The Palazzo Vecchio, Florence,* $24\frac{1}{2} \times 20$, (City Art Gallery. Glasgow)

D-Day and After

IN the public eye the Italian campaign was eclipsed, the day after the fall of Rome, by the Normandy invasion, and the Second Front was to remain the focus of attention as the attack moved across France and up through Belgium and Holland into Germany itself.

Preparations for the invasion of France had begun more than two and a half years before – and it was covered better by artists than any other episode of the war. As a preliminary, Anthony Gross, after six months in India and Burma on secondment to the Indian Government,[289] was attached to the 21st Army Group to draw the men and officers of the 50th (Northumbrian) Division and the US 1st Infantry Division, detailed to take part in the invasion – 'The HEROES and ACTORS presented to the Public before the CURTAIN goes up.'

Then as the invasion day neared, artists were sent to the Channel ports – most notably Barnett Freedman to Portsmouth, to make an elaborate study of the War Room from which the Allied expeditionary operations were to be conducted (*Headquarters Room**). At the same time Ardizzone, furious at not being there on the day for once, was almost getting himself arrested in Southsea by stalking Wrens in order to draw them.

On D-Day itself, the WAAC could not have been better served, with one artist attached to the airborne troops who launched the assault, and another with the seaborne forces going in over the beaches.[290] The most closely involved in the proceedings was Albert Richards, the youngest official war artist and, in the words of Graham Sutherland, 'the one real discovery of the war'. Richards was born in 1919 into a working-class family in Wallasey. In 1939 he won a scholarship to the RCA, but after only one term he was called up into the Royal Engineers. Life as a sapper was tedious and he sought consolation when he could in painting, finding most of his subjects in the preparations throughout 1940 for the German invasion which never

Albert Richards

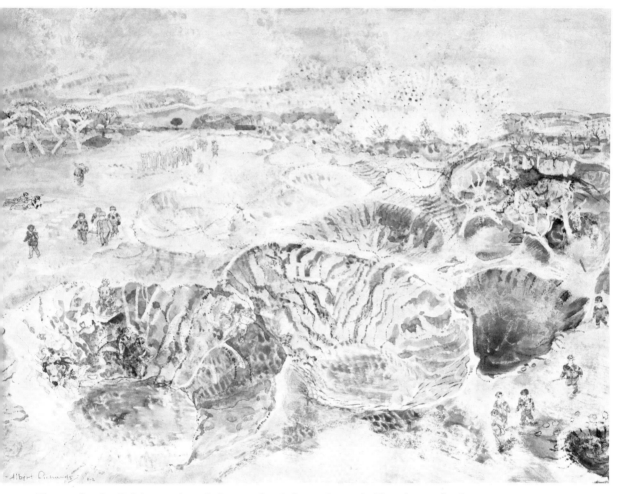

Albert Richards, *Withdrawing from the battery after the battery's guns had been destroyed – the M.O. set up his R.A.P. in a bomb crater* (watercolour), $21\frac{1}{4} \times 29$, (Tate Gallery)

came – pill-box construction in Northumberland and anti-tank ditches on the Suffolk coast. These pictures he submitted to the WAAC and some were bought.

Richards then became a paratrooper. The parachutist as a pictorial image – one used by Paul Nash and Christopher Wood, both artists whom he much admired – had long fascinated him,[291] and he had made some use of it in his work; now he came to love the parachute jump itself as 'a beautiful experience'. His army life had suddenly become so much more interesting that when the Committee offered him a short-term commission he refused lest it jeopardise his career as a paratrooper. However, he accepted a full-time post, becoming the first serving soldier to be taken from fighting duties,[292] chosen partly for his youth in view of 'the rigours of campaigning ahead'.

Between March and June 1944 Richards sent the Committee various pictures of paratroop preparations, but on 5 June he wrote to the Secretary of the WAAC, 'Tomorrow I shall be in France. The beginning.' At midnight he dropped near Merville, to the east of Sword Beach, with a unit of the 6th Airborne Division detailed to put out of action a battery covering the beach. By the time all had landed Richards, having been made an Honorary Captain as a war artist, was the only officer left in his platoon. He took command and helped achieve the objective two hours before the land troops were due.

Richards's ambition was, according to his parents, 'to paint the greatest picture of the war'; but on the beaches he was able only to make a few sketches. These he worked up shortly afterwards during a brief visit to England, finally producing *The Landing – H-Hour–6 – In the distance the glow of the Lancasters bombing the battery to be attacked**, *Withdrawing from the battery: after the battery guns had been destroyed. The MO set up his RAP in a bomb crater*; *At the village of La Plein*, and *Gliders crash-landed against a bridge.* He was still dazed, and working in watercolour, in which he did not yet feel confident: 'In painting them, my mind was always full of pictures of my gallant Airborne friends, who gave their lives so readily. It's the first time I have ever witnessed death in this crude form. Somehow I am hoping that it will all help me to paint the pictures I want to paint yet feel so unable to do.'

Further to the west, on the afternoon of 6 June, Gross landed with the men whose portraits he had drawn on the 'Jig' section of Gold Beach, wading ashore laden with materials, his drawing-board held high over his head – 'Quite a feeling of unbelief as I trod the sands of France again.' He was then to spend several weeks in the area behind the three British beachheads, between Bayeux and Caen. On June 11 he was joined by Ardizzone who, during his week's stay, found the bustle and confusion on the beaches hard to come to grips with: he seems to have been most impressed by the self-heating tins of soup with which the troops were issued as emergency rations, and by the hideousness of Normandy's seaside architecture. The most visible feature of the beachhead scene was the influx of supplies for the landing forces, facilitated in the British landing area at least by the 'Mulberry', an artificial deep-water harbour positioned at Arromanches. Richard Eurich, without being told what it was, had been sailed round the Mulberry in a DUKW and painted it while it was being partially assembled at Selsey Bill in May 1944. Stephen Bone had witnessed the cross-Channel journey (*An Important Tow*) of one of the 'Phoenixes', the 200-foot concrete caissons which were the largest components of the Mulberry.[293] Now Freedman, crossing to Normandy at the end of June, laboured over a five-foot drawing of the Mulberry in place,[294] working 'on a panel ripped out of this shelled house and so if I get capsized on my way home . . . I might float awhile on my own drawing.'

However, only a few miles inland the fighting was to remain bitter well into August as Allied troops struggled to link the five beachheads and break out. Thomas Hennell recorded with a mixture of exaltation and sorrow the battle and its impact on the French summer countryside – 'There is a real splendour about fresh battlefields which quickly fades.' Hennell had arrived on 16 June, impressing Ardizzone with the 'string in his shoulder straps, his shy manner and moral courage'; amidst the chaos of camps and transport and wreckage, 'his absorption in the drama of the elements remained unabated', manifest in such pictures as *A field-gun position in the rain, Normandy June*

1944, Sunset on the beach, Normandy June 1944 (troops cooking their evening meal), and *High tide, wet and rough.* He borrowed a bicycle and pedalled about the area from various billets (one with three millers) near Caen, whose capture he recorded on 10 July. In an article called 'The Work of a War Artist'[295] Hennell wrote of the 'sense-haunted ground' which the armies left in their wake. 'The shot-threshed foliage of the apple orchards was fading and just turning rusty, fruit glowed against the sky; there were ashes of burnt metal, yellow splintered wood and charred brown hedge among the shell pits; every few yards a sooty disintegrated hulk.'

By the time the break-out came, most of the war artists had left France. As the British forces advanced out of Normandy, Hennell was one of only three to advance with them.[296] The high point of Gross's career since D-Day had been an encounter with Montgomery. Sent to do a portrait of the General in the Forêt de Cérisy during the battle of the breakthrough, Gross had

Thomas Hennell in France (photograph reproduced by kind permission of Rex Wailes, OBE)

arrived pouring blood from a newly extracted tooth;[297] he received little sympathy and, having asked to draw Montgomery among his advisers, was rebuffed with the remark, 'What do you want them for?'[298]

Gross next embarked on a trip into Brittany under the auspices of the FFI (Forces Françaises de l'Intérieur), the military arm of the French Resistance – not entirely a pleasant experience, as the maquis were in the process of 'cleaning up' opposition, both from pockets of Germans and from collaborators. 'They used to take me and show me their prisons.' Nevertheless, he painted several stirring pictures – among them *Liberation and Battle of France, 1944: 'La Compagnie Tito', members of the 'Maquis' in the Maquis de Callac.* He then headed east, to accompany the triumphal procession of the Free French into Paris: his pictures of the occasion are among his most dramatic of the war – *General Leclerc's Division entering Paris by the Route d'Orléans, 25th August, 1944* and *Liberation and Battle of France: Frightened crowds in the Place de la Concorde, Paris after the attempted shooting of Général de Gaulle from the housetops: the afternoon of Saturday, 26th August, 1944.*

As de Gaulle reached Paris, the 21st Army Group under Montgomery was crossing the Seine upstream at various different points between the capital and the coast. With them was Richards, who on his return to France had instructions to turn his attention from airborne to land troops. He followed the advance in a jeep that resembled a mobile studio, and the titles he gave each series of pictures reveal the stages in the campaign

Frank Wootton, *Rocket-firing Typhoons at the Falaise Gap, Normandy, 1944* (oil on canvas), $41\frac{1}{2} \times 59\frac{1}{2}$ (purchased by the WAAC, 1944)

as he saw it – 'the beginning of the advance', 'the breakthrough', 'the Pockets'. Detailed to concentrate on 'cemeteries of German transport', he recorded not only the burnt-out petrol tankers but also the contorted remains of dead horses from a horse-drawn division caught in 'Typhoon Orchard' near the entrance to the largest 'pocket' of all, the Falaise Gap.[299]

While Richards accompanied the British Second Army inland, Hennell struck off for the coast with the Canadian First Army. For nearly two months he travelled between the invasion ports (Dieppe, Boulogne and Calais), moved both by the pathetic detritus of war – thousands of dirty and dejected German prisoners of war at Thiberville, near Dieppe – and by the dramatic austerity of the coastal plain in autumn. 'Once I was very lucky,' he wrote, 'for I left my paintbox behind and had with me only a bottle of liquid grey colour and a cake apiece of ochre and umber. These were the means of formalising the brown earth, dusty broken walls and curdled sky into better related colour than I could have found in a full palette. . . . The subject itself – it was the ruined field of Calais Nord – had become half identified in my mind with a great empty ploughed field near my father's house in Kent. . . . It is in this half-nostalgic, half-severe mood, that the scenes of battle seize one's mind most strongly.'

In the course of his journey up the coast Hennell had twice stopped to record the traces of what, shortly after D-Day, had become one of the most detested of German weapons – the V-1 flying bomb, or 'doodlebug'.[300] Hennell had been attracted by the pictorial possibilities of the paraphernalia of the rocket-launching sites, rockets still being something of a novelty. However, the subject was equally important from the propaganda point of view: the WAAC was anxious to record and publicise the overrunning and destruction of the 'secret weapon' bases. V-1s were followed closely by V-2s, less demoralising but more destructive, and in December 1944 Graham Sutherland was sent on the Air Ministry's behalf to Northern France – his first trip abroad – to record abandoned V-2 sites. This proved impossible,[301] and he turned instead to V-1 storage depots[302] – the caves at St Leu d'Esseren, thirty miles north-west of Paris, normally used for growing mushrooms. The RAF had recently bombed them, and Suther-

Thomas Hennell, *Nijmegen Bridge and Belvedere Tower from the south: seen from Ubbolgsche Weg* (watercolour), $17\frac{3}{4} \times 19\frac{3}{4}$

land recorded: 'The bombs made holes in the top of the hills. It was fascinating to look up inside the caves and see blue sky. . . . There was a terrible sweet smell of death.'

By this time the Allies were deep into Belgium and Holland, and the war artists were spending a cold and dismal winter charting the advance – the Walcheren operation, the aftermath of the landings at Arnhem, and the fighting round the Nijmegen bridge.[303] Richards, after a brief visit in December to the Ardennes,[304] was with the British 2nd Army as they reached the Maas, and revelling in a new type of warfare which in the flooded winter landscape amounted to 'island hopping on a small scale'. It had its disadvantages, however, and at the end of February 1945 he wrote to the WAAC: 'I'm not very good at waiting in traffic hold-ups . . . and I've developed the bad habit of trying to find a new road. On our map there are several possible routes and I try them. This is where the badness of the habit shows up. For I usually end up at a blown bridge . . . or I get my car bogged in some deep mud, miles from help. . . . To me, the fighting seems to be the hardest we have met in this war. Perhaps it is the end.' On the night of 5 March he set off to paint a night attack on the retreating Germans across the river; misunderstanding the instructions he received from the engineers in charge of a minefield, he turned off the road and into the fringes of the field. The engineers heard the explosions and for the rest of the night they heard his moans, but at dawn when they found him, he was dead.

Three weeks later, as the British and Americans crossed the Rhine, with Russian forces spread out along the Oder, the end of the war in Europe was in sight. All British eyes were on the triumphal progress across Germany – and in Italy Ardizzone was agitating for an immediate transfer to the 21st Army Group. Terribly anxious to be in at the finish, he arrived in time to accompany the push to the Elbe.

Ardizzone was attached to the 8th Hussars, and with them advanced through the pine forests of North Germany towards Bremen. Though there were white flags on most of the houses and the population in general seemed pathetically shocked and cowed, there were occasional spurts of resistance, often from Hitler Youth members, and the atmosphere was profoundly uneasy. 'That bloody forest . . . mile after mile, and you couldn't get out of your tank to do a pee because you'd be probably shot at by some bloody boy round a tree . . . something very nasty about it.'[305] Ardizzone's only welcome memory was of the day when the Hussars liberated Stalag 257, one of the many British prisoner of war camps in North Germany. He drew the scene (*Scout-cars of a regiment of Hussars liberating a Stalag*), commenting, 'It was pleasant to see little groups in the country outside the cage, but many still lined the wire as if out of long habit.'

Life behind the wire was minutely recorded for the WAAC by John Worsley who, shortly after his experiences at Salerno, had been captured during an unsuccessful joint operation with Yugoslav partisans in the North Adriatic; suspected because of his association with the partisans of being some kind of agent or spy, he was put in solitary confinement for two months, under constant interrogation. The only Naval POW camp in Germany was Marlag 'O', twelve miles from Bremen, with Milag Nord, for captured merchant seamen, less than half a mile away. This latter camp had a hospital hut, and Worsley contrived to have a minor operation so that for two weeks he could make drawings of life in Milag Nord as well. Worsley was, in fact, to put

Edward Ardizzone, *Scout-cars of a regiment of Hussars liberating a Stalag* (watercolour), $22\frac{3}{4} \times 30\frac{3}{4}$, (Tate Gallery)

his painting materials to fairly subversive uses. As well as producing a large number of pictures which vividly conjure up the makeshift, stubborn, inventive and faintly gung ho atmosphere of PoW life – *An Illicit Alcohol Still, Milag Nord*; *Cricket Match – Milag Nord v. Marlag 'O' at Marlag 'O'*; *Naval officers filling in a discovered escape tunnel*, and so on – he was regularly employed as a forger, becoming adept at simulating identity photographs with lead pencil. But his greatest coup was the manufacture of 'Albert', a dummy with a papier-mâché head (courtesy of the *Volkischer Beobachter*), hair contributed by the prisoners, and eyes of halved ping-pong balls, painted with oils supplied by the Swedish Red Cross. Albert was assembled in the shower-room of Marlag 'O' and 'marched' out with the other prisoners as a stand-in for an escaper who remained hidden in the bath-house till nightfall when he made his break – a story later made into Ealing Studios' *Albert RN*, on which Worsley acted as technical adviser. Worsley himself was not to escape and was repatriated only after

John Worsley, *Naval officers filling in a discovered escape tunnel* (watercolour), $11\frac{1}{8} \times 16\frac{1}{8}$

an eighty-mile forced march ahead of the Allied advance under heavy strafing from the RAF; he recorded the experience in a large oil in which he leads the procession, the work of two years slung from his shoulder in three containers made out of 'Klim' tins.

Other camps were being opened as the Germans retreated – Ardizzone had commented on the pathetic straggle of freed slave labourers and Russian prisoners of war on the roads of North Germany. Stephen Bone, sent to Norway to record captured naval bases,[306] saw the kind of camps in which they had been kept: of 'Death Camp' at Kitdal he wrote, 'In these hovels Russian prisoners spent an arctic winter. They died in hundreds and were either buried in mass graves or left unburied.'

These atrocities paled into insignificance beside those revealed when, on 15 April, Belsen was handed over to the British, the first of the German concentration camps to be opened to the world. The artist chosen to go to Belsen for the WAAC was Leslie Cole – perhaps because he had already demonstrated his ability to detail dispassionately the worst excesses of man's inhumanity. In March 1945 he had been required to make a record of the British effort to resist the armed take-over of Greece after the German

Leslie Cole, *Belsen Camp: the compound for women* (oil on canvas), $26 \times 35\frac{1}{2}$

withdrawal by the Communist-led ELAS – the last stage in their struggle against the liberal-republican EDES, in which the support of the rural masses was compelled by the judicious use of terrorism. The titles of Cole's pictures reveal precisely what he saw – *A pathologist and Greek National Guards recover mutilated civilians from a well, Greece*; *Corpses floating in well, Monument Hill, Athens*; *Mother mourning the death of a village priest*.

Now he was confronted with a camp of sixty thousand victims, of whom five hundred were dying every day of starvation or typhus; his first picture was of *One of the death pits, Belsen. SS Guards collecting bodies.* Of *Belsen Camp. The compound for women* Cole wrote, 'During my visit the victims were still dying in the open and the woman at the centre of the picture collapsed while I was drawing. There are many bodies lying about clothed and unclothed. . . . If [a] body disappeared at night it was alive.'

Mervyn Peake, following close behind Cole,[307] made a large number of drawings of Belsen victims. He also drew on his experiences in the writing of *Titus Alone*, and in his poem 'The Consumptive. Belsen 1945' he raises a question of ethics which every war artist exposed to violent action and its aftermath must have had to resolve for himself –

> *If seeing her an hour before her last*
> *Weak cough into all blackness I could yet*
> *Be held by chalk-white walls and by the great*
> *Ash-coloured bed, and the pillows hardly creased*
> *By the tapping of her little cough-jerked head –*
> *If such can be a painter's ecstasy*
> *(Her limbs like pipes, her head a china skull)*
> *Then where is mercy? And what*
> *Is this my traffic? For my schooled eyes see*
> *The ghost of a great painting, line and hue*
> *In this doomed girl of tallow.*

It fell to Anthony Gross to record the final stage of the German war: on 26 April, with a large party of American journalists, he travelled to Torgau to preserve for posterity the formal rendezvous between the Russians and the Americans on the Elbe – or as Kenneth Clark put it, 'the barbarians from the East meeting the barbarians from the West'.

None of the artists pressed on to Berlin and, as in the First World War, none was present to record the signing of the Armistice. It remained only to commemorate the meting out of retribution to the defeated survivors of the Third Reich, and in January 1946 the WAAC sent Dame Laura Knight, at her own suggestion, to the Nuremberg Trials. Commissioned to produce one large picture of the trials, which were held in the main courtroom of the Bavarian Central Courts of Justice, Dame Laura took up her position in an unoccupied American broadcasting box, with a steep, oblique view at close range of the defendants – Goering, Hess, Ribbentrop, Streicher, Doenitz, Speer and fifteen others. 'I had the feeling that if I threw out a handkerchief I could have covered that force which for so long almost held the whole world.'[308] For three months she battled with the technical problems posed by strip-lighting, which cast a sickly greenish hue over the proceedings, and she contrived, amidst constant interruptions from press, photographers and the American Military Police (known as 'Snowdrops' for their white helmets) to produce a large watercolour sketch of the composition, which she intended to work up in oils virtually without alteration. However, before she left Nuremberg she had changed her mind.

Dame Laura was not unduly sensitive, and she prided herself on her capacity to concentrate on the aesthetic aspects of a scene to the exclusion of its moral or emotional implications. To her husband she wrote before leaving Nuremberg, 'My one dread is that I may lose aloofness – not likely.' Taking no chances, she kept the window of the press box closed, to shut out the pervasive air of tension in the courtroom, and she tried not to listen to the running translation coming through the earphones which she would not wear. However, in her journeys to and fro between her hotel[309] and the courtroom she could not ignore the misery of the Nurembergers, living like rats in the rubble of their devastated city; and in the background of her picture, where the blank wall of the courtroom should have been, emerged 'a sort of mirage of a ruined city'. To Harold Knight she wrote firmly, 'I used this vision . . . from pure aesthetic emotion only – for colour, composition, balance and line. . . . Above all, for space.' But to the Committee she unbent: 'In that ruined city death and destruction are ever present. They had to come into the picture.'

Laura Knight, *The Nuremberg Trial*, 1946 (oil on canvas), 72 × 60

CHAPTER THIRTY-NINE

The Far East

A FTER the overwhelming Japanese onslaught of the spring of 1942, when Hong Kong, Singapore and Rangoon fell in rapid succession, British military activity in the Far East was confined principally to Burma. This unpalatable fact, and the subsequent agreement between Churchill and Roosevelt to give overall priority to the war against Germany, are both clearly reflected in the WAAC's records. Of the six artists selected to cover the eastern theatre, five were appointed only in mid-1945, when the war in Europe was over; by this time, however, their area of potential operations had expanded – from Burma to the coast of Japan itself.

The one artist sent to the East before the tide of battle turned was Anthony Gross. During 1942 there had been growing speculation in England that under the pressure of Gandhi's campaign of civil disobedience, India might withdraw from the war, shattering the notion of the Empire united and wrecking the British war effort in terms of both men and manufacturing capacity. At the request of the India Office, the MoI set out to promote the image of British–Indian solidarity, the most conspicuous example of which was the fighting on the Burma Front. With a push into the Arakan planned for the dry season 1942–3, it was suggested to the WAAC that Anthony Gross (then in Cairo) might be despatched to record the action.

In 1943 Gross travelled by train across the Indian sub-continent from Karachi to Calcutta and thence to Cox's Bazaar on the Burmese border – interestingly seeing little sign of the growing resentment of the British presence in India.

From Cox's Bazaar he travelled to the Front Line in the Arakan, near Rathedaung – part of the way by sampan down the River Mayu, with the helmsman brewing tea in the stern, and obstinately refusing to relinquish the current in mid-stream for the shelter of the bank which alone offered cover from passing Japanese planes – a journey he recorded in *Battle of Arakan, 1943: A Sampan convoy on the Mayu River*.

The likelihood is that Gross was intended to record British and Indian troops united in victory; instead he arrived in Burma in the last disastrous weeks of the winter campaign, with the Japanese advancing inexorably, to be stopped in May 1943 only by the rains and the terrain itself. Morale was at a low ebb – Gross encountered in the ranks of the Lancashire Fusiliers at Rathedaung a real horror of the Japanese infiltration methods, entering tents at night, slitting a few throats at random, and leaving undetected. He was gratified to find his own presence acting as a minor tonic for men who had been in the jungle for months; the arrival of an outsider was itself a relief – 'Thank God someone realises we're still alive,' he was told – and one who took a positive interest, even better; to this extent his drawings of British and Indian troops served an immediate and practical purpose.

Moving on to visit the Rajputana Rifles, Gross was taken to the top of a hill overlooking the Japanese positions and encouraged to reconstruct the heroic charge by Jat

Sepoys which had occurred a few days before[310] – his escort, despite protests, insisting on holding aside the protective curtain of foliage, thus (mutually) improving the view.

Gross found himself in the bamboo jungle of Rathedaung with, for once, an obvious advantage over the camera. The diffused light filtering without sun or shadow through the screen of bamboo, which made photographs 'flat', was ideally suited to his ink and wash technique, the sables and sepias of the desert replaced by translucent greens. 'For me it was beautiful. It was like Italian Renaissance paintings – they used to paint under tents in their courtyards. This was the same sort of light: you could see every detail of a face.'

He soon learnt to make his own way about the area, and having discovered the rules about snipers, travelled north by mule to Dombaik. Here he was even closer to the Front Line, was strafed by Zero fighters en route, and a drawing he made from an artillery observation post (*Battle of Arakan, 1943: Gunners pinpointing Japanese positions on the Dombaik Front*) reveals the middle distance spotted with the bodies of Inniskilling Fusiliers and Punjabi troops. At one point he ventured to within twenty yards of the Japanese lines – being warned to speak in whispers, less to conceal his presence than to disguise his nationality, it being the Japanese practice to open fire with mortars when they heard English rather than Hindustani spoken.

From Dombaik, he travelled by horse over the Arakan Hills to the line west of Laungchaung, the town itself being Japanese held. In this area he made some of his most memorable drawings – of a Buddha overturned by shell-fire in a jungle clearing; a Jammu State Mountain Battery in position on the approaches to the town; and Sikhs of the 7th Rajput Regiment proudly displaying a geisha parasol captured during a raid.

But with the Japanese advance now accelerating, Gross returned to the coast – joining a flotilla of Indian Navy motor launches on an expedition to bombard positions to the rear of the enemy – before leaving the Arakan and heading for the more northerly part of the Line to spend the remainder of his appointment drawing some of the British Army's more unusual allies.

Gross travelled first into the Naga Hills on the border with Assam. It was here in northern Burma that Orde Wingate's Chindits had crossed the Chindwin River in February on their first sortie behind Japanese lines, but Gross was not on hand to record either their departure or, six weeks later, their return with forty per cent casualties. He made, however, several drawings of the Naga ('naked men') tribesmen whom, despite their head-hunting habits, he found friendly and decorative.

He then made his way three hundred miles south to the Chin Hills, the northern flank of the Arakan and the scene of much fighting, in which the British were receiving invaluable assistance from the local tribesmen. The Chin levies – some ex-Burma Rifles, others raw recruits equipped with their own antique flintlocks and gunpowder homemade from the saltpetre in goat droppings – closely patrolled their own territory to provide early warning of enemy movements, and had been holding up the Japanese for months. Gross took pains to distinguish the various tribes, each with its own distinctive head-dress – and found himself with ample time to contemplate his drawings of Chins and Gurkhas, the other British levies in the area, when the Japanese advance succeeded in cutting the British supply route to India and isolating the Chin Hills.

Anthony Gross, *Chins at war: a platoon of Chin village levies of the Sokte tribe* (pen and wash),
15 × 22

When the route was eventually reopened, Gross emerged to trek back to civilisation.[311] It was, however, for other artists to record eventual British success against the Japanese in 1944 and 1945.

The culmination of the campaign for Burma was witnessed by Vivian Pitchforth,[312] for whom the Committee had secured a commission as Temporary Captain, RM, to record naval operations in the South-East Asia Command.[313] Arriving at the Navy's principal base in Ceylon, he sent back numerous paintings of Colombo harbour before joining the combined amphibious and airborne assault on Rangoon, reaching the city in time to paint *The first British troops in Rangoon*.

On its way, Pitchforth's commando unit had moored its assault craft in an inlet and proceeded overland to the capital. To minimise the threat of aerial attack, the artist was asked to camouflage the ships against the mud banks: so effective were his efforts at disguise that there was an interval of several days before all of them were rediscovered.

Rangoon was the last of Pitchforth's official work: contracting a severe lung ailment, he was removed to hospital in Durban where he remained until the spring of 1946.

In the meantime two other official artists had been sent out to cover events in SEAC – Thomas Hennell (now a salaried Air Ministry artist) and Leslie Cole (continuing his War Office appointment). Both reached Burma in May 1945 at the start of the monsoon season: Hennell was seized almost at once with lumbago, and Cole wrote gloomily of 'mushrooms in my boots . . . and my watercolours all coated with fungus'.

Hennell was based at an airfield fifteen miles from Rangoon and for several weeks his principal subjects were the constant repairs necessary to maintain the airstrip, and Liberators and Dakotas grounded by the rain – though the more records-minded of the WAAC were delighted also to receive a watercolour of *Lord Louis Mountbatten at Rangoon Victory Parade*. His main interest, however, was in the Burmese people themselves, and their crafts – 'a friendly and peaceable race, they can build with bamboo, pegs and wire as scientifically as our own engineers with steel. . . . They weave their own cloth and I shall try to get some.'

Cole, more adventurous, accompanied men of the Queen's Own (Royal West Kent) Regiment on patrols into the jungle, on one occasion attending and recording a meeting of Burmese guerrillas – 'Reindeer Force 136' – planning an attack on Japanese troops in a neighbouring village. The two artists subsequently met and compared notes in Pegu, where they worked companionably together for some time.

Not long after the capture of Burma, however, Hennell contracted amoebic dysentery. On 14 August, whilst he was still recuperating in Kandy, Japan surrendered, and he forced himself from his sick-bed to accompany the naval force, led by the aircraft carrier HMS *Hunter* sent from Colombo, to reoccupy Penang. The sketches he made of Admiral Walker signing the settlement with the Japanese admiral he never worked up, and he was much better pleased with the watercolours he made aboard en route – of the carrier's flight deck, sick bay, operations room, and so on.

Moving on to Singapore by flying boat, Hennell was reunited with Leslie Cole who, after the horrors of Belsen, had been exposed once again to scenes of hideous suffering at the opening of the Japanese camps – PoWs suffering from starvation and beriberi, limbless officers and men checking out from Changi Gaol, and British women and children interned at Syme Road.

From Singapore, both men travelled south – Hennell to Java, Cole more circuitously to Borneo, as a guest of a Gurkha regiment, and then to Java – where he learned that Hennell was reported missing. He had been with a party at a hotel in Surabaya when the building was besieged by Indonesian nationalists demonstrating against the re-establishment of Dutch colonial rule. What happened has never been established, but two Sergeants 'also in the show – who knew Hennell' told of the artist trying to defend his companions and 'firing a Sten gun into an angry mob of Indonesians'. It was later reported that he had not been killed immediately, but had been taken into the jungle as a prisoner, having probably been mistaken for Dutch.[314]

Cole wrote sadly to the Committee, 'The whole thing puzzles me because it's so out of character – Tom was unwarlike – I can't imagine him armed or firing guns even in an extremity.' Ironically, Hennell had also made passivity a primary principle in his art: 'The artist has but one duty, to observe and record – the moment he is tempted to interfere or play an active part himself he ceases to perform his duty as an artist.'

While the British forces were progressing south through Burma, the US and Australian forces were advancing northwards through the Philippines and Pacific islands, the British contribution in this latter theatre of war being largely confined to the activities of the British Pacific Fleet, established in November 1944. As early as December 1944 the Committee had discussed sending an artist to the BPF, and in the event sent two – Leonard Rosoman and James Morris.

Rosoman, whose work for the Home Office had up till now denied him an official artist's post, was commissioned Temporary Captain, RM, and commenced a six-month commission from the Committee on 1 April 1945.[315] The appointment began disastrously: he travelled out to Sydney, the base of the BPF, on a troopship whose captain forbade him to paint, and on arrival in Australia he spent a frantic two weeks hunting for his irreplaceable painting equipment, which had been wrongly routed: 'People didn't sympathise much – apparently it's a common occurrence in the Navy.'

He quickly settled down, however, encouraged by letters of introduction to Sydney Nolan and Australian war artist William Dobell. During a visit to the Fleet in port, he was immediately attracted by Admiral Vian's flagship, the aircraft carrier HMS *Formidable*, undergoing repairs to her flight deck where a kamikaze had struck. When she sailed on operations, he sailed with her – sending a dramatic report back to the Committee: 'I hope you . . . are able to read this letter – the truth of the matter is the ship is doing a fast run out of the strike area and the vibration tends to make one's hand a little unsteady. I'm with the BPF in the flagship carrier and we're off the coast of Japan – only just off, I may add!'

In his first series of paintings the sea rarely appears, all his attention being concentrated within the aircraft carrier herself – not on her crew, but on her armament – 'I've become interested in all sorts of strange devices like RADAR indicators, pom-poms and planes with wings that fold up like a moth's.' The thirteen paintings (oil and gouache) which Rosoman based on his *Formidable* experiences offer, with Paul Nash's series of aerial creatures, the most consistent and penetrating insight into the machinery of war in the Committee's collection. Unlike his Admiralty predecessor Ravilious, he was moved by more than simply the novel design of the hardware surrounding him: 'To watch a man sitting, trapped almost, in the flower-like interior of a radar predictor was beautiful. The aeroplane folds its wings and crouches on the flight deck. These things must be felt with the senses, not just used in terms of interesting shapes.'

Rosoman did much of the work on these pictures in a studio in Sydney, as on the *Formidable* herself there was no space in which to work. 'I have a cabin but it has artificial light and is so small I practically have to paint in bed. Then there's the heat, which is unbelievable. . . . I paint absolutely nude when I'm in the cabin and as I'm a very untidy painter I tend to look like an Early Briton in warpaint.'

OPPOSITE ABOVE, Charles Cundall, *The withdrawal from Dunkirk, June 1940* (oil on canvas), 40 × 60. BELOW, Richard Eurich, *Survivors from a torpedoed ship* (oil on canvas), 14 × 24, (Tate Gallery)

Edward Bawden, *Tobruk: the harbour* (pen and watercolour), $17\frac{3}{4} \times 45\frac{1}{2}$, <small>(Tate Gallery)</small>

Edward Bawden, *A Creek in Shaikh Muzhir Al-Gassid's section of the Hatcham tribe territory* (watercolour), $15\frac{1}{2} \times 20$

OPPOSITE, William Coldstream, *Havildar Ajmer Singh (Sikh)* (oil on canvas), $31 \times 22\frac{1}{4}$, <small>(Tate Gallery)</small>

TOP, Barnett Freedman, *Headquarters Room* (watercolour), 20 × 29   ABOVE, Edward Ardizzone,
Naval control post on the beaches, Normandy, 1944 (watercolour), $11\frac{1}{2} \times 14\frac{3}{8}$

OPPOSITE ABOVE, Albert Richards, *The landing: H Hour minus 6 – in the distance glow of the
Lancasters bombing battery to be attacked* (watercolour), $21\frac{1}{4} \times 29$, (Tate Gallery). BELOW, Albert
Richards, *Germany 1944: the Siegfried Line between Heerlen and Aachen* (oil on panel), $22\frac{1}{4} \times 30\frac{1}{8}$

TOP, Leonard Rosoman, *'Angry aeroplanes' – two Avengers on the flight deck of HMS Formidable* (gouache), $15\frac{3}{4} \times 20\frac{1}{2}$ ABOVE, Ken Howard, *Long Kesh* (watercolour) (destroyed by fire, 1977)

OPPOSITE ABOVE, Anthony Gross, *Battle of Arakan, 1943: Colonel M. E. Pocock at his Battalion HQ overlooking the plain of Rathedaung, 8 Battalion, 6 Rajputana Rifles* (pen and wash), $14\frac{1}{8} \times 21\frac{1}{8}$. BELOW, Thomas Hennell, *Calais Nord, 11th November, 1944* (watercolour), $18\frac{3}{4} \times 24\frac{1}{2}$

Humphrey Ocean, *Rescuing the Dan Buoy* (acrylic on canvas), $35 \times 56\frac{1}{2}$

BELOW LEFT, Anthony Eyton, *Mess Night* (oil on canvas). RIGHT, Edward Burra, *Skull in Landscape* (black chalk and watercolour), 22×30

Leonard Rosoman, *A Chinese merchantman sunk in Hong Kong harbour* (gouache), $9\frac{3}{4} \times 13\frac{3}{4}$

Rosoman completed his official work with a series of eight paintings (oils, gouaches and watercolours) of Hong Kong. He visited the Colony in October, the time of year when the humidity drops and the light resembles that of the Mediterranean, and he found the landscape 'a revelation. Instead of the subtle tones and muted colours of Chinese painting there were strident reds and chrome greens spattering the hills.' Against this setting he found his subjects in the damage done during the Japanese occupation – *A Crater in the Naval Dockyard, Hong Kong*; *A Chinese merchantman sunk in Hong Kong harbour*; *A looted Chinese coffin house*.

The WAAC had hoped that he would then be able to travel on to Japan to record the devastation at Hiroshima and Nagasaki: fortunately for Rosoman, he was unable to arrange transport and made his way back to England via Sydney. Thus the Committee's only artist to reach Japan[316] was Signalman James Morris, the last official

James Morris, *The Imperial Japanese Army Headquarters, Tokyo* (watercolour), $20\frac{1}{4} \times 28\frac{1}{2}$

artist to be appointed, becoming a salaried Admiralty artist (and a Second Lieutenant, RNVR) on 26 June 1945.

Morris had the most unconventional background of any of the official artists, having been successively a miner in South Wales and an interior designer for Harrods. After joining the Royal Navy in 1939, he spent the early years of the war on Arctic convoys (one of which had the misfortune to be shelled by the *Tirpitz*) and in 1944 the Committee purchased his Russian convoy sketchbook and several of the pen and wash drawings made from it – including the cheery *A British Soldier and the Artist Entertain Wounded Soldiers with a Russian Folk-Dance at Archangel Military Hospital 1944*.

The members saw in his lively and literal graphic style a perfect complement to Rosoman's more painterly approach, and with their encouragement Morris travelled widely to Rangoon, Hong Kong, Formosa (where he witnessed the handing-over of the airstrip at Kiirung to the British) and Shanghai – which he saw from HMS *Argonaut*, the first British ship to enter the port after the Japanese surrender. His numerous pictures provide a fascinating documentary record of surrender and liberation scenes in the Far East, culminating in a visit to Japan where he recorded the blitzed areas of Yokohama (though not Hiroshima or Nagasaki) and, as an icon of victory, *The Imperial Japanese Army Headquarters, Tokyo*.

CHAPTER FORTY

Propaganda, Uses and Dispersal

DESPITE the industry of the WAAC and the enterprise of its artists, its continued existence throughout the war was never secure. At least twice the Treasury suggested an end to its operations, and after Clark's resignation as Controller of Home Publicity towards the end of 1941[317] the MoI itself displayed increasing hostility. The outcome was to be compromise – survival, but with a reduced budget.

It was the Committee's application for renewal of its Vote in the autumn of 1940 which found the Treasury, at Britain's 'finest hour', 'not . . . convinced that the production for posterity of an artistic record of England at war is . . . essential for the effective prosecution of the war'. The comment reveals that, like many observers and like several members of the WAAC itself, the Treasury minimised, not to say discounted, the propaganda function of official war art which, in truth, alone made it a proper function of the MoI.

The issue was brought into the open by Frank Pick, the MoI's new Director-General (appointed in August 1940). As the past Chairman of the Council for Art and Industry and Vice-Chairman of the London Passenger Transport Board, Pick had been for over twenty years a leading advocate of the utility of fine art in industry, and had done a great deal to raise standards of design in advertising, architecture and so on. He took a keen interest in the WAAC's work, offering several appealing suggestions for pictures which were unfortunately never painted – a series by the Nashes on the English seaside, for example, or 'intimate interiors' of Churchill and others by William Nicholson in the style of his famous portrait of Sydney and Beatrice Webb.[318]

Now he declared that the Treasury was 'sadly wrong and I am surprised. Propaganda and culture should be combined. They are properly related if propaganda is good. We should boldly claim to go on. . . . Let us ask for more money.' Pick's support was decisive. The increased Vote was granted[319] – and at the same time he galvanised the WAAC into a more positive use of its pictures. It was not by natural inclination a propagandist body. Unlike its First World War predecessors, it had no professional propagandists within its ranks. Kenneth Clark, its most senior MoI representative, had made his attitude to propaganda quite clear in a radio broadcast early in the war: 'A sensitive artist might well feel that propaganda tended to coarsen his style and degrade his vision, and many artists could only be used to persuade in a very indirect manner.' No attempt was ever made to induce artists to compromise their integrity by producing overtly propagandist images: several of the artists themselves – most notably David Bomberg and Paul Nash – were considerably more convinced of the propriety of utilising artists in this way than the Committee's artist members.

Nevertheless official war art had been entrusted to the MoI rather than the Services on the grounds that it was 'publicity' and not 'news', and both the MoI and the Service representatives at least were resolved that publicity it should be. Straightforward

Laura Knight, *Ruby Loftus screwing a breech-ring* (oil on canvas), 34 × 40

recording for posterity was to be the province of the Pilgrim Trust and its project for 'Recording Britain', and wholly disinterested patronage of the arts (whatever Clark's original intentions for the WAAC), the province of CEMA.

Kenneth Clark made it clear that no pictures were commissioned purely for propaganda purposes. Nevertheless, some lent themselves more readily than others to the task of publicising Britain's war effort. Records of heroic incidents and other landmarks of the war could obviously be deployed to uplifting effect – the struggles of the small ships at Dunkirk, the Battle of Britain, the siege of Malta GC, the arrival of the first American troops in Britain, and so on; a majority of these pictures were prompted by the Admiralty and Air Ministry representatives.

Portraits, both civil and military, were a similarly useful tool. From January 1943 onwards, for example, at the instigation of the Ministry of Production's representative, there was a deliberate increase in portraits of production workers, in an effort to combat the discontent and disillusionment manifested in the growing number of days lost to strikes. Two distinct types of portrait are discernible – the very numerous one-off 10-guinea commissions for drawings of 'types' and workers engaged in characteristic activities which, by the very presence of the artist/observer in the factory, boosted morale; and the fully fledged set-pieces in oils of workers of particular significance to be held up as an example to others – a prime example being *Ruby Loftus screwing a breech-ring*.[320] Ruby, an exceptionally talented machinist in a Royal Ordnance Factory in Newport, Monmouthshire, became nationally, even internationally famous through Laura Knight's portrait. The image of a twenty-one-year-old girl succeeding in what had traditionally been a male preserve was intended both as a challenge to men and an inspiration to women, and it was circulated widely to the press, discussed on the radio, and reproduced in poster form for distribution to other factories.

The Committee struck a rich and much more unexpected source of material in the work of Moore and Sutherland, whose distancing of the unpleasant realities of the Blitz was, paradoxically, a positive advantage in propaganda terms. Moore's Underground dwellers, for example, had a dignity quite absent from Ardizzone's more literally represented shelters, which the Minister of Health, for one, found simply 'depressing'. And Sutherland's City drawings could be exhibited and reproduced where photographs of the collapsed jerry-built terraces of Stepney were stopped by the Censor.

Remarkably, the pictures of Moore and Sutherland had a wide popular appeal. Moore has remarked that the shelter drawings made him a household name; a contemporary review in *Good Housekeeping* confirms this, hailing him (with Sutherland, Piper, John Armstrong and Pitchforth) as 'apostles of the ordinary men and women of this country who stood up to it and took it, recorders of what German *Kultur* succeeded in doing to our buildings and failed to do to our souls.'

In November 1940, Clark wrote to Paul Nash, 'We are making a real effort to use artists in order to provide people with something to carry about in the mind's eye'; and after its *raison d'être* had been queried by the Treasury, the WAAC made various efforts to exploit the persuasive power of its pictures. In the hope of goading the members into action, Pick had circulated his own set of *The Western Front*, which found its Second World War counterpart in the Oxford University Press *War Pictures by British Artists* – two series of booklets, four in each series and approximately fifty pictures in each booklet.[321] The WAAC did not believe the Treasury would countenance a publication which could only appeal 'to the intelligentzia' and, priced at 1*s* 3*d* in editions of up to 24,000, the *War Pictures* were twice as cheap (and half as well reproduced) as *The Western Front* or *British Artists at the Front*.

The format was, however, much the same – the careful blend of selected image and discreetly propagandist text pioneered by Masterman and Montague. Each picture had a short caption (Ethel Gabain's *Building a Beaufort Fighter*, for instance: 'No new type of aeroplane has been more successful than the "Beaufighter". Our airmen deserve the best machines, and these girl workers are determined that they shall have them'), and each booklet an introduction, by an intriguing selection of authors.

The first four introductions, composed by two representatives of the Services (Colin Coote and Admiral Sir Herbert Richmond) and two writers associated more closely than most with the 'spirit of England' (J. B. Morton – 'Beachcomber' – and H. E. Bates), delivered their messages without inhibition. The reader of J. B. Morton's 'Blitz' volume, for example, glancing at a heap of rubble meticulously rendered by Randolph Schwabe and labelled 'The Guildhall, once the heart of London's civic life', was assured, 'In the midst of all the destruction and suffering, that sense of humour which is so pecu-liarly English has remained.' Sir Herbert Richmond, endeavouring to explain the ab-sence of conventional 'battle' pictures in his 'War at Sea' volume, concluded, 'In this war there are no great fleets composed of massed bodies of ships of the line : for Germany has (since the sinking of the *Bismark*) but three of them . . . while the original half-dozen or so of the Italian fleet have never tarried to fight and could by no possible skill of the artist be brought into the same canvas which shows the British fleet.' The authors of the second series – Cecil Beaton, Stephen Spender, William Coldstream and Laura Knight – all preferred, with the exception of Dame Laura, to concentrate more closely on the art than on the war.

In addition to the booklets, postcards, calendars and other ephemera were produced by the publications department of the National Gallery, which was also responsible for lithographic reproductions of Paul Nash's *Battle of Britain*, Spencer's *Burners*, Ardiz-zone's *Shelter Scene* and Barnett Freedman's *1 5-inch Gun Turret, HMS Repulse*, produced in ten colours with a special grant of £1000 from the Treasury, specifically for sale to canteens and British Restaurants. Other large colour reproductions were contracted out to commercial firms.

The official pictures were also reproduced in a plethora of unofficial publications. The most notable of these was a collection of Eric Kennington's RAF portraits,[322] with an introduction by J. B. Priestley, published by Kennington's brother for free distribu-tion in his factory. (Beaverbrook, the Minister of Aircraft Production, was much struck by the morale-boosting potential of the publication and ordered 50,000 copies for wider circulation.) A selection from Henry Moore's shelter sketchbooks was published in 1944 by Editions Poetry London. Further useful (unofficial) publicity was given to a selection of the artists and their war work by Jill Craigie's film, *Out of Chaos* (described as 'the first attempt to reproduce British contemporary painting on the screen'), which showed Sutherland at work in the quarries, Spencer in the shipyards, and Moore in the mines. The first issues of the Penguin Modern Painters series (edited by Kenneth Clark) – amongst them the issues devoted to Moore, Nash and Sutherland – also appeared in the later years of the war, and examined the artists' official war work in the context of their careers up to that point.

The choice of pictures for exhibition offered another obvious opportunity for bringing particular themes to the attention of the public – an opportunity which seems only to have been taken in exhibitions designed for overseas, handled principally by the MoI. Between 1941 and 1944 exhibitions were sent to the USA, Canada, Mexico, South America,[323] the West Indies, South Africa, Australia and New Zealand. Pictures of pertinent subjects, especially portraits, were commissioned for exhibition in particu-lar countries, and catalogues, markedly propagandist in tone, were individually pre-pared. Attempts were also made in 1942 to send to Russia 'an ostensibly straightfor-ward Art Exhibition [which] might serve as the key to admit the first British publicity about Britain in the Soviet Union'. The exhibition was vetted and approved at the National Gallery by the Head of Tass in Britain, but cancelled by 'higher [British] auth-ority', in agreement perhaps with the observer to whom the pictures presented the general impression of 'a very bourgeois country putting itself out to only a moderate extent'.

The very first effort abroad was a collection of small black and white photographs of the war artists' work sent to Tokyo in 1940. This singularly ineffective attempt to divert Japan from her course was followed by an altogether more successful exhibition at the Museum of Modern Art in New York, which went on to tour the USA and Canada. It is a sign of the personal prestige which was such an asset to the WAAC that Clark was able to arrange this show in a brisk exchange of four cables totalling less than fifty words, the last of which were (from Alfred H. Barr Jr., the Director of the Museum of Modern Art), 'Committee [of the Museum] trusting to your taste approves enthusiastically.'

'Britain at War' comprised some 110 pictures, including the best 'modern' work, displayed alongside 200 photographs and panels depicting all aspects of civilian life, military preparedness and plans for reconstructing post-war Britain. It was opened on 22 May 1941 – just before Roosevelt's 'unlimited emergency' proclamation – with an elaborate ceremony conducted by means of a trans-Atlantic radio hook-up between Lord Halifax and John Hay Whitney in New York and Clark and Harold Nicolson in London, and it provoked an overwhelming response: Monroe Wheeler wrote, 'We have never had more publicity for any exhibition,' and added, 'A movement has already been started to set up in our country a committee similar to yours to record our own defense effort.'

The exhibition also highlighted the value of art as low-key propaganda. Until Pearl Harbor (7 December 1941), the USA remained neutral and the British Government, acknowledging the strength of isolationist feeling and the resentment of foreign propaganda (due in part to the success of Masterman's efforts), officially restricted itself to 'giving out information on demand, leaving the task of making its case to its American friends'. An art exhibition, however, could hardly give offence.[324]

'Britain at War' was in fact the second major British art exhibition to tour the USA in eighteen months, the first being the collection at the New York World's Fair of 1939, which was subsequently toured by the British Council.

It might seem that the WAAC was with its foreign exhibitions trespassing in the British Council's domain. Early in the war, however, an informal line of demarcation was established: the British Council undertook not to exhibit war pictures, (presumably to avoid carrying over any taint of war propaganda into the post-war world), and this held until towards the end of the war, when the Council began to tour exhibitions including war art in liberated areas.

One issue which, in the later stages of the war, the MoI wished particularly to air abroad was Britain's fighting effort in South-East Asia Command, the magnitude of which was felt to be insufficiently appreciated by her American and Anzac allies, whose attention was fixed on their own 'island-hopping' advance in the Pacific Ocean areas. War art had a significant part to play: in February 1944 the MoI concluded that, 'The imminence of major action in Burma would make it good propaganda to direct Australia's attention by all methods, to the heroism and endurance of the UK troops on that Front. One excellent method at our disposal is the set of drawings by Anthony Gross . . . in the "India in Action" exhibition.'[325] This exhibition, consisting principally of Gross's Burma drawings, was already on show at the National Gallery with the rather different objective of advertising the 'comradeship in arms of Indians and

Britons'; however, in the summer of 1944 the pictures were packed up and despatched to Australia; 'India in Action' opened in Melbourne in September 1944, and in the spring of 1945 the exhibition was transferred to the United States. The determination to raise the British profile is obvious also in the instructions issued to Rosoman and Morris to send their pictures of the British Pacific Fleet home via the Naval Information Centre in Washington, 'so that suitable reproductions might help British publicity in America'.

In marked contrast, exhibitions at home – which were organised by Clark and the successive Secretaries to the WAAC, operating outside the MoI through other, non-propagandist bodies – showed no didactic intent. Catalogues were neutral and informative; such selection of pictures as there was – and the great majority were exhibited eventually – was made almost entirely on grounds of artistic merit. The object of these shows was primarily to entertain; they formed one facet of the extraordinary upsurge of artistic activity throughout the country, partly fuelled by CEMA, with which people attempted to relieve the inevitable drabness of wartime life.

The principal centre for the exhibition of official war art at home was the National Gallery where the first official display was opened to the public on 3 July 1940. From that moment until the Armistice, with one short break after some of the unused rooms were bombed, there was a continual changing display of war pictures which, coupled with the lunchtime concerts organised by Myra Hess, made the National Gallery 'a defiant outpost of culture, right in the middle of a bombed and shattered metropolis'.[326]

From the National Gallery display, smaller exhibitions were subsequently withdrawn to tour the provinces. Five separate selections of up to eighty works each were circulated round the larger provincial galleries by the Museums Association, timed to coincide whenever possible with local War Weapons Weeks, and a further three, composed of smaller pictures, round towns, villages and army camps by the British Institute of Adult Education as part of its 'Art for the People' programme.

It is unfortunately no easier to assess the effectiveness of fine art propaganda in the Second World War than in the First. The OUP booklets, cheap and a manageable size, with a striking cover design by John Piper, sold uniformly well; the lithographs and larger photographic reproductions generally did not. Attendances at exhibitions were good; but precisely because of the wide exposure of the pictures at regular intervals up and down the country, there was no one major 'unveiling' comparable to the Royal Academy exhibition of 1919–20 through which the general critical reaction might be judged.

The broadest of generalisations are possible. The initial response was hesitant: the comments of those invited to the first private view at the National Gallery ranged from ungrudging praise bestowed by the IWM to a reprimand from HMSO for wasting valuable Civil Service manhours – 'One wonders whether the French débâcle was not largely due to the French High Command spending their time looking at pictures in the Louvre.' Some observers were disappointed with the pictures, many of which inevitably reflected the atmosphere of the Phoney War – the dearth of incident and the apparent lack of profound involvement. Several of the artists themselves were among the most outspoken critics – Henry Carr describing much of the work of others as 'pansy', Kennington dismissing it as 'pretty-pretty'. Six months later Paul Nash wrote, 'I very fre-

Michael Ford, *War Weapons Week in a country town* (oil on canvas), 26 × 36

quently hear the complaint that the war pictures are too detached, too decorative, too quaint and amusing.' But John Piper probably spoke for the majority of critics in concluding that as the war itself became more disturbing, the pictures too became more powerful: 'It is not camouflage nor uniforms nor the clean lines of a gun, nor even heroic profiles that make good subjects for war pictures, it is death and destruction, and the agony that stays about the rubbish pile and the grave.'

It is clear that despite the considerable efforts made by the WAAC to turn its pictures to account, there was a significant element within the MoI which remained unconvinced of its value as a function of the Ministry. The principal ground for resentment seems to have been the demands made by the Committee on the administrative resources of the MoI – finance, photographic and exhibitions sections; conversely, its executive independence may have aroused jealousy. In the summer of 1943, the WAAC was subsumed more firmly within the MoI and put under Divisional control – a move which resulted almost at once in MoI interference in matters of artistic policy.

The Committee reacted aggressively, by reaffirming its original terms of reference – 'We wish to make it clear that although the use of the pictures for propaganda in a wide sense at the present time looms large . . . we have not forgotten that our chief task is to build up for posterity a collection of artistic war records of the highest quality' – and, in May 1943, by moving out of the MoI building in Malet Street to the offices of the National Gallery.

Clark's intention was that, as of 1 April 1944, the WAAC should become independent, with its own grant from the Treasury administered through the National Gallery. The Treasury, however, would not countenance this – 'It would not be appropriate to make a purchase grant to the National Gallery for the work of the War Artists' Advisory Committee. The Tate Gallery would be the more natural recipient' – and suggested instead that the Committee should close down entirely. This would no doubt have suited various members of the MoI; fortunately they were not sufficiently senior, and once again official war art was saved from extinction by the intervention of a sympathetic Director-General – this time Cyril Radcliffe, himself a patron of the arts.

The price was compromise: three of the WAAC's own official salaried artists' posts were axed, and the budget for 1944–5 was reduced. It was not long, however, before the Committee's activities were in any event being run down, with the exception, after D-Day, of the artists in liberated Europe. At home the most significant developments during 1945 were the portraits commissioned to fill the gaps in the roster of senior military staff, and the attempts to make some record of the vital role played by scientists throughout the war. W. T. Rawlinson was commissioned to make a series of paintings of the Chain Home early-warning system of coastal radar installations; Charles Ginner was sent to the National Physical Laboratory at Teddington; Ethel Gabain painted Sir Alexander Fleming, the discoverer of penicillin, in his laboratory. Portraits were commissioned of several of the scientists involved in atomic research, though there is no contemporary official artistic record of the weapon they helped produce, or of its effects.

Until the end of 1945, responsibility for official war art continued to rest with the WAAC, but with the demise of the MoI, the committee was dissolved (after 197 meetings) and administration of the collection passed once again to the IWM which, after some debate, had finally been declared principally responsible for records of the Second World War. Muirhead Bone, no doubt with a strong sense of *déjà vu*, found himself the Chairman of a newly formed Art sub-committee which was given a small grant for the period up to 31 March 1946, to bring the official scheme to a tidy close.

This committee's otherwise ordered existence was much disturbed by the efforts to extract from Wyndham Lewis his *A Canadian war factory*, begun and paid for (handsomely)[327] in 1943. The Committee had been induced to offer the commission by Kennington, who was well aware of Lewis's near-destitution in Canada; however, the pressing need for readier money led Lewis to take a series of more immediately rewarding jobs, and in 1945 when he returned to England the work was still unfinished. He explained the delay in terms of the change of artistic approach which was characteristic of his painting of the 1940s: 'I switched from the "impressionistic" [approach] to a

OPPOSITE, Wyndham Lewis, *A Canadian war factory* (oil on canvas), $45 \times 33\frac{3}{4}$, (Tate Gallery)

more solid and detailed one. . . . One part after another took body and bristled with factual stuff so that at last it *all* had to be brought into far more solid pattern.' But even with the stylistic dilemma resolved, he could not be persuaded, even by the threat of legal action, into parting with the canvas; and the problem of its recovery was inherited from the IWM by the Tate, to whom the picture had (notionally) been assigned.[328]

Clark did not join the IWM committee. Instead he was appointed the Chairman of an entirely separate new committee, responsible to the Treasury for the dispersal of the pictures. In the Second World War, there was no Beaverbrook figure to fight for the preservation of the collection as a unity. The National Gallery, as the Treasury had pointed out, had no legitimate interests in contemporary art; nor was any formal claim made by the IWM on the basis of its custody of the previous war's pictures. There was, on the other hand, irresistible pressure from other national institutions for the collection to be shared. John Rothenstein's plea to Clark was typical: 'It would be lamentable if . . . all the more important works produced during the period were to find their way into the various Service museums only, as happened during the last war, with the result that there is virtually a lacuna in the representation at the Tate of contemporary British art between the years 1914 and 1919.'

The Allocations Committee set about its task by dividing the pictures roughly under the headings of 'art' and 'record', and establishing within these categories some kind of pecking order. Where 'art' was concerned, the Tate had priority, and the British Council second choice, with the other major national institutions and provincial galleries close behind. Through Bone's good offices the IWM received a representative selection of 'art' as well as priority in the field of 'records', other than those of naval activities, a large proportion of which went to the National Maritime Museum at Greenwich.

The showcase for the pictures, and the symbolic end to the official war art scheme, was, as in the First World War, a large exhibition at the Royal Academy in the autumn of 1945, after which applications for the pictures were invited. Besides the national institutions, any other body which could claim a genuine interest in specific pictures – by virtue of a local connection, for example – was entitled to make a claim for them. In this way, pictures were allotted to galleries, regiments, embassies, even libraries and town halls, not only throughout Britain but across the world, from the Sudan to New Zealand. However, the work of the Allocations Committee was not finally approved by Parliament until 25 March 1947, when the physical distribution at last began of the 5570 pictures accumulated by the WAAC, at an estimated cost to the nation of £96,000.

PART III

THE POST-WAR PERIOD

Y

Sketches of these →

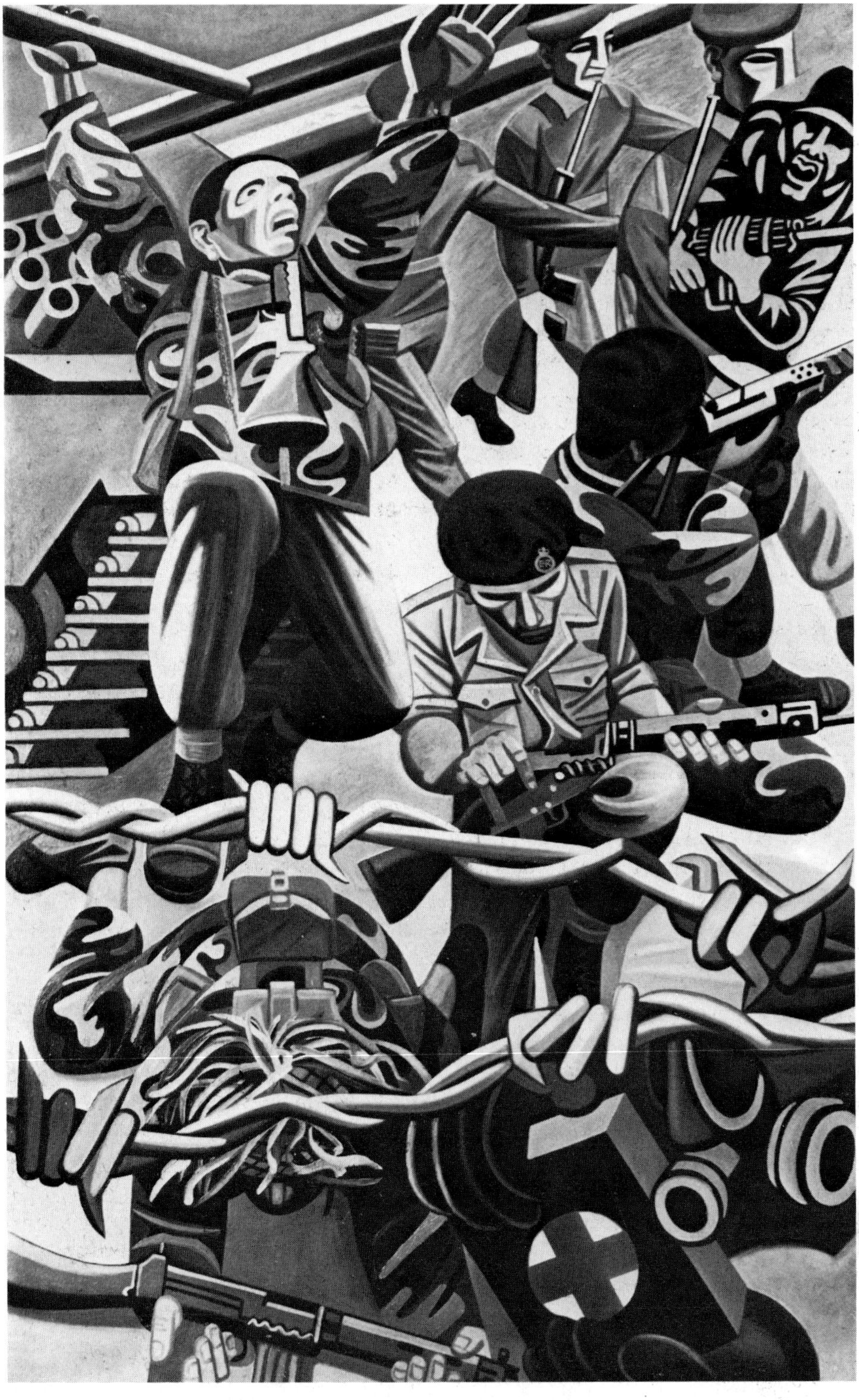

CHAPTER FORTY-ONE

War Art since 1946

I N 1946 the IWM found itself once again the guardian of the greater part of the national war art collection. For the next twenty-five years, however, it was to be prevented by an acute shortage of money from achieving much more than the conservation, exhibition and loan of the existing pictures.

A few additions were made: the Trustees purchased such pictures of the First and Second World Wars as they could afford, and were happy to secure pictorial records of contemporary conflicts when from time to time these were offered. In 1956, for example, they bought three oils of RAF operations against the Mau Mau by Lady Rathdonnell of Lisvanagh; and in 1957 they acquired from the same artist two pastels of operations against EOKA in Cyprus and salvage operations at Suez after the 1956 crisis. But there was no attempt to carry on through new commissions the systematic recording of British military activities.

Official war art, deprived of one of its principal champions by the death in 1953 of Sir Muirhead Bone, revived only in 1972 with the establishment of the IWM's Artistic Records Committee, set up after the suggestion was made by Lieutenant-General Sir Harry Tuzo, C-in-C Northern Ireland, that some record be made of British activity in that province. Prodded into a reassessment of the utility of war art the Museum instituted a committee whose terms of reference were to commission and acquire works of art 'as historical records of conflicts or aspects of them which are now taking place or which may in the future break out and which are in the IWM's field of interest.'

Its members were Frederick Gore, RA, already a Trustee of the IWM and a natural choice as Chairman, Edward Ardizzone, recruited on the strength of his own war artist experience, and, as military adviser, General Sir Charles Jones. The Secretary was Joseph Darracott, Keeper of the Department of Art; as the custodian of the archives of the official war art schemes,[329] he was keenly aware of the tradition which the ARC was perpetuating, and took Yockney and Dickey as his mentors.

The ARC's first act was to commission the suggested eyewitness records of the Army in Northern Ireland. With a pleasing sense of continuity, its choice was an artist with a tangible link with the war art of the past – Ken Howard, who now works from what was Orpen's studio in his heyday. He was appointed on the basis of the expert draughtsmanship evident in his earlier, largely topographical work,[330] with an added recommendation from Carel Weight, one of his tutors at the RCA, who was aware of his recently revived interest in figure drawing. Howard saw the subject of his commission as 'figures with architecture to animate them', the architecture in this case being a dirty and part-derelict industrial environment reminiscent of the area of North

OPPOSITE, Ray Walker, detail from *Army Recruitment* (oil on canvas), triptych, each section 96 × 60

London around Neasden where he was born and learned to draw.

He spent five weeks in Northern Ireland in August and September 1973, dividing his time between Belfast, Londonderry and 'the country' – Belleek, Cosford Castle and Long Kesh. He worked in various mediums (watercolour, tonal drawing and oils) and adapted his techniques to meet the demands of each situation: the Creggan Estate, Londonderry's 'hardest' area and no place to loiter with a sketchbook, he drew largely from memory, and in the Lower Falls Road, where patrols were well advised to keep moving, he reluctantly used a camera wherever absolutely necessary.

Howard had made a conscious decision before he started as to the kind of pictures he wanted to produce – a record of the everyday existence of the soldier, of hours of planning and briefing in operations rooms, of waiting and watching in observation posts or 'sangars', of intelligence-gathering and routine foot patrols. He felt that the horror and violence of Northern Ireland's 'incidents' were best left to television and the photographer: where a draughtsman could excel was in recording the 'continuous event'.

His aim was a scrupulous objectivity, although he acknowledges that the fact of his association with the Army necessarily limited and selected the subject-matter accessible to him. He also learned quickly the sort of accuracy expected of him by the Army, not so much in the recording of buttons and badges, but in the details of routine operational procedure – the precise distances between men on patrol, the points at which a patrol would stop, or run, or spread out, and so on.

He went out with patrols, on foot or in armoured cars (he particularly remembers his first trip in a Saracen through the Creggan, and the noise of the bricks and paint tins bouncing off the sides) and spent hours sketching on the streets. He drew soldiers in 'the Coffin', an observation post where two men had already been shot (the first after being enticed outside by a woman, the second in the attempt to rescue him); the 'wriggly tin', the 'peace' line between the Protestant Shankhill and Catholic Falls Road; the graffiti which seemed to cover every wall in Belfast, the Protestant pictures and slogans executed with logic, care and precision, the Catholic ones more emotional, 'sloshed on, like natural abstract expressionist paintings'; the wire at Long Kesh, an image of Northern Ireland which remained with him for a long time.

After this promising new beginning, however, the ARC achieved very little; the budget for 1974 was absorbed in other museum purchases, and the members found themselves unable to use the Northern Ireland pictures to best advantage as an argument for a larger grant, it having been decided that it would be inadvisable to display them, 'simply asking for trouble'. Though they were reproduced in the national press when first completed, the pictures remain in store, consigned involuntarily to the category of records for posterity.

At the end of 1976, at the instigation of Sir Peter Masefield, the functions of the ARC were reconsidered and the Committee was reconstituted, still under Gore's chairmanship, with wider terms of reference – limited no longer to acquiring 'historical records' – and with a larger membership. General Jones was succeeded by Field-Marshal Lord Carver, and Edward Ardizzone by Leonard Rosoman; in addition the Trustees appointed the historian Alistair Horne, who has since been succeeded in the same capacity by The Rt Hon Sir Kenneth Robinson. The Keeper of the Department of Art became a member ex officio, and a new Secretary, Susan Burgess, was appointed from the Museum's directing staff; in 1983 the IWM's Director, Dr Alan Borg, also joined the Committee.

Since its first meeting in July 1977, the reconstituted ARC has met approximately four times a year and in recommending the commissioning of new artists can be counted among the few present-day patrons of contemporary art. Although one member has remarked a little ruefully on the English tendency to pigeonhole, the Committee has no unalterable preconceptions about the style of work required; but, as in the Second World War, the necessity of securing a reasonably accessible record inevitably imposes some constraints. It is also acknowledged that there are many artists who would not consider military subjects.

Similarly there are some restrictions on the choice of subject-matter – certain subjects being excluded for security reasons, others for the practical difficulties involved (Rhodesia, for example), and civil disturbances, where there is no military involvement, are in any case outside the Museum's terms of reference. Artists are briefed in varying degrees of detail by the Committee and facilities are very often arranged through the Services Directors of Public Relations in the Ministry of Defence. However, while the arrangement resembles that made in the Second World War, there is no longer, in peacetime, a Government propaganda function for war art: the ARC is a Committee of an ad hoc statutory Board of Trustees, Government-funded (and accountable to the Exchequer and Audit Department) but not responsible to a Minister in Cabinet, and its work is an expression of the Museum's Trustees' policy rather than of Government policy in the larger sense.

The Committee has in recent years used its artists purely for purposes of record to cover far-flung subjects, from the South China Sea to the South Atlantic, but its first commission after reconstitution was again Ken Howard, sent back to Northern Ireland in March 1978 to execute further pictures to replace his earlier ones, many of which had been lost in a fire.

The atmosphere he remembered from 1973 had been much tenser, with ill-feeling against the Army more apparent; now sectarian violence had partly supplanted it, and retracing his steps, this time with the BBC looking over his shoulder, Howard found it harder to respond with the same combination of suspense and spontaneity. But with the authenticity of one picture at least he was well satisfied – a drawing of soldiers keeping surveillance on top of the Divis Flats, at the heart of Republican territory, in a sangar so cramped that Howard had to make the drawing lying flat on his stomach. Moreover, to reach the hideout he had had to ascend eight floors in a lift, recalling uneasily that on several occasions in the past the lift had been stopped on intermediate floors and its occupants machine-gunned as the doors opened.

The next artist commissioned was John Devane, then still a student at the RCA. Devane appealed to the ARC as a highly praised figurative painter, and a defender of representational painting against the then fashionable view that only modernist work can convey messages of contemporary relevance. He was sent to Cyprus in the summer of 1978 to record the work of the Army and RAF on the Sovereign bases and with the UN peacekeeping force: the IWM received seventeen watercolours and two oils.

Ken Howard, *Divis Flats, 41 Commando Royal Marines Belfast 5.3.78* (sepia, ink and wash), 15 × 22

In order to maintain an equitable balance between the Services, a naval work was now suggested. The subject chosen was 'life in the Royal Navy today', in particular life aboard HMS *Broadsword*, the first of a new class of anti-submarine frigate, armed also with Exocet missiles. At the suggestion of Leonard Rosoman, the commission was offered to Humphrey Ocean, whose *Triumph* (a self-portrait with friend) was receiving high praise at the 1979 RA Summer Exhibition.

Despite his mildly unconventional appearance, and a past career as an actor and rock musician as well as a painter,[331] Ocean's reception on *Broadsword* was sympathetic. Throughout five days of exercises in the Channel, the various messes vied for the honour of 'having the artist in', and, given the privileges of an officer, he had access to most areas of the ship.

But while he enjoyed the novelty of life at sea, in pictorial terms he found the military environment alien and unappealing – 'very butch and unyielding, no curves anywhere' – and he looked vainly for a composition with some 'give' in it. Anxious to make his picture a genuinely personal expression rather than the dutiful record of externals which seemed a distinct risk, he decided to soften the rigidity and make sense of the military greyness of the scene by focusing on the people inhabiting it, thus transforming the painting into a group portrait of the kind in which he was already skilled, portraits in which the subjects and their environment are mutually dependent.[332]

Recovering the Dan Buoy* depicts one stage of an exercise in which the Dan Buoy, (a warning buoy which can be detected by sonar), is brought aboard by crane. To supplement the picture, the ARC selected five of the sketches which Ocean had made of all ranks and every aspect of life on *Broadsword*.

A more orthodox portrait was to be commissioned in 1980 – an oil of the Marshal of the RAF, Sir John Grandy, by Ruskin Spear, RA. However, the next artist detailed to depict forces at work was Paul Hogarth, appointed at the end of 1980 to record the role of the forces serving in Berlin. Hogarth was selected as one of Britain's leading illustrators,[333] the *chef d'école* of travel reportage, with a particular fondness for the cityscape; his aim, as a specialist in the personality of locations, was to communicate the uneasy blend of offence and defence along the Wall and the atmosphere of mutual and unremitting suspicion.

In December 1980 he went on a week's reconnoitre of the Wall arranged by the Army, making preliminary notes and sketches in ink and wash of possible compositions; he then returned for a month in May 1981 to work up his chosen subjects (he finally delivered twenty-five drawings) in a studio rented for him at the Akademie der Kunst.

The British sector of West Berlin naturally provided the majority of his subjects: the changing of the guard at Spandau Prison in honour of its lone inmate, Rudolf Hess; *Sunrise on the Spree* at a point where the river, narrow enough to offer a crossing, is electrified by a high tension cable; the barricaded Brandenburg Gate, symbol of the city's division, and the Freedom Flame in Theodor-Heuss-Platz (once Adolf-Hitler-Platz) burning day and night as a symbol of the hopes for its reunification. He was also, however, given access to both French and American sectors – to Bernauerstrasse, where crosses and wreaths on the pavement commemorate those who have died in

Paul Hogarth, *Finkenkruger Weg* (watercolour), $18\frac{1}{2} \times 24\frac{3}{4}$

the attempt to leave East Berlin; to Checkpoint Charlie, turned by the Press into a symbol of East-West tension; and the Oberbaum Bridge, where John le Carré's Karla defects to the West.

Working conditions were complicated when travelling with patrols by the need to maintain a brisk pace in order to reach checkpoints at given times. Hogarth took photographs where he could and, where security precautions imposed too great a distance between him and his subject, he used binoculars through which he could see the East German guards in their 'goon towers' angrily waving him off and, on one occasion, unleashing the 'war dogs', trained to attack on sight.

There was no attempt by the Army to influence Hogarth's work, though certain obvious topics were recommended to him – Allied Forces Day, for example, the ceremonial highpoint of the Berlin garrison's year – the Wall was by 1981, in media terms at least, something of a dead subject, and he experienced no more pressure than on the average magazine assignment. His record of life in West Berlin, completed in time for the twentieth anniversary of the Wall, forms an interesting counterpart to the drawings made by Ronald Searle in 1961, the year the Wall was built.[334]

During 1981 the ARC focused on the RAF, acquiring from Geoffrey Staden an oil and five drawings (made the previous year) of air/sea rescue and from Patrick George, an oil of the early-warning radar station at Neatishead in Norfolk. However, in July, it turned its attention back to the Army, and this time in a spirit of experiment, commissioning a triptych on the subject of *Army Recruitment* from Ray Walker, well known as a mural painter.

Walker's brief was 'three different stages in the progress of a new recruit to the Army', an updating perhaps of Carel Weight's *Recruit's Progress* with however one major difference: Weight's series, deeply coloured by personal emotion, was essentially a record of actual experience. Walker, although he visited a Recruiting Office in Sutton Coldfield and the Training Centre at Pirbright, developed his pictures less from observation than from beliefs he already held. The visits were useful principally for the purpose of gathering the visual imagery through which to express and substantiate his attitude to the Army – what he perceives as the brutalising effect of military training, and its futility 'in an age of possible thermo-nuclear destruction'. To this extent the triptych was less a record than an interpretation of its theme – which Walker, in any case, extended well beyond the process of army recruitment itself to include what he sees as its inevitable consequences.

The first panel attempts 'to provide the key to the sociological and psychological make-up of a kid joining the Army' at a time of massive unemployment, making play with the incentives and allurements – the portrait of the Queen, the photographs of water-skiing, and so on. The second focuses on the training for 'big deeds' – the physical toughening and mental regimentation required in order to kill. The third represents the 'deeds' themselves on the streets of Ulster, in 'a theatre call of popular revolt and military reaction', studded with the symbols of bloodshed in Northern Ireland – the grenade, the plastic bullet, the sandalled foot of a dead child.

As he reflected on his theme, Walker found himself at times inhibited by the limitations of even so large a set of canvases (each one 96×60); had he been executing the work as a mural, he would have liked, for example, to explore the wider implications

Ray Walker, *Army Recruitment* (oil on canvas), triptych, each section 96 × 60

of British rule in Ireland, the relationship between governments and armies in history, and so on. To incorporate as much as possible, he dovetailed his images and symbols into an ingenious jigsaw using all the picture planes equally to give a kaleidoscopic view of a scene which is itself constantly changing.

Four months after Ray Walker finished his recruiting triptych, the Army, with the other two Services, found itself in the midst of one of the largest and most rapid mobilisations since the Second World War; and with the despatch of the Task Force to the South Atlantic in April 1982, the ARC was confronted with a situation which, though not yet a war, very obviously called for pictorial record. The Committee would have liked to send several artists to the Falkland Islands – both draughtsmen and painters, objective recorders and more subjective and imaginative artists. In the event there was neither time nor money for more than a single artist to be chosen, and at the suggestion of both Rosoman and Gore, the ARC appointed Linda Kitson, a tutor in illustration at the RCA with a reputation for rapid and accurate draughtsmanship under pressure.

Her assignment lasted some three months – the greater part of it spent, for reasons entirely outside her own control, away from the spearhead of the advance. Prevented by virtue of her sex from travelling on a Royal Navy vessel, she arrived on East Falkland after the first troops had landed, and in all she experienced less than two weeks of battle conditions before the ceasefire came into operation on 14 June. Her pictures, and her own published record,[335] reflect this fact, being devoted for the most part to

[283]

the preparations for battle, and its gruelling aftermath.

One of Linda Kitson's interests as an artist is the 'behind-the-scenes' view of people at work.[336] The three weeks she spent on the voyage out, on the *QE II* and later the *Canberra*, offered her just such a perspective – of the Army in training, at uncomfortably close quarters. Crouched under the stairway leading to the boat-deck, she drew men monotonously 'deck bashing' in full kit; crammed into the band-room amidst a tangle of microphones and drum-kits, she sketched gunners on the dance floor at work on a Rapier missile-tracking unit; and she recorded 'heli-training' with the Sea Kings both from the air and on the flight-deck cocooned in earmuffs and goggles, with her sketchbook clipped to her sleeve.

During her brief exposure to the fighting, much of her energy was devoted to staying upright and mobile in the mud and freezing cold. It was in the month after the ceasefire that she became 'the only Task Force attachment on this isle *not* desperate to get off it' – absorbed as she was in making her most effective records of service in the Falklands, as it appeared to all except those involved in the front line fighting: the efforts to neutralise the threat that remained – mine detection at Stanley Airport, the collection and storage of abandoned Argentinian ammunition[337] – and to come to terms with the damage that had been done. She made perhaps her most dramatic drawing at this time – of the *Sir Galahad*, a week after the crippling attack by Skyhawk and Mirage jets, still blazing as it was sunk as a war grave with forty men of the 1st Battalion, Welsh Guards entombed. She also made her most disturbing – the business-like clearing and sorting of the belongings of the dead.

Kitson was neither disappointed nor relieved by her distance from the violent action, which it had never been her intention to record. She interpreted her brief as being to convey to the public only the experiences they could genuinely share – not the crises themselves, but the life going on around the crises, the current of ordinary human behaviour in extraordinary circumstances. Thus she was quite happy to leave to the cameraman both the split-second incidents of technological warfare and the appalling human debris they left behind.

In making little record of the horrors she saw, Kitson is at one with many, perhaps most, of her predecessors in the official war art schemes – and it is interesting to see her work as part of a tradition and not, as critics have tended to take it, in isolation. She shared with the artists of the Western Front the disabling cold and omnipresent mud of trench warfare, and with Bone in particular the frustrations of having to adjust artistic techniques accordingly: 'I hoped that aesthetically one would turn corners. Not a chance. . . . Operating from the bottom of one's skill is very painful.' She shared with the Dunkirk artists the desire to disassociate herself from the Press, whose priorities and needs – the hunger for news and incident – were entirely alien. Like Orpen, Sargent and Hennell, she found herself much moved by the sight of the defeated enemy – the Argentinian youths brought aboard the *Canberra* for medical treatment, many of them carrying their father's call-up cards and shaking with the fear instilled in them by their officers that, once captured, they would be eaten. Like Henry Moore, she was much struck by the frequent incongruity in war of an event with its setting: but whereas Moore responded to the stimulus of normal behaviour – eating, sleeping, dressing – out of place in the abnormal environment of the tube tunnel, Kitson chose to empha-

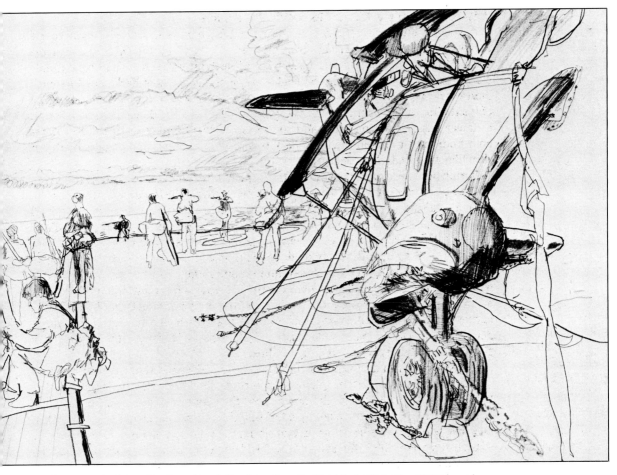

Linda Kitson, *2nd Battalion Scots Guards live firing from the flight deck, QEII, May 1983* (conté crayon and ink), $16\frac{3}{8} \times 23\frac{1}{4}$

sise the bizarre and somewhat macabre appearance of the military machine in the bland and humdrum setting of the *QE II* – the armaments bristling above the sports deck, the 4th Field Regiment HQ in Cosmetics and Jewellery, the Signals Squadron in the Rudolf Steiner Hairdressing Salon.

The one obvious difference between Linda Kitson and her predecessors seems ultimately unimportant. She was the first woman to accompany troops in the battle-zone[338] – and the Press seized on this gratefully, lingering over her competition with the Gurkhas for the small sizes in Arctic wear, her cast-off Argentinian tin hat, her red-white-and-blue legwarmers. It is a tribute to her professionalism, however, that once on the Falklands she expected, and received, very few concessions.

The ARC's most recent acquisitions are the product of a commission offered before Linda Kitson's, but pre-empted by the Falklands War, to a rather different kind of artist – perhaps the furthest removed of any of the post-war appointees from the realm of

illustration. Schooled in the ideology of the Euston Road group, Anthony Eyton is considered one of the principal guardians of 'an honourable . . . tradition' of figurative
painting, but insistent within these boundaries on the importance of personal expression, intuitive and painterly.

He was sent in April 1982, at Lord Carver's suggestion, to Hong Kong, to record
the British garrison there, paying particular attention to the Gurkha regiment. The
Gurkha pictures were in fact among the hardest to achieve: by the time Eyton arrived,
the Falklands War had stirred up a fresh surge of popular enthusiasm for Gurkhas,
and the Gurkha Field Force was besieged at its base in the New Territories by photographers and journalists. A 'set piece' of Gurkhas in ethnic dress, practising with the kukri,
was arranged, but the models drooped in the heat and Eyton found more promising
material in the less formal side of their life in the Colony – on the basketball pitch,
for example, and in the schools for Gurkha children.

He was anxious also to capture the atmosphere of colonial Army life – polo players,
full-dress dinner in the officers' mess, and troops drawn up for inspection by the Governor on the parade ground overhung by the extraordinary and oppressive Hong Kong
city skyline – aspects of an existence which, as an ex-officer with what he describes
as an 'eccentric' army past, Eyton enjoyed very much in the knowledge that he was
free to leave.

Perhaps his most successful pictures, though, are those which fall into no category,
scenes which arrested his attention during frequent forays over the outlying islands
and along the border with China – army mechanics gambling; soldiers on patrol in
the north-east corner of the New Territories, near the village of Sha Tau Kok whose
main street the frontier bisects; and the capture at night of forlorn illegal immigrants
from the People's Republic.

Over the next two years the ARC will cover further new ground by sending artists
to Belize; to branches of the womens' Services throughout Britain; and, in 1984–5,
to cover aspects of life with the British Army on the Rhine.

In its commissions the Committee is continuing, clearly and deliberately, in the existing tradition of official war art. It is in the field of purchases – each initiated by the
Keeper of the Department of Art and paid for out of that Department's separate grant
– that a further stage in the evolution of the national collection both as a document
of war and as an art collection is evident. In the late 1970s, under Joseph Darracott,
the Department's purchase grant was considerably increased, which made it possible
to make some notable acquisitions – war pictures painted before the start of the First
World War scheme, for example, and works by artists otherwise inadequately represented.[339] It was also a good time for additions to the scanty collection of war sculpture,
the price of small bronzes then being relatively low.

In the 1980s, under Angela Weight, who succeeded Joseph Darracott as Keeper
in 1981, one interesting development has been the effort to supplement the ARC's
historical records of particular military operations with works which attempt to interpret the phenomenon of war on a more general level, and to express contemporary
attitudes to war – works which will in themselves have some historical importance
as evidence of the impact of war on a country's culture. This aim was apparent in
the purchase in 1982 of Edward Burra's *Skull in Landscape** (1946), a powerful expres-

sion of post-war *angst*, evocative of the landscapes of both the Western Front and the nuclear holocaust.

The Art Department's objective is to make its pictures better known, not only as a unique historical record but as one of the most striking and comprehensive collections of twentieth-century British art; and in the process it is hoped to remove the stigma which has long been attached to war art. The suggestion that it is in some way morally inferior by virtue of its subject-matter has regularly resulted in an artist's war work being minimised, even omitted entirely, from accounts of his development. Interest in war is often assumed automatically to imply a pro-war stance: but the national war art collection in peacetime accommodates criticism of war more pointed, and pacifist views more explicit, than would ever have been tolerated before – expressed not only in Ray Walker's *Army Recruitment*, but also, more forcefully, in Graham Ashton's *81568 1945* or *The Hiroshima Cartoon* (the title incorporating the precise time of the dropping of the bomb on Hiroshima), and *Beach girl: nuclear victim 1966* by Colin Self.[340]

This is a single facet of the Art Department's policy, and the past is not forgotten. Angela Weight continues to fill out the First and Second World War collections: in 1983 the Art Department made one of its most exciting and important acquisitions, one of the earliest and best of British war pictures and a principal source of inspiration for official war art in the twentieth century – Eric Kennington's *The Kensingtons at Laventie*.

Colin Self, *Beach Girl: nuclear victim 1966* (fibre glass and hair), 11h × 67w × 22¾d

Acknowledgements

A great many people have contributed to this book, and we should like to thank them all –

Jennie Davies and Joe Stern, for their initial enthusiasm and unwavering support for the project throughout its tortuous life; Angela Weight, Keeper of the Department of Art at the Imperial War Museum, and her staff, Vivienne Crawford, Michael Moody and Jenny Wood, who gave us daily help, encouragement and advice; also at the IWM, Dr Gwyn Bayliss, Susan Burgess, Penelope Ritchie-Calder, Jonathan Chadwick, Diana Condell, Christopher Dowling, Angela Godwin, Frederick Gore, Brad King and James Lucas; and at the Tate Gallery, Iain Bain, David Brown, Clare Colvin and Mandy Green.

We are most grateful to the war artists and war art administrators who talked to us – Edward Bawden, the late Lord Clark, Sir William Coldstream, Richard Eurich, Anthony Eyton, Anthony Gross, Paul Hogarth, Ken Howard, Linda Kitson, Henry Moore, Humphrey Ocean, John Piper, Leonard Rosoman, Ray Walker and John Worsley. We should also like to thank Mrs Catherine Ardizzone, Mrs Mary Bone, Mrs Nancy Carline, Miss Gabriel Cross, Miss Elizabeth Hennell, Professor Neville Masterman, Mrs Maeve Peake, Gerald Pitchforth, Sir John Rothenstein, Miss Shirin Spencer, Miss Unity Spencer and Mrs Ann Ullmann – with especial thanks to Sue Yockney and Peter Murray Lee for their kindness in supplying us with pictures and in giving us access to the private papers of Alfred Yockney and Colonel Arthur Lee. Our thanks also to Victor Bonham-Carter, Patric and Sheila Dickinson, Allen Freer, Bridget Harris, Ronia Hinds, Mr and Mrs V. Johnson, Michael Macleod, W. P. Mayes, Angela Sims, Rex Wailes and Emily Wheeler.

For their help in the preparation of the final text of the book, we are particularly indebted to Joseph Darracott, Angela Weight, Jenny Wood and Vivienne Crawford. For the book's design we are very grateful to Penny Mills; to Jim Simmonds, in charge of the IWM's Art Store, for his invaluable advice in the selection of illustrations; to Mrs Eileen Tweedie and John Webb, who photographed many of the pictures reproduced, and to Peter McClure, for the maps which comprise the endpapers.

We have reproduced much copyright material, and in each case have named the source of the quotation or the holder of the picture; we have made every effort to contact the owners of copyright, and would like to thank all those named in the picture captions and the list of sources – in particular the Trustees of the Imperial War Museum and the Trustees of the Tate Gallery, the Paul Nash Trustees, and John Lewis and the John Nash Trustees.

FOOTNOTES

1. We have not included under the heading of propaganda the recruitment and savings campaigns etc., conducted by various Government ministries: for an account of these, and also the extensive but unofficial propagandist activities of the press, see Cate Haste, *Keep the Home Fires Burning* (Allen Lane, 1977).
2. He was successively Under-Secretary of the Local Government Board and Under-Secretary at the Home Office.
3. Robert Cumming – 'Recorder of a World at War', *Country Life*, 23.2.78 – attributes this ability to combine meticulous attention to detail with a coherent overall structure to a peculiarity of Bone's eyesight: he was long-sighted in one eye, short-sighted in the other.
4. His contract was subsequently renewed at six-monthly intervals until the end of the war.
5. Joseph Pennell (1861–1926), American lithographer, best known as Whistler's faithful disciple, publicist and biographer. Earlier in 1916 he had applied on his own initiative to tour munitions factories; in return for the facilities granted, Wellington House had the use of his drawings, but they were published privately. He was not regarded as an official war artist.
6. It covered, in fact, every aspect of his war work, the ten issues being: 'The Western Front', 'The Somme Battlefield', 'Trench Scenery', 'The Upper Hand' (military superiority at the Front, rooted in women's munitions work at home), 'The British Navy and the Western Front', 'Deserts', 'Behind the Front', 'Soldiers' Travel', and 'Ship-Building'.
7. McBey had learned to be cautious: while sketching by the river in Aberdeen early in the war, he had got up from his stool to stretch himself and been arrested for signalling to German submarines.
8. In fact, in every case the artist was permitted to take advantage of immediate topical interest and sell the pictures during the war.
9. Cowans was rewarded for his efforts to make Orpen's stay in France more comfortable by an obituary poem 'Midnight. April 16, 1921. (J.S.C.)', in which he was described as 'noble', 'strong' and 'lovable'.
10. Copies of Lee's diaries were presented to the IWM in 1982 by his son, Peter Murray Lee.
11. 'Do you remember,' Orpen wrote to Lee in 1924, 'the days I used to journey to Cassel and get blotto at Bumpherie [Beaumerie-sur-Mer] on the way – you dirty dog!' (from the collection of copies of Lee's letters presented to the IWM by Peter Murray Lee in 1982).
12. 'The Colonel' referred to in *Onlooker* is incorrectly believed to have been Lee – a confusion stemming from Lee's promotion to Colonel in 1918. As Lee's diary makes clear, the object of Orpen's spleen was Hutton-Wilson.
13. Interestingly, Lavery leaves his war pictures out of the catalogue of 'Pictures in Public Galleries' appended to *Life of a Painter*, although they are periodically displayed in the art galleries at the IWM.
14. Depicting a returning British plane tracked by the 'Archie' bursts of which Nevinson had complained.
15. The official exhibition poster can be seen in the background of Walter Bayes' picture *The Underworld*, which shows people taking shelter from an air-raid in the London Tube.
16. It is not clear whether the picture ever went on show in this state, but Nevinson certainly had posters printed from it.
17. Kennington was in France for two weeks at the private invitation of Adjutant-General Macready.
18. On the 'Efforts and Ideals' series, see Chapter 14.
19. This curious and ill-drafted clause was included in Nevinson's agreement but not in that originally drawn up by Dodgson and signed by Orpen, nor in later agreements. For suggestions as to its origins and purpose, see Chapter 22.
20. Kennington was never reduced to such extremes as Francis Dodd, who made the studies for one of his most popular war pictures, *Interrogation*, on sheets of lavatory paper.
21. The Bantam Regiment, for men who wished to fight but failed to meet the army's height requirement, was created in response to pressure from volunteers – principally from industrial and mining areas. Recruits could be between 5′ and 5′2″, but had to have the standard chest measurement.
22. The fourth issue to be published (in July 1918), it contained fifteen colour plates, a biographical essay by Dodgson, and an introduction by C. E. Montague called 'Trench Housekeeping' – criticised, not unreasonably, by the DoI as concentrating on a single, unromantic aspect of the soldier and his life in France.
23. Kennington's bark was often worse than his bite. In addition to the pictures he sold at concessionary prices to the War Museum in 1918, he also presented seven free in 1919 and 1920; and between 1934 and 1938 he presented a further twenty-one, including the oil painting *Gassed and Wounded* (28 × 36).
24. Bone considered that he had been seduced by a better offer – from Edwin Lutyens, to do a large frieze for Lutyens' church, St Jude-on-the-Hill, Hampstead Garden Suburb – but that disenchantment with the official British scheme had contributed. His services were taken over by the Canadians, for whom he worked throughout 1919.
25. Kennington's only war oil on that scale was done for the Canadians – *The Conquerors*, so-called by official request: Kennington's original title was *The Victims*.
26. His son, Dr Christopher Kennington (in his introduction to the exhibition of Kennington's work at the Maas Gallery in 1981) makes a further point: 'His unashamed admiration for the courage and strength of fighting men . . . has not induced sympathy from a world longing to enjoy peace.'
27. Unveiled in 1924. His other well-known sculptures include the war memorial to the missing at Soissons; the life-size figure of Thomas Hardy in Dorchester; the effigy of T. E. Lawrence at St Martin's Church, Wareham, and the carved brick frieze on the Memorial Theatre at Stratford-upon-Avon.
28. In *Outline*, his unfinished autobiography, Nash remembers envying Kennington his apparent freedom to concentrate on art. 'The highest forms at St Paul's were different sorts of eighths – the History 8th, the Science 8th, and so on . . .

Kennington comprised the Drawing 8th.' Nevinson at the Slade he describes as something of a bully who, from the security of cloak and sombrero, sneered at Nash for looking like an 'engineer' in stiff collars.

29. Paid largely from the Secret Service funds at Buchan's disposal.

30. Throughout his stay Nash kept minutely detailed accounts which must have been a considerable strain for one of self-confessed mathematical 'inaptitude'.

31. *The place was rotten with dead; green clumsy legs*
    High-booted, sprawled and grovelled along the saps;
    And trunks, face downward in the sucking mud,
    Wallowed like trodden sand-bags loosely filled.
    'Counter-attack' by Siegfried Sassoon. From *Counter-attack and other poems*, published by Viking Press.

32. Remarkably, this letter was written at the same time as the chatty epistles to Masterman on the subject of chauffeurs and valets. Nash's aspirations as a poet are very obvious in his letters to his wife, suitably suppressed in his official correspondence.

33. There is a striking parallel also in the growing disillusionment felt by other members of Edward Marsh's circle – most notably Siegfried Sassoon, who in the summer of 1917 had refused to go back to the Front on the grounds that 'the War is being deliberately prolonged by those who have the power to end it.'

34. This statement, unexplained, is one of several tantalising loose ends in Nash's 'Notes for the Continuation of his Autobiography' relating to his official appointment.

35. A remark he made in 1929 (to Charles ffoulkes, Curator of the IWM – IWM:NASH, Nash/ffoulkes, 2.4.29) – 'The trouble is that the chaps who painted away from the battles seem to have made such much better pictures' – seems to reaffirm his earlier judgement.

36. In 1905, for example, he wrote a letter to *The Times* and obtained many distinguished signatories to it, deploring the growing rift between the two countries; and in 1906, at the banquet which followed a Knightsbridge exhibition of German art, it was Rothenstein who proposed the toast to 'Our Guests the German artists'.

37. He was assisted in the drawing by Kennington, who also painted in some of the architectural detail. The painting was exhibited half-finished at the Royal Academy in 1916, and never fully completed.

38. The exhibition did not receive official support – a symptom of his relations with the propaganda authorities.

39. Rothenstein and Kennington spent Christmas Day 1917 at the American base, and Rothenstein observed somewhat wryly, 'The names called out, as each man walked up to receive his present from the tree, amused us. Private Schwartz, Private Schmidt, Corporal Prellwitz, Sergeant Bergman, and so forth.'

40. In fairness, this was equally to do with finance – see Chapter 15.

41. In November 1917 there were two artists in France besides Orpen – Kennington and Nash; between January and March 1918 there were still three altogether – Orpen, Kennington and Rothenstein.

42. On the Canadian war art scheme, see Chapter 15.

43. Orpen agreed to make two copies of the Rhys-Davids portrait – one (free) for his father, the other (£250) for Eton 'as an inspiration to future generations of Etonians'.

44. Orpen's ping-pong prowess was famed: C. E. Montague wrote caustically to Francis Dodd, 'To stand artists' war-work a man must be like Orpen and do as much boxing and ping-pong as painting. The French art critics at the Allied Press can't find words to express their admiration of Orpen's ping-pong.'

45. One of *The Times's* leading war correspondents.

46. This was the version swallowed whole by Lady Diana Manners and reproduced in her autobiography *The Rainbow Comes and Goes* (Hart-Davis, 1958) – with the story of her subsequent enlightenment.

47. A matchbox decorated with Bone's *Tank* on one side and his portrait of Haig on the other achieved some popularity.

48. The mailing list for the first issues of *The Western Front* is informative: copies went to, among others, the King, Queen, Prince of Wales, Archbishop of Canterbury and Cardinal of Westminster.

49. Likened by P. G. Konody to the mile-long banqueting hall in D. W. Griffiths's 'Intolerance'.

50. It was also used as a poster for the propaganda film *Britain Prepared* both in England and in Italy.

51. The eighteen artists were Muirhead Bone, Frank Brangwyn, George Clausen, Edmund Dulac, Maurice Greiffenhagen, Archibald Hartrick, F. E. Jackson, Augustus John, Eric Kennington, Gerald Moira, C. R. W. Nevinson, William Nicholson, Charles Pears, Charles Ricketts, William Rothenstein, Charles Shannon, Claude Shepperson and Edmund J. Sullivan.

52. Although 'Efforts and Ideals' did not in fact *sell* well in America, their *succès d'estime* was considered to have proved the value of art propaganda; one British representative in New York even attributed to them the initiation of America's own official war art scheme.

53. Lloyd George had already raised him from knighthood to a peerage (as Lord Beaverbrook) in the month of the coup.

54. Though in fact the MoI did come to play a significant part in home propaganda as the NWAC's agent for the organising of film shows (which at their peak drew audiences of twenty million a week) and the supplying of official photographs.

55. Bennett always claimed to have been appointed on the strength of his knowledge of the French mind, as displayed in his novel *The Pretty Lady* (about a French courtesan in London) which Beaverbrook much admired.

56. The MoI representative in Russia was author Hugh Walpole.

57. Bennett first met Masterman in September 1914 at the conference arranged by Wellington House to rally support from writers: others present included Barrie, Bridges, Chesterton, Conan Doyle, Galsworthy, Hardy, Masefield and Wells; Kipling and Quiller-Couch sent messages offering their services.

58. Bennett suggested Sickert as the ideal choice for subjects of this kind.

59. Both Dodd and Lavery did, however, continue as official artists under the auspices of the IWM and Admiralty – see Chapter 24.

60. Tonks also made the Slade's studios available in the vacation for use by official war artists.

61. Edward Wadsworth, working on camouflage for the navy, applied for consideration only when the war was nearly over.

62. Matthew Smith also applied for an official appointment, from a prisoner of war labour camp in France where he was

working, but by the time his request was received the Ministry's scheme was being wound up.

63. The caricatures were reproduced in three successive issues of *Reveille*, the wartime magazine for disabled servicemen, of which four issues were produced in 1918–19. A further Beerbohm drawing – *Demobbed* – is a portrait of Eric Kennington.

64. Gertler's *Merrygoround* (1917) had already achieved a certain notoriety for its implicit condemnation of the war.

65. The proposal was made in an open letter to the BWMC dated 8.4.18 – a document of great importance in the evolution of the Ministry's scheme.

66. Several of the older artists – including Tonks and Clausen – objected to this condition on the grounds that it offered an affront to their dignity, and in their cases it was waived.

67. Not all were anxious to avail themselves of this privilege; Cameron, for instance, wrote, 'I love to see the flames curling round them, they do embrace so lovingly.' (IWM:CAMERON, Cameron/Yockney, 6.3.19)

68. Bayes was a respected artist-teacher, who in 1918 succeeded his mentor Sickert as head of the Westminster Art School.

69. Holmes was as a painter perhaps less eminent than the others, but was a leading figure in the art establishment, having been successively manager of the Vale Press, editor of the *Burlington Magazine*, Slade Professor of Art at Oxford (1904–10), Keeper of the National Portrait Gallery (1909–16), and, in 1918, Director of the National Gallery and a Trustee of the Tate.

70. The '*total* output' condition was strictly enforced. Bernard Meninsky, extremely impoverished after his discharge from the army as a neurasthenic, took two days a week teaching at the Central School in order to support his wife and baby; he was discovered and required to make up the days lost to the Ministry at the end of his appointment.

71. *Honorary* commissions carried no pay of rank – only those artists with actual commissions received military pay. It was later ruled that a serving officer could not receive military and civil pay simultaneously, and the MoI was obliged also to pay the equivalent of the artist's military pay.

72. In the event Rothenstein never took up the lecturing job in France; the French authorities objected, as he explained, to 'my dear old father having come from a village near Hanover nearly seventy years ago'. (Rothenstein/John Drinkwater, 23.10.18 – quoted in Mary Lago, *Max and Will*, John Murray, 1975, p. 106.)

73. The following paragraphs are a summary of the shape the 'art memorial' plans took over several months (April-July 1918) and many meetings: the BWMC minutes in the IWM provide a step-by-step account of the Committee's complicated and not always consistent deliberations.

74. He applied shortly after completing for Derrick's 'Efforts and Ideals' a thunderously allegorical 'Ideal' entitled *The Dawn*.

75. The cartoon was exhibited in the exhibition of CWMF pictures at the Royal Academy in January 1919 and, while the Canadians were still hoping for the completed picture, was subsequently offered to the IWM for £1,000: it was turned down.

76. We are grateful to an anonymous member of the IWM's Art Department for having spotted this association.

77. His large picture *General Officers of World War I, 1914–18*, commissioned by Sir Abe Bailey for the National Portrait Gallery, illustrates well the difficulties he experienced in composing without a model. Not surprisingly he had no trouble in making the separate studies for the individual generals, but found constructing the overall scheme for the picture extremely problematical. He wrote to Evan Charteris in September 1920, 'I am handicapped by the idea that they never could have been altogether in any particular place – so I feel deterred from any sort of interesting background and reduced to painting them all standing up in a vacuum'. *General Officers* is widely acknowledged to be one of his least successful paintings (though it is worth noticing that he received £5,000 for it, in contrast with the £600 the BWMC paid him).

78. He did need, however, to refresh his memories of the hospital tents. Yockney wrote to him after his return from France, 'I think you will find in [Richmond] Park between the Roehampton Gate and the Robin Hood Gate the material you require. There are canvas buildings of all kinds from small bell tents to Balloon hangars.' (IWM:SARGENT, Yockney/Sargent, 27.12.18)

79. *Gassed** was also much commercialised. In 1934 Odhams Press attempted to use it to advertise a series of articles in *The People* on Edith Cavell. Commented a scandalised IWM official, 'A colossal figure of Nurse Cavell appeared, looming up behind the soldiers in the picture . . . The design looked like a pill advertisement.' (IWM:SARGENT, note by Ernest Blaikley, 9.3.34.).

80. The fourth super-picture, on Colonial co-operation, at one time tentatively allocated to Henry Lamb (Australian by birth), never got beyond the idea stage.

81. In 1887, he was house surgeon to Sir Frederick Treves, doctor to the 'Elephant Man'.

82. Some of these drawings, now at the Royal College of Surgeons, were used to illustrate Gillies' manual on plastic surgery. The drawings for Gillies' book do not form part of the official war art collection. We are indebted to Angela Sims for access to her unpublished thesis on the early history of plastic surgery.

83. Tonks's picture was not ultimately 'Uccello'-sized, but the smaller alternative size of 72×86.

84. Sims' 'strangeness' later developed into diagnosable mental illness, and in 1928 he drowned himself while the balance of his mind was disturbed.

85. Konody had suggested that in view of Paul's inexperience in oils, the Nashes should both be employed to *collaborate* on a 'memorial' picture.

86. Roberts had spent some time in the early years of the war making bomb parts in a munitions factory in Tufnell Park.

87. The philosopher-critic T. E. Hulme, an erstwhile friend of Lewis, was killed in September 1917 a few hundred yards away from Lewis's battery.

88. Strang was later appointed under Scheme 3.

89. According to William Roberts (*The Listener*, 21.3.57), Lewis used Edward Wadsworth, with or near whom he was staying in the summer of 1919, as a model for the group.

90. The principal picture of the Italian campaign in the National Collection, Elliott Seabrooke's *Bombardment of Gorizia* (42×60), was purchased outside the MoI scheme in 1919 – see Chapter 26 (Bone Fund). Several other Italian Front pictures were commissioned by the Air Services Section of the IWM – see Chapter 25.

91. See Chapter 26. Although the MoI was formally dissolved in

December 1918, the Art sub-committee of the IWM took over its responsibilities: it received and paid for pictures already commissioned and, in addition, commissioned in 1919 some new works from artists considered in 1918 by the MoI. These were to fit within the old MoI 'memorial' series and were paid for from funds allocated by the Treasury to meet outstanding MoI commitments. Hence our inclusion as MoI artists of some who began work only in 1919.

92. Henry Lamb, Neville Lewis and Harold Squire were all proposed, but the War Office refused to release any of them.

93. In *The Resurrection of Soldiers*, the altar-piece of the Oratory of All Souls, Burghclere, one of the resurrecting soldiers is wreathed in barbed wire, from which another is extricating him with wire-cutters.

94. Steer's MoI canvas is *Dover Harbour, 1918*. A further five oils were acquired in 1919 by the IWM – one presented by the artist, four puchased from the Bone Fund (see Chapter 26).

95. Fergusson's *Portsmouth Docks* was purchased by the IWM in 1975.

96. This picture was destroyed by fire in 1977.

97. Its report was put before Parliament on 3.8.18.

98. Pemberton Billings, a barrister and orator, was sued for libel in April 1918 by theatre producer J. Grein and dancer Maud Allan, whom he had denounced as agents of German subversion for their production of Wilde's *Salome*. Ross, who had worked for many years to have Wilde's plays restored to the standard repertoire, was implicated as a witness for the prosecution.

99. Bennett was an old friend of Ross who, as Compton Mackenzie describes ('My Life and Times', octave 3, pp. 271–2), had had him elected to the Reform Club.

100. The subject – more specifically the Worcesters at Gheluvelt – was a curious choice for Jagger, who had not been at First Ypres but had an extremely distinguished record of service elsewhere – at Gallipoli, and at Neuve Chapelle, where he had won the MC. He later executed much successful (free-standing) war sculpture, including the figures for the Artillery Memorial at Hyde Park Corner.

101. The MoI was formally dissolved on 31.12.18; most of the staff were sacked, but a few were transferred to the Foreign Office, to continue a semblance of propaganda work during the Peace Conference.

102. The museum, originally dubbed the 'National War Museum', was, subject to Cabinet approval, renamed the 'Imperial War Museum' in the interim report of Lord Crawford and Balcarres' Committee, dated 14.12.17, at the request of the Dominions sub-committee.

103. ffoulkes was subsequently promoted to the rank of Major, RM.

104. Trophies were also exhibited for propaganda purposes in America. (IWM:WWI ARCHIVE A1/4, War Trophies Committee minutes 6.6.18)

105. Ross died in October 1918, at the age of 49.

106. It is likely that Epstein's portrait bust *Sergeant Hunter, VC* was the product of sittings arranged by Bone for the bas-relief, a consolation prize for the cancellation of the larger commission.

107. Tonks was not among the artists Brereton employed.

108. Lavery was still completing his DoI assignment at that time.

109. The Admiralty sub-committee was the first to exhibit its pictures, at the 'Sea Power' exhibition at the Grosvenor Galleries in December 1918.

110. This was invariably much less than they would have received in peacetime; Lavery, in fact, having originally reduced his fee by half, eventually presented his whole output to the Museum.

111. Allfree was employed at 2 guineas per day, Connard at £2 16s 6d a day, Dawson at £25 per week, and Pears at £25 a week.

112. This was much resented by artists employed later who *had* already seen active service; Donald Maxwell, who had commanded a motor launch for some time, wrote bitterly of artists 'swanking in spurs, with nothing but seahorses in sight, as Majors of Marines'. (IWM:MAXWELL, Maxwell/Blaikley, 15.1.29)

113. In his article 'Dazzle Painting in the First World War', (*Antique Collector*, April 1975), Paul Atterbury has argued convincingly that dazzle painting was not, as it might appear, the result of a practical application of Cubist and Vorticist theories of colour and abstraction. The designs were in fact worked out on strictly scientific principles by a team of traditional marine painters in studios in the basement of Burlington House: the modernists were, if anything, influenced by dazzle, and not vice versa. Edward Wadsworth, for example, whose woodcuts of dazzled ships helped to make his name, played no part, as has been suggested, in the development of dazzle designs; his job as Dazzle Officer in Liverpool Docks was merely to supervise the physical application of the paint.

114. Bone was in fact technically already in the MoI's employ; Brownrigg appears, temporarily at least, to have been poaching on behalf of the Admiralty and IWM.

115. Bone's pictures were published in book form with a text by his brother, as *Merchantmen at Arms* (Chatto and Windus, 1919).

116. This picture seems also to have been partially based on an official German aerial photograph of Jerusalem.

117. In the making of these models – dummies, many of them life-size, of women engaged in war work – she engineered the appointment, rather improbably, of Charles Ricketts as a consultant.

118. With the possible exception of Austin Spare, whose pictures came to the Women's Work Section when Brereton's medical pictures were distributed.

119. The IWM also acquired by gift three watercolours of the British Caspian Fleet by G. L. Parnell.

120. The original commission for one large picture at £3000 was later modified to three large pictures at £2000 each.

121. The figures of the two soldiers were based on an earlier drawing – *Blown-Up: Mad*.

122. The incident had a curious sequel when, after Haig's death in 1928, Orpen painted out the offending soldiers and cherubs and presented the picture of the flag-draped coffin in the empty Hall to the IWM as a memorial to the Field-Marshal – 'one of the best friends I ever had' (IWM:ORPEN, Orpen/IWM, 20.2.28) – thus turning it from a tribute to the Unknown Soldier into a tribute to perhaps the best-known soldier in the army.

123. Many MoI artists received post-war commissions in this way – notably Colin Gill (Jacka, VC), Alfred Hayward (Generals Birdwood and Furse), Walter Russell (General Godley), and John Wheatley (Crichton, VC).

124. These unfortunately included works invited from Gertler, Grant and Philpot.

25. The remarkable similarity to one another of the soldiers depicted is to be explained by the fact that Underwood's brother modelled for them all.

26. This represented the proceeds from the sale of two sets of war lithographs – the 'Efforts and Ideals' series and another set of Clydeside scenes – and the copyright fees from *Merchantmen at Arms*. Bone had already donated £1200 to the Belgian Relief Fund and was understandably sensitive to suggestions that he had made money out of the war.

27. Bone's offer was accepted in November 1918: in January 1919, Yockney's suggestion that he be invited to join the Art sub-committee was rejected on the grounds that it was 'undesirable that an artist should be on the Committee'. (IWM 401a/8, Art sub-committee minutes, 10th meeting, 8.1.19) It is not impossible that the IWM had hoped, in his absence, for a free hand in the spending of the Fund. However, Bone seriously mistrusted the Services representatives' artistic intentions (he felt 'that beastly Air . . . Committee' in particular was simply wasting money – IWM:BONE, Bone/ Yockney, c.25.10.19); his practice was to buy the pictures and send the IWM the bills – and he went so far as to stipulate that in the event of his death, control of the Fund was to pass to Charles Aitken, by then the Director of the Tate Gallery.

28. With the IWM due to open its doors to the public for the first time (at its first home, Crystal Palace) in June 1920, it is curious that the administrators should have chosen to exhibit one of its main collections prematurely. The answer may lie in Mond's desire to rival the success of the CWMF's pictures.

29. The 104 Orpens, which would undoubtedly have featured largely, were unfortunately still in America and he was poorly represented.

30. This was not a new tendency: Mark Gertler's *Eve* was defaced on its first appearance at the Goupil Gallery in 1915, with a label marked 'Made in Germany', and Epstein's *Rock Drill* met the same fate.

31. The question was tabled by Sir Clement Kinloch-Cooke on 23.2.20.

32. Not all gifts were accepted, however: in 1924, after consulting Arnold Bennett, the IWM turned down Sickert's *1914* on the (by now) spurious ground that only eyewitness accounts were acceptable.

33. CIAD could also give direct financial relief, but did not commission work.

34. CIAD and the *Domesday Book* project were both administered from the National Gallery. Clark was invited to join the advisory panel of Paul Nash's Arts Bureau, he was Chairman of the Ministry of Labour's Publicity Artists Committee, and he was one of the founders of CEMA.

35. As early as 1934. See generally Michael Balfour, *Propaganda in War 1939–45: Organisations, Policies and Publics in Britain and Germany* (Routledge and Kegan Paul, 1977), Ian [McLaine,] *Ministry of Morale* (Allen and Unwin, 1979) and Evelyn Waugh, *Put Out More Flags* (Chapman and Hall, 1942).

36. Hitler's reoccupation of the demilitarized zone of the Rhineland and Mussolini's invasion of Ethiopia.

37. In his autobiography, *The Other Half – A Self-Portrait* (John Murray, 1977) p. 22, Clark writes, 'A few weeks after the outbreak of war I set in motion a plan by which artists should be commissioned to make a record of the war. I was no doubt thinking of the Canadian war artists scheme in the 1914–18 war. . . .'

138. He was a member of the London Group.

139. In 1940 he was put in charge of 'priority matters' at the Ministry of Aircraft Production.

140. Clark was promoted from Head of Films to Controller of Home Publicity in 1940.

141. £650 for the War Office artists and £1000 for the Admiralty.

142. Originally titled simply the 'Artists' Advisory Committee'. Both titles were in current usage during the war; the Committee met under one or other of them 197 times between 1939 and 1945.

143. To the early meetings the MoI also sent Leigh Ashton, its Head of Finance (and best man at Kenneth Clark's wedding), and R. A. Bevan, from its General Productions Division.

144. The Services representatives were: for the Admiralty, R. M. Y. Gleadowe, ex-Slade Professor at Oxford, Head of the Admiralty's Honours and Awards Section (succeeded after his death by others from this section – Armide Oppé and Oliver Warner); for the War Office, Colin Coote, a well-known journalist, later the Editor of the *Daily Telegraph* (succeeded towards the end of the war by Selwyn Jepson); and for the RAF, W. P. Hildred (succeeded by Harald Peake and Lord Willoughby de Broke).

145. The WAAC's proceedings were themselves classified as 'Secret'.

146. Now Sir Muirhead Bone, knighted in 1937.

147. Russell had been in 1895 Assistant Professor at the Slade and an active member of the NEAC.

148. Most notably Gilbert Ledward, one of the first sculptors employed in the First World War scheme, who urged the Committee to 'leave some records for the benefit of the Outer Mongolian Archaeological Society when they come to excavate London about AD 3000'. (IWM:GP/46/81, Ledward/ Dickey, 14.1.40).

149. In the index (now in the IWM) of artists considered for appointment, Ben Nicholson's card simply bears the inscription 'Abstract. No recommendation.'

150. Although the Artists General Benevolent Fund, in settling his rent debts in October 1942, at the same time recommended that he seek cheaper accommodation than his present flat in Edwardes Square.

151. Documented in the Bomberg papers in the Tate Gallery Archives (TAM 22 I-M, 23, 24A).

152. In his radio broadcast, 'The Artist in Wartime', printed in *The Listener*, 26 October 1939.

153. For the RAF's operations outside the scope of the WAAC, see Chapter 30.

154. Art critic of *The Sunday Times*, and an enthusiastic supporter of the official war art scheme.

155. Where a serving artist showed particular merit, the WAAC undertook to ask his commanding officer to give him facilities to paint.

156. The only exception was the £500 paid for Laura Knight's picture of Nuremberg.

157. Names were initially drawn from a list compiled for the WAAC by Armide Oppé; daughter of connoisseur-historian Paul Oppé, she had built up an encyclopaedic acquaintance with contemporary art as a picture researcher for the *London Mercury*. Her list included Ardizzone, Bawden, Stephen Bone,

Coldstream, Connard, Cundall, Dodd, Freedman, Kennington, Laura Knight, Lamb, Wyndham Lewis, Medley, John and Paul Nash and, interestingly, David Jones and C. R. W. Nevinson.

158. Roberts was later rehabilitated, and recorded scenes in ARP control rooms and at railway stations under wartime conditions.

159. Gabain applied to draw the evacuation of children to America – an issue which was believed to exacerbate class hostilities – but was not given facilities.

160. Commissioned in March 1940 to make twelve drawings of ARP subjects for 100 guineas.

161. It was during this period that John Piper was commissioned to paint in ARP control rooms in Bristol.

162. Medley was a Slade graduate, a member of the London Group, and an exhibitor at the Surrealist Exhibition in London in 1936.

163. *Little Tim and the Brave Sea Captain* (OUP, 1936), *Lucy Brown and Mr Grimes* (OUP, 1937), and *Tim and Lucy Go To Sea* (OUP, 1938).

164. The murals were destroyed by bombing in 1941, and replaced by Bawden alone in 1958.

165. Eves, finding his occupation gone as the generals dispersed, had gone home straight away.

166. In his book *Baggage to the Enemy* (John Murray, 1941), Ardizzone describes vividly the events between the invasion and the fall of France.

167. *Aircraft Runway in course of construction at Thélus.*

168. When he got home he worked these up into watercolours such as *The Entrance to an Air-Raid Shelter, Dunkirk* and *In the Square at Dunkirk (before the embarkation).*

169. Coastal Command was to be placed in 1941 under the operational control of the Admiralty.

170. Kennington was sure that the Air Ministry representative would be 'distressed when he sees that Squadron-Leader Beamish [who had interrupted his sitting to destroy two Messerschmitts, four flak ships and various troops on the ground] has been presented with his top button undone and his tie hanging out.' (IWM:KENNINGTON, Dickey/Clark, 22.1.41)

171. He took, at the MoI's expense, a variety of magazines from *Aeronautics* to *Picture Post.*

172. See his article, 'Photography and Modern Art', *The Listener* 27.7.32.

173. 'Raiders' were followed in October 1940 by another series of watercolours and an oil on the same theme – both entitled 'Marching against England'.

174. Summarized later in print – *Vogue*, March 1942, 'The Personality of Planes'.

175. He delivered in October 1940 a related watercolour series and a large oil of his 'aerial creatures' actually in the air, with the title 'Flying against Germany'. He was also asked by Clark in 1944 to paint the 'robot planes' or V-1s as 'a beautiful (if rather insistent) emanation of your idea of this war as a combat of inanimate monsters' (Clark/Paul Nash, undated; Tate Gallery Archives, 7050 358), but the picture never materialised.

176. The navy displayed similarly gentlemanly scruples: Harold Nicolson reported the MoI's naval adviser's explanation as to why no pictures had been obtained of the sinking of the *Bismarck*: 'After all, an Englishman would not like to take snapshots of a fine vessel sinking.' (Nicolson, diary entry for 10.6.41 – *Diaries and Letters 1939–45*, Collins, 1967)

177. Kennington was repeatedly urged by the WAAC and eventually by the Air Ministry to diversify, and repeatedly refused.

178. Nash complained half-jokingly that one of his planes in the National Gallery 'has an unholy job standing up to the dive-bombing of Kennington's glamour boys, each one twice as large as the machine'. (IWM:PAUL NASH, Nash/Dickey, c.12.5.41)

179. Thomson also spent some time at RAF hospitals and produced a gruesome but valuable record of some aspects of the rapid advances made during the Second World War in plastic surgery and the treatment of burns.

180. Further large number of RAF portraits were either purchased (e.g., many by Cuthbert Orde, including a drawing of Josef Frantisek, who is thought likely to have been the RAF's highest scoring ace in the Second World War) or commissioned from non-salaried artists, such as Allan Gwynne-Jones, T. C. Dugdale and Oswald Birley.

181. With a short interval March-July 1941 during which he was returned on loan to the Admiralty.

182. This picture, and another of the RAF Training Station in Windsor Great Park, was sold by special request to King George VI.

183. Held in May 1942 and visited by 21,000 people in three weeks.

184. Dame Laura also painted several WAAF heroines and a Stirling bomber crew.

185. H. W. Hailstone, for example, made interesting records of RAF operations with the partisans in Yugoslavia, and of the recapture of the Channel Islands; Stafford-Baker covered in detail the effects of RAF bombing on Berlin, and was present at the International Military Tribunal for the Far East, the Japanese equivalent of the Nuremberg Trials.

186. Nash was not made a salaried artist, as he made it clear that he resented being kept from doing outside work; he was given instead a commission for £500-worth of pictures to be allocated by mutual agreement. This sum was used up between January 1941 and May 1942. Thereafter he was offered no formal contract, but was invited to give the WAAC first refusal on all his work.

187. Cultural propaganda was an important element in the Arts Bureau manifesto of 1939 and in 1941 Nash went so far as to propose a 'Ministry of Imaginative Warfare'. (IWM:PAUL NASH, undated memorandum by Nash, possibly c.April 1941)

188. The MoI appears to have been unconvinced of the collages' persuasive power and they were not used. *Above the Clouds* was acquired for the national collection in 1977.

189. Evidence for this series is to be found in letters to Nash from the Neutral Countries Division of the MoI (Tate Gallery Archives, 7050.843 and following). In one of these montages a fungus stem blossoms into four heads of Hitler.

190. Submitted in February 1941.

191. The evidence for this is to be found in letters Lambe/Nash, 2.12.41 and Day/Nash, 28.1.42. (Tate Gallery Archives, 7050.834 & 841)

192. The canvas was never used.

193. Though he completed the set of oils and produced

watercolours of the 'antagonists' ('Raiders' and 'Marching against England') and Bomber Command ('Aerial Creatures' and 'Flying against Germany'), the watercolours for Fighter and Coastal Commands were never started.

4. Submitted in November 1941.

5. Even for the vapour trails Nash used photographs: in a letter to the MoI's Photographic Division (IWM:PAUL NASH, 6.5.41) he asked for pictures of 'aerial doodles'.

6. Submitted in April 1942.

7. Submitted in September 1944.

8. It is worth noting that while *Battle of Britain** and *Defence of Albion* were willingly commissioned by the WAAC in fulfilment of the £500 fee, Nash had to press *Battle of Germany* upon them once the £500 was exhausted.

9. Published a year later by Counterpoint Publications.

0. Hailstone was also commissioned by the WAAC to paint civil defence subjects in 1941, and in 1943 he was appointed as a Ministry of War Transport artist.

1. Devas had generously asked that the commission be given to a serving artist, one who, unlike himself, did not have the opportunity to paint – but he was eventually persuaded by the Committee to accept it.

2. See Richard Morphet, catalogue to the Meredith Frampton exhibition, Tate 1982.

3. Both drawn as part of a 50-guinea commission at the end of October 1940 from the WAAC for 'life in London during air-raids'. (IWM:TOPOLSKI MoI/Topolski c. end October 1940)

4. At the suggestion of Julian Huxley.

5. Aggravated by an abnormally low tide in the Thames which restricted water supplies.

6. None of Moore's devastation scenes were offered to the WAAC.

7. For 'general subjects'.

8. The WAAC purchased a second aeroplane picture *Camouflaged Bombers* on 15.8.40 from the Leicester Galleries exhibition.

9. John Armstrong was also commissioned at this time to record damage in Wales, and in Essex.

0. A position that was renewed with short breaks until 31 March 1945.

1. Randolph Schwabe was also sent to draw Coventry Cathedral in accordance with the WAAC's policy of acquiring pictures of air-raid damage of 'two kinds: records in which the real motive is the original excellence of the architecture, and damage which is picturesque in itself. The former should be done by architectural draughtsmen such as Schwabe; the latter by artists with a sense of pictorial drama like Sutherland and Piper.' (IWM:SCHWABE Clark/Dickey 29.11.40)

2. *Coventry Cathedral November 15th 1940*. Piper also painted in Coventry *Interior of Coventry Cathedral* and *Ruins of St Michael Baptist Church*.

3. Clark insisted on the omission of the first couplet as 'rather idealistic'. (IWM:PIPER Clark/Pick 22.11.40)

4. In three watercolours of *Shelter experiments near Woburn, Bedfordshire*.

5. Clark suggested Ardizzone on 12.9.40.

6. The commission was satisfied by the delivery of 9 shelter subjects in March and April 1941, and on 23 April a further 2 drawings were purchased. The Committee completed its acquisitions by commissioning a further 2 drawings on 7 May 1941: these were delivered on 24 September, when a further work was purchased for 10 guineas, bringing the Committee's total of

shelter drawings to 18 (one of which was subsequently lost by enemy action – see Chapter 40, Footnote 323). It is interesting to note that a single shelter drawing was recently sold at auction in London for £38,000.

217. Recorded in Evelyn Dunbar's *The Queue at the Fish Shop*, Grace Golden's *An Emergency Food Office*, and Leslie Cole's *Kitchen of the first British Restaurant at Hull*.

218. Rupert Shephard's *Road Transport in the Blitz* and Henry Carr's *Interior of a Railway Carriage at Night on the Great Western, 1941* illustrate two different aspects of the black-out's hazards and inconveniences.

219. e.g., Evelyn Dunbar's *A Knitting Party*; Ethel Gabain's series of lithographs of 'Children in Wartime', of which *Boys from South East London gathering sticks in Cookham Wood* is typical; and Adrian Allinson's *The AFS Dig for Victory in St James's Square*.

220. Frank Dobson was commissioned in 1943 to portray *An Underground Room in the BBC Building*, but his suggestions for further BBC subjects were turned down.

221. See for example Hennell's *The Countryman at Work* (Architectural Press).

222. As a gesture, the WAAC briefly switched John Piper to recording land reclamation in January 1944; he produced 3 watercolours including 'Swaffham Prior showing excavators at work with centuries old bog oak being grubbed up'. (IWM:GP/46/96)

223. On 13.7.41 Moore was commissioned for 25 guineas to make drawings at medical aid posts in London; nothing came of this commission and it was superseded by the coalmining commission. (See IWM/WAAC Minutes, 53rd Meeting, 13.7.41)

224. The WAAC in fact acquired 10 of Moore's coalmining drawings. 4 were delivered on 28.5.42 in satisfaction of the first commission, and 4 more were purchased for 25 guineas on the same date; (on 11.6.42 an extra 30 guineas was voted towards these 8 to bring the price up to the average paid for the shelter drawings). On 17.7.42 2 more coalmining drawings were purchased for 10 guineas each. (See IWM:WAAC MINUTES for these dates.)

225. Many tin mines were reopened by the Government because of the emergency demand.

226. Sutherland's first six-month commission on bomb damage expired on 30.6.41. He was given a second six months by the WAAC from 1.8.41 to visit the steel works at Dowlais and Port Talbot. His third six-month commission dates from 1.6.42, for the Cornish tin mines. His fourth six-month commission commenced on 1.1.43, was extended by three weeks into July, and on 1.8.43 was renewed for a further six months; during this time Sutherland worked on subjects in an ICI underground factory, in limestone quarries at Buxton, and at open-cast coal mines at Wakefield. On 1.2.44 he was given a two-month commission, followed on 1.4.44 by a four-month commission, during which time he worked at Woolwich Arsenal. (He began to lose interest in production subjects at this point; in June 1944 he asked the Committee if he might visit the Second Front, but the request was refused.) On 1.8.44 he received a three-month commission, and on 1.11.44 a further three months – during which he was able to visit France (see Chapter 38). On 1.2.45 he received his last commission of two months. The intervals between commissions were a result of the delay in submitting sufficient

drawings to justify the fee, and the need to accommodate holidays.

227. The Committee first purchased a drawing in 1942, then in 1944 Richards was commissioned to make more on the same theme; he was not satisfied with the results and the commission was subsequently cancelled.

228. Ayrton was one of the loosely knit group of young artists – John Minton, John Craxton, Keith Vaughan and Rodrigo Moynihan were others – who met regularly in the early 1940s at the studio of Colquhoun and MacBryde in Campden Hill.

229. He was employed by the MoI as a propaganda artist from 5.10.42 until 30.1.43, and evolved his 'An Exhibition of the Artist Adolf Hitler' series.

230. Peake did not finish his glassblowers pictures until December 1943 when, despite their admitted excellence, the WAAC adjudged them insufficient in quantity to warrant full payment of his salary. He was therefore sent to an RAF Bomber Station in Sussex and completed his commission with the oil painting *Interrogation of Pilots* and some sketches in December 1944.

231. *Going to Work* (oil, 18 × 24) was commissioned on 31.12.42; the subject is Mather and Platts, Newton Heath, Manchester. In addition the WAAC purchased Lowry's *St Augustine's Church, Manchester* in June 1945.

232. Hailstone was in 1945 to be sent to South-East Asia Command, where he painted successful portraits of many of the General Officers Commanding, including Mountbatten, Sir Miles Dempsey and Sir Keith Park.

233. The outcome of a 1929 commission from the Empire Marketing Board.

234. During the war Spencer visited Port Glasgow in April 1941, September-October 1942, September-October 1943, May-July 1944, and August 1944-March 1945.

235. Explaining his choices of the triptych form, Spencer wrote: 'In each activity there seems always to be a central climactic aspect which belongs as far as I can see always to the verticle [*sic*] tall portion.' (Tate Gallery Archives, Spencer Notebook 34, 733.3.34 – quoted by kind permission of Shirin and Unity Spencer.)

236. His oil painting *Caulkers* was a detail only of an intended larger panel which was never completed.

237. During the early part of the war Spencer stayed in Gloucestershire with Mr and Mrs George Charlton, and moved to Epsom probably in May 1941 to be with his children, who were being looked after by his first wife's mother. In January 1942 he returned to Cookham, where he lived throughout the war – except for his increasingly extended visits to Port Glasgow.

238. *The Template* was delivered in May 1942; *Bending the Keel Plate** in July 1943; *The Riggers* in July 1944; *Plumbers* in March 1945; and *The Furnaces* in March 1946.

239. For the details of Stephen Bone's later appointments, including his coverage of the Normandy landings and his assignment in Scandinavia, see Chapter 38.

240. Increased to two in July 1940.

241. Nash's sentiments were interestingly echoed by another First World War veteran, Henry Lamb – 'I must face the fact that my contact with [army life] is just that of a journalist and the experiences can hardly come from within as they did in my pictures of the other war.' (IWM:LAMB, Lamb/Dickey,

12.7.40)

242. Ravilious, like John Nash, contributed illustrations to the Nonesuch *Natural History of Selborne* (1937).

243. After failing to obtain reasonable terms from commercial publishers, Ravilious arranged to have the series of 10 printed at his own expense. Despite the WAAC's enthusiasm for the project they acquired none of the lithographs (which were exhibited at the Leicester Galleries in April 1941), preferring instead to purchase at £2 10s each the original drawings (two of which were, however, lost by Ravilious).

244. Dickey's successors were Arnold Palmer (appointed in July 1942), G. Elmslie Owen (appointed in September 1942), and Eric Gregory (appointed in July 1943).

245. Ravilious's place in Iceland was taken by Thomas Hennell, who volunteered immediately on hearing of his friend's death. Hennell was in Iceland between August and November 1943 working mainly in Reykjavik with occasional forays to the north of the country; he produced some 60 watercolours of the activites of British and US troops.

246. See Chapter 37.

247. All but one of the men pictured in *Gun Turret* survived.

248. Freedman's work continued for the Admiralty – see Chapter 38.

249. Epstein did however sculpt his brother *Sir Alan Cunningham*. The WAAC's other Epstein busts were: through purchase, a cast of his *Maisky*; by commission in 1942, *Sir Charles Portal* in April 1945, by commission, *Ernest Bevin*; by commission August 1945, *Sir John Anderson*; and, by commission, *Sir Winston Churchill* (started in November 1946, and completed probably in 1948).

250. Pears's work was acquired by a mixture of purchases and commissions.

251. 53 of these canvases are at the National Maritime Museum, Greenwich, and one at the Royal United Services Institution.

252. Cundall was subsequently employed as an official salaried Admiralty artist between July 1940 and February 1941 to record the work of the Merchant Navy. In February 1941 he was transferred as an official salaried RAF artist, replacing Paul Nash.

253. Eurich was elected an ARA in 1942 (RA 1953) on Reginald Eves's nomination; he was elected to the NEAC in 1943.

254. See Chapter 38.

255. He preferred to use photographs only for the finest details, not for the broad outlines of the scene.

256. Made for Alexander Korda.

257. Replacing Barnett Freedman at the end of February 1941.

258. Moynihan had been commissioned by the WAAC to paint 2 RAF subjects in July 1940, before being called up in October 1940. He submitted pictures for puchase sporadically but did not escape the rigours of signalling until 1942 when he was transferred to Camouflage and shortly afterwards invalided out. The WAAC employed him as one of its salaried artists in September 1943: apart from *Medical Inspection*, which displays clearly his awareness of the indignities of army life, the great part of his work until 1945 was portraits.

259. 8 watercolours were purchased in September 1942.

260. Arthur Marwick points out (*The Home Front*, Thames and Hudson, 1976, p. 37) that several early photographs of the Home Guard, or Local Defence Volunteers as they then were, were stopped by censors for fear of ridicule of their

'disconcertingly amateurish appearance'.

1. In May 1943 in Colchester he could find no subject more appealing than a post-mortem: in October 1944, sent to Southampton Docks to record interesting activities, he gave up altogether.

2. A journey described in van der Post's *First Catch Your Eland*, (Hogarth Press, 1977).

3. On the way to Siwa Bawden was delighted to find embodied an imaginary landscape he had used as the background to a wallpaper designed in the 1930s for an Egyptologist at the British Museum.

4. Gross had been sent out by the WAAC in November 1941 to record life on board a Middle East convoy round the coast of Africa, calling at Freetown, Cape Town and Aden. He arrived in Cairo in January 1942, having completed some 50 pictures of the journey out.

5. British forces had been based in Iraq since the Anglo-Iraqi Treaty of 1930.

6. In a letter to Dickey (IWM:RAVILIOUS, 15.6.42), Ravilious described as 'wonderful and improbable' a newspaper report that Bawden was 'helping the Australians keep the pubs open at Tobruk!'

7. Gross's travel notes, as yet unpublished, cover the whole period of his official appointment in outline, and his travels in the Middle East and Burma in detail.

8. Gross's pictures of these casualties were stopped by the censor – a decision Gross felt was misguided, as the public *expected* soldiers to be hurt: only to see civilians hurt, as they were in air-raids throughout the war, gave 'the wrong impression'.

9. Although no other artists were commissioned to cover North Africa, the WAAC made several valuable purchases from soldier-artists as eye-witness illustrations of incidents in the Desert War – most notably Lieutenant Colin Hayes's *An Italian medium tank demolished by Sappers (near Bir El Gubi, March 1942)* and watercolours of actions at Second Alamein and on the Mareth Line by Alex Ingram, a Corporal in the Royal Tank Regiment.

'0. The WAAC purchased an eye-witness record from a 22-year-old Flight-Lieutenant, Denis Barnham – a pilot's view of *Battle over Malta, 1942* (dated 23 March 1942) from a Spitfire attacking JU88s and being embroiled in a dogfight with ME109s.

'1. Of subjects such as life on minesweepers, bomb manufacture, dentistry during a gas practice, and balloon maintenance. The WAAC had also given him occasional small commissions – to paint the embarkation of tanks for Russia, the manufacture of gliders, and others.

'2. Ardizzone did remember making 'pretty complete' sketches whilst working at home in 1940 on blitz and shelter subjects; but abroad, near the front, he seems rarely to have had time.

'3. Between July 1943 and May 1945 Ardizzone filled four diary-sketchbooks: these were published in 1974 by The Bodley Head, after which the originals were presented to the IWM.

'4. Bawden informed his wife (Bawden/Charlotte Bawden, 28.12.44–7.1.45) that Ardizzone in company 'has all the graces of a rural dean, and to see his portly figure in a dance bobbing with the lightness of a cork, combining the ridiculous with dignity, warms the heart'.

'5. A member of the Army Film and Photographic Unit, also attached to PR.

276. As well as *On the Road to Fuka: Looting from a Disabled Truck*, he drew *Troops and Civilians looting in the town of Reggio, Italy* (which was immediately stopped by the censors), and, again, a scene of troops rifling the Castle of the Malatestas at Castel St Angelo.

277. Ardizzone was among the first British forces to reach Brussels in the attempt to check the German advance in May 1940; he witnessed the breakthrough at Second Alamein and the fall of Tripoli; he landed in Sicily on the first day, was at Reggio for the landing in Italy, went into Naples and Rimini with the investing forces; and was to be among the first British forces to go into Denmark, even before the Germans had officially surrendered.

278. By September, as Admiralty artist in the Mediterranean, Worsley had already recorded aspects of the Sicilian campaign (e.g., a series of watercolours of the Melilli Caves, used to store Italian mines, and pictures of the bombardment of Augusta).

279. The Euston Road School of Drawing and Painting was founded in 1937 by Coldstream, Claude Rogers and Victor Pasmore. The school closed down at the outbreak of war, but the term 'Euston Road School' had by this time been introduced by Clive Bell into the language of art criticism to refer to the type of realism of which Coldstream's work is characteristic.

280. Coldstream served in 1940 as a gunner in a Field Training Regiment, first outside Dover in 'a charming Napoleonic fort ... with a grandstand view of the Battle of Britain' (Coldstream, interview in series 'Artists in an Age of Conflict', IWM 3184/03), and then near Loch Lomond; he next transferred to Farnham Castle to train as a camouflage officer, and was subsequently employed on the camouflage of gun sites in the West Country, before being posted to Anti Aircraft Command at Bushey, Herts.

281. Von Thoma had been captured at Second Alamein, and was imprisoned with other *prominenten* at Trent Park, the Sassoon family home. The picture was not completed when Coldstream left, and he would have found it impossible to work away from the sitter; considering the portrait unsatisfactory in its unfinished state, he scraped the canvas down.

282. Henry Carr, a pupil of William Rothenstein's at the RCA, was established as both a portraitist and landscape artist. He was sent out to the Middle East in February 1943 after the Treasury had sanctioned the appointment of a further official war artist 'in view of the activity in North Africa'. (IWM:WAAC MINUTES, 103rd Meeting, 9.12.42)

283. The heat did make the oil paint bubble on occasion; this is noticeable in *Havildar Ajmer Singh.**

284. Again there was some overlap with Henry Carr; directed to do fewer portraits, by March 1944 he was painting war landscapes in Italy – *Cassino*, *Vesuvius in Eruption*, *The Liri Valley*, and so on.

285. He also tended to compare his own life in wartime Italy with that of his brother, who had gone in through the beachhead at Salerno. 'Nor was I really in as much danger as my poor old parents in Hampstead.' (Coldstream, interview with the authors, 7.2.83.)

286. Rome had been liberated on 5 June 1944.

287. Ardizzone would seem to be the only one to have produced any pictures of Rome during this period – *Troops in the Sistine Chapel, Rome*, a companion to *Soldiers waiting to be admitted to a Papal Audience, Rome*, drawn on an earlier visit in September.

288. This was after a long struggle to get Weight released in order to paint; the War Office first refused in December 1942 – and final success came only in March 1945 when Weight was appointed a full-time artist for the War Office.
289. See Chapter 39.
290. Wilkinson was offshore on HMS *Jervis*; he had been told to go ashore at Portsmouth, but as he had by then heard the briefing, he had to be allowed to stay and sketched the action in relative comfort.
291. This point is discussed in detail by Allen Freer in his introduction to the catalogue for the exhibition 'The Rose of Death', Arts Council and IWM, 1978.
292. John Worsley and James Morris were both taken from active *naval* duty.
293. Stephen Bone finally arrived in Normandy in mid-July and spent several weeks recording scenes both ashore and afloat. On the beaches he was much bothered by the omnipresent dust and sand, and Muirhead Bone told Gregory that he needed a special box for his wet oils – 'I remember Orpen travelled with several of these – he needed them on the Somme – I remember that!' (IWM:MUIRHEAD BONE, Bone/ Gregory, 12.8.44)
294. From which he was commissioned to do a large oil, not finished until 1947.
295. Written apparently for Oliver Warner, the Admiralty representative on the WAAC in late 1944. Excerpts from the article are reproduced by kind permission of Miss Elizabeth Hennell, the artist's sister.
296. Freedman, to his annoyance, had fallen seriously ill and been rushed home for an emergency operation. Stephen Bone remained at the beachhead throughout August, while Richard Eurich went backwards and forwards between England and France gathering material for a D-Day triptych – the left panel depicting the initial bombardment, the centre the troops running ashore, and the right panel the destruction of Caen. Leslie Cole visited the 41st Commandos of the Royal Marines at the end of August to record their attacks on German strongpoints east of Caen, but his stay, though eventful – as his picture of Commandos crossing a girder over a stream under fire in Pont l'Evêque with the town in flames shows – was short.
297. Gross had no luck with his teeth; in Cairo an Army dentist had broken his jaw, trying to remove a wisdom tooth.
298. Gross's picture was, as usual, watercolour. A more formal portrait was done in oils by John Worsley at the WAAC's request in 1946; and another, still more ceremonial, was commissioned by the Trustees of the IWM in 1948 from Oswald Birley.
299. Perhaps the most famous picture of the Falaise Gap – Frank Wootton's eye-witness account *Rocket-Firing Typhoons at the Falaise Gap, Normandy, 1944* – was purchased by the WAAC in 1944.
300. Harold Nicolson's diary for the weeks after their first use over London testifies to the peculiar power of the V-1 (*Vergeltungswaffe*, or Reprisal Weapon, 1) to terrify – largely due to the nerve-racking wait for the motor to cut out and the bomb to fall.
301. The majority of V-2s were in fact launched from the Hague, and the sites were only put out of action when that city fell to the Allies in March 1945.
302. He also recorded the bombed marshalling yards at Trappes.
303. Stephen Bone accompanied a Bombardment Unit on *HMS Roberts* in the last week of the naval expedition against Walcheren Island; Hennell painted several watercolours of th■ Nijmegen Bridge, which was still under German fire in January 1945, four months after Operation 'Market Garden' – among them *Defence by a Bofors Gun-Crew of Nijmegen Bridg■ from Water-borne Attack on the River Waal*.
304. He was the only official war artist to have visited the scene of the Battle of the Bulge, but would seem to have produced no pictures during his stay.
305. He did nonetheless a spirited series of drawings entitled 'With the 8th Hussars in Germany' – e.g., *German Villagers waving white flags at the approach of our tanks*, *Tanks in a burning village* and *A German woman rescuing her pig*.
306. At Trondheim he drew *Hitler's Yacht 'Grille'*, at Tromsö the *Interior of the Upside-Down 'Tirpitz'*; and on 7 June 1945 he sailed into Oslo in HMS *Norfolk* with Haakon, King of Norway to record the royal return after five years of exile in England.
307. These were published in June-August 1945 in *The Leader*, by which magazine Peake was sent out; this was not an official commission.
308. She was the only artist to have this view of the proceedings, all the others being confined to the more distant visitors' gallery.
309. She was staying in the Grand Hotel, in a private suite built especially for Hitler – who had before the war been refused entry to the Grand as a 'common agitator'.
310. This drawing he later worked up into one of his very few wartime oils – *Arakan Campaign: The Battle of Rathedaung 1943. 6th Rajputana Rifles attacking Hill North 75.*
311. He reached England in July 1943.
312. After completing his RAF work, Pitchforth had been transferred to Admiralty subjects; initially salaried by the Mo■ on 6 October 1943 he became a salaried Admiralty artist (replacing Muirhead Bone). In the early months of his appointment he painted coastal motor boats in action, and travelled on convoys to the Azores and to Gibraltar.
313. John Worsley was selected to be a second Admiralty artist to cover the same sphere of operations, but it was at about this time that he was taken prisoner in the Adriatic by the Germans.
314. One source reported that Hennell had made plans to travel to Sumatra by junk with a Dutch ex-Pow. (See Michael Macleod's essay on Hennell in the catalogue 'Drawn from Nature', a touring exhibition of the work of Hennell, Vincent Lines and A. S. Hartrick, January-July 1979.)
315. Later extended by three months.
316. The WAAC also purchased two pictures of the International Military Tribunal for the Far East by Julius Stafford-Baker.
317. In *The Other Half – A Self-Portrait* (John Murray, 1977, p. 22), Clark explains his exit from the MoI after Bracken's appointment as Minister: 'I belonged to the old, amateurish, ineffective, music-hall-joke Ministry, and had long been an unnecessary member of that ramshackle body. Cyril [Radcliff■ the MoI's new Director-General] was a friend of mine, for whom I had a great admiration. He told me to leave in the kindest possible manner.'
318. Balfour (op. cit., p. 62) puts Pick's eventual dismissal by Duff Cooper down to a similar flight of fancy – as part of a series

for the Christmas of the blitz, he commissioned a poster by John Piper 'showing a tulip blooming in a bomb site. Duff, who had to defend such fancies in the House was by no means enchanted.'

19. The WAAC's acquisition grant for the war years was – 1939–40, £5000; 1940–41, £9000 (plus £1000 additional expenses); 1941–2, £14,000 (plus an additional £500 for Admiralty portraits); 1942–3, £14,000 (plus £500 for Admiralty portraits); September 1943–March 1944, £8000; April 1944–March 1945, £10,750; April-August 1945, £4500; September–December 1945, £3600; January–31 March 1946, £3000.

20. The Americans circulated a remarkably similar portrait of a woman factory worker, *Rosie the Riveter* (Edna Reindell, US Army Center of Military History).

21. The 'First Series', published in 1942, comprised: 1. *War at Sea* (introduction by Admiral Sir Herbert Richmond); 2. *Blitz* (introduction by J. B. Morton); 3. *RAF* (H. E. Bates); 4. *Army* (Colin Coote). The 'Second Series', published in 1943, comprised: 1. *Women* (Dame Laura Knight); 2. *Production* (Cecil Beaton); 3. *Soldiers* (William Coldstream); 4. *Air-Raids* (Stephen Spender).

22. William Rothenstein's *Drawing the RAF* does not fall into the same category, as the majority of his portraits were not official war art.

23. The vessel carrying the pictures to South America was torpedoed in August 1942. All 96 pictures were lost, including 3 by Paul Nash, 2 by Sutherland, one by Moore, and one by Piper. Separate arrangements were made for a part of the USA touring exhibition to be diverted to South America.

24. That the exhibition was propagandist is shown by the internal 'Proposal for Final Approval' memorandum of 18.3.41 put to the MoI's Overseas Planning Committee; this gave as 'Objective and supporting reasons: propaganda value in the USA'. (IWM: GP/46/24/4/B)

25. Additional valuable propaganda for the British Navy was obtained by sending Wilkinson's 'The War At Sea' series to Australia and New Zealand in June 1945 – 'The number of men from the Australian Forces who were there [Canberra] was noteworthy. . . . It emphasised the vital importance of seapower.' (IWM:WILKINSON, High Commissioner for Australia/MoI, 24.7.45)

26. The Artists International Association organised lectures at the National Gallery on Sunday afternoons on 'War and Art'. There were also exhibitions other than war art at the National Gallery during the war.

27. Lewis, at his own insistence, was paid the sum (£300) which he had received in the First World War for *A Battery Shelled*.

28. Eventually received in 1948.

29. The IWM's Art Department holds all the files relating to war art of Wellington House, the Department of Information, and the 1918 Ministry of Information, and the Minutes and all the artists' files kept by the WAAC.

30. Which includes some of the cover designs for GPO telephone directories throughout Britain.

31. In the BBC's 'Explorers' series, Ocean played the part of Captain Cook's artist-in-waiting in Samoa; in 1976 he toured America as Paul McCartney's artist-in-waiting; as a musician he worked with Ian Dury and also released his own modestly successful single 'Whoops a Daisy'.

32. In 1982 Ocean's group portrait *Lord Volvo and his Estate* won the Imperial Tobacco Portrait Award.

333. Hogarth succeeded Ardizzone as the RCA Senior Tutor in Illustration in 1964; in 1966 he published *The Artist as Reporter* (to be republished shortly in an expanded form). He has collaborated on many travel books with such writers as Doris Lessing, Brendan Behan, Malcolm Muggeridge, Robert Graves and Stephen Spender.

334. Purchased by the Artistic Records Committee in 1980.

335. Linda Kitson, *The Falklands War – A Visual Diary* (Mitchell Beazley, 1982).

336. Her drawings of the *Times* offices during the upheavals of 1981–2 – *Newspapers and Newspeople* – played a large part in her appointment.

337. She had already recorded the destruction of the napalm store discovered at Goose Green on 8 June.

338. Stella Schmolle, a Sergeant in the ATS employed as a draughtswoman, had been sent to France and Belgium under ATS auspices around the end of 1944; but she returned without having ever progressed beyond the lines of communication, her attempts to work at the front totally frustrated by the restrictions imposed on her as a woman by the military authorities. (In 1939 Coote had warned Dickey of the difficulty of employing women war artists overseas: 'It will amuse you to know that no woman is allowed to wear trousers in France for fear of being mistaken for one who practises wearing nothing at all.')

339. Joseph Darracott was especially pleased with the acquisition of one of the studies for C. R. W. Nevinson's *Returning to the Trenches* – the gouache *Marching Men, 1916*; and J. D. Fergusson's *Portsmouth Docks*, bought in 1975.

340. Both bought in 1980.

SOURCES

page/line

1/17 John/John Quinn, 16.2.16 – quoted
in Michael Holroyd, *Augustus John*
(Heinemann, 1974)

1/22 Tonks/D. S. McColl, 19.9.14 – quoted
in Joseph Hone, *The Life of Henry
Tonks* (Heinemann, 1939)

1/28 *Memories of the War to End War*
(published privately, 1974), p. 1

1/34 Wyndham Lewis, *Blasting and
Bombardiering* (Eyre & Spottiswoode,
1967), p. 184

1/38 Epstein/John Quinn, 12.8.14 –
quoted in Holroyd, *op. cit.*

2/9 Wyndham Lewis, *op. cit.*, p. 114

2/12 C. R. W. Nevinson, in the *Daily
Express*, 25.2.15

2/16 John Lavery, *The Life of a Painter*
(Cassell, 1940), p. 139

2/36 Spencer, draft autobiography (Tate
Gallery Archive 733.3.86) – quoted
in Richard Carline, *Stanley Spencer at
War* (Faber, 1978)

2/38 Nash/Margaret Nash, 4.4.17 – in
Paul Nash, *Outline* (Faber, 1949)

3/15 IWM :KENNINGTON – Campbell
Dodgson/Masterman, 2.4.17

3/21 *Burlington Magazine*, September/
October 1916

3/38 Sir Kenneth Clark, 'The Artist in
Wartime', in *The Listener*, 26.10.39

4/11 William Rothenstein, *Men and
Memories – Volume II, 1900–22*
(Faber, 1932), p. 305 ff.

4/13 Leon Wolff, *In Flanders Fields*
(Longman, 1960) – introduction by
Major-General J. F. C. Fuller, p. xi

4/16 Charles A'Court Repington, *The First
World War 1914–18 : Personal
Experiences* (Constable, 1920) – diary
entry, 19.4.16

4/20 Rothenstein, *op. cit.* p. 305

4/22 *The Times*, 19.2.16

4/25 *Times* editorial of 5.5.16 – quoted by
Dr. Susan Malvern in her doctoral
thesis 'Art, propaganda and
patronage' (Reading University,
1981)

4/29 Stanley Jackson, *The Sassoons*
(Heinemann, 1968), p. 148

5/11 Alexander Woolcott, 'The Sacred
Grove', in *While Rome Burns*
(Penguin, 1937), p. 17

5/27 *British Propaganda During the War
1914–18 : The History of Propaganda.*
For this chapter see generally :
a) Public Record Office INF 4/5
Report of the Work of the Bureau

established for the purpose of laying
before Neutral Nations and the
Dominions the case of Great Britain
and her Allies* (7.6.15)
b) *Second Interim Report on the Work
Conducted for the Government at
Wellington House* (1.2.16) (IWM)
c) *Third Report on the Work Conducted
for the Government at Wellington
House* (September 1916) (IWM)
d) *British Propaganda During the War
1914–18 : The History of
Propaganda* (undated – ?1919–20
report by Foreign Office?) (IWM)

7/10 *Second Report, op. cit.*

7/37 Cecil Roberts, *Nottingham Journal*,
25.2.21

7/42 *Evening Standard*, 18.11.27

8/6 Masterman/Lucy Masterman,
Christmas 1908 – quoted in Lucy
Masterman, *C. F. G. Masterman – A
Biography* (Nicholson & Watson, 1939)

8/17 Masterman/Lucy Masterman,
undated – *op. cit.*

8/20 Masterman/Lucy Masterman,
undated – *op. cit.*

9/5 *Times* obituary, 23.10.53

10/16 IWM : BONE – Bone/Yockney,
31.10.18

10/28 IWM : M999 Part 1 – Bone/Gowers,
30.9.16

11/2 IWM : M999 Part 1 – Bone/
Masterman, 12.11.16

12/10 IWM : BONE – Gertrude Bone/
Yockney, 18.8.17

13/12 H. G. Wells, *Experiment in
Autobiography* (Gollancz, 1934),
p. 682

13/20 Quoted by Oliver Elton, *C. E.
Montague – A Memoir* (Chatto &
Windus, 1929)

13/32 *Manchester Guardian*, 30.8.17

13/33 IWM : BONE – Bone/ffoulkes, 31.3.29

13/37 Introduction to the second volume of
the collected edition of *The Western
Front* (1918) – 'War As It Is'

14/4 IWM : DODD – Masterman/H.M.
Treasury, 21.12.16

14/20 IWM : DODD – Dodgson/Gowers,
19.12.16

14/29 IWM : DODD – Dodd/Gowers, 6.2.17

16/4 IWM : M999 Part VII – Dodd/
Yockney, 27.10.17

16/12 William Rothenstein, *Men and
Memories*, Vol. I, p. 156

16/15 IWM : DODD – Dodd/Blaikley,
January 1938

16/16 IWM : DODD – Cavan/Masterman,
14.12.17

16/19 IWM : DODD – Hunter-Weston/
Buchan, 7.3.18

16/25 IWM : DODD – Masterman/Hunter
Weston, 11.3.18

16/32 Brownrigg, *Indiscretions of a Naval
Censor* (Cassell, 1920), p. 162

16/37 IWM – DODD – reminiscences
pencilled on artist's proofs

18/2 IWM : DODD – de Chair/Dodd, 11.2.1?

18/5 IWM : DODD – Bethel/Dodd, 6.1.18

18/24 IWM : DODD – Buchan/Masterman,
18.4.17

18/26 British Museum, Additional
Manuscripts 45,910 – Montague/
Dodd, 12.10.17

18/30 IWM : DODD – Masterman/O'Neill,
undated

18/49 IWM : DODD – Gerard T. Meynell/
Wellington House, 1.1.18

19/1 *Manchester City News*, 13.11.18

20/13 IWM : G4010/17 – Masterman/Buchan,
28.3.17

20/22 Public Record Office, INF 4/9

20/29 Public Record Office, INF 4/9

21/6 Charteris, *At G.H.Q.* (Cassell, 1931),
diary entry for 25.9.16

21/30 Lucy Masterman, *op. cit.*

21/45 Public Record Office INF 4/IB. G.32.
Report on the DoI made to Sir
Edward Carson by Buchan,
September 1917

22/33 Public Record Office INF 4/11,
'Propaganda Enquiry : Evidence
taken at Wellington House' (by
Robert Donald) – Evidence taken
from Masterman, 28.11.17

23/2 IWM :McBEY – Dodgson/Masterman,
22.1.17

23/13 *The Early Life of James McBey – An
Autobiography 1883–1911* (Oxford
University Press, 1977), edited with
intro. by Nicholas Barker

23/32 Robin Johnson, catalogue for IWM
exhibition, 'James McBey
1883–1959', Spring 1977

24/15 IWM : McBEY – Willson/McBey,
28.4.17

25/3 McBey's own note on *The Suez Canal
by Night* (1413)

25/9 Quoted by Nicholas Barker, *op. cit.*

25/12 IWM : McBEY – McBey/G.H.Q.,
26.9.17

25/19 IWM : McBEY – McBey/Masterman,
6.11.17

26/1 Basil Liddell-Hart, *T. E. Lawrence : In*

page/line

Arabia and After (Cape, 1934), p.248
26/5 McBey's own note (1516)
/27 *Morning Post*, 5.4.19
/37 McBey/William Hutcheon, early 1918 (Nicholas Barker, *op. cit.*)
27/5 Ernest Blaikley, *The Studio*, December 1942
27/7 IWM : McBEY – McBey/Masterman, 21.5.18
7/20 *Morning Post*, 10.5.19
7/30 McBey's own note (1568)
7/33 *Morning Post*, 12.4.19
7/39 IWM : McBEY – McBey/Yockney, 16.12.18
/16 Brigadier-General John Charteris, *At G.H.Q.*, diary entry 7.4.17
/35 IWM : $\frac{G4010}{17}$ – Charteris/Masterman, 12.3.17
/26 Sean Keating, 'William Orpen – A Tribute', in *Ireland Today*, 1934 (quoted by Bruce Arnold, *Orpen – Mirror to an Age*, Jonathan Cape, 1981, p. 301)
/28 Wyndham Lewis, *Blasting and Bombardiering*, p. 169
31/2 William Rothenstein, *Men and Memories*, Vol. II, p. 2
31/8 Edward Marsh, *A Number of People* (Heinemann, 1939), p. 104
/31 IWM : ORPEN – Cowans/Masterman, 24.3.17
2/18 War diary – entry for 10.6.17
2/24 IWM $\frac{323}{17}$ – Lee/Yockney, 4.10.19
2/28 Lee's diary – entry for 10.7.17
2/31 Lee's diary – entry for 26.9.17
2/33 Lee's diary – entry for 27.1.17
2/34 Lee's diary – entry for 6.4.17
2/37 Lee's diary – entry for 6.4.17
33/8 *An Onlooker in France*, Williams and Norgate/Ernest Benn, 1923, p. 21
3/12 IWM : ORPEN – Masterman/Orpen, 14.5.17
3/16 IWM : ORPEN – Masterman/Buchan, 10.10.17
3/18 IWM : ORPEN – Masterman/Orpen, 27.9.17
4/10 *Life of a Painter*, p. 197
4/13 Cassell, 1940
5/10 *Life of a Painter*, p. 141
5/17 Special Permit issued to Lavery through M.I.5 on 3.8.17
5/19 IWM : LAVERY – Yockney/Lavery, 13.8.17
5/24 *Life of a Painter*, p. 146
5/44 *Life of a Painter*, p.183
36/3 *Life of a Painter*, p. 148
36/7 *Life of a Painter*, p. 40
37/5 Montague/Dodd, 16.6.18, (British Museum. Add. Ms. 45,910)
38/7 Methuen, 1937

page/line

38/33 'The Six Hundred, Verestchagin and Uccello', *Notes and Vortices No. 3* (reproduced in *Wyndham Lewis, the Artist : from 'Blast' to Burlington House*, Laidlaw and Laidlaw, 1939)
38/36 *Daily Express*, 25.2.15
39/20 P. G. Konody, *Modern War – Paintings by C. R. W. Nevinson* (Grant Richards, 1917)
39/26 IWM : NEVINSON – Masterman/ Charteris, 3.5.17
39/35 *Paint and Prejudice*, p. 103
40/20 IWM : NEVINSON – Masterman/ Buchan, 18.5.17
40/6 IWM : NEVINSON – Nevinson/ Masterman, 30.7.17
40/12 IWM : NEVINSON – Nevinson/ Masterman, 30.7.17
40/15 *Paint and Prejudice*
40/22 Catalogue for exhibition, Leicester Galleries, March 1918
40/35 IWM: NEVINSON – Derrick/ Masterman, 16.10.17
40/38 IWM : NEVINSON – Masterman/ Hudson, 29.10.17
42/1 IWM: NEVINSON – Nevinson/ Masterman, 3.12.17
42/4 *Paint and Prejudice*, p. 106
42/15 *Paint and Prejudice*, p. 72
44/2 Nevinson/Ross, 11.6.18, (quoted in Margery Ross, *Robert Ross – Friend of Friends*, Cape 1952.)
44/7 Osbert Sitwell, introduction to *Contemporary British Artists : C. R. W. Nevinson* (Ernest Benn, 1925)
44/8 Catalogue for exhibition, Leicester Galleries, March 1918
44/31 IWM : $\frac{323}{17}$ – Lee/Yockney, 14.12.18
44/43 IWM : NEVINSON – Yockney/ Dodgson, 21.11.17
44/44 IWM : NEVINSON – draft letter (not sent) from Nevinson to Lee, c. November 1917
45/4 IWM : NEVINSON – Nevinson/ Masterman, 25.11.17
45/7 IWM : NEVINSON – Lee/Yockney, 13.12.17
45/14 IWM : NEVINSON – Yockney/ Masterman, 4.12.17
45/15 IWM : NEVINSON – Nevinson/ Masterman, 3.12.17
45/21 Montague/Dodd, 7.1.18. (British Museum. Add. Ms. 45,910)
45/29 IWM : NEVINSON – Nevinson/ Masterman, 9.1.18
45/33 IWM : NEVINSON – Nevinson/ Masterman, 4.1.18
46/9 IWM : KENNINGTON – Kennington/ Masterman, mid-February 1917
46/18 IWM : KENNINGTON – Dodgson/

page/line

Masterman, 2.4.17
46/26 IWM : KENNINGTON – Derrick/ Masterman, 28.9.17
46/37 IWM : KENNINGTON – Kennington/ Masterman, end of 1917
47/8 IWM : KENNINGTON – Kennington/ Masterman, 23.9.17
49/4 Rosenberg/Laurence Binyon, Autumn 1916 (quoted in *The Collected Works of Isaac Rosenberg*, ed. Ian Parsons, Chatto & Windus, 1979)
49/9 IWM : KENNINGTON – Kennington/ Masterman, ?September 1917
49/16 IWM : KENNINGTON – Note for catalogue to exhibition, Leicester Galleries, June 1918
49/23 IWM : KENNINGTON – Kennington/ Masterman, December 1917
49/39 IWM : KENNINGTON – Kennington/ Masterman, December 1917
49/41 IWM : KENNINGTON – Kennington/ Yockney, 16.6.18
50/2 IWM : KENNINGTON – Kennington/ Masterman, 4.10.17
50/6 *Men and Memories*, Vol. II, p. 328
50/8 IWM : KENNINGTON – Kennington/ Yockney, 16.6.18
51/5 IWM : KENNINGTON – Kennington/ Yockney, 11.6.18
51/15 IWM : KENNINGTON – Kennington/ Yockney, 23.6.18
51/33 IWM : KENNINGTON – Kennington/ Yockney, 6.6.18
52/9 John Rothenstein, *Modern English Painters*, Volume 2, p. 101
52/17 Wyndham Lewis, *Blasting and Bombardiering*, p. 148
52/23 Nash/Margaret Nash 4.4.17. (quoted in *Outline*)
53/3 IWM : PAUL NASH – Nash/Marsh, 7.7.17
53/9 IWM : PAUL NASH – Marsh/Buchan, 17.8.17
53/16 IWM : PAUL NASH – Stopford/ Buchan, 16.8.17
53/21 IWM : PAUL NASH – Masterman/ Buchan, 15.9.17
53/22 IWM : PAUL NASH – Dodgson/ Masterman, 18.10.17
53/25 IWM : PAUL NASH – Buchan/ Masterman, 14.12.17
54/1 Nash/Bottomley, early December 1914 (quoted in *Poet and Painter – being the correspondence between Gordon Bottomley and Paul Nash, 1910–46*, O.U.P., 1955)
54/5 Nash/Bottomley, 1.1.17, (quoted in *Poet and Painter*)
54/18 Nash/Margaret Nash, 13.11.17. (quoted in *Outline*)

page/line

54/21 IWM : PAUL NASH – Nash/ Masterman, c. 4.11.17

54/25 IWM : PAUL NASH – Nash/ Masterman, c. 4.11.17

54/28 IWM : PAUL NASH – Nash/ Masterman, c. 4.11.17

54/33 IWM : PAUL NASH – Nash/ Masterman, 16.11.17

54/37 IWM : PAUL NASH – Nash/ Masterman, 16.11.17

54/43 IWM : PAUL NASH – Nash/ Masterman, 22.11.17

55/3 IWM : PAUL NASH – Nash/ Masterman, 22.11.17

56/7 Nash/Margaret Nash, 6.4.17 (quoted in *Outline*)

56/12 Nash/Margaret Nash, 7.3.17 (quoted in *Outline*)

56/15 Nash/Margaret Nash, 6.4.17 (quoted in *Outline*)

56/17 Nash/Margaret Nash, 18.4.17 (quoted in *Outline*)

56/21 Nash/Margaret Nash, 7.3.17 (quoted in *Outline*)

56/26 Nash/Margaret Nash, 13.11.17 (quoted in *Outline*)

57/2 Nash/Bottomley, 23.8.17 (quoted in *Poet and Painter*)

57/6 Nash/Margaret Nash, 12.5.17 (quoted in *Outline*)

57/17 Nash/Bottomley, 16.7.18 (quoted in *Poet and Painter*)

58/9 IWM : PAUL NASH – Nash/ Masterman, 30.1.18

59/1 IWM : 323 – Lee/Yockney, 2.5.18

59/8 IWM : PAUL NASH – Nash/ Masterman, 16.11.17

59/24 Nash/Bottomley, 16.7.18 (quoted in *Poet and Painter*)

59/30 IWM : PAUL NASH – Nash/ Masterman, 12.6.18

59/33 *The Observer*, 2.2.19

59/35 Letter to William Rothenstein, 1919 (quoted in *Paul Nash : Memorial Volume*, ed. Margot Eates, Lund Humphries, 1948)

59/40 IWM: PAUL NASH – Nash/ffoulkes, 2.4.29

60/32 Rothenstein/Robert Ross, 2.3.05 (quoted in *Robert Ross – Friend of Friends*)

61/3 IWM : Rothenstein/Dodgson, 12.12.17

61/8 Rothenstein/Frances Cornford, undated (quoted in Robert Speaight, *William Rothenstein*, Eyre & Spottiswoode, 1962)

61/14 *Men and Memories*, Vol. II, p. 299

61/16 Rothenstein/Marsh, 11.9.18 (quoted in Speaight, *op. cit.*)

61/25 IWM : ROTHENSTEIN – Rothenstein/ Dodgson, 10.1.18

61/43 *Men and Memories*, Vol. II, p. 328

61/44 *Men and Memories*, Vol. II, p. 326 and p. 333

62/4 Introduction to catalogue for exhibition 'On the Péronne Front' at the Goupil Gallery, April/May, 1918

62/13 *Men and Memories*, Vol. II, p. 327

63/6 Galbraith/Kenneth Towndrow (quoted in Speaight, *op. cit.*)

63/17 Orpen/Tonks, undated (quoted in Arnold, *op. cit.*, p. 330)

62/30 Rothenstein/Beerbohm, 20.3.18. (quoted in Speaight, *op. cit.*)

63/26 *Men and Memories*, Vol. II, p. 336

63/29 G. C. E. Simpson/Kenneth Towndrow (quoted in Speaight, *op. cit.*)

63/34 C. E. Montague, diary entry for 29.3.18 (quoted in Oliver Elton, *C. E. Montague – A Memoir*)

63/37 *Men and Memories*, Vol II, p. 336

63/38 Rothenstein/Alice Rothenstein, 22.3.18. (quoted in Speaight, *op. cit.*)

63/45 IWM : ROTHENSTEIN – Rothenstein/ Yockney, 28.6.18

64/7 *Blasting and Bombardiering*, p. 220

64/12 IWM : ROTHENSTEIN – Sir Whitworth Wallis/Conway, 16.1.19

64/14 IWM : ROTHENSTEIN – Yockney/ Sheringham, 3.5.18

64/21 IWM : ROTHENSTEIN – Rothenstein/ Yockney, 30.6.18

65/7 IWM : ORPEN – Orpen/Masterman, undated, c. October 1917

65/27 Orpen/Rothenstein, undated (quoted in Arnold, *op. cit.*, p. 331)

66/1 IWM : ORPEN – Orpen/Buchan, end October 1917

66/13 IWM : ORPEN – Orpen/Ross, 7.2.18

66/17 Arnold, *op. cit.*, Appendix B, p. 432

66/27 Orpen/Tonks, undated (quoted in Arnold, *op. cit.*)

66/33 *An Onlooker in France*, p. 26

66/37 *An Onlooker in France*, p. 36

69/1 IWM : ORPEN – Yockney/ Masterman, 4.3.18

69/6 Orpen/Rich, 17.11.17 (British Museum. Add. Ms. 42711)

70/1 *An Onlooker in France*, p. 16

70/3 *An Onlooker in France*, p. 58

70/10 *An Onlooker in France*, p. 58

70/18 Undated ; Arnold, *op. cit.*, p. 237

70/26 *An Onlooker in France*, p. 60

70/45 Orpen/Rich, 19.6.18 (British Museum. Add. Ms. 42711)

72/13 'Mr. Punch's Personalities. V.' – *Punch*, 9.12.25

72/22 Quoted in *Life of a Painter*, p. 143

72/27 *An Onlooker in France*, p. 40

72/31 *An Onlooker in France*, p. 20

72/40 'Our Empire' I (the first of three collections of unedited original notes made on the spot by Orpen, entitled 'Have We Forgotten ?')

73/6 IWM : NEVINSON – Masterman/ Edward Hudson, 29.10.17

74/1 IWM : DODD – Yockney/Willson, 12.12.17

74/4 IWM : ORPEN – W. M. Meredith/ Major-General C. E. Callwell, 12.4.1

74/13 IWM : BONE – Ministry of National Service/Yockney, 21.1.18

74/16 Public Record Office INF4/1B – Claud Schuster, Chief Executive of Wellington House/Robinson, 3.12.14

77/4 *The Western Front*, Introduction to Part VII, July 1917

77/11 *The Western Front*, Part VIII, August 1917

77/16 *The Western Front*, Part 1, December 1916

77/19 *The Western Front*, Part IX, September 1917

77/29 Harold Lasswell, *Propaganda Techniques in the World War* (Kegan Paul, Trench, Trubner, 1927), pp. 138–49

77/39 IWM : DODD – Masterman/Treasury 21.12.16

78/29 IWM : M999 Part VIII – Yockney, memorandum 1918

78/32 IWM : M999 Part IV – R. Harold Paget/A. S. Watt, 10.3.17

78/40 These papers are now in the possession of Mrs. Sue Yockney

81/14 IWM : 14 – Butler/Ministry of Information, 9.7.18

81/19 Catalogue to Fine Art Society exhibition, July 1917

82/5 *British Propaganda During the War 1914–18 : the History of Propaganda* (IWM Library)

82/15 *British Propaganda During the War 1914–18 : the History of Propaganda* (IWM Library)

83/8 IWM : 174 – *Morning Post*, 28.2.18

83/13 Bennett/Beaverbrook, 19.10.18. (quoted in *Letters of Arnold Bennett*, edited by James Hepburn, O.U.P. 1966–70)

84/15 IWM : 7 – anonymous and undated document

84/21 *The Referee*, 19.5.18

84/43 *Star*, 7.2.18

87/2 Bennett/F. S. A. Lowndes, 6.4.18. (quoted in *Letters of Arnold Bennett*, Volume 3, *op. cit.*)

87/24 IWM : BWMC Minutes – Derrick/ Masterman, 6.5.18 (discussed at 10th Meeting of BWMC)

page/line

/39 IWM :BWMC Minutes – Bennett, memorandum to BWMC 9.3.18

5/26 Bennett/Hugh Walpole, 12.12.19 (quoted in *Letters of Arnold Bennett*, Volume 3, *op. cit.*)

89/1 IWM : BWMC Minutes – Beerbohm/ Bennett, undated (considered at 10th Meeting of BWMC, 15.5.18)

9/32 IWM : ERIC GILL – quoted in Yockney/Masterman, 18.7.18

9/36 Epstein/Quinn, 20.7.17 (quoted in Michael Holroyd, *Augustus John*, Volume 2)

9/42 IWM : BWMC Minutes, 15.5.18

90/1 IWM :GERTLER (Post-war file) – Gertler/Yockney, 23.3.18

90/28 Wyndham Lewis, *Blasting and Bombardiering*, p. 94

91/4 IWM : BWMC Minutes – Preliminary meeting of the BMWC, 6.3.18

91/28 IWM : CAMERON – Cameron/ Yockney, 28.9.18

92/15 IWM : BWMC Minutes – Kennington/ Ross, memorandum read to the 4th Meeting of the BWMC, 27.3.18

92/17 IWM : BWMC Minutes – Konody/ BWMC, 6th Meeting, 17.4.18

92/26 Evan Charteris, *John Sargent* (Heinemann, 1927), p. 177

92/30 *Times*, 27.11.17 (quoted by Holroyd, *Augustus John*, Volume 2, p. 63)

92/31 Lytton Strachey/Clive Bell, 4.12.17 (Holroyd, *Augustus John*, Volume 2)

93/1 IWM : NEVINSON – Nevinson/ Masterman, 10.3.18

94/4 IWM : BWMC Minutes – Ross/ Bennett, 23.4.18

94/28 IWM : BWMC Minutes – Bone/BWMC (discussed at 11th Meeting of BWMC, 22.5.18)

94/29 IWM : BONE – Bone/IWM Art sub-committee, 29.1.19

94/32 IWM : BWMC Minutes – Bone/BWMC (discussed at 11th Meeting of BWMC, 22.5.18)

94/37 IWM : BWMC Minutes – Bone/BWMC (discussed at 11th Meeting of BWMC, 22.5.18)

94/41 IWM : BONE – Bone/IWM Art sub-committee, 29.1.19

95/7 IWM : BWMC Minutes – Ross/BWMC, 8.4.18

95/30 Wyndham Lewis, *Blasting and Bombardiering*, p. 200

95/32 John/Tonks, 21.2.18 (Holroyd, *Augustus John*, Volume 2)

96/1 John/Oliver St. John Gogarty, 24.7.18 (Holroyd, *Augustus John*, Volume 2)

96/8 IWM :JOHN – Dodgson/Masterman,

page/line

1.9.17

96/13 John/Cynthia Asquith, ?1917/ ?1918 (Holroyd, *Augustus John*, Volume 2)

96/17 *Reveille*. See Footnote 63

98/15 Sargent/Evan Charteris, 24.7.18 (quoted in Charteris, *John Sargent*)

98/18 IWM :$\frac{488}{12}$ – Yockney/Masterman, 18.6.18

98/19 IWM : SARGENT – Lee/Yockney, 5.10.18

99/6 Sargent/Charteris, 11.9.18 (quoted in Charteris, *John Sargent*)

99/15 IWM : SARGENT – Yockney/Bone, 5.11.18

99/16 Sargent/Charteris, 11.9.18 (quoted in Charteris, *John Sargent*)

99/17 IWM : SARGENT – Sargent/Yockney, 4.10.18

99/23 IWM : SARGENT – Yockney/Bone, 10.10.18

99/40 IWM : ORPEN – Orpen/Yockney, 18.4.19

101/2 Tonks/Ross, 16.8.18 (quoted in Margery Ross, *Robert Ross – Friend of Friends*)

101/5 IWM : TONKS – Tonks/Yockney, 25.7.18

101/10 Tonks' diary, ?June, 1919 (quoted in Joseph Hone, *The Life of Henry Tonks*)

102/1 Tonks/Ross, 1.9.18 (Ross, *Robert Ross – Friend of Friends*)

102/27 IWM : CAMERON – Cameron/ Yockney, 8.11.19

103/9 IWM : PAUL NASH – Nash/Yockney, 29.10.19

103/13 IWM : PAUL NASH – Nash/Yockney, 1.7.18

103/17 Nash/Bottomley, 16.7.18 (quoted in *Poet and Painter*)

103/32 Nash/Bottomley, 16.7.18 (quoted in *Poet and Painter*)

104/3 Nash/Bottomley, *c.*25.4.19 (quoted in *Poet and Painter*)

104/8 Reproduced in *Outline*

104/9 Nash/Bottomley, *c.*25.4.19 (quoted in *Poet and Painter*)

104/17 IWM : JOHN NASH – Yockney/John Nash, 25.3.19

104/29 John Nash in a letter to David Brown, 15.1.74

104/36 IWM : NEVINSON – Nevinson/Ross, 21.4.18

104/43 IWM : NEVINSON – Nevinson/Ross, 21.4.18

105/2 *Daily Express*, 28.3.19

105/10 Secretary, Canadian War Memorials Fund/Roberts, 28.12.17 (quoted in William Roberts, *Memories of the War to End War 1914–18*, published

page/line

privately, 1974)

106/6 IWM : ROBERTS – Roberts/Yockney, ?May 1919

106/13 *Blasting and Bombardiering*, p. 170

107/2 Wyndham Lewis, *Blasting and Bombardiering*, p. 170

107/5 Wyndham Lewis, *Blasting and Bombardiering*, p. 190

107/9 Wyndham Lewis, *Blasting and Bombardiering*, p. 195

108/1 *Blasting and Bombardiering*, p. 201

108/24 *Blasting and Bombardiering*, p. 125

108/29 *Blasting and Bombardiering*, p. 148

108/36 John/Alick Schepeler, February 1919 (Holroyd, *Augustus John*, Volume 2)

109/24 IWM :$\frac{9}{2}$ – Lamb/Yockney, 23.5.19

109/34 *Observer*, 21.12.19

110/16 IWM : TONKS – Tonks/Yockney, 12.10.18

110/18 IWM: STANLEY SPENCER – Spencer/ Yockney, 16.11.19

110/25 Spencer/Jas Wood, 3.3.18 (quoted in Richard Carline, *Stanley Spencer at War*, Faber 1978)

110/28 Spencer/Florence Image, 3.6.18 (Carline, *Stanley Spencer at War*)

110/33 Spencer/Desmond Chute, 3.6.18 (Carline, *Stanley Spencer at War*)

111/1 IWM : STANLEY SPENCER – Spencer/ Yockney, August 1919

111/10 IWM : STANLEY SPENCER – Spencer/ Yockney, 6.1.19

111/17 Spencer's draft autobiography, (Tate Gallery Archive 733.3.86) – quoted in Carline, *Stanley Spencer at War*)

111/24 IWM : STANLEY SPENCER – Spencer/ Yockney, 12.7.19

111/27 IWM : STANLEY SPENCER – Spencer/ Yockney, 27.7.19

111/39 D. S. McColl, *Life, Work and Setting of Philip Wilson Steer* (Faber, 1945), p. 118

111/43 Steer/Geoffrey Blackwell, 12.7.18 (quoted in McColl, *op. cit.*)

111/44 Steer/Geoffrey Blackwell, 12.7.18 (quoted in McColl, *op. cit.*)

112/1 Steer/Ronald Gray, 12.8.18 (quoted in McColl, *op. cit.*)

112/4 Steer/Geoffrey Blackwell, 25.9.18 (quoted in McColl, *op. cit.*)

112/8 IWM : FERGUSSON – Fergusson/ Yockney, 4.8.18

112/11 IWM : DERRICK – Derrick/Yockney, 11.9.18

112/18 IWM:WHEATLEY – Wheatley/ Yockney, 28.6.18

112/22 IWM:WHEATLEY – Wheatley/ Yockney, 31.1.19

112/24 IWM:WHEATLEY – Wheatley/ Yockney, 1.10.18

page/line

112/33 IWM : BAYES – Bayes/Bone, 12.6.18

113/7 IWM : SCHWABE – Schwabe/ Yockney, 4.9.18

113/24 IWM : RUSHBURY – Yockney/ Rushbury, 31.10.19

113/30 Brigadier-General John Charteris, *At GHQ*, p. 8

114/15 IWM : BWMC Minutes – Beaverbrook/William Jury and Bertram Lima, 2.4.18

114/21 Public Record Office INF 4/1B – *1st Report of the War Office Cinematograph Committee*, September 1918

114/26 Chairman of NWAC/General Smuts, *c*. 27.4.18 House of Lords Library. Beaverbrook Papers, Ref. 202

115/35 Bennett/Beaverbrook, 12.6.18 House of Lords Library. Beaverbrook Papers, Ref. 202

116/3 IWM : ~~481-5~~ – Catalogue *War Paintings and Drawings exhibited under the auspices of the Ministry of Information, London* (U.S.A., 1919)

116/6 IWM : ~~481-5~~ – Catalogue *War Paintings and Drawings exhibited under the auspices of the Ministry of Information, London* (U.S.A., 1919)

116/19 Needham/Beaverbrook, 19.8.18 House of Lords Library. Beaverbrook Papers, Ref. 308

117/4 IWM : PPC Minutes – 3rd Meeting of the PPC, 30.10.18

117/5 IWM : PPC Minutes – 3rd Meeting of the PPC, 30.10.18

117/11 Needham/Treasury, 4.11.18 House of Lords Library. Beaverbrook Papers, Ref. 308

117/13 H. M. Treasury/Beaverbrook, 29.11.18 House of Lords Library. Beaverbrook Papers, Ref. 308

118/25 IWM : WWI CENTRAL ARCHIVE A1/ 3 – War Cabinet 87 Minutes 5.3.17

120/12 IWM : WWI CENTRAL ARCHIVE A1/ 3 – War Cabinet 87 Minutes 21.8.17

121/3 Charles ffoulkes, *Arms and the Tower* (John Murray, 1939), p. 15

121/25 IWM : WWI CENTRAL ARCHIVE A1/ 2 – Mond/Lloyd George, 18.5.17

121/33 IWM : WWI CENTRAL ARCHIVE A/ WW General – General Committee Minutes 2.8.17

122/12 IWM : ORPEN – Conway/Mond, 25.3.18

122/20 IWM : WWI CENTRAL ARCHIVE A/ WW General – General Committee Minutes 15.7.18

122/32 IWM : ~~491a~~/8 – Art sub-committee Minutes 10.10.18

123/3 IWM : WWI CENTRAL ARCHIVE – 1st Annual Report of the Committee

of the IWM, 1917/18

124/1 IWM : DUGDALE – Dugdale/Yockney, 14.11.19

125/13 IWM : HILL – ffoulkes/Hill, 14.6.18

126/6 IWM : HILL – ffoulkes/Donald, 15.2.18

127/10 Undated letter to *The Times*, 1908 (quoted in *Epstein : An Autobiography*, Vista, 2nd edition, 1963)

127/15 IWM : EPSTEIN – Conway/Donald, 3.1.18

127/18 IWM : EPSTEIN – Epstein/Shaw, 5.12.17

127/22 IWM : EPSTEIN – Shaw/IWM, 6.3.18

127/40 IWM : EPSTEIN – Lady Randolph Churchill/Beaverbrook, 4.4.18

129/6 *Pearson's Magazine*, October 1924

130/16 IWM : ~~491~~ – Walcott/ffoulkes, 1.5.18

130/30 IWM : ~~491~~ – Walcott, memorandum *c*. December 1917

131/14 *Colour*, June 1917

131/15 Obituary in *The Times*, 5.1.27

131/39 IWM : NELSON DAWSON – Admiral Roger Keyes/Brownrigg, 1.2.18

131/44 *Indiscretions of a Naval Censor*, p. 165

132/9 *Life of a Painter*, p. 148

132/16 IWM : PEARS – Pears/Walcott, 7.1.18

132/31 *Indiscretions of a Naval Censor*, p. 170

133/4 Seeley Service, 1969

134/44 *Life of a Painter*, p. 146

135/6 IWM : BONE – James Bone/Yockney, *c*. November 1918

135/6 IWM : BONE – Bone/Yockney, 23.11.18

136/1 Introduction to *British Artists at the Front – Part 1* : C. R. W. Nevinson.

135/17 IWM : ~~35~~ – MacLean/Sir Hugh Trenchard, 21.11.18

136/23 IWM : NEWLING – MacLean/Colonel E. B. Gordon, 5.9.18

136/30 IWM : RICHARD CARLINE – Conway/MacLean, 29.4.18

138/22 IWM : FLEMING-WILLIAMS – Yockney/ffoulkes, 20.3.19

138/24 IWM : FLEMING-WILLIAMS – MacLean/Insall, 5.4.19

138/25 IWM : FLEMING-WILLIAMS – General Committee minute 3.4.19

138/29 IWM : FLEMING-WILLIAMS – Insall/ Gwynne-Vaughan, 29.4.19

138/35 IWM : FLEMING-WILLIAMS – Insall/ Fleming-Williams, 30.10.19

138/38 IWM : DOBSON – Yockney/Dobson, 11.4.19

139/12 IWM : SYDNEY CARLINE – Letter home from Sydney Carline, 5.3.18

139/19 IWM : SYDNEY CARLINE – Letter home from Sydney Carline, 5.10.18

139/27 IWM : SYDNEY CARLINE – ffoulkes/

MacLean, 12.6.18

139/30 IWM : SYDNEY CARLINE – MacLea Sydney Carline, 12.9.18

139/38 IWM : DOCUMENTS DEPARTMEN Sydney Carline's diary, 23.1.19

139/39 Letter home from ?Richard Carline 28.2.19 (published in *The Draconia No. 96*, April 1920)

140/2 IWM : SYDNEY CARLINE – referen to diary entry, 15.2.19

140/8 Letter home from ?Richard Carline 28.2.19 (published in *The Draconia No. 96*, April 1920)

140/14 IWM : SYDNEY CARLINE – Sydney Carline/MacLean, 26.3.19

140/25 Letter home from ?Richard Carline 8.10.19 (published in *The Draconia No. 96*, April 1920)

140/44 IWM : HAROLD WYLLIE – Lambe/ Wyllie, 29.6.20

141/1 IWM : RICHARD CARLINE – Lamb (drafted by Wyllie) to Richard and Sydney Carline, 6.2.20

142/23 IWM : LAVERY – Norman/Lavery, 22.7.19

142/33 IWM : ~~492~~ – Women's Work sub-committee Minutes, 21.11.19

142/34 IWM : ~~308~~/2 – Agnes Conway/Victoria Monkhouse, 15.9.18

143/3 IWM : ~~492~~ – Reported at meeting, 16.1.19

144/11 IWM : ~~308~~/2 – Agnes Conway/Wood, 7.2.19

144/19 IWM : ~~308~~/2 – Stanhope Forbes/Norma 27.2.19

144/27 IWM : LAVERY – Norman/Lavery, 1.3.19

144/31 IWM : LAVERY – Agnes Conway/ Lavery, 2.5.19

144/33 IWM : LAVERY – Agnes Conway/ Lavery, 2.5.19

145/5 IWM : TONKS – Tonks/Yockney, 22.7.19

146/1 Joseph Hone, *The Life of Henry Tonk* p. 159

146/11 Orpen/Rothenstein, 23.2.18 (quote in *Men and Memories*, Vol. II, p. 33

146/13 IWM : ORPEN – Orpen/Yockney, 1.3.19

146/18 IWM : ORPEN – J. T. Davis/Mond, 12.2.19

146/20 IWM : ORPEN – J. T Davis/Mond, 12.2.19

146/30 *An Onlooker in France*, p. 104

146/36 IWM : ORPEN – Orpen/ffoulkes, 19.2.22

146/40 IWM : ORPEN – Orpen/Yockney, 18.4.19

146/41 *Evening Standard*, 7.5.23

146/45 IWM : ORPEN – Orpen/ffoulkes,

page/line

19.2.22
47/2 IWM:ORPEN – ffoulkes/Conway, 3.1.23
47/6 *Daily Herald*, 8.5.23
47/7 *The Patriot*, 5.10.23
48/6 *Sunday Express*, 20.5.23
49/1 *Liverpool Echo*, 10.5.23
49/27 IWM : CLAUSEN – Clausen/Yockney, 19.11.20
49/31 IWM : ROYAL ACADEMY – Yockney's Report on the R.A. Exhibition *c*. February, 1920
50/4 *Men and Memories*, Vol. II, p. 363
50/14 IWM :$\frac{19}{1}$ – Minutes of IWM/R.A. Hanging Committee, 20.5.19
50/22 IWM :$\frac{31}{1}$ – Yockney/Bone, 24.4.19
50/34 *Paint and Prejudice*, p. 125
152/3 *Manchester Guardian*, 12.12.19
52/12 Letter to *The Graphic*, *c*. January 1920
52/15 *Morning Post*, 24.12.19
52/18 *Manchester Evening News*, 22.3.20
52/19 *Daily Mirror*, 15.12.19
52/24 *The Graphic*, 31.1.20
52/29 *The Graphic*, *c*. 30.1.20
52/31 *The Graphic*, 9.2.20
52/37 Mond's response to Sir Clement Kinloch-Cooke's question in Parliament, 23.2.20
156/7 Letter to *The Times*, 18.9.39
56/11 *Evening Standard*, 2.10.39
56/33 Clark, *Another Part of the Wood: A Self-Portrait*, (John Murray, 1974), p. 211
56/39 IWM : WEIGHT – Weight/Clark, 17.12.39
57/11 Michael Balfour, *Propaganda in War 1939–45 – Organisations, Policies and Publics in Britain and Germany*, (Routledge and Kegan Paul, 1979), p. 53
57/20 Clark, *The Other Half : A Self-Portrait*, (John Murray, 1977), p. 9
57/22 *Ibid.*, p. 22
57/29 IWM : GP/46/B – Clark/Scorgie, 27.8.40
57/36 *The Navy in Peace and War* – catalogue to exhibition at Portsmouth Navy Week, 1–8 August 1936
57/42 Sir Stephen Tallents, *The Projection of England*, (Faber, 1932), p. 39
158/2 IWM : GP/46/4 – Lloyd/Macmillan, 27.9.39
158/5 IWM : GP/46/4 – Lloyd/Macmillan, 2.10.39
159/1 For full details of the formation of the WAAC see IWM/GP/46 A & B
59/27 IWM : GP/46/A – Waterfield (Deputy Director-General)/Director-General memorandum 6.11.39
60/18 Clark, *Another Part of the Wood*, *op. cit.*, p. 59

page/line

160/27 Clark, *The Other Half*, *op. cit.*, p. 23
160/36 IWM:GP/46 – Waterfield/Needham, 21.9.39
160/44 *Tatler*, 14.2.40
161/5 Circulated to WAAC members on 23.11.39
161/16 IWM : GP/46/81 – Clark/Scorgie, 6.5.41
161/27 'War Artists at the National Gallery', *The Studio* CXXIII, January 1942, p. 586
161/37 Henry Moore, interview with the authors, 17.2.83
161/41 *The Studio*, *op. cit.*
162/9 IWM : BOMBERG – Bomberg/WAAC, 12.2.42
162/15 IWM : BOMBERG – Bomberg/Dickey, 28.4.42
162/16 *Ibid.*
162/17 IWM : BOMBERG – note 12.6.42
162/23 Tate, TAM 22 L 174/350 (quoted by kind permission of Mrs Mary Bone)
162/38 IWM:NEVINSON – Nevinson/Dickey, 14.11.40
163/5 IWM : NEVINSON – Nevinson/Bracken, 30.12.42
164/10 Eric Newton, *War Through Artists' Eyes*, (John Murray, 1945), p. 7
164/24 IWM : JOHN – Beaverbrook/Monckton, 30.4.41
164/22 IWM : BONE, Gregory/Bone, 30.3.45
165/1 IWM:GP/46/A – WAAC Paper No. 1, 'Categories of Work for War Artists'
165/9 IWM:WAAC MINUTES – 2nd Meeting, 29.11.39
165/13 IWM : WAAC MINUTES – 23rd Meeting, 19.6.40
165/15 IWM : KENNINGTON – Kennington/Dickey, 15.7.40
166/4 IWM : PITCHFORTH, Dickey/Clark, 22.7.40
166/12 IWM:MEDLEY – attendance note of meeting between Dickey, R. A. Bevan, Leigh Ashton and Medley, 29.12.39
166/14 IWM : MEDLEY – Clark/Dickey, 9.1.40
167/9 IWM : RUSHBURY – Dickey/Sturch, 3.3.41
167/15 *War Pictures by British Artists* – First Series, No. 1, *War at Sea*, (OUP, 1942), p. 59
167/22 IWM : BONE – Bone/Dickey, 7.8.40
167/35 *The Daily Telegraph*, 8.6.40
168/23 Bawden, interview with Julian Andrews in series 'Artists in an Age of Conflict', IWM 004622/05
168/37 IWM : FREEDMAN – 'Report' by Freedman, 28.5.40
168/42 Ardizzone, *Baggage to the Enemy*, (John Murray, 1941), p. 7

page/line

170/10 *Ibid.*, p. 121
170/17 Bawden, interview with the authors, 30.1.83
171/17 Len Deighton, *The Battle of Britain*, (Jonathan Cape, 1980), p. 32
172/3 IWM : PAUL NASH – Nash/Dickey, 31.3.41
172/10 IWM : WAAC MINUTES – 27th Meeting, 14.8.40
173/4 *Spectator*, 6.9.40
173/11 *Vogue*, March, 1942
173/22 *Sunday Times*, 1.9.40
174/9 IWM : KENNINGTON – Kennington/Dickey, *c*. 9.7.40
174/14 *The Statesman and Nation*, 8.8.41
174/28 IWM : DRING – Dring/Gregory, 17.3.45
176/9 Janet Dunbar, *Laura Knight*, (Collins, 1975), p. 11
176/10 *World of Art*, April 1939 ; quoted in Dunbar, *op. cit.*, Chapter 13
176/12 IWM : LAURA KNIGHT – Knight/WAAF 22.12.41
176/15 *Daily Express*, *c*. 6.5.42
177/2 IWM : PAUL NASH – Clark/Nash, 3.3.41
177/15 IWM : PAUL NASH – Nash/Clark, 8.11.40
178/4 IWM : PAUL NASH – Nash/Dickey, ?18.3.41
178/7 IWM : PAUL NASH – Nash/Clark, 11.3.41
178/14 IWM : PAUL NASH – Nash/Dickey, 13.3.41
178/28 IWM : PAUL NASH – Note on *Defence of Albion*, Nash/Clark, 27.5.42
178/31 Nash's note on *Battle of Britain*, *c*. November 1941
178/33 IWM : PAUL NASH – Clark/Nash, 22.10.41
178/37 IWM : PAUL NASH – Nash's explanatory note to Clark, 27.5.42
179/2 Nash/Ravilious, January 1942 – quoted by Andrew Causey, *Paul Nash*, (Clarendon Press, 1980), p. 457
179/4 IWM : PAUL NASH – Nash/Dickey, 29.4.42
179/6 IWM : PAUL NASH – Nash/Dickey, *c*. 20.3.42
179/10 IWM : PAUL NASH – Nash/Gregory, 22.9.44
179/13 IWM : PAUL NASH – Nash/Gregory, 6.4.44
179/18 IWM : PAUL NASH – Nash/Clark, 2.9.44
179/19 IWM : PAUL NASH – Nash's manuscript note for Clark, 1.10.44
179/26 IWM : PAUL NASH – Nash/Clark, 2.9.44

page/line

179/28 IWM : PAUL NASH – Nash/Gregory, 5.2.45

179/33 Tate, 7050.343, Clark/Nash, 1.5.44 (quoted by kind permission of Lord Clark)

179/36 Tate, 7050.361 Clark/Nash 3.10.44 (quoted by kind permission of Lord Clark)

179/43 IWM : NASH – Nash/Gregory 26.2.45

180/9 IWM/Dept. of Sound Records Accession No. 000323/05 interview John Nash/David Brown and Joseph Darracott

180/16 IWM : DOBSON – Dobson/Dickey 5.6.41

180/25 IWM : ARDIZZONE – Ardizzone/ Dickey 13.10.40

180/28 IWM : DODD – Dodd/Dickey 24.9.40

181/7 Leonard Rosoman, interview with authors, 2.3.83

181/10 *War Pictures by British Artists (Second Series) Air Raids* – introduction by Stephen Spender (OUP, 1943)

181/20 IWM : THOMSON – Thomson/Dickey 3.7.41

185/1 IWM : DEVAS – Devas/Dickey *c.* 9.9.41

186/9 IWM : WAAC MINUTES – 52nd Meeting 30.7.41

186/15 IWM : SCHWABE – Dickey/Schwabe 17.11.40

186/23 IWM : GRANT – Clark/Grant 7.7.41

186/33 IWM : PITCHFORTH – Pitchforth/ Dickey, received 26/3/41

186/38 IWM : BIOGRAPHIES

186/43 IWM : WAAC MINUTES – 22nd Meeting, 5.6.40

187/3 IWM : SUTHERLAND – Dickey/ Sutherland, , 3.8.40

187/7 IWM : SUTHERLAND – Dickey/ Sutherland, 8.8.40

188/1 IWM : SUTHERLAND – Sutherland/ Dickey, 22.8.40

188/4 IWM : SUTHERLAND – Sutherland/ Dickey, 4.9.40

188/6 IWM : SUTHERLAND – Sutherland/ Dickey, 1.10.40

188/25 *Daily Telegraph Magazine*, 10.9.71, and following

189/1 IWM : SUTHERLAND – Sutherland/ Dickey, 16.5.41

189/6 John Piper, interview with the authors, 28.2.83

189/24 *Ibid.*

189/26 IWM : WAAC MINUTES – 24th Meeting, 3.7.40

189/29 IWM : PIPER – Piper/Dickey, 7.12.40

189/30 IWM : WAAC MINUTES – 33rd Meeting, 7.11.40

190/8 Piper, interview with the authors, 28.2.83

190/10 *Ibid.*

190/13 IWM : WAAC MINUTES – 43rd Meeting, 26.3.41

190/30 'John Piper : 50 Years of Work, Paintings, Drawings and Photographs 1929–79' (1979 exhibition, Museum of Modern Art, Oxford, and Minories, Colchester) – 'A Biographical Outline' by John Betjeman

192/7 IWM : WAAC MINUTES – 35th Meeting, 5.12.40

192/28 Moore, interview with the authors, 17.2.83

192/42 Alan G. Wilkinson, *The Drawings of Henry Moore*, (Tate Gallery in collaboration with the Art Gallery of Ontario, 1977), p. 213

194/19 IWM : TOPOLSKI – WAAC/Topolski, 15.4.43

195/15 IWM : GP/46/96 – Clark/Bracken, 15.6.43

196/14 IWM : MOORE – Moore/Dickey, 24.11.41

196/33 Moore, interview with Joseph Darracott, IWM : Department of Sound Records, Accession No. 000785/01

197/11 *Daily Telegraph Magazine*, open letter to Edwin Mullins, 10.9.71

198/8 *Ibid.*

198/10 Sutherland/Clark, undated – quoted in Roger Berthoud, *Graham Sutherland – A Biography*, (Faber, 1982)

199/2 Edward Sackville-West, *Graham Sutherland*, (Penguin Modern Painters, 1943), p. 16

200/7 *War Pictures by British Artists, Second Series – Production*: introduction by Cecil Beaton (OUP, 1943), p. 6

201/1 IWM : GP/55/95 – MacBryde/Dickey, 15.11.40

201/19 IWM : WAAC MINUTES – 59th Meeting, 29.10.51

201/45 IWM : PEAKE – Peake/Dickey, 15.4.42

202/10 IWM : PEAKE – WAAC commissioning letter to Peake, 26.1.43

203/2 John Watney, *Mervyn Peake*, (Michael Joseph, 1976), p. 155

203/4 *The Glassblowers*, (Eyre and Spottiswoode, 1950)

203/25 IWM : DOBSON – Burton/Dobson, 7.6.44

203/43 IWM : PIPER – Piper/Gregory, 18.7.44

204/4 Piper, interview with the authors, 28.2.83

205/1 IWM : SPENCER – Dudley Tooth/ Clark, 25.12.39

205/11 IWM : SPENCER – attendance not Dickey, 19.3.40

205/14 IWM : SPENCER – WAAC commissioning letter, 19.3.40

205/22 IWM : WAAC MINUTES – 17th Meeting, 27.3.40

205/24 IWM : WAAC MINUTES – 21st meeting, 22.5.40

205/39 IWM : SPENCER – Spencer/Dickey 21.10.40

206/11 Tate, 733.3.34, p. 2 (quoted by kind permission of Unity and Shirin Spencer)

206/19 Tate, 733.3.34, p. 12 (quoted by kind permission of Unity and Shirin Spencer)

206/27 Tate, 733.3.34, p. 10 (quoted by kind permission of Unity and Shirin Spencer)

206/32 Spencer/Gilbert Spencer, undated quoted in 'Stanley Spencer : War Artist on Clydeside 1940–45' (catalogue to exhibition, Scottish Council, Third Eye Centre, Glasgow)

206/35 Andrew Causey, 'Stanley Spencer and the Art of his Time' – catalogue to R.A. exhibition, 1980 (Weidenfeld and Nicholson, 1980), p. 31

206/37 *War Pictures by British Artists – War at Sea*, (OUP, 1942), p. 60

208/5 IWM : SPENCER – Spencer/Dickey 7.11.41

208/25 IWM : SPENCER – Spencer/Palmer 7.10.42

208/36 IWM : SPENCER – Spencer/IWM, 20.11.46

208/43 IWM : WAAC MINUTES – 105th Meeting, 30.12.42

209/24 IWM : STEPHEN BONE – memorandum to WAAC 18.5.43

210/5 IWM : JOHN NASH – Nash/Dickey 10.6.40

210/7 IWM : JOHN NASH – Nash/Dickey *c.*6.8.40

210/11 IWM : JOHN NASH – Nash/Dickey *c.* 1.5.40

210/16 IWM : JOHN NASH – Nash/Dickey 10.6.40

211/2 Tate, 7050.933, John Nash/Paul Nash, undated (quoted by kind permission of John Lewis and the John Nash Trustees)

211/4 IWM : JOHN NASH – Nash/Dickey 23.8.40

211/8 IWM : JOHN NASH – Nash/Dickey 2.9.40

page/line

1/13 IWM : WAAC MINUTES – 29th Meeting, 12.9.40

1/17 Tate, 7050.930, John Nash/Paul Nash, undated (quoted by kind permission of John Lewis and the John Nash Trustees)

1/22 IWM : PAUL NASH – Paul Nash/Dickey, c. 6.6.41

12/5 IWM : RAVILIOUS – Ravilious/Dickey, 15.2.40

12/9 IWM : RAVILIOUS – Ravilious/Dickey, c.22.6.40

2/13 Harold Nicolson, *Diaries and Letters 1939–45*, (Collins, 1967), entry for 4.6.41

2/18 IWM:WAAC MINUTES – 28th Meeting, 29.8.40

2/20 IWM : RAVILIOUS – Ravilious/Dickey, 19.7.40

2/23 IWM : RAVILIOUS – Ravilious/Dickey, 2.8.40

2/28 IWM : RAVILIOUS – Ravilious/Dickey, c. 24.9.40

13/8 IWM : RAVILIOUS – Ravilious/Dickey, c 13.12.41

14/7 IWM : WAAC MINUTES – 68th Meeting, 7.1.42

4/10 IWM : RAVILIOUS – Ravilious/Dickey, 19.1.42

4/22 IWM : RAVILIOUS – Ravilious/Dickey, c. 11.7.42

4/35 Catalogue 'Eric Ravilious 1903–42' (exhibition, Minories, Colchester, January–February 1972)

215/6 IWM : FREEDMAN – Coote/Dickey, 12.7.40

5/15 IWM : FREEDMAN – Freedman/Dickey, 4.11.40

5/19 IWM : FREEDMAN – Freedman/Dickey, 18.7.41

5/35 Armide Oppé, interview with the authors, 2.1.83

216/2 IWM : WAAC/GP/46/B – Dickey/Clark, undated memorandum, c. June 1941

217/9 IWM : WAAC MINUTES – 83rd Meeting 27.5.42

17/12 IWM : WAAC MINUTES – 76th Meeting 25.3.42

17/14 IWM : DRING – Dickey/Dring 11.9.42

17/35 IWM : NORMAN WILKINSON – Wilkinson/Prime Minister 10.4.49

218/4 Catalogue : *Richard Eurich RA – A Retrospective Exhibition* Preface by Richard Eurich (1980 Bradford Art Galleries, The Fine Art Society, Southampton Art Gallery)

218/9 IWM : EURICH – Eurich/Dickey 10/6/40

18/19 Denys Brook-Hart, *Twentieth Century*

page/line

British Marine Painting (1981 Antique Collectors Club Ltd) p. 317

218/33 IWM : EURICH – Eurich/Dickey 18.1.41

218/41 IWM : Dept. of Sound Records Accession No. 003818/04, interview with Richard Eurich

220/36 IWM : COXON – Coxon/Dickey 29.9.40

221/3 IWM : LAMB – Lamb/Dickey 24.7.41

221/5 IWM : LAMB – Lamb/Dickey 13.8.41

221/10 IWM : MOYNIHAN – Moynihan/Dickey 10.11.40

224/15 Edward Bawden, interview with Julian Andrews, IWM 004622/05

224/20 Bawden/Charlotte Bawden, 4.12.40 (In 1980 Bawden presented to the IWM a collection of his wartime letters to his wife)

224/37 Bawden/Charlotte Bawden, 11.4.41

225/4 Bawden, interview with Julian Andrews, *op. cit.*

225/6 Bawden/Charlotte Bawden, ?July 1941

226/3 *Ibid.*

226/21 Bawden/Charlotte Bawden, 15.11.41

226/26 Bawden/Charlotte Bawden, 7.1.42

226/27 Bawden/Charlotte Bawden, 16.2.42

227/23 Bawden, interview with the authors, 30.1.83

228/2 IWM : BAWDEN – Bawden/Dickey, 16.10.41

228/4 Bawden/Charlotte Bawden, 19.1.44

228/6 Bawden/Charlotte Bawden, 22.6.42

228/41 IWM : BAWDEN – Bawden/Dickey, 22.6.42, and following

230/7 IWM : BAWDEN – Bawden/Gregory, 29.11.43

230/9 Bawden, interview with the authors, 30.1.83

230/13 Bawden/Charlotte Bawden, 18.12.43

230/23 GHQ Middle East Force, press release 26.11.43

230/27 IWM : BAWDEN – Bawden/Gregory, 5.5.44

230/30 Bawden, interview with Julian Andrews, *op. cit.*

230/32 IWM : BAWDEN – Bawden/Gregory, 5.5.44

231/1 IWM : BAWDEN – Bawden/Gregory, 14.7.44

231/5 Bawden/Charlotte Bawden, 5.6.44

231/7 Bawden, interview with Julian Andrews, *op. cit.*

231/8 Bawden, interview with the authors, 30.1.83

233/6 'The Campaign in Greece and Crete', official War Office publication, ?1941

233/20 Ardizzone, unpublished diary, 2.11.42

page/line

234/9 Ardizzone, interview with Conway Lloyd-Morgan in series 'Artists in an Age of Conflict', IWM 004525/05

234/15 *Ibid.*

234/21 *Ibid.*

235/18 *Ibid.*

236/19 IWM : COLE – Dickey/Peake, 12.6.41

236/36 IWM : COLE – Cole/Coote, 6.7.43

236/40 *Ibid.*

237/2 Ardizzone, interview with Conway Lloyd-Morgan, *op. cit.*

237/16 *Ibid.*

237/22 Ardizzone, *Diary of a War Artist*, (Bodley Head, 1974), diary entry for 9.9.43

237/26 Ardizzone, diary entry for 16.7.43, *op. cit.*

237/29 Ardizzone, diary entry for 17.7.43

237/36 Ardizzone, interview with Conway Lloyd-Morgan, *op. cit.*

238/3 Ardizzone, interview with Conway Lloyd-Morgan, and following

239/3 Ardizzone, diary entry for 3.9.43

240/12 IWM : WORSLEY – Worsley/IWM May 1983

240/22 Ardizzone, diary entry for 1.10.43

240/25 Ardizzone, diary entry for 1.10.43

240/34 Ardizzone, interview with Conway Lloyd-Morgan, *op. cit.*

241/25 Coldstream, interview in series 'Artists in an Age of Conflict', IWM 3184/03

241/31 Coldstream, interview with the authors, 7.2.83

242/38 Coldstream, interview, IWM 3184/03

242/8 *Ibid.*

242/18 Bawden/Charlotte Bawden, 30.11.44

243/12 Bawden/Charlotte Bawden, 8–13.1.45

243/19 IWM : BAWDEN – Bawden/Gregory, 22.2.45

243/22 Bawden/Charlotte Bawden, 13.1.45–10.2.45

244/2 IWM : BAWDEN – Bawden/Gregory, 22.2.45

244/6 IWM : BAWDEN – Bawden/Gregory, 22.2.45

244/14 Bawden/Charlotte Bawden, 13.1.45–10.2.45

244/17 Ardizzone, diary entry for 30.3.45

244/21 Weight, interview in series 'Artists in an Age of Conflict', IWM 3171/03

244/37 IWM : WEIGHT – Weight/Gregory, 21.9.45

244/38 Weight, interview, IWM 3171/03

244/46 *Ibid.*

246/10 IWM : GROSS – Gross/Gregory, 17.9.44

page/line

246/25 Reported by Allen Freer, in letter to the authors, 21.2.83
247/6 IWM : RICHARDS – Richards/WAAC, 1.9.43
247/10 IWM : WAAC MINUTES, 139th Meeting, 10.11.43
248/1 IWM : RICHARDS – Richards/ Gregory, 5.6.44
248/7 IWM : RICHARDS – Mr and Mrs G. Richards/WAAC, 20.3.45
248/12 IWM : RICHARDS, Richards/Gregory, end June 1944
248/18 IWM : GROSS – Gross/Gregory, 24.7.44
248/33 IWM : FREEDMAN, Freedman/ Gregory, 9.7.44
248/38 Hennell, unpublished article 'The Work of a War Artist'
248/39 Ardizzone, diary entry 16.6.44
248/41 Vincent Lines, introduction to catalogue of Hennell memorial exhibition, Leicester Museum and Art Gallery, November 1955
249/3 Hennell, 'The Work of a War Artist'
249/26 Gross, interview in series 'Artists in an Age of Conflict', IWM 004621/02
249/30 *Ibid.*
249/45 IWM : WAAC MINUTES – 163rd Meeting, 30.8.44
250/8 Hennell, 'The Work of a War Artist'
251/15 Sutherland, open letter to Edwin Mullins, *The Daily Telegraph Magazine*, 10.9.71
252/7 IWM : RICHARDS – Richards/ Gregory, ?end February 1945
252/9 *Ibid.*
252/28 Ardizzone, interview with Conway Lloyd-Morgan, *op. cit.*
252/33 Ardizzone, diary entry for 16.4.45
254/7 IWM : STEPHEN BONE – Bone's notes on pictures delivered 31.7.45
255/9 IWM : COLE – Cole's undated note on pictures submitted to WAAC, ?May 1945
256/4 Peake, 'The Consumptive, Belsen 1945', published in *The Glassblowers*, (Eyre and Spottiswoode, 1950)
256/18 Quoted by Gross, interview, IWM 004621/02
256/28 Knight/Harold Knight, undated – quoted in Janet Dunbar, *Laura Knight, op. cit.*, p. 173
256/38 Knight/Harold Knight, undated – Dunbar, *op. cit.*, p. 182
257/2 Knight/Harold Knight, ?March 1946 – Dunbar, *op. cit.*, p. 201
257/3 Knight/Harold Knight, ?March 1946 – Dunbar, *op. cit.*, p. 201
257/5 IWM : LAURA KNIGHT – Knight/ Oxford – Coxall, 11.5.46

258/36 Gross, interview, IWM 004621/02
259/9 *Ibid.*
261/4 Guy Hartcup, *Camouflage – A History of Concealment and Deception in War*, (David and Charles, 1979)
261/11 IWM : COLE – Cole/Gregory, 24.8.45
261/17 IWM : HENNELL – Hennell/Gregory, 14.6.45
261/42 IWM : COLE – Cole/Gregory, 19.4.45
262/1 *Ibid.*
262/4 Hennell, 'The Work of a War Artist'
262/17 IWM : ROSOMAN – Rosoman/ Gregory, July 1945
262/24 *Ibid.*
262/30 *Ibid.*
262/36 Catalogue – 'Leonard Rosoman' (exhibition at the Fine Art Society, 1974) : introduction by Rosoman
262/40 IWM : ROSOMAN – Rosoman/ Gregory, July 1945
263/6 Catalogue – 'Leonard Rosoman', *op. cit.*
265/7 IWM : GP/46/B – Barlow/Scorgie, 19.8.40
265/22 IWM : GP/46/B – Pick/Scorgie, 30.9.40
265/29 'The Artist in Wartime', printed in *The Listener*, 26.10.39
267/14 IWM : ARDIZZONE – Dickey/Clark, 26.10.40
267/28 *Good Housekeeping*, September 1942
267/31 IWM : PAUL NASH – Clark/Nash, 22.11.40
267/39 IWM : GP/46/20 – Minutes of meeting between HMSO, Leigh Ashton Bevan, H. R. Francis and Dickey, 4.12.39
267/44 *War Pictures by British Artists*, Second Series, *Women* (OUP, 1943), p. 60
267/54 *War Pictures by British Artists*, First Series, *Blitz*, (OUP, 1942), p. 5
268/3 *War Pictures by British Artists*, First Series, *The War at Sea*, (OUP, 1942), p. 7
268/26 Tate, 7050.471 press release
268/40 IWM : GP/46/84 – Serota/Smollett, 7.1.42
268/45 IWM : GP/46/84 – Lawrence/ Smollett, 27.1.42
269/7 IWM : GP/46/24/4/B – Barr/Clark, 25.9.40
269/16 IWM : GP/46/24/4/B – Wheeler/ Clark, 12.6.41
269/23 Balfour, *op. cit.*, p. 166
269/38 IWM : GP/46/24/14 – Anderson, memorandum 25.2.44
269/43 Catalogue – 'India in Action' (exhibition National Gallery, 1944) ; introduction by L. S. Amery

270/4 IWM : WAAC MINUTES – 175th Meeting, 14.2.45
270/18 Herbert Read, introduction to catalogue for 'Britain at War' (Museum of Modern Art, New York 1941)
270/37 IWM : GP/46/24/A – HMSO/Clark 28.6.40
270/42 IWM : CARR – Carr/Dickey, 22.7.
270/43 IWM : KENNINGTON – Kennington Dickey, c. 9.7.40
270/44 IWM : PAUL NASH – Nash/Dickey 18.3.41
271/3 Piper, *Spectator* 23.5.41
273/2 IWM : WAAC MINUTES – Interim Report for – Third Year of the War August 1942 (Paper 1052, Apper
273/9 IWM : GP/46/B – Treasury/Bamfo 6.1.44
273/43 IWM : WYNDHAM LEWIS – Lewis MacDonald, 19.1.44
274/14 IWM : GP/46/48 – John Rothenst Clark, 4.2.41
274/35 IWM : WAAC MINUTES, p. 172 – Treasury Minute laid before Parliament, March 1947
277/19 IWM : ARTISTIC RECORDS COMMITTEE – Board Paper 1972, Item 6 (Enclosure A)
277/34 Howard, interview with Joseph Darracott, Department of Sound Records, Accession No. 000329/0
278/36 Joseph Darracott, interview with authors, 9.2.83
280/2 IWM : ARTISTIC RECORDS COMMITTEE – 'List of Commission produced for the ARC of the IWM since 1977'
280/10 Ocean, interview with the authors 15.2.83
280/13 *Ibid.*
282/9 Hogarth, interview with the autho 20.2.83
282/24 IWM : WALKER – Chadwick/Walk 14.7.81
282/32 IWM : WALKER – Walker/ARC, 21.9.81
282/36 WALKER, interview with authors, 26.2.83
282/39 *Ibid.*
282/41 Walker, unpublished note on *Army Recruitment*, January 1983
284/17 IWM : KITSON – Kitson/Chadwick 1.7.82
284/39 *The Daily Telegraph*, 28.10.82
286/2 Catalogue – 'Anthony Eyton' Southwark, May 1980 : introducti by William Packer
286/18 Eyton, interview with the authors, 25.2.83

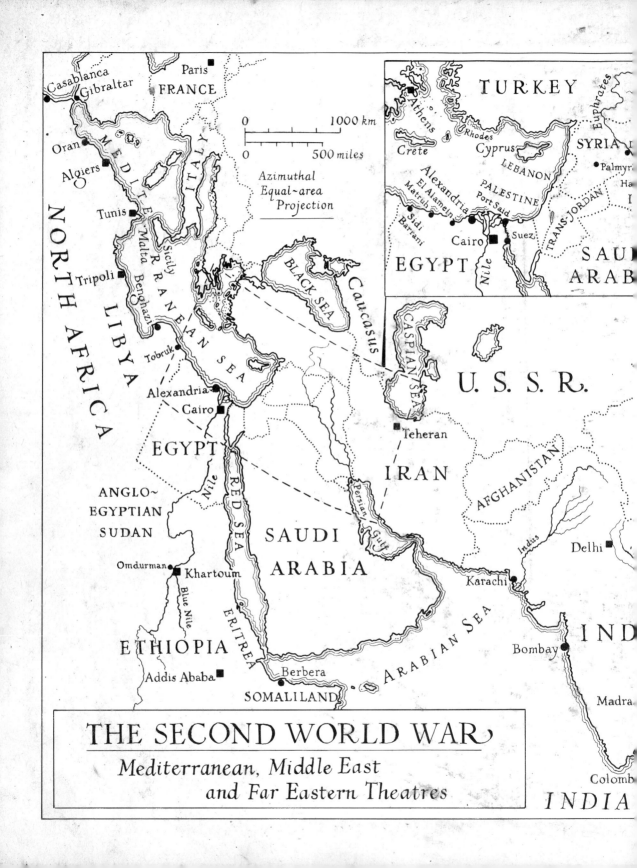

THE SECOND WORLD WAR
*Mediterranean, Middle East
and Far Eastern Theatres*